To James,

Thank you for all your help with publicity,

Best wishes

Gary James

P/ Hope you didn't mind being called "The original Junior Blue" on one 'Thank You' page!

THE PRIDE OF MANCHESTER

A history of the Manchester derby matches

By Steve Cawley and Gary James

Published by ACL Colour Print & Polar Publishing (UK) Ltd

THANK YOU

Dedicated to:

Sue, Joe and Rosie Cawley
& Paul and Marjorie James
also
a special dedication to the memory of
Joe Mercer,
one of football's true gentlemen.

First published in Great Britain by
ACL Colour Print & Polar Publishing (UK) Ltd
2 Uxbridge Road, Leicester LE4 7ST, England

ISBN 0 9514862 1 7

Dust Cover Design
Bernard Gallagher, Sports Projects Ltd

Edited by
Julian Baskcomb

Printed by
ACL Colour Print & Polar Publishing (UK) Ltd
2 Uxbridge Road, Leicester LE4 7ST, England
Telephone: (0533) 610800

Firstly our indebted thanks go to the two men who have done so much for Manchester football - Sir Matt Busby, CBE and the late Joe Mercer, OBE. For these great men to each find time to write the foreword to our book is indeed a great honour and privilege. The two men are not just former managers, they are the greatest and are still the main reasons why both City and United are such important clubs.

We were particularly saddened by the death of Joe Mercer during the 18 months taken to research and produce this book, and will both treasure for a lifetime the opportunity to interview one of the true legends of the game. Both Mr Mercer and his extremely kind wife Norah could not have been more helpful or gone to greater lengths to ensure we were made most welcome.

There have been a number of people who have helped us during the course of our extensive research. Many provided so much assistance that a thank you is simply not enough. Falling into this category is Ray Goble who has, over many years, spent considerable time collating his wealth of facts and figures on Manchester City. His detailed derby statistics and his own vast knowledge helped us to include much of the statistical information in the publication.

Heidi Ward must be acknowledged for her considerable time spent proof-reading, typing and generally assisting in all areas of research. Her willing nature and constant encouragement helped 'the Blue' half of the writing partnership throughout the months of 'hard slog'.

Tommy Docherty on Piccadilly Radio and Jim Reeve (the original Junior Blue) assisted with publicity as did Radio Manchester, the South Manchester Reporter and the following fanzine editors; Noel Bailey, Mike Kelly, Bill Burrows and Dave Wallace. Granada Television's Bob Greaves provided a number of photographic leads for us to follow.

Particular thanks are due to Jackie Sen, deputy head of lending services at the Rylands library, Manchester who kindly sifted through hundreds of photographs from the Daily Mail collection. Thanks too to the newspaper for kind permission to reproduce many of those pictures.

Stuart Renshaw of Dawn Covers provided a wealth of first day covers and information much of which is included in this book.

City's Phil Critchley and Geoff Durbin with United's Cliff Butler all assisted with publicity as well as providing certain other information included. Ken Smallwood, Des Layton, James Thomas, John Hewit, Iain McCartney, Michael Wells, Mike Cox and Mike Davage all supplied various pieces of memorabilia and derby information, with particular regard to early Christian names. Eddie Harrison and Michelle Amella kindly allowed us to scrutinise their scrap-books.

We both owe a considerable debt to the patience and ever helpful assistance of numerous librarians as we have pored over miles of Manchester newsprint and numerous other publications besides. Particular thanks are due to the British Library's newspaper library at Colindale and Manchester Central Library.

Julian Baskcomb at ACL & Polar needs thanking for taking on this enormous project and for his tremendous support. There were various unavoidable set-backs and delays but without Julian and his colleagues the book might even now still be in the planning stage. They have put much time and effort into making this publication one of depth and quality. Special thanks must also go to Bernard Gallagher and Phil Lees of Sports Projects Ltd for the layout and design of the book.

Of course, the greatest thank you goes to you, the reader, and the many Blues and Reds who have subscribed to this publication.

Thank you one and all.

CONTENTS

FOREWORD

IT pleases me that a long overdue book devoted to the Manchester derby has finally been published. I am also delighted that Gary and Steve have given me, along with my good friend Matt Busby, the chance to introduce their fine publication.

This book details not only match statistics but also gives a report on the unique background information for every League and Cup game between the Manchester greats, allowing all of us the chance to relive our favourite match. One period of particular interest to myself is the late 1960's, a time when both City and United were continually challenging for all the game's top honours. The atmosphere and tension at the derby matches during this period clearly illustrated the importance of derby success. These years as manager of the Blues were among the happiest of my managerial career and I well remember the feeling of elation when City beat United in the vital derby of 1968 which set us up for the championship that year.

I'm sure that all Manchester supporters and followers of football in general will find this remarkably in-depth publication one of the most interesting, entertaining every generation with games from the very first encounter through to the modern day.

One amazing feature of this book is the fact that it has been written by two dedicated supporters, one Blue, one Red, who have, by working closely together, produced a well-balanced, well thought out publication that is of interest to us all. I remember well the fantastic support both Manchester clubs have always enjoyed and feel that two men who have experienced that special aura that derby matches bring about are best equipped to tell us the story of 'The Pride of Manchester'.

Joe Mercer O.B.E.   *31st May 1990*

AS a player with City and Manager at United I had the privilege to be involved in the Manchester derby matches with both sides and they can be amongst the most demanding of any on the fixture list. Like all major cross-city rivalries; Rangers and Celtic, Athletico and Real Madrid, Liverpool and Everton, Inter and Milan, etc.,the games between the Reds and Blues have an appeal, atmosphere and tension all of their own.

Most United and City supporters are fiercely proud of their respective clubs and rightly so, for both have brought honour and distinction to Manchester. So it's not really surprising that the temperature rises when the two clubs meet.

I have been involved in many such matches and I always find them amazingly tense occasions with neither side wanting to lose because that means that they have to suffer the taunts until the next opportunity arrives to redress the balance.

Although I was born in Scotland, close to Glasgow and a very proud Scotsman, Manchester has always meant a great deal to me and to have played a small part in the City's sporting history is indeed an honour. I applaud Steve Cawley and Gary James for writing this book which will take its place alongside the best of historical football literature. They chose a fascinating subject and I'm sure all football fans, not just those dedicated to United or City, will take great pleasure from adding it to their collections.

Sir Matt Busby C.B.E.   *1st June 1990*

*Captains of Scotland and England respectively, **Matt Busby** and **Joe Mercer** take the field at Hampden Park in April 1945. It was to be Busby's final international. Not only did England win 6-1, but Frank Swift - seen immediately behind Mercer - saved Busby's penalty-kick.*

INTRODUCTION

THE derby match is, and has been, over the last century probably the most important match in the soccer calendars of both Manchester City and Manchester United. The term 'the derby' has some rather confusing origins. Some soccer historians refer back to AD 217 and the ferocious cross-country battles between the two halves of the Derbyshire town of Ashbourne, where the 'derby' still occurs today every Shrove Tuesday. Whereas other sources talk of the term coming from the annual match last played in Derby on Shrove Tuesday 1846 between the parishes of St Peters and All Saints.

Whatever the origins of the term there is no doubting the importance of a fixture that started officially between the Manchester clubs one hundred years ago in 1891. Regardless of the triumphs or the disasters of a particular season, to become or remain the major club in the city until the next contest comes about, has always been of paramount importance. Both for players and supporters alike the pride evoked by these parochial encounters is well worth attaining and the effects of the triumph or disaster can be long lasting in the pubs, clubs and homes of Manchester.

Syd Robinson's cartoon culled from a 'United Review' of the late Fifties encapsulates delightfully the critical nature of these games in the minds of the supporters from the cradle onwards! For supporters, once the allegiance is gained at birth there is no going back, it's Blue or Red forever. Mike Summerbee, the City winger of the Sixties and Seventies summarised perfectly when asked to describe the Manchester derby: "These games are not like League matches, they are a one-off about pride".

Although there had been many games between the West Gorton and Newton Heath clubs as they were then known, the first official League encounter occurred some 97 years ago in 1894 when both teams were in the League's Second Division. The derby contest quickly became the highlight of the fixture lists of both clubs. These early games evolved around the ambition to reach the First Division, where the elite sixteen clubs in the country played. Newton Heath had tasted life in the top flight between 1892 and 1894, but were relegated at the end of the 1893-94 season.

From their opening 5-2 victory it was the Newton Heath (United) club that enjoyed the superiority of these initial games and it seemed highly likely that they would be the first Manchester club to gain promotion to football's top flight. However, football's unpredictable nature can never be discounted and it was City who went up in 1899, bringing the first series of derby matches to a close. The early years of this century saw both clubs in their rightful place in the League's First Division, and indeed all League derby matches have been First Division affairs, a mark of these two famous clubs' standing in the game.

Now the context of the Manchester game was on a higher plane as the two clubs attempted to win the game's major honours. Again the capricious nature of football prediction came to the fore. City looked the team likely to dominate affairs as their experienced and talented team became the first Manchester side to win a major honour when they lifted the FA Cup in 1904.

However, shortly after this fate took a hand and within four years the balance of power between the Manchester clubs had been totally reversed in the most dramatic fashion. The bribes scandal which rocked City in 1905 had a devastating effect on the club. Not only did it deprive them of their best players (leading to a stagnation of the club's progress) but agonisingly for the supporters they saw some of their best players join United once their bans were completed.

The legendary Billy Meredith and such stalwarts as Sandy Turnbull and Herbert Burgess started playing for United in 1907. Not surprisingly shortly after this, United entered their first golden era, winning the League twice and the FA Cup for good measure. When one considers the dramatic nature of this recruitment to the Reds' colours it is hardly surprising that there has never really been any tradition of large transfers between the clubs to this day. So it was United (as they had been renamed in 1902) who continued to dominate the derby contest up until the outbreak of the First World War.

The derby was a less frequent event during the yo-yo years of the Twenties and Thirties as both United and City suffered the indignity of relegation during that period. City's highly unpredictable reputation could well have been forged during this time. In retrospect, nothing was more typical than City's 1925-26 season. The men from Maine Road were having a terrible time of it in the League and relegation seemed a certainty from an early stage. United with only a moderate side themselves at the time must have looked upon that season's home derby as a banker. Yet when that fateful 36th derby match came about it was City that established the record derby victory by inflicting a drubbing on their neighbours.

In a sense this is a theme which has run through many derby matches. The form book does not always apply and many surprise results have come about that have no bearing on other events at the time. City though showed the result was no fluke as later that same season the clubs met in the FA Cup semi-final (the nearest the derby has come to a Wembley venue) and again it was the Blues who came out on top with a comfortable 3-0 victory.

This era of history was generally a dismal one for United as City held the upper hand whilst the Reds wrestled with a constant struggle to survive both on and off the field. However, despite their problems, again the lure of local pride proved a spur.

In the dreadful 1936-37 season when relegation was virtually assured by Christmas, one of only eight United League victories came against the high-flying Blues. City, though, retained their top dog status in emphatic fashion by deservedly picking up their first League Championship at the end of that season. City being City, they were relegated the following season and with the war intervening the fans had to wait until 1947 before the derby contest recommenced.

The advent of Matt Busby to the management of United after the war changed the picture entirely. The man who had graced the City team in the early Thirties galvanised United to make them not only the power in Manchester but in England and, subsequently, Europe over the next twenty five years.

The austere years immediately following the war showed the other side of the neighbourly link between the two clubs. United's Old Trafford ground had been badly damaged by wartime bombing and City generously allowed the Reds to play their home fixtures at Maine Road. So, for the fans those post-war derbies were slightly confusing affairs - United were at home ..... but they were also away!

Despite this Matt Busby quickly inspired his first great side to win the FA Cup and the Championship. City, though taking time to record their first derby win after the war, soon entered a purple patch in these contests during the early Fifties. Les McDowall's Revie plan for a couple of seasons outfoxed the Reds and United suffered one or two painful defeats in League and Cup. Indeed, the 1954-55 season was a particularly triumphant one for the Blues as they recorded three straight wins with an aggregate of 10-0!

Matt Busby though showed he was never a man to stand still and his second great side, the immortal Busby Babes, soon put matters to rights and a series of crushing defeats restored the balance of power to United. The tragedy of the Munich air crash wiped out a wonderful side and left the whole city of Manchester devastated by grief.

The slowly rebuilt United side of the late Fifties and early Sixties proved too good for a City side beginning to enter their own period of gloom when the club seemed to have an annual fight against the threat of relegation. When the day for the drop inevitably arrived in 1963 it came in a most dramatic derby when either club could be relegated. In an acrimonious affair it was the team from Maine Road that went down.

The late Sixties saw Manchester as the soccer capital of England. Matt Busby's third great side of entertainers built around the legendary triumvirate of Law, Charlton and Best were sweeping all before them in inimitable style. Yet City had themselves been galvanised by the management team of Joe Mercer and Malcolm Allison and it was they who began to challenge United's right to dominate not just Manchester, but in England and Europe as well.

The 78th League derby in March 1968 proved to be something of a watershed. United, on the threshold of a European Cup and League double, were pipped, almost by surprise, by their neighbours. It was now City's turn to dominate events playing similarly attacking football with their own

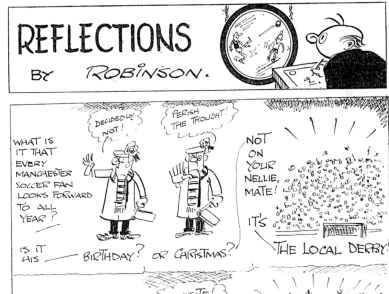

NOTES ON TEXT

trio of stars in Bell, Lee and Summerbee.

The early Seventies saw some crushing defeats for the former aristocrats from Old Trafford, as United struggled to replace the Busby recipe for success. Matters came to a head in the infamous derby of 1974. This proved to be almost a replica of 1963, only this time United were the doomed team and in one of the most ironic moments of derby history it was their former hero Denis Law who applied the coup de gras.

City's golden period under genial Joe did not last as long as perhaps it should have done and by the time Tommy Docherty's exciting young United side had developed, City's derby mastery was at an end.

The mid to late Seventies saw some of the best derby matches as United and City boasted two of the finest sides in the country. For City fans though - bar one notable exception - that was where the derby glories finished as from 1981 onwards the club became almost permanently involved in a struggle to stay in the division. Indeed, for four years during the decade City played in the Second Division as the club were twice relegated. United, under the extrovert Ron Atkinson won cups and were clearly the top side in Manchester.

Bringing the story up to date does not diminish the derby contest's capacity to surprise, and recent seasons have been no exception to this. The 111th League derby played in September 1989 saw City's 5-1 thrashing of their millionaire neighbours to equal their record home victory in the long series of matches. The February derby of that same season was the 100th derby to be played in the First Division - the premier League to which a century earlier both clubs had striven so hard to gain membership. The division has been graced by one or other of these great clubs ever since.

An even more recent derby in October 1990 saw the Blues fans cheering home their favourites to what seemed a certain victory, only for United to stage a grandstand finish and restore their pride. Once again the match showed that when local pride is at stake it would take a foolish man to risk a forecast. As their next century of encounters gets under way the faithful supporters of both clubs hope that this situation may long continue - but of course only if their particular favourite comes out on top and becomes the Pride of Manchester.

Steve Cawley & Gary James

Manchester, May 1991

ALTHOUGH this publication is laid out in a largely chronological format we believe a small amount of explanation may be required to enable you, the reader, to enjoy it to its fullest.

The book is broadly divided into three sections with the major part devoted to Section One. This details every one of the twelve Second Division and 102 First Division derbies played between the two great Manchester sides.

Each game in this section commences with the score and scorers, teams, date, division, venue and attendance. Following the facts and figures we have provided background details on the two clubs. This background information details any major signing, gives an outline guide as to how the season was progressing and mentions any important events that may have a bearing on the derby match. For example, the signings of Dennis Tueart for City and Bryan Robson for United are detailed as of significance as both players made their League debuts in a derby match. Following the background information we have provided a basic League record of that season for both clubs prior to the match. Hopefully this gives a comparison between the fortunes of the two clubs leading up to derby day.

The match verdict follows the League record and this is, simply, a resume of the match. It includes the major incidents of the game and tries to detail impartially which side produced the better performance, although we admit, that we have all probably got our own views and recollections of many of the games. Following the match verdict for the second derby of each season we also detail the position of the two clubs at the end of the campaign and list any major trophy won. Again we hope this enables the reader to make a straight comparison between the fortunes of the Reds and the Blues after every season.

The Second Section of the book details all FA Cup, League Cup and Charity Shield matches between the two Manchester giants. For these games we still have the match verdict, but the background is replaced by a record of progress through the previous rounds of the relevant competition. For instance, for the League Cup semi-final of 1969-70 we detail both City's and United's previous matches by listing the opponents, the score, attendance, scorers and the venue. After the match verdict we detail the progress of the surviving club in a similar way.

The Third Section of the book is basically a statistical record of all other derby games and a selection of various facts and figures. Also, in this section we have picked our greatest United and City teams based solely on the criteria of matches between the two clubs.

That broadly, is the book, although as we hope you can appreciate there is an awful lot more inside than we have detailed above. The true story of the derby saga is a tale that cannot be easily told and we, as loyal supporters, have agonised over much of it. We both know that as supporters of either City or United there are certain matches we would perhaps simply have preferred not to include!

However, it was always our intention to produce as complete a record as possible of the Manchester derby regardless of personal preference. We believe we have managed to achieve that and trust on the whole our fellow supporters will agree with us. We hope you enjoy the wealth of history and memories that lie behind 'The Pride of Manchester' and that it brings you as much pleasure reading it as it did us compiling it.

EARLY DERBY DAYS

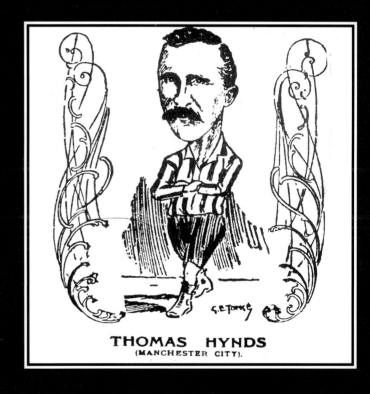

THOMAS HYNDS
(MANCHESTER CITY).

The Championship of Cottonopolis 1894-1903

1

MANCHESTER CITY 2
(Meredith 2)

NEWTON HEATH 5
(Smith 4, Clarkin)

DATE	3rd November 1894
DIVISION	Two
VENUE	Hyde Road
ATTENDANCE	14,000

Manchester City		Newton Heath
George HUTCHINSON	1	William DOUGLAS
Harry SMITH	2	John McCARTNEY
John WALKER	3	Fred ERENTZ
George MANN	4	George PERRINS
Joseph NASH	5	James McNAUGHT
Fred DYER	6	William DAVIDSON
Billy MEREDITH	7	John CLARKIN
Pat FINNERHAN	8	Robert DONALDSON
Sandy ROWAN	9	James DOW
James SHARPLES	10	Richard SMITH
Bob MILARVIE	11	James PETERS

BACKGROUND

Both sides had joined the Football League in 1892 when Ardwick (Manchester City) entered the newly formed Second Division and Newton Heath (Manchester United) joined the enlarged First Division. At the end of this first season Newton Heath finished bottom of the First Division and Ardwick in fifth place in Division Two.

Newton Heath survived in the top flight by succeeding in the Test matches that were used to decide promotion and relegation in the early years of the League. The 1893-94 season saw Ardwick finish 13th out of 15 teams in the Second Division, whereas Newton Heath were again bottom of the First Division. This time The Heathens were unsuccessful in the Test matches and were relegated, joining Ardwick in Division Two.

During the close season Ardwick had been reformed as Manchester City and were determined to make an impact. A number of new players had been signed by City secretary Joshua Parlby, including one William Meredith. The derby was to be Meredith's home debut. Prior to the derby, City had won only four games out of eleven in the League, although they had scored thirty goals including four in their previous game - a 5-4 defeat at Newcastle United! Newton Heath had lost only once in the League at Burton, and so entered the match as very much the team in form.

BEFORE THE GAME							
	P	W	D	L	F	A	Pts
NH	7	3	3	1	17	11	9
CITY	11	4	1	6	30	30	9

Richard Smith – Newton Heath's hero scored a record four goals in the opening derby match

Manchester City 1894/95. **Back:** *Iles (Trainer), McDowall, Hutchinson, Skerratt (Assistant Secretary), Chapman (Chairman), Lumsden.* **Middle:** *Dyer, Bowman, Douglas, Bennett.* **Front:** *Tomkinson, Johnston, Nash, Baunatyne, Milarvie.*

MATCH VERDICT

This was the first ever League match between the Manchester clubs. It proved to be an exciting game of end to end attacking football leading to a conclusive victory for Newton Heath. Smith, Newton's inside left was in irresistible form and set up derby history by scoring most goals in a single match. City were well beaten on the day, finding The Heathens' defence and McNaught in particular, difficult to break down. Some consolation came from the goal-scoring home debut of the legendary Billy Meredith, who was to give both clubs such wonderful service. For goal hero Smith this match marked the high point of a splendid first season for the club. His record four goals were part of 17 strikes in 29 games. During this season and the next he remained a consistent marksman for The Heathens, but thereafter, lost form and his team place, before leaving the club in 1900.

"The Umpire" sports newspaper of the day described the build up to the first ever League derby and recorded the first derby goal as follows:

"This League match was looked upon as the local Derby in Association football, and in spite of the dull and threatening weather the much-improved ground at Hyde Road presented an animated spectacle. When play started the weather was still dull, but the crowd rolled in fast, until probably over 10,000 were present. The City played towards the hotel end, and the sun coming out strongly was much against them early on. The excitement was intense as Meredith raced away and centred finely but the defence was equal to it and sternly repelled. At the other end the home side were not equally fortunate, as after Hutchinson had placed a beauty over the bar, Smith headed past him and opened the scoring for Newton after thirteen minutes play".

"The Umpire" then summarised the first ever League derby in the following terms:

"Although some allowance must be made on account of Smith (Harry) being hurt, it must be admitted that on the day the winners were the better team. Their combination was excellent and hardly a fault could be found with any of the players. Douglas made amends for his somewhat poor form of the previous week and, judging by the cheers with which he was greeted, he is still a great favourite on the Ardwick ground. All the backs played finely, but the highly finished display of McNaught is deserving of special mention. Dow played about his best game so far this season, one good feature being his unselfishness. Donaldson played as hard as ever, although he is not quite so unselfish as he might be. On the City side Hutchinson had little chance with any of the goals scored against him, albeit he gave one the appearance of being far from safe. Walker however, played very finely, but Dyer was by no means brilliant at half, in which position Mann was about the most conspicuous. The winning half-backs were clearly too good for the opposing forwards, but the play of the young Welsh player, Meredith and Finnerhan, was far superior to that of any other".

Newton Heath 1894/95
Back:
Albut (Secretary), Paley (Trainer), Dow, Douglas, Palmer (Director), Erentz, Davidson, Faulkner (Director).
Middle:
Crompton (President), Perrins, McNaught, Stewart, Jones (Vice-President).
Front:
Clarkin, Donaldson, Cassidy, Smith, Peters.

2

NEWTON HEATH 4
(Clarkin 2, Donaldson, Smith)

MANCHESTER CITY 1
(Sharples)

DATE		5th January 1895
DIVISION		Two
VENUE		Clayton
ATTENDANCE		12,000

Newton Heath		Manchester City
William DOUGLAS	1	Charlie WILLIAMS
John McCARTNEY	2	John WALKER
Fred ERENTZ	3	David ROBSON
Harry STONES	4	Harry SMITH
James McNAUGHT	5	Robert JONES
William STEWART	6	John McBRIDE
John CLARKIN	7	Billy MEREDITH
Robert DONALDSON	8	Pat FINNERHAN
James DOW	9	Sandy ROWAN
Richard SMITH	10	William McREDDIE
James PETERS	11	James SHARPLES

BACKGROUND

By the time the two clubs met for the second time in the League it was clear both were destined for quite different seasons. Newton Heath were enjoying a successful first season in Division Two and were up among the pacemakers. Beaten only three times in 19 games - all away from home - they were hot favourites. City however, were struggling to find consistency, a fact highlighted by a 4-1 beating of the Woolwich Arsenal on 15th December and then an 8-0 reverse on Boxing Day at Burton Wanderers. However two consecutive victories over Crewe and Rotherham prior to the derby put them in better heart. The Heathens' 3-0 defeat at Lincoln seven days before the derby, suggested the game could be closer than seemed likely earlier in the season.

MATCH VERDICT

City were unable to gain revenge for the early season derby defeat at Hyde Road. Although soundly beaten, most commentators felt the scoreline rather flattered The Heathens who led after seven minutes through Clarkin's goal and, despite an evenly balanced half, went in with a 2-0 lead due to a mistake by Robson, who let in Clarkin again for a second goal. It was certainly against the run of play when The Heathens made it 3-0 through Donaldson, and although Sharples' dramatic overhead kick allowed City some hope, this was soon doused by Smith's speculative shot for the fourth goal.

BEFORE THE GAME							
	P	W	D	L	F	A	Pts
N H	19	11	5	3	48	26	27
CITY	18	7	2	9	42	51	16

*The young **Billy Meredith** pictured here had an enormous influence on the early history of both clubs. A giant of Manchester football, he enjoyed a remarkable career. He played for City in two spells, from 1894-1906 and late in his career from 1921-24, making a total of 394 League and Cup appearances for the club, scoring 151 goals. For United he made 332 League and Cup appearances and scored 35 goals between 1906-20.*

"The Umpire" sports newspaper of the day reported on the match as follows:

In no previous season, it may truly be asserted, has the meeting of local rivals been looked forward to with such a great amount of interest in Manchester football circles. And this interest has by no means diminished as a result of the Heathens winning the first game at Hyde Road by 5 goals to 2, for since then the City team has been greatly strengthened, resulting in several brilliant performances, and, although their neighbours have been going great guns, a hard and fast game was anticipated. Unfortunately for Newton Heath, Perrins and Davidson were on the injured list, letting in Stones and Stewart, whilst Millar was shelved for Dow. On the other hand, the City were fully represented. The day was beautifully fine, and at the start there would be quite 10,000 persons present.

Newton Heath started in promising style, as after Clarkin had fallen when in a good position, some grand play by the home front rank resulted in Donaldson hitting the upright with a fast shot, whilst from the return Smith shot over. A run by Meredith developed an attack on the Heathens goal, but after some exciting play dangerously near, Stewart and Erentz cleared well on two occasions, and after Peters had taken the ball well down, it was, however, returned. McNaught who was playing very finely, put the sphere in goal, and Clarkin scored for the Heathens seven minutes from the start. Clever play at different times by McBride gave the City players a look in, but the forwards were bottled up on each occasion by the home defence. Be this as it may, the home team gave more than they received, and the City goal twice underwent the narrowest of shaves, one of which was a grand save by Williams from Smith, Clarkin soon after shooting rashly over the top. From this point however, the visitors played up in surprising fashion and following some grand work by the whole of the Heathens' backs, the City were awarded a couple of free kicks a few yards from their opponents' goal, from the latter of which Douglas saved in a style little short of marvellous, the ball bobbing about in the goal mouth until the player named placed it over the top. The leather was at last got away, and Peters taking a pass from Dow, raced along and centred. Unfortunately Robson missed his kick and Clarkin scored again from an awkward position.

The play was pretty evenly divided for some time after, and after Williams and his men had an anxious time at one end, Douglas was similarly placed at the other, although in the latter instance the Heathens would certainly have fallen but for two magnificent efforts by Douglas and Erentz.

At the restart the play for some time went in favour of the visitors, and after Meredith had forced a corner which resulted in a keen tussle in front of Douglas, a free kick for Newton Heath relieved the pressure. The latter were forced to play a strictly defensive game for a little time, during which Rowan should certainly have scored from a fine pass by McReddie. Dow at length passed cleverly to the right, and Clarkin and Donaldson outdoing McBride, Donaldson scored Newton Heath's third goal with a high shot. Play continued to hover round Williams and he and his men had a merry time. Peters, however, made poor use of his several chances of centering. The City players got to the other end, McBride took a free kick and Sharples with an overhead kick scored the visitors' first goal. The Heathens were again on the attack, and Walker was loudly cheered for saving a certain goal, and Williams later kept out a capital one from McNaught. Douglas soon after saved equally well as two or three times near the end, whilst from a free kick, Stones ran the ball out. A minute later Smith added the Heathens' fourth point with a long shot, Williams falling in trying to keep it out. For the last eight minutes of the game Clarkin retired injured and Newton Heath finished the game with ten men.

There was not such great superiority in the play of the Heathens as one would be inclined to suppose, judging by the score. The great failing of the losers was in a direction in which Newton Heath were seen to great advantage - the latter's readiness to seize opportunities to score which presented themselves, and the winners all round played a capital game from start to finish. In fairness to the losers', however, it must be said they experienced cruel luck two or three times and with all due deference to Douglas' excellent goalkeeping, he was certainly assisted by an element of luck.

AT THE SEASON'S END

CITY: Finished 9th on 31 points

NEWTON H: Finished 3rd on 38 points
(missed out on promotion by losing the Test match play-off 3-0 to Stoke City)

Pat Finnerhan – was a tricky inside-right who partnered Billy Meredith in the City attack.

3

NEWTON HEATH 1
(Clarkin)

MANCHESTER CITY 1
(Rowan)

DATE	5th October 1895
DIVISION	Two
VENUE	Clayton
ATTENDANCE	12,000

Newton Heath		Manchester City
William DOUGLAS	1	Charlie WILLIAMS
James DOW	2	James HARPER
Fred ERENTZ	3	David ROBSON
George PERRINS	4	George MANN
James McNAUGHT	5	Thomas CHAPMAN
Walter CARTWRIGHT	6	John McBRIDE
John CLARKIN	7	Billy MEREDITH
William KENNEDY	8	Pat FINNERHAN
Joe CASSIDY	9	Sandy ROWAN
Richard SMITH	10	William McREDDIE
James PETERS	11	James SHARPLES

BACKGROUND

Both sides had made excellent starts to the campaign for promotion from Division Two. Billy Meredith scored the only goal in City's opening away victory at Woolwich Arsenal while Newton Heath beat Crewe 5-0 at Clayton. City then won their next two home games against Rotherham and Leicester Fosse. However, the defence gave some cause for concern in a 5-0 defeat at Grimsby and it was with some relief that they chalked up a 1-0 victory over Woolwich Arsenal in the game prior to the derby. Newton Heath's second game was away at Loughborough where they drew 3-3, but The Heathens won their two games prior to the derby in convincing fashion, beating Burton 5-0 and Crewe 2-0.

BEFORE THE GAME							
	P	W	D	L	F	A	Pts
CITY	5	4	0	1	6	5	8
N H	4	3	1	0	15	3	7

George Perrins – another of Newton's regulars in the early days of the club.

Fred Erentz – one of Newton's early defensive stalwarts.

MATCH VERDICT

Derby fever had really caught on and, as the contemporary match report claimed, this was now the eagerly awaited "championship of Cottonopolis", requiring extra accommodation for the large crowds it attracted. The match was played in a typical Manchester downpour which may well have accounted for some elementary errors. City were the better side in the first half putting the home defence under constant pressure. Despite this they went in at half time a goal down, following a mistake by goalkeeper Williams. City justifiably drew level ten minutes into the second half, Rowan finishing off Robson's good work, while Williams atoned for his earlier error, keeping out a rejuvenated Heathens in the frantic final minutes.

"The Umpire" newspaper of the day recorded the enormous enthusiasm now already accorded to the Manchester derby match.

*City goalkeeper **Charlie Williams** who produced a great save in the final moments.*

"Certainly never in the Association football history of Manchester has there been greater interest taken in the match for the championship of Cottonopolis. Needless to state, the contest took place on the Heathen's ground at Clayton, the officials of which, anticipating a mammoth crowd, had provided extra seating accommodation, one item being the erection of an additional stand behind one of the goals. The gates were opened at one o'clock, at which time rain, however, commenced to fall, and as a consequence, the attendance only numbered between 10,000 and 11,000. The ground was on the heavy side, but the visitors felt their feet, so to speak, and several pretty movements caused the Heathens the greatest anxiety. Douglas saved a fine effort by McBride, and then after Cassidy, in taking a pass from Peters, had rattled the crossbar with a grand shot, Meredith made a number of capital centres, but none were taken advantage of, to the intense chagrin of the Cityites.

With twenty-five minutes gone Clarkin opened the scoring for the Heathens, the ball rolling across the goalmouth, and Williams missing, it went through - a somewhat lucky goal.

It was still raining when the players resumed and the City continued to play the smarter game and several runs and centres had a decided element of danger about them, but the home backs managed to chip in at the right moment, until at length McReddie got through. He was ruled offside, being palpably so, but a minute later Robson outdid Cassidy, and McReddie, getting the better of the half-backs opposing him, passed to the centre and Rowan put the finishing touch to a very fine piece of work. Performing with the utmost spirit again and yet again the visiting forwards bore down upon the Newton Heath goal, but they just failed to do the trick. In the last minute the home players made a magnificent dash to gain the lead and but for a truly marvellous save by Williams they would have succeeded, the latter and Robson keeping out stinging shots when surrounded by opponents".

*The young and brilliant **Billy Meredith** was always a favourite subject for cartoonists of the day. In this 1895-96 season he scored 12 League goals in 29 games.*

MANCHESTER CITY 2
(Hill, Meredith)

NEWTON HEATH 1
(Cassidy)

DATE	7th December 1895	
DIVISION	Two	
VENUE	Hyde Road	
ATTENDANCE	18,000	

Manchester City		Newton Heath
Charlie WILLIAMS	**1**	William DOUGLAS
Bert READ	**2**	James DOW
David ROBSON	**3**	Fred ERENTZ
George MANN	**4**	David FITZSIMMONS
Thomas CHAPMAN	**5**	James McNAUGHT
John McBRIDE	**6**	Walter CARTWRIGHT
Billy MEREDITH	**7**	John CLARKIN
Pat FINNERHAN	**8**	William KENNEDY
Sandy ROWAN	**9**	Joe CASSIDY
Hugh MORRIS	**10**	Richard SMITH
Robert HILL	**11**	James PETERS

BACKGROUND

Since the previous derby at Clayton in October, City had enjoyed a good League run and confidence was sky high. A 4-1 defeat by Burton Wanderers and a draw with the same club were the only matches they had failed to win.

The Heathens' form had been somewhat more erratic. Most of their matches had been high scoring affairs; a 5-5 draw with Lincoln, a 5-2 victory over Liverpool but also a 7-1 defeat at Liverpool! Indeed, City entered the game as League leaders, optimistic that they could record their first derby victory.

BEFORE THE GAME

	P	W	D	L	F	A	Pts
CITY	14	10	2	2	27	18	22
N H	13	7	3	3	38	24	17

Joe Cassidy - levelled with a splendid goal for Heathens.

MATCH VERDICT

Table-toppers City chalked up their first derby victory in front of an appreciative capacity home crowd at Hyde Road. City got off to a wonderful start with Hill finishing off Meredith's skilful wingplay. Despite City being well on top Cassidy brought Newton back into the game with a splendid goal. Shortly before half time the first ever derby penalty was awarded to the Heathens, who promptly missed it! A game of fluctuating fortunes was finally settled by a memorable individual goal by man of the match, Meredith.

"The Umpire" newspaper of the day reported on City's triumph as follows:

"The position of both these local clubs added to the usual attractiveness of this return fixture at Hyde Road. That the home executive anticipated an extraordinary attendance was shown by the improvements on the ground, accommodation even being provided for about 600 spectators on the cinder track. The weather materially improved by 1-30 and at this time there would be four or five thousand spectators on the ground, and by half-time there were 16,000 people present. At 2-15 the City entered the field, amid enthusiastic cheering, followed immediately by the Heathens, who received a round of cheers from their supporters, who were very much in evidence. The City won the toss and kicked off towards Galloway's. Tricky work by Hill gave McBride a chance and he forced Douglas to throw away. The City pressed, and Meredith centring, Finnerhan forced Douglas to handle. Returning to the attack, Meredith got away, and, sending well in, Hill scored a beautiful goal four minutes from the start. Finnerhan beat Erentz and passing to Meredith, he sent in a grand shot which just went outside. The City still pressing, nice work by Finnerhan and Hill enabled McBride to have a pop, the ball going wide of the posts. Newton broke away and Cassidy shot, but Robson saved, only to see Clarkin put in a fast shot just outside. A foul against Read close in menaced the City goal, and Williams cleared splendidly twice in succession. From good passing by the City, Meredith raced away, and sending in a terrific shot, Douglas just tipped it over the bar. From the flag-kick Newton got to the other end, but good work by Hill, Rowan and Morris relieved, and Morris sent in a good shot which Dow kicked away. Brilliant work by McBride and Rowan gave Meredith a chance, but he had to put in a screw shot with the left foot which cannoned off the post. Good work by Fitzsimmons, Kennedy and Clarkin looked ominous for the City, but Robson saved grandly. A pass by Rowan to Meredith looked a certain goal, the ball just skimming the bar, and Cartwright and Erentz could not stop Meredith from putting in some brilliant work. Twice Chapman shot, but in each instance, the ball was luckily deviated by the Newton backs. Newton broke away, and Cassidy, getting possession, sent in a lovely shot which scored. A pass by Finnerhan intended for Rowan was nicely intercepted by McNaught and Read conceded a corner. From the flag-kick a penalty was given against Chapman five yards from goal, but Hill cleared and the City getting away, Morris gave Douglas a handful which he cleared. Immediately on resuming, the Heathens went away in earnest on their left wing, but Smith's shot was put far out, a splendid opportunity thus being lost. After Cartwright had robbed Finnerhan, Cassidy gained a lot of ground uselessly, as Chapman was too strong for him. Both the extreme wing players for the City essayed shots, McNaught being here there and everywhere as occasion arose. The crowd cheered Meredith for dodging Cartwright, and working round Erentz, he beat Douglas with a magnificent shot, the uproar being tremendous. Still keen but fair football continued to be the order, and Williams put out three or four times in quick succession. Though a corner was awarded to Newton Heath in the last minute, it proved ineffectual, and City won a good game, in which much better football was shown than is usual in local contests. That the City won on their merits will be the verdict of the fair-minded observers. They combined better, and were quicker on the ball than their rivals, their passing being of a very high order. The coffers of both organisations will benefit largely, the takings amounting to £410".

Division Two	P	W	L	D	F	A	Pts
Manchester City	**15**	**11**	**2**	**2**	**29**	**19**	**24**
Burton Wanderers	15	10	2	3	32	15	23
Liverpool	17	11	5	1	49	24	23
Newton Heath	**14**	**7**	**4**	**3**	**39**	**26**	**17**
Woolwich Arsenal	14	7	5	2	29	19	16
Burton Swifts	13	7	6	0	23	25	14
Grimsby Town	12	6	5	1	31	22	13
Newcastle United	10	5	3	2	26	19	12
Darwen	14	4	6	4	38	30	12
Notts County	14	5	8	1	30	33	11
Leicester Fosse	11	4	5	2	19	18	10
Rotherham Town	13	3	8	2	15	28	8
Burslem Port Vale	10	3	6	1	19	38	7
Loughborough	11	2	7	2	13	28	6
Crewe Alexandra	12	3	9	0	15	35	6
Lincoln City	11	1	8	2	16	33	4

The League table after the match. Note how the old style tables placed the 'lost' column before the 'drawn' column.

AT THE SEASON'S END

CITY: Finished 2nd on 46 points
(Level on points with Liverpool, but missed out on promotion on goal average as only one team went up).

NEWTON H: Finished 6th on 33 points

MANCHESTER CITY 0
NEWTON HEATH 0

DATE	3rd October 1896
DIVISION	Two
VENUE	Hyde Road
ATTENDANCE	20,000

Manchester City		Newton Heath
Charlie WILLIAMS	1	Frank BARRETT
James DITCHFIELD	2	Harry STAFFORD
Dick RAY	3	Fred ERENTZ
George MANN	4	William DRAYCOTT
Charlie BANNISTER	5	Caesar JENKYNS
John McBRIDE	6	Walter CARTWRIGHT
Billy MEREDITH	7	Billy BRYANT
Pat FINNERHAN	8	Robert DONALDSON
Robert HILL	9	Joe CASSIDY
William LEWIS	10	James McNAUGHT
William TOWNLEY	11	Richard SMITH

BACKGROUND

Both Manchester clubs were determined to have successful seasons and matters certainly started well for both teams. The Heathens were in excellent form suffering just one defeat, away at Grimsby, and were at the top of the League going into the match. In the two games prior to the derby they had won 3-2 at Walsall's Hilary Street ground and thrashed Newcastle 4-0 at Clayton, Cassidy scoring a hat-trick, while goalkeeper Barrett also made his debut in the same game. City entered the derby unbeaten, but with just two victories over Darwen (4-1) and Lincoln (3-0).

BEFORE THE GAME							
	P	W	D	L	F	A	Pts
N H	7	6	0	1	19	8	12
CITY	5	2	3	0	11	5	7

Newton Heath 1896-97 – *the year they narrowly failed to gain promotion back to Division One.* **Back:** *A. Norris (Trainer), J. Taylor (President), Harry Stafford, Frank Barrett, Fred Erentz, A. Albut (Secretary), W. Healey (Director).* **Middle:** *William Draycott, James McNaught, Caesar Jenkyns, Walter Cartwright.* **Front:** *William Bryant, Robert Donaldson, Hugh Boyd, Matthew Gillespie, Joe Cassidy.*

MATCH VERDICT

The largest derby crowd yet witnessed the first scoreless match which was all rather a disappointment considering both clubs' promising starts to the season. Rain was again the culprit, making playing conditions extremely difficult. The Heathens had the balance of much of the play but could not transform their superiority into goals.

"The Umpire" sports newspaper of the day recorded the events as follows:

"The City team entered upon this match with the distinction of being the only organisation in the second division of the league who held an unbeaten certificate, and in spite of the splendid form shown by the Heathens, it was generally admitted they would have to go the full 90 minutes to deprive their rivals of that distinction.

A drizzling rain set in a few hours before the commencement, but notwithstanding this drawback, it was apparent the crowd would tax the limits of the accommodation. The scene was an exceedingly animated one, presenting as it did, an unbroken sea of faces. It is difficult to estimate with any degree of accuracy a crowd of such character, but it may be safe to venture the opinion that very few short of 20,000 witnessed the start.

Both teams met with a heavy reception, and Jenkyns having won the toss, Hill off kicked towards Galloway's end. After a few exchanges, McNaught got away nicely, and passed to Smith, who crossed, and Bryant just headed past the posts. The ball was, however, called back for a foul near the City goal. Tough scrimmages were contested in the Heathens' citadel, and the ball coming out to Ditchfield, the City back, had a try, which just went by. The home players were also several times penalised, notably in one instance by Ditchfield, who tripped up Cassidy when sailing along in dangerous fashion. The game had been very fast, but it must be admitted that the Heathens had the better of it up to this stage.

The City attacks were ragged indeed, while the backs, usually a strong quintet, were much below their standard. The result was that several corners were awarded as the outcome of miskicks, whilst on one occasion, Erentz placed the ball in grandly from a fine kick and Bryant only just missed the post with a header.

Lewis and Hill changed places hereabouts and there was a slight improvement in the City display, and following a run by Meredith a long shot went over Barrett's charge. Some more nice work by the Citizens in which Mann and McBride played a prominent part, gave the home side a look in, when Barrett, to a bouncing shot by Ditchfield, tipped the ball over the bar. Nothing came from the corner and at the interval nothing had been scored. On resuming the Heathens had the advantage for a moment or so, but then a fine run by Finnerhan altered the aspect again. The visitors scrambled out of difficulty by giving a corner, and the ball shortly came out to Mann, who let fly, but just as the sphere was going through at the corner, being completely out of the reach of Barrett, Draycott met it with his head - a good, and at the same time, lucky save.

By degrees the Heathens gained a footing in the home half, and, after Williams had cleared with a ponderous kick, Ray gave a corner. This was nicely sent across the goalmouth, but McNaught, with a splendid opening, put outside. The Hyde-roaders retaliated and Meredith, working his way into position, sent in a grand shot, which was, however, capitally kept out by Barrett, who received some hearty applause for the effort.

At the other end, Bryant came bounding along and Ray, coming in the way, gave a corner when a goal seemed inevitable. A loud groan shortly afterwards proclaimed the fact that Hill had missed a golden opportunity of scoring from a capital centre by Meredith. From this point the game went much in favour of the Heathens who strove hard to gain the lead. Every man was on his mettle. Cassidy was robbed by Bannister when getting dangerous, whilst Williams had to fist away from McNaught. Then Cartwright got his feet in the way of Meredith when getting in position to shoot, and in doing so, gave a corner from which Jenkyns did a grand piece of work by sending away. Neither side could claim much advantage subsequently, and the game ended in a draw".

The table after the match looked like this:

Division Two	P	W	L	D	F	A	Pts
Newton Heath	**8**	**6**	**1**	**1**	**19**	**8**	**13**
Notts County	6	5	1	0	16	9	10
Grimsby Town	7	4	1	2	15	10	10
Manchester City	**6**	**2**	**0**	**4**	**11**	**5**	**8**
Burton Swifts	5	3	1	1	10	8	7
Leicester Fosse	5	3	2	0	11	7	6
Woolwich Arsenal	5	2	1	2	9	5	6
Gainsborough Trinity	6	1	1	4	6	6	6
Blackpool	5	2	2	1	12	9	5
Small Heath	6	2	3	1	14	11	5
Newcastle United	5	2	3	0	11	14	4
Walsall	6	1	3	2	6	9	4
Lincoln City	6	2	4	0	7	13	4
Darwen	6	1	5	0	6	21	2
Burton Wanderers	6	1	5	0	5	17	2
Loughborough	6	1	5	0	4	13	2

6

NEWTON HEATH 2
(Smith, Donaldson)

MANCHESTER CITY 1
(Hill)

DATE	25th December 1896
DIVISION	Two
VENUE	Clayton
ATTENDANCE	18,000

Newton Heath		Manchester City
Frank BARRETT	1	Charlie WILLIAMS
Harry STAFFORD	2	James HARPER
Fred ERENTZ	3	Dick RAY
William DRAYCOTT	4	George MANN
Caesar JENKYNS	5	Charlie BANNISTER
James McNAUGHT	6	John McBRIDE
Billy BRYANT	7	Billy MEREDITH
Richard SMITH	8	Pat FINNERHAN
Joe CASSIDY	9	Robert HILL
Matthew GILLESPIE	10	John GUNN
Robert DONALDSON	11	Fred WILLIAMS

Robert Donaldson – on target to give Newton Heath a Christmas Day victory over City.

BACKGROUND

Immediately after the September derby City's form suffered. A 3-3 draw at Notts County and three straight defeats pushed them down the table. November brought a welcome victory (Blackpool) but also defeat (Walsall). A much needed confidence booster came in the shape of two home victories prior to the derby, a 2-1 victory over Burton Wanderers and a 3-1 defeat of Grimsby Town. The Heathens had mixed fortunes between derbies. A draw (Small Heath) and two defeats (Blackpool and Gainsborough Trinity) knocked the club off the top of the League. The prolific Cassidy improved things with all the goals in the 3-0 defeat of Burton. However, confidence was low as they entered the derby following two away defeats at Small Heath (1-0) and Notts County (3-0).

BEFORE THE GAME							
	P	W	D	L	F	A	Pts
N H	15	8	2	5	29	21	18
CITY	15	6	5	4	31	25	17

This picture shows the unusual roof pavilion on the old main stand at Bank Street, Clayton - the home ground for Newton Heath between 1893 and 1910.

MATCH VERDICT

A Christmas Day derby (in subsequent years the holiday period was often considered a good derby date) brought a capacity crowd to Clayton. As the match report outlines, such was the crowd pressure that there was a danger of the match being abandoned at half time. In heavy conditions, apparently not to City's liking, Newton proved easy victors, with the visitors reportedly 'fagged out'. The key to the victory had been the superb defensive performance of McNaught, who marked Meredith out of the game. The derby had now established itself as the major attraction on the Manchester soccer calendar - witness the 18,000 crowd and healthy gate receipts of £546.17s.

The reporter of the day, using the pen name 'Nibbes' recorded the match as follows for "Athletic News"

"Holidays are suitable for Derby Day matches, and the two Manchester clubs were wise in selecting Christmas Day for their return League encounter at Clayton. The crowd was an enormous one, fully 18,000 being present, and I never saw so many lads at a football match. They were really the cause of the encroaching in the first half, for they were continually creeping under the rails, and as a natural consequence their elders were bound to follow if they were to get a glimpse of the game. The hoarding behind the goal lines gave way in several places, and as a result of one smash, two lads had to be led off the ground. The game had to be stopped in the first half, but at the interval, Mr J. Parlby, one of the League Management Committee, told the crowd point blank that if they did not keep beyond the touch line, the game could not proceed, and the Newton Heath Club would have to suffer the consequences. His words had the required effect. The ground was in a wretched condition, which was certainly in favour of the home team, for the City are never at home on a heavy ground. This was easily to be seen in the second half, for they were fagged out, whereas the Hea-

thens were going as strong as ever, and it was their stability that enabled them to gain their victory. They were undoubtedly the better team, and as they have gained three points out of City this season, they have a fair claim to superiority; indeed, their record against the City is very favourable to them. One of the secrets of the Heathens' success was the bringing of McNaught to left half to face Meredith and Finnerhan, and so successful was he in his shadowing tactics that the City crack forwards could make no headway whatever. The only forward who was at all brilliant was Gunn, who did the work of two men, and was very effective into the bargain. I had not seen Donaldson previously at outside left, but on Friday he was a great success, Mann being of little use against him. Harper and McBride were the only ones who shone in the defence, but on the other hand the Heathens were strong behind, the half-backs contributing in no small measure to the victory. Jenkyns' head seemed to be continually getting in the way of the ball: indeed, all round the winners were the superior lot".

CITY: Finished 6th on 32 points

NEWTON H: Finished 2nd on 39 points
(Again lost promotion chance in Test match play-offs).

Billy Meredith – wearing a Welsh International cap. The City wing-wizard had made his debut for Wales in 1895.

NEWTON HEATH 1
(Gillespie)

MANCHESTER CITY 1
(Ray)

DATE	16th October 1897
DIVISION	Two
VENUE	Clayton
ATTENDANCE	20,000

Newton Heath		Manchester City
Frank BARRETT	1	Charlie WILLIAMS
Harry STAFFORD	2	Bert READ
Fred ERENTZ	3	Dick RAY
James McNAUGHT	4	Bobby MOFFATT
Caesar JENKYNS	5	William 'Buxton' SMITH
Walter CARTWRIGHT	6	William 'Doc' HOLMES
Billy BRYANT	7	Billy MEREDITH
Robert DONALDSON	8	William 'Stockport' SMITH
Hugh BOYD	9	Billy GILLESPIE
Matthew GILLESPIE	10	Fred WILLIAMS
Joe CASSIDY	11	Patrick LEONARD

BACKGROUND

City were top of the table and riding high. Seven straight wins and an average three goals a game made them clear favourites. There had been big victories over Gainsborough Town (3-0), Darwen (4-2) and Woolwich Arsenal (4-1), while William 'Stockport' Smith was in prolific form with eight goals in the last five games. City had at this time two players called William Smith and so they were both nicknamed after the towns they came from - Buxton and Stockport. Newton Heath also started the season well beating Lincoln (5-0) and Burton Swifts (4-0). However, they were somewhat inconsistent after this with victories (Blackpool and Leicester Fosse) but also defeats (Luton and Newcastle). They needed to be on top form to resist City.

BEFORE THE GAME

	P	W	D	L	F	A	Pts
CITY	7	7	0	0	22	3	14
N H	6	4	0	2	13	4	8

Newton Heath in 1897/98 **Back:** *A. Norris (Trainer), H. Erentz, F. Erentz, W. Draycott, F. Barrett, H. Stafford, J. McNaught, W. Morgan.* **Front:** *W. Cartwright, J. Collinson, H. Boyd, M. Gillespie, W. Bryant, J. Cassidy. The trophy is the Lancashire Cup.*

MATCH VERDICT

League leaders City dropped their first point of the season in a typically hard fought contest with their neighbours. In the first half Newton Heath had all the play and Williams needed to be on excellent form to keep The Heathens' forwards at bay. Eventually Newton Heath scored, following a spell of sustained pressure on the City goal and Gillespie shot home to give The Heathens a half time lead. In a close fought second half City were unlucky on a number of occasions not to create an equaliser. However, with only one minute remaining, Ray charged half the length of the pitch and scored with a spectacular high cross shot. City had narrowly retained their unbeaten record, although Burnley knocked them off the top of the table on goal average.

"The Umpire" reported on the derby at Clayton as follows:

"Owing to the friendly rivalry that exists between these two clubs, a great amount of interest was centered on the game, and in consequence there were about 20,000 spectators, in fact, the numbers far exceeded any previous game on this ground. Both clubs turned out their strongest teams, and the weather was all that could be desired, the sun shining brilliantly. A few minutes before the time for kicking off (three o'clock), the home representatives stepped onto the field amid encouraging cheers, and directly afterwards loud shouts announced the appearance of the City men.

Newton Heath won the toss and decided to play with the wind but against the sun. Punctual to time, Gillespie kicked off for the visitors amid much excitement, and the City men at once made tracks for the home goal, but Erentz kicked back to the centre when a free-kick was awarded to the home players for a foul. This was nicely put in, but after some exciting play the ball was put over the line and a goal-kick was the only result. Some tricky play by both sets of forwards ended with play settling down at the centre for a time. Newton Heath then worked the ball to the other end, and Cassidy put in a climbing shot. A goal looked certain, but Williams had to be reckoned with. He jumped up and fisted the ball amid loud cheers from the City supporters. It was a grand shot and a brilliant save. Donaldson and M.Gillespie were next prominent and Newton were now having all the best of the game. McNaught put in a grand piece of work, and the final kick just landed the ball on the net. The visitors now had a turn at pressing and for two or three minutes were very dangerous. Several good shots were put in, but Barrett, Erentz and Stafford kept them all out. Bryant too did some excellent work and along with Jenkyns sent the ball well down the field, but City returned to the attack with some equally excellent work by Meredith and Smith. The game was now very fast and exciting and if anything slightly in favour of the home team. Twice more Williams saved but the home team were not disheartened and renewed the attack with vigour. Boyd and Donaldson showed good combination and sent the ball in to M.Gillespie whose shot opened the score for Newton much to the relief and loud cheers of the home supporters. Soon after City had an excellent chance of equalising the score, but Smith shot over. The City were coming again when McNaught kicked well down field in brilliant style. Boyd got the ball and had a clear chance for goal. He made a grand attempt but Williams was in the way.

After a brief half-time refreshment the game was resumed, the City players now having the advantage of the wind. Boyd kicked off, but for a time neither side could gain an advantage, the ball crossing and recrossing the centre line with great rapidity. Then City got going but although they tried hard they could only place the ball over the line, a goal-kick thus being the only result. From this Cassidy got possession and raced away to the City end; a corner was the result. This was well put in and the City had a most anxious time as they could not get the ball away, and just when Newton looked as if they would score, the whistle was blown for a foul against the home team. Again City attacked, and they had an excellent chance of scoring but Leonard, who made a gallant effort just failed to find the net. Newton were going in fine style to the City goal when they were pulled up for a foul. From the free-kick the ball went to Moffatt who made a long shot for goal. This was a long way off the mark, but Smith soon after put in a better shot which just went over the bar. Newton still kept on the attack much to the delight of the home partisans. Time after time the City tried to break away, but Stafford and Erentz who were playing a fine game returned the ball on each occasion. A goal to Newton now looked certain but Ray cleared just in time. The last-named player and Read had plenty of work to do, and right well they did acquit themselves. Holmes too was conspicuous with some good effective work. Much to the relief of the City, Moffatt got the ball and kicked well down field and the City men, following up well, took the ball to the home half. Donaldson, however, with a splendid run transferred the play to the other end. Here the Newton men became dangerous more than once, but do as they would, they could not find the net. The City men, who were not playing with the same dash as in the first half broke away occasionally, but they were never really dangerous. Smith, one of the City forwards was loudly cheered for a grand piece of individual work but he had little support and the effort was quickly neutralised by the Newton men. As time drew near the excitement was intense, both sets of players being called upon to do their utmost. The City men now played better and rushing down the field scored a clever goal with a high cross shot which was well done. The excitement was intense at this point, and the City partisans did not fail to show approval of this stage of the game when they had made up their minds for a defeat. Only a minute remained for play, and neither side did anything more, and the game was left drawn".

Billy Gillespie – a bustling centre-forward who scored 126 League goals during his eight years with City. His brother Matt played for Newton Heath and scored the Heathens goal in this match.

Bobby Moffatt – City's half-back was a great provider for winger Billy Meredith and played a prominent role in this derby.

MANCHESTER CITY 0
NEWTON HEATH 1
(Cassidy)

DATE	25th December 1897
DIVISION	Two
VENUE	Hyde Road
ATTENDANCE	16,000

Manchester City		Newton Heath
Charlie WILLIAMS	1	Frank BARRETT
Bert READ	2	Harry STAFFORD
Dick RAY	3	Fred ERENTZ
Bobby MOFFATT	4	William DRAYCOTT
William 'Buxton' SMITH	5	James McNAUGHT
William 'Doc' HOLMES	6	Walter CARTWRIGHT
Billy MEREDITH	7	Billy BRYANT
James WHITEHEAD	8	James CARMAN
Billy GILLESPIE	9	Hugh BOYD
Fred WILLIAMS	10	Joe CASSIDY
Patrick LEONARD	11	William DUNN

BACKGROUND

City maintained their excellent start to the season. It was not until the tenth game that they tasted defeat (3-1 at Burnley). They quickly put this reverse behind them, recording further victories over Leicester Fosse and Grimsby. With ground advantage City entered the game hot favourites. Inconsistency had dogged The Heathens' progress. They had thrashed Walsall 6-0 but lost to Small Heath, Lincoln and Newcastle.

BEFORE THE GAME							
	P	W	D	L	F	A	Pts
CITY	13	10	2	1	36	12	22
N H	14	6	3	5	25	12	15

Frank Barrett – one of Newton's finest early goalkeepers, he was a Scottish international, signed from Dundee in 1896.

Harry Stafford – an accomplished full-back with Newton Heath, he went on to become one of the great captains of the club.

MATCH VERDICT

The Heathens' hoodoo over their City rivals continued in a result that upset the form book. Cassidy's first half goal proved enough to win a close fought match. City (as had been the case in previous encounters) had a lot of the play but failed to take advantage of their many chances. This was City's first home defeat of the season and at the time a severe blow to their hopes of making the top Division.

"The Umpire" sports newspaper recorded City's home defeat in the following fashion:

"In the Second Division the match of the day was, of course, the eighth contest between Newton Heath and Manchester City, and as a result of it, the Heathens have been able to record their fourth win, the City only having proved successful in one instance, while three games have ended in draws. It was a characteristic local contest, fast and hard rather than scientific play being witnessed, and in the end Newton Heath won an exciting game by one goal to nil - a point which accrued as the outcome of a scrimmage in goal, and which, though the Manchester City men strove with might and main, they were never able to neutralise.

Newton Heath certainly owed their victory to the fine character of their defence, and while giving them credit for their success, which was undoubtedly gained by downright hard work, they must count themselves somewhat lucky to come out of the contest with a couple of points to their credit. In the first half and again in the second, the City players did rather more of the pressing, but the Clayton halves were going great guns and whatever they were unable to perform was accomplished in the most capable manner by Stafford, Erentz and Barrett. Against their combined efforts, the City forwards rarely shone in the matter of combination, a remark which applies with equal force to the winning side, Cassidy missing a couple of good chances of beating Williams. But he was not the only delinquent, the shooting of the whole five being anything but deadly. As the end approached and the much needed goal did not appear to be forthcoming the Manchester men threw themselves with the greatest zeal into the contest, and shot after shot was poured into the Newton Heath goal, but they were as often sent out again by Barrett and the men in front of him, and when at last the referee sounded his whistle for the last time, the City had lost their first game at home this season, a result that somewhat blights their prospect of appearing in the test games. They at least deserved a point from yesterday's contest".

Walter Cartwright – a dedicated left-half who gave Newton sterling service during the club's earliest years.

AT THE SEASON'S END

CITY: Finished 3rd on 39 points
(6 points behind 2nd placed Newcastle)

NEWTON H: Finished 4th on 38 points

Hugh Boyd – a prolific goalscorer with Newton during this period, he netted 32 League goals in just 52 appearances between 1896-98.

9 NEWTON HEATH 3
(Cassidy 2 (1 pen), Boyd)
MANCHESTER CITY 0

DATE	10th September 1898	
DIVISION	Two	
VENUE	Clayton	
ATTENDANCE	20,000	

Newton Heath		Manchester City
Frank BARRETT	1	Charlie WILLIAMS
Harry STAFFORD	2	Bobby MOFFATT
Fred ERENTZ	3	Bert READ
William DRAYCOTT	4	William 'Doc' HOLMES
William MORGAN	5	William 'Buxton' SMITH
Walter CARTWRIGHT	6	Stuart MUNN
Billy BRYANT	7	Billy MEREDITH
John COLLINSON	8	William 'Stockport' SMITH
Hugh BOYD	9	Billy GILLESPIE
Joe CASSIDY	10	James WHITEHEAD
Matthew GILLESPIE	11	Fred WILLIAMS

BACKGROUND

The previous season was the first in which neither Manchester side had appeared in the promotion Tests. It was also the last year of the play-offs following a suspicious result in the game between Stoke and Burnley when the convenient 0-0 draw allowed both clubs to gain promotion. Both Manchester clubs were naturally keen to gain automatic promotion at the first attempt, especially Newton Heath who had failed so many times in the Test matches. Both sides won their opening game of the season, The Heathens beating Gainsborough Trinity 2-0, O.J.Jones scoring both goals in his only appearance for the club. City meanwhile were among the goals in a 7-2 win at Grimsby where Meredith and Gillespie both netted hat-tricks.

BEFORE THE GAME							
	P	W	D	L	F	A	Pts
CITY	1	1	0	0	7	2	2
N H	1	1	0	0	2	0	2

MATCH VERDICT

The Heathens were taking an ascendancy in derby encounters, this being their sixth victory to City's single success over the course of nine matches. Indeed, the consistently large crowds certainly whetted local appetites for the day when the two clubs would play their derby games in the premier Division. In this match Newton Heath enjoyed a conclusive victory, including the first successfully converted derby penalty, given for a foul by Read on Bryant and scored by The Heathens' Cassidy, who in other reports was also credited with the first goal. City laboured with the handicap of being reduced to only ten men after the injured Holmes was forced to leave the field.

"The Athletic News" reported the early season meeting as follows

"With such a vast crowd as we had at Clayton on Saturday in mind it makes one wonder why we do not possess a First Division club in Manchester, and a successful one at that. The

The cover of the first Official Programme for a Manchester derby match.

abolition of the Test matches and the elevation of Burnley and Newcastle United to a higher state should provide a fine opening for the two socker clubs of Cottonpolis, and I think we shall have one, if not two, representatives among seniors twelve months hence. The two clubs are certainly no weaker than they were last season, and as they then finished together after a pair who qualified for the Test matches, I see no reason why our consummation should not be fulfilled.

As a proof of the enthusiasm of Mancunians for the game I need only mention the fact that there would be fully 18,000 on the Clayton enclosure on the occasion of the first meeting of the old rivals. It is rather early in the season for such serious matches, for neither side could scarcely have been wound up, but such weather as we are now enjoying is a big inducement for crowds and I suppose a big turnover is not to be despised. The two clubs may always be depended upon to produce a stiff struggle, no matter what the standard of the football might be, and it is worthy of note that although they met on no fewer than half a dozen occasions last season only one goal divided them on the aggregate, that in favour of the City who, however, in League matches from the very commencement never seemed to make much headway.

There have been great improvements effected in the Heathens' enclosure since last season, a fine uncovered stand having been erected on the Clayton side in place of the one which stood at the opposite end, while the apology for a covered stand has also received attention; in fact, there has been quite a brush-up, for the turf itself has never been in better condition.

As usual, both teams commenced as though the game was only to be of a quarter of an hour's duration, and indeed, twice during that period was the ball netted once by each team, but only Newton's counted. The City first got through, Meredith putting on the finishing touch from a pass by Williams, but the referee ruled that the latter was offside. Newton's legitimate goal was gained as the result of a free kick taken well up the field by Stafford, who planted the ball right into the goalmouth, and into the net it went off somebody's back - whose was a matter of controversy. Soon after this Holmes was injured, but, though useless, he kept his place, but as it dawned on him that he would be better off the field he retired for the rest of the game, so that the City were heavily handicapped, particularly as Holmes was playing exceedingly well up to his injury.

The City kept up surprisingly, although it must not be forgotten that the Heathens were playing against both wind and sun, which at times was rather dazzling. There was no further scoring, so that the Heathens turned round with a lead of one goal to none and under the circumstances it was fully anticipated that they would further increase their lead after the interval. After Holmes' retirement the City brought B.Smith to left-half and played four forwards, which they continued on resuming, but Williams was transferred to extreme right and Meredith went inside. The City again

played up pluckily, and once Stafford let Meredith in, but happily Erentz intervened. Their weakened forces told its tale however and a second point was put up against them. Gillespie had got the ball from the half-backs, and running well down he shot in from the near flag, a favourite bit of his. The ball went across squarely, but other white shirts were in close vicinity, and Boyd, rushing up, made no mistake in collaring the ball and whipping it past Williams, who was beaten a third time ere the close from a penalty given against Read. Cassidy was entrusted the kick, and keeping the ball low, his sterling play during the whole of the afternoon was rewarded by a goal".

Reproduced above is a page from the first Official Programme for a derby match. At this time it was a combined publication for both the Manchester clubs and the rugby teams Broughton Rangers and Salford.

Billy Meredith - *"was like a bull in a china shop rushing about without much good result" said 'Athletic News'.*

MANCHESTER CITY 4
(F.Williams, Meredith, Gillespie, Dougal)
NEWTON HEATH 0

DATE	26th December 1898
DIVISION	Two
VENUE	Hyde Road
ATTENDANCE	25,000

Manchester City		Newton Heath
Charlie WILLIAMS	1	Frank BARRETT
Bert READ	2	Harry STAFFORD
Di JONES	3	Fred ERENTZ
Bobby MOFFATT	4	William DRAYCOTT
William 'Buxton' SMITH	5	Frank PEPPER
William 'Doc' HOLMES	6	Walter CARTWRIGHT
Billy MEREDITH	7	Billy BRYANT
William 'Stockport' SMITH	8	John COLLINSON
Billy GILLESPIE	9	Joe CASSIDY
Fred WILLIAMS	10	William BROOKS
George DOUGAL	11	Matthew GILLESPIE

A plan of City's Hyde Road ground before the turn of the century.

BACKGROUND

City had lost just once since the last meeting, 3-1 at Lincoln City. They were scoring plenty of goals with the irrepressible Billy Meredith leading marksman with 15 goals in 16 games. Sitting at the top of the table they were confident of beating their old rivals. The Heathens had shown nothing but see-saw inconsistency as heavy defeats (5-1 by Burton Swifts and 5-1 by Woolwich Arsenal) were balanced by unlikely results such as the 9-0 demolition of Darwen just two days before the derby.

BEFORE THE GAME

	P	W	D	L	F	A	Pts
CITY	16	11	3	2	43	20	25
N H	16	11	1	4	38	21	23

MATCH VERDICT

A wonderful victory for City as goals by four of their five forwards capped a thrilling display of attacking football that demolished their keen rivals. The two clubs were involved in a fierce race for promotion to the First Division and this derby result proved the conclusive spur as far as City were concerned. Conditions were poor with rain before and during the match but City took an interval lead as Read sent in Dougal whose shot was parried by Barrett and Fred Williams scored from the rebound. Dougal had a fine effort ruled out for offside but intense second half presssure saw Meredith bundle the ball in from close range after a series of corners. From a further flag-kick Fred Williams and Gillespie barged Barrett into the net with the ball in his possession, but the referee allowed the goal to stand. A fine combination between Dougal and Williams down the flank then opened up the Heathens' defence again, with Dougal slotting a fourth goal. It was City who climbed into the top flight, and it would be three seasons before the clubs would meet again.

AT THE SEASON'S END

CITY: Promoted as Division 2 Champions

P	W	D	L	F	A	Pts
34	23	6	5	92	35	52

NEWTON H: Finished 4th in Division 2
(9 points behind City)

'CLIMBING THE GOLDEN STAIRS'
This contemporary cartoon refers to the fact that both clubs were locked in a close battle for promotion. City's 4-0 victory helped them to ultimately achieve that prized goal as champions at the end of the season.

Manchester City's 1898/99 Second Division championship winning team.

11

MANCHESTER UNITED 1
(Pegg)

MANCHESTER CITY 1
(Meredith)

DATE	25th December 1902	
DIVISION	Two	
VENUE	Clayton	
ATTENDANCE	40,000	

Manchester United		Manchester City
Herbert BIRCHENOUGH	1	Jack HILLMAN
Harry ROTHWELL	2	John McMAHON
Thomas READ	3	Robert DAVIDSON
Alec DOWNIE	4	Sammy FROST
William GRIFFITHS	5	Tom HYNDS
Walter CARTWRIGHT	6	William McOUSTRA
Alf SCHOFIELD	7	Billy MEREDITH
Thomas MORRISON	8	Jimmy BANNISTER
Ernest PEGG	9	Billy GILLESPIE
John PEDDIE	10	Sandy TURNBULL
Arthur BEADSWORTH	11	Fred THRELFALL

BACKGROUND

A great deal happened to the two Manchester clubs between the date of the last meeting on Boxing Day 1898 and this next Christmas-time encounter in 1902. Manchester City had a fairly successful first season in Division One, finishing seventh, but the following season saw the Blues slip to eleventh place. The 1901-02 season however brought misery; the first five games were all lost, only eleven matches were won and City were relegated back to the Second Division. Across at Clayton, Newton Heath had also found life increasingly difficult. The Heathens finished season 1889-90 in fourth place in Division Two but were not attracting the sizeable crowds of their neighbours. Newton's average crowd hovered around the 6,000 mark, whilst City were supported by 17,000. The situation deteriorated further the following season with the club finishing tenth and the parlous state of the Newton Heath finances was illustrated by the fact that the team's rail fare to some away games had to be paid for by the generosity of supporters.

At the end of the 1901-02 season Newton Heath sank to their lowest position since formation, fifteenth out of eighteen. The season ended on 23rd April and with it effectively, so did Newton Heath. The club was in dire financial straits and faced complete closure. The only remedy was a relaunch, and by 28th April, largely due to the financial acumen and generosity of local brewery owner John Davies, the club was saved and re-emerged as Manchester United.

Johnny McMahon – made his debut in the Christmas Day Mancunian derby match.

Jimmy Bannister – was rated by Meredith as one of the best footballing partners he ever had.

BEFORE THE GAME							
	P	W	D	L	F	A	Pts
CITY	16	12	1	3	40	17	25
UNITED	12	6	3	3	15	11	15

Playing in their new strip of red shirts and white shorts, United started the 1902-03 season in optimistic fashion winning their first two games, and by Christmas were comfortably placed in midtable. City, like United, started the season with a victory and kept in touch with the top of the table via a series of successful results. Their 4-1 win over Woolwich Arsenal five days before the derby suggested United would do well to take any points at all from this encounter.

MATCH VERDICT

In front of the largest ever derby crowd to date the new Manchester United entertained their table topping neighbours. It proved to be a closely contested match but a gusty wind often made control of the ball difficult. In general, City were unlucky not to record a victory, Meredith being particularly unfortunate to hit the woodwork twice in the match. Victory seemed in sight early in the second half when Meredith finally found the net and United were temporarily reduced to ten men as goalkeeper Birchenough - injured when the goal was scored - was carried off. However the Reds' fortitude in these fixtures shone through once again with Pegg's late equaliser.

A newspaper report of the day commented on the match as follows:

Jack Hillman - the City goalkeeper was just one of several new faces to line up as the two great rival teams met for the first time in four years.

"These local rivals met at Clayton before an immense crowd, fully 35,000 spectators being present. Both sides had alterations, Schofield and Morrison playing on the United side, while City played Hillman and McMahon. City won the toss and played with a strong wind behind them. The game in the first half was of a one-sided character, City doing all the attacking, but Birchenough and his backs played a splendid game, and prevented any score, although Gillespie, McOustra and Threlfall narrowly missed scoring. On one occasion Meredith shot with great force, only to see the ball hit the upright and go out. Now and again United made towards the City goal, and Hillman twice saved by fisting away, with a crowd of players around him. Half-time arrived with no score. With the wind behind them United were thought to have the game well in hand, but City played with surprising dash, and early on, after clever work by Threlfall, Meredith scored. Unfortunately Birchenough, in trying to save, injured himself, and had to be carried off the field, but after ten minutes rest resumed. City were showing clever combination and threatened the United goal time after time, but they could not increase their score. The City half-backs were always to the front, and repeatedly broke up the United efforts to break through. Twenty minutes from the finish, a free kick was awarded to United and Pegg received, tricked Frost and shot through, thus equalising the scores. From this point up to the close exciting play was the order, and with less than five minutes to go Meredith dashed away, his final shot striking the cross-bar and rebounding into play. At the other end three corners were conceded, but brought no result, and a splendidly contested game (though somewhat spoilt by the wind) ended in a draw of one goal each".

*The benevolent **Mr John Davies**, who came up with substantial money to ensure the club survived and that the re-named Manchester United grew to prominence under his Presidency.*

12

MANCHESTER CITY 0
MANCHESTER UNITED 2
(Holmes og, Schofield)

DATE	10th April 1903
DIVISION	Two
VENUE	Hyde Road
ATTENDANCE	30,000

Manchester City		Manchester United
Jack HILLMAN	1	Herbert BIRCHENOUGH
John McMAHON	2	Harry ROTHWELL
William 'Doc' HOLMES	3	Thomas READ
Sammy FROST	4	Walter CARTWRIGHT
Tom HYNDS	5	William GRIFFITHS
William McOUSTRA	6	Alec DOWNIE
Billy MEREDITH	7	Alf SCHOFIELD
Jimmy BANNISTER	8	Thomas ARKESDEN
Billy GILLESPIE	9	Ernest PEGG
Sandy TURNBULL	10	John PEDDIE
Fred THRELFALL	11	Thomas MORRISON

BACKGROUND

Following the Christmas-time draw City's season continued to be successful. The Blues lost only one game between derbies, a 1-0 defeat at Lincoln City. On their return to the Second Division City were looking a far superior side to the rest. They entered the derby top of the table following crushing victories over Burnley (6-0), Burslem Port Vale (7-1) and Gainsborough Trinity (9-0). United were struggling to find consistency but had recorded some encouraging victories such as the 3-0 win over Woolwich Arsenal. However, they must have entered this derby against all-conquering City with some trepidation.

BEFORE THE GAME

	P	W	D	L	F	A	Pts
CITY	31	23	4	4	90	27	50
UNITED	28	12	7	9	43	32	31

*An early team group of **Manchester United** in 1903*

MATCH VERDICT

Again a massive crowd gathered at Hyde Road to see the local rivals play but United upset all the pre-match odds by recording another victory, with goals at the beginning of each half. City showed a good deal of endeavour but their finishing, particularly in the first half, was woefully wayward. In derby terms the result was a sweet one for United as it put a last minute question mark against City's hopes of returning to Division One.

A newspaper of the day reported on the match as follows:

"The keen rivalry in play which exists between these teams attracted a great crowd to Hyde Road yesterday. When they met at Clayton on Christmas Day, both clubs were running very closely together for First Division honours, and the game ended in a draw of one goal each. Throughout the season the Manchester City team have played very consistent football, not having lost a match since January 3.

Manchester United won the toss, but little was gained as there was only a slight wind. The game was only five minutes old when a stroke of luck fell to United. From a throw-in Arkesden got hold and centred, and Morrison, who was lying well up, put in a tame shot, but in transit the ball struck Holmes and then the upright, and rolled into the net. The City men seemed a good deal demoralised by this early reverse, and chances were thrown away by wild shooting, Threlfall especially being at fault. On one occasion Turnbull gave him a judicious pass and the outside man had only Birchenough to beat when he shot wide. Cartwright gave Meredith very little scope, and it was seldom that the City captain was seen to advantage. Read, before the interval arrived, nearly put the ball through his own goal, but Birchenough just managed to tip it over the bar.

When the teams crossed over United were leading by one goal to none. Like the opening of the first half, United again scored ere the game had been restarted three minutes. Hillman, from a shot by Peddie, kicked behind, and from the ensuing corner Schofield easily scored a second and this was the last goal. From this point City never looked like scoring; their passing quite lacked finesse compared with that of the United team, whose play throughout was splendid. Arkesden and Peddie in this combined work showed fine judgement, but found a tough opponent in Frost. Cartwright and Downie bore the brunt of the half-back line, and their play had a great deal to do with the result. Birchenough had more to do than Hillman, but managed to preserve a clean sheet. Read and Rothwell withstood all the efforts made by the City men to score, and Read's kicking was certainly a prominent feature of the match. Of the City play little more need be said than that Frost, McOustra and Turnbull were the pick of a team that from some cause or other, appeared to be beaten after the first five minutes of their work on the field".

Alf Schofield - scored United's second goal to make the game safe.

John Peddie – a useful goalscorer who was signed from Newcastle, he ended the season with 11 League goals in 30 appearances.

Alec Downie was to prove a tremendous servant to the club as a totally committed wing-half. This was his first season after joining United from Swindon. He went on to make 191 senior outings

AT THE SEASON'S END

CITY: Promoted as Division 2 Champions

P	W	D	L	F	A	Pts
34	25	4	5	95	29	54

UNITED: Finished 5th on 38 points

Manchester City *in 1905. Many believed this Blues squad were poised for great things after lifting the 1904 F.A. Cup, but the bribes scandal ripped the heart out of the club, with many of the eleven players pictured here fined and suspended. Five of them subsequently joined United and formed the basis of the Reds success towards the end of the decade.*
Back: *Broad, McMahon, Moffatt, Mr. Forrest, Hillman, Mr. Davies, Pearson, Booth, Mr. Maley (Secretary).*
Front: *Turnbull, Burgess, Jones, Meredith, Frost, Hynds.*

Manchester United *with the 1909 F.A. Cup. The core of this squad also won two League Championships in 1908 and 1911, but this first great Reds team owed much to the loss of a handful of City's best players who crossed Manchester to join the 'other' club in the wake of the Blues bribes scandal.*
Back: *J.E. Mangnall (Secretary), F. Bacon, Picken, Edmonds, Mr. Murray (Director), Moger, J.H. Davies (Chairman), Homer, Mr. Lawton (Director), Bell, Mr. Deakin (Director).* **Middle:** *Meredith, Duckworth, Roberts, A. Turnbull, West, Stacey.* **Front:** *Whalley, Hofton, Halse, Wall.*

FIRST HONOURS

Bribes Scandal... City's Loss, United's Gain 1906-1915

MANCHESTER CITY 3
(Stewart 2, Jones)

MANCHESTER UNITED 0

DATE	1st December 1906
DIVISION	One
VENUE	Hyde Road
ATTENDANCE	40,000

Manchester City		Manchester United
Walter SMITH	1	Harry MOGER
Percy HILL	2	Robert BONTHRON
Frank NORGROVE	3	Dick DUCKWORTH
George DORSETT	4	Alec DOWNIE
Bill EADIE	5	Charlie ROBERTS
James BUCHAN	6	Alec BELL
George STEWART	7	John BEDDOW
Billy Lot JONES	8	Dick WOMBWELL
Irvine THORNLEY	9	Alex MENZIES
James BLAIR	10	John PICKEN
Jimmy CONLIN	11	George WALL

BACKGROUND

The period in between derby matches saw City bring the F.A. Cup to Manchester for the first time and finish as League runners-up but it also saw the Blues involved in a quite amazing bribes and illegal payments scandal. City had become the first truly successful Manchester side during this period but it could be argued that, indirectly via the bribes scandal, they enabled United to become successful later. Investigations into City's affairs following their final game of the 1904-05 season resulted in 17 players, including Billy Meredith, being suspended along with manager Tom Maley. Five of City's best players who were banned from appearing for the club ever again eventually transferred to United and formed the basis of future success for the Reds. United eventually gained promotion to the premier Division in 1906, finishing runners-up to Bristol City. Star of the team was United's first England International Charlie Roberts, bought from Grimsby for £400 in 1904. A strong attacking centre-half he became kingpin of the defence and was a future captain. City meanwhile had finished that season fifth in the First Division. After an optimistic start in the top flight with victories over Bristol City and Sheffield United the Reds gradually found the high-life more difficult. Confidence was ebbing away prior to the derby following a 4-2 home defeat by Bury.

However, City were faring much worse. The season started disastrously with three straight defeats including their record reverse, a 9-1 away thrashing at Everton. They had to wait until the 15th September to record their first point while their first victory, a 3-2 away win at Middlesbrough, did not arrive until the end of that month.

It was against this rather disappointing form background that the scene was set for the first derby to be played in Division One.

*Pictured here is **Manchester United's** 1905-06 Second Division promotion team, the core of which turned out for the first derby meeting for four seasons. **Back:** Downie, Moger, Bonthron. **Middle:** Ernest Mangnall (Manager), Picken, Sagar, Blackstock, Peddie, Bacon (Trainer). **Front:** Beddow, Roberts, Bell, Arkesden.*

BEFORE THE GAME

	P	W	D	L	F	A	Pts
UNITED	14	5	4	5	19	25	14
CITY	14	2	5	7	20	36	9

The illustration is captioned with the following handwritten notes:

Manchester City's Victory.

A centre by Wall off Hill's head.

Bonthron scored for his opponents.

Charlie Roberts was the mainstay of United.

Jones converted a centre from Thornley.

Eadie was here, there, and everywhere!

Smith, the new idol at Ardwick.

How the 'Athletic News' depicted City's convincing 3-0 victory

MATCH VERDICT

"CITY'S GREAT WIN...UNITED OUTPLAYED" recorded 'The Umpire' magazine for December 1906.

The largest derby crowd to date had gathered with high expectations as both clubs now figured in the upper circle. The gates were closed with an estimated 40,000 crowd inside Hyde Road. In a rather frenetic start United looked dangerous but it was City who soon took control, particularly through the creative wing-play of Conlin. The home followers exploded with delight after 20 minutes as the Blues scored twice in three minutes, Billy Lot Jones stylishly finishing a neat move and then, disastrously for the visitors, Bonthron deflected an effort by Stewart through his own goal. Early in the second half Stewart put the game beyond the Reds when he nipped between dithering defenders Duckworth and Bonthron

and fired past Moger. City goalkeeper Smith had virtually nothing to do in the second half but this still did not stop an enthusiastic band of supporters carrying him from the field shoulder high at the close.

Billy Lot Jones - on target with a stylish goal in City's convincing victory.

MANCHESTER UNITED 1
(Roberts)

MANCHESTER CITY 1
(Dorsett pen)

DATE	6th April 1907
DIVISION	One
VENUE	Clayton
ATTENDANCE	40,000

Manchester United		Manchester City
Harry MOGER	1	Walter SMITH
Robert BONTHRON	2	Percy HILL
Herbert BURGESS	3	Tommy KELSO
Dick DUCKWORTH	4	James BUCHAN
Charlie ROBERTS	5	Bill EADIE
Alec BELL	6	James BLAIR
Billy MEREDITH	7	George DORSETT
John PICKEN	8	Robert GRIEVE
Alex MENZIES	9	Irvine THORNLEY
Sandy TURNBULL	10	Billy Lot JONES
George WALL	11	Jimmy CONLIN

BACKGROUND

United's first game of 1907 was a special one as it marked the debut of former City favourites Billy Meredith, Herbert Burgess, Jimmy Bannister and Sandy Turnbull. As an indication of good things to come in the future, Turnbull scored to beat Aston Villa 1-0 on New Year's Day and United entered the derby in excellent heart, with a number of good victories behind them, not least a 1-0 win over reigning Champions Liverpool just five days before the game. City's inconsistent form continued to dog them, a fact reflected by their beating of Champions Liverpool but defeat at relegation bound Stoke.

BEFORE THE GAME							
	P	W	D	L	F	A	Pts
UNITED	34	15	7	12	44	53	37
CITY	34	10	10	14	48	67	30

*City goalkeeper **Walter Smith** saves and avoids United's **Alex Menzies**, while (inset) United captain **Charlie Roberts** checks City's **Robert Grieve**. Note the spectators on the stand roof.*

MATCH VERDICT

On the day Meredith, Burgess and Turnbull faced their old club for the first time it was City who could claim the moral victory and indeed, three points out of four for the season. City, much the sharper in the first half, took a 12th minute lead and the goal proved a particular embarrassment for Burgess. He handled in the area and Dorsett scored from the penalty spot. Excellent handling by both goalkeepers was a feature of the half but again it was an unfortunate injury to a player, City's Eadie, that was a turning point. Hurt in a collision with Meredith at the start of the second half, he was helped from the field and failed to return. The remaining ten men battled gamely but, 15 minutes from the close, with Smith unsighted, Roberts shot home from Wall's corner. City were however still bitterly disappointed to be denied victory when a late shot from Conlin was ruled out for offside.

The 'Athletic News' of the day reported on the big match as follows - although their reporter 'Harbicus' was more than a little indignant about the facilities for the Press!

"The return match between the two premier clubs of Manchester attracted unusual attention by reason of the fact that the three ex-City players would appear against their old club for the first time. When the United lost the first game by three clear goals at Hyde Road, Meredith, Burgess and Turnbull were resting, as they say in the theatrical profession, and consequently the United people were confident that the return game would end in favour of their side. As a matter of fact, they were rather fortunate to draw 1-1, so that as the City have secured three points from them this season, their supporters may naturally claim that Manchester City is the best team in Manchester. I am not personally sure of that, but figures are difficult to overcome, and no doubt the City portion of the 35,000 or so spectators at Clayton will stick to figures. I considered that United were fortunate to acquire one point for this reason: During the first half when it was an eleven-a-side contest, the City were the smarter team - though it must not be forgotten that they had a very strong wind behind them which blew the rain into the faces of their opponents - and then, when United had their opportunity against ten men for the whole of the second half, they failed to secure any advantage. The United forwards could not even score one goal, for it was a half-back who saved them from defeat.

Play had been in progress just over twelve minutes, when the first goal accrued from a penalty-kick. Dorsett got nicely away and almost ran to the goal line ere he centred. Burgess put himself in the way of the ball. He did more; he raised his hand to it, and from the resultant penalty-kick Dorsett scored, Moger hesitating at the shot. Moger, however, saved many good shots, as did Smith; indeed, the goalkeeping was one of the features of the first half, which concluded with City still retaining their penalty goal lead. Both Meredith and Eadie had retired for a few minutes in the initial half, and Eadie retired altogether after about a minute following the resumption. Dorsett fell back to centre-half, and then right half-back, four forwards being played. Play toned down and there seemed little likelihood of any more scoring. With about a quarter of an hour to go however, Wall forced a corner off Dorsett. The outside-left took the flag-kick, and the ball going straight to Roberts the latter put it into the net, Smith being shocked to find the ball had passed him. He seemed to be unsighted. Conlin afterwards shot a fine goal, but was adjudged offside. City supporters did not like the decision, but I am prepared to stand by Fred Kirkham's judgement in this matter, that it was not a legitimate goal. My view was obscured by a hat fitted on the head of a lady who stood in front of me, and also by one of the thick posts which support the stand. I have by the way a bone to pick with the United club. I arrived on the ground an hour and a quarter before the time of starting and was informed that there was no accommodation in the Pressroom, which was largely occupied by people whose business it would be interesting to know. I tried three different doors with different tickets, apart from the Press ticket which I possess, without success, but at last was turned into a dirty pen, which I am informed is a sort of overflow Press-box. It was used as a special stand on Saturday and I certainly object to having to work amongst a lot of partisans, and particularly with ladies standing on the seat below me. A club of the position of Manchester United should treat the representative of the recognised national football paper with respect. But why does not the club provide a proper Press-box like all the other first class-clubs?

However, to the game. To be candid I must confess I have seen much better games this season, and the second half in particular went very stale. The City certainly created a more favourable impression on me, being stronger in every department, except perhaps in goal. Particularly in attack did the United compare unfavourably, and no player disappointed me more than Meredith. I am of the opinion that the Welsh international has no superior, but he got a nasty knock on the head in the first half, and it seemed to take all the fire out of him. Turnbull, likewise was not a success against his old club, being too slow, and the best of the attackers were Wall and Picken. Bonthron, who found the tricky City left-wing pair very troublesome is to be complimented on the gentle manner in which he dealt with them, for they must have exasperated him at times. Moger was an excellent goalkeeper, and is a very greatly improved man from when he first came to Clayton. Indeed, he is now an accomplished custodian.

The City were a far different side than when I saw them last. The tricky left-wing of Lot Jones and Conlin were very smart, Jones being perhaps the cleverest of the quintette. Blair was a splendid left half-back, and, considering that he was until recently a forward, the City directors are to be congratulated on the successful outcome of their experiment. Hill and Kelso are a couple of fine backs, but with very opposite methods. Hill is a defender after the style of Spencer, while Kelso is a rusher. He made one rush that might have ended very disastrously to his limbs. He certainly requires a little toning down. Smith, like Moger, was a capital goaler".

Charlie Roberts – stabbed in the equaliser. A cornerstone of a player for United during this era, he was to help develop what eventually became a formidable half-back line-up alongside Alec Bell and Dick Duckworth.

The great **Billy Meredith** appeared in United's colours for the first time, but his performance against his old club was affected by a nasty blow on the head in the first half.

AT THE SEASON'S END

UNITED: Finished 8th on 42 points

CITY: Finished 17th on 32 points

15 MANCHESTER UNITED 3
(Wall, A. Turnbull 2)

MANCHESTER CITY 1
(Eadie)

DATE	21st December 1907
DIVISION	One
VENUE	Clayton
ATTENDANCE	35,000

Manchester United		Manchester City
Harry MOGER	1	Walter SMITH
Dick HOLDEN	2	Percy HILL
Herbert BURGESS	3	Frank NORGROVE
Dick DUCKWORTH	4	James BUCHAN
Charlie ROBERTS	5	Bill EADIE
Alec BELL	6	James BLAIR
Billy MEREDITH	7	George DORSETT
Jimmy BANNISTER	8	John WOOD
Jimmy TURNBULL	9	Irvine THORNLEY
Sandy TURNBULL	10	Billy Lot JONES
George WALL	11	Jimmy CONLIN

BACKGROUND

In the period prior to the derby United were riding high, scoring plenty of goals and dropping few points. They had suffered only two defeats in a 17 game sequence that also included a run of ten straight wins, and were storming away at the top of the table. The ex-City players were forming the backbone of the side and their most impressive victory of the season (6-1 away at Newcastle) showed just what heights they were capable of reaching. City's season kicked off in promising fashion with a 5-2 victory at Sunderland, with Robert Grieve, City's signing from Morton in August 1906, scoring a hat-trick. Their form became rather more patchy nearer the derby, sustaining defeats at Arsenal, Bristol City and Middlesbrough. However, a 4-2 home victory over Nottingham Forest the previous week put them in a more confident frame of mind.

George Dorsett - a regular for City at wing-half, he was involved in the incident which led to Turnbull's dismissal.

'Sandy' Turnbull - the competitive former City forward scored twice and became the first player to be sent off in a Manchester derby as United recorded an eventful victory.

BEFORE THE GAME

	P	W	D	L	F	A	Pts
UNITED	17	14	1	2	51	22	29
CITY	15	6	6	3	31	25	18

MATCH VERDICT

"CITY'S DEFEAT". . . "REGRETTABLE INCIDENTS". . . "TURNBULL ORDERED OFF". . . recorded 'The Umpire', the leading sporting newspaper of the day.

After a close fought opening quarter of an hour it was United who took the lead with winger Wall shooting home via the unfortunate Smith's face after the goalkeeper had parried two shots. City fought back but good defence particularly by Holden, Burgess and Moger kept them at bay. However, United grasped a stranglehold on the contest with a crucial second goal. Meredith, fouled by Norgrove, took the free-kick himself, floating it towards Sandy Turnbull who, outjumping his marker, headed into the far corner of the net. United then raced into a three goal lead early in the second half when ace marksman Turnbull dispossessed Norgrove and shot past Smith. City immediately struck back, Eadie heading in from a corner kick but the Reds, struggling with only ten men after Burgess was forced to retire injured, reverted to an offside game to keep their rivals at bay. A degree of ill feeling subsequently crept into the game, and sensationally, as full time approached, Sandy Turnbull became the first player to be sent off in a derby. Referee Tom Campbell ordered him from the field after he had punched Dorsett. 'The Umpire' newspaper commented on the "regrettable" nature of the incident and added that Manchester was rapidly acquiring a bad name as Turnbull now joined City's Stewart as "the only players sent off so far this season" United finished as comfortable winners but hardly surprisingly, proceedings ended on a sour note.

This delightful cartoon from 'The Athletic News' humorously comments on the sea of Manchester mud. The 'Clayton Reception' mentioned at the start refers to the noxious smoke and smells that emanated from nearby industrial chimneys.

MANCHESTER CITY 0
MANCHESTER UNITED 0

DATE	18th April 1908	
DIVISION	One	
VENUE	Hyde Road	
ATTENDANCE	40,000	

Manchester City		Manchester United
Walter SMITH	1	Herbert BROOMFIELD
Bert JACKSON	2	Dick DUCKWORTH
Frank NORGROVE	3	George STACEY
James BUCHAN	4	Alec DOWNIE
Bill EADIE	5	Charlie ROBERTS
James BLAIR	6	Alec BELL
Charles WEBB	7	Billy MEREDITH
Irvine THORNLEY	8	Jimmy BANNISTER
George DORSETT	9	Jimmy TURNBULL
Billy Lot JONES	10	Sandy TURNBULL
Jimmy CONLIN	11	George WALL

BACKGROUND

By the time this fixture arrived United were assured of their first Football League Championship. A glorious moment in their history and a remarkably quick turnaround in fortunes from the near extinction of 1902. A lot of the credit rightly went to their shrewd and innovative Manager Ernest Mangnall and the stewardship of Chairman John Davies. City fans must have mused enviously on what might have been as they saw the decisive roles played by their former players, especially the talented Meredith and prolific forward Sandy Turnbull who entered this match with 25 goals from 26 games.

City were however also having a good season and as the derby approached were in contention for runners-up spot to the Reds. Chelsea visited Hyde Road for the first time on 4th April and gained an easy 3-0 victory, making City's task harder. However a 2-1 win over Birmingham the day before the derby increased their hopes of success on the day. Perhaps even more significantly, for the first time it could be said with conviction that Manchester football was now a dominant force within the English game.

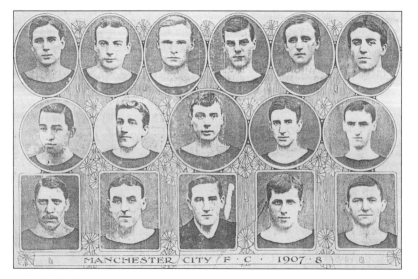

Manchester City's 1907-08 squad that clinched third place in the table.
Back: Blair, Wood, Hill, Jones, Eadie, Grieve. *Middle:* Stewart, Jackson, Thornley, Conlin, Kelso. *Front:* Dorsett, Ross, Smith, Buchan, Norgrove.

BEFORE THE GAME

	P	W	D	L	F	A	Pts
UNITED	34	22	4	8	76	43	48
Final Championship Record							
	38	23	6	9	81	48	52
CITY	35	16	8	11	62	54	40

City finished 3rd on 43 points
(the same total as Aston Villa in 2nd place)

MATCH VERDICT

Even though with United Champions and nothing really dependent on the match, the derby was played in the usual competitive spirit. The "Umpire" newspaper commented on the fractious nature of the match "players with noses close together...explaining by the movements of their hands what the other deserved". A rough game saw players occasionally leaving the field for treatment but it was United who generally showed the greater class and could have won it on the basis of the better first half chances but the ever dependable Smith in goal and a little fortune with the woodwork kept the Blues in the game.

'The Manchester Guardian' reported the April derby as follows under the headline "POINTLESS BUT ONE-SIDED GAME":

"At the close of the match between Manchester United and Manchester City at Hyde Road on Saturday the score - no goal on either side - pointed to an even game between two well-balanced teams. The score, however, was the only point in which the teams were really equal. Everywhere else, the balance went decidedly in favour of the United - in pace, in combination, in opportunities of scoring and the general run of play. The City team played as so many individuals, strenuously and often cleverly. The United men played as so many parts of a well-constructed machine. They worked as a whole on a more scientific and co-operative method, and in addition, their individual play was mostly better than that of their opponents. Their failure to win was due to two things - to their exceedingly bad luck (or was it want of judgement?) in shooting at the goal and to the splendid efforts of the City goalkeeper, who anticipated attacks with a sort of prophetic understanding, and met them without a single mistake. Even so, however, the City goal had some very narrow escapes. Twice the ball struck the posts, at least half a dozen times it must have passed just outside, and once J.Turnbull from a distance of six yards nearly bowled Smith over into the goal with the force of a low shot, and yet somehow the ball wriggled its way out as usual.

Nothing of importance really depended on the match. The United were in any case sure of the championship of the League, and if the City had won, it would only have brought them a stage nearer to the champions. But this made no difference to the spirit in which the game was fought. The spectators seemed mostly in favour of the City team, and as the play went in favour of the other side they watched it amid constant sweats and fears. This fierce rivalry communicated itself to the players and the play at times was a little too personal to be pleasant. Occasionally one saw a couple of players with their noses close together talking excitedly at each other and obviously explaining by the movements of their hands what they thought the other deserved. Then the referee (Mr Campbell) would step up and end the quarrel.

Free-kicks were fairly numerous, and some of the players were temporarily disabled. Eadie, for example, had to leave the field at an early stage of the game, and as soon as he re-appeared, Webb went off for temporary treatment. Some of the charging was pretty fierce, but on the whole, considering the excited temper in which the game was played, the casualty list was satisfactory, only at times the players sailed rather near the wind.

On the United side there was only one weak spot. A. Turnbull, playing in bandages, was quite unable to do himself justice and the attack might have been strengthened by a deputy. The City players worked very hard, but they struck one as being not quite of the same class as their opponents. Conlin and Jones made a very smart left-wing, and they might with advantage have been used more. In the last ten minutes Conlin made some clever runs into the corner and centred the ball most skilfully. He got through in this way a few minutes before the close, screwed the ball into the mouth of the goal, and Dorsett, leaping up, headed it just outside the post. That was the narrowest escape the United goal had. A goal to City in the last five minutes, after United's repeated failures to score at the other end, would have given a last touch of irony to the match".

Bill Eadie – the City half-back had to leave the field early on for treatment during what was at times a physical match.

Manchester United's 1907-08 Championship squad. **Back:** Burgess, Bannister, Berry, Wall. **Middle:** F.Bacon (Trainer), Menzies, Meredith, Moger, J.Turnbull, Mills, Stacey, Williams, Bloomfield, McGillivray, E.Mangnall (Manager). **Front:** Dalton, Picken, Whiteside, Holden, Thomson, Bell, A.Turnbull.

MANCHESTER CITY 1
(Thornley)

MANCHESTER UNITED 2
(J. Turnbull, Halse)

DATE	19th September 1908	
DIVISION	One	
VENUE	Hyde Road	
ATTENDANCE	40,000	

Manchester City		Manchester United
Walter SMITH	1	Harry MOGER
Tommy KELSO	2	Dick DUCKWORTH
Bert JACKSON	3	George STACEY
James BUCHAN	4	Jimmy BANNISTER
Bill EADIE	5	Charlie ROBERTS
James BLAIR	6	Alec DOWNIE
Charles WEBB	7	Billy MEREDITH
Billy Lot JONES	8	Harold HARDMAN
Irvine THORNLEY	9	Jimmy TURNBULL
David ROSS	10	Harold HALSE
George DORSETT	11	George WALL

BACKGROUND

United, the reigning Champions, started the season magnificently with three successive victories prior to the derby. Jimmy Turnbull, a centre-forward who had arrived at United in 1907, was the man making the headlines, with some phenomenal scoring. Two in the first game (3-0) at Preston), two in the second (2-0 home to Bury) and four in the 6-3 defeat of Middlesbrough. Together with his Charity Shield hat-trick (United beat Q.P.R. 4-0) Turnbull had netted eleven times in just four games!

City placed their hopes in the previous season's top-scorer, England International Irvine Thornley. The Blues opened the season with a 1-0 victory over Sunderland. Two draws followed, 3-3 at home to Blackburn (Thornley scoring twice) and a 0-0 at Bradford. Both sides therefore entered the 17th derby unbeaten.

Jimmy Turnbull – took his tally of goals for the season to 12 with a vital headed equaliser in the derby match.

George Wall – a derby regular for United whose crosses were always a source of goals.

BEFORE THE GAME						
	P	W	D	L	F	A	Pts
UNITED	3	3	0	0	11	4	6
CITY	3	1	2	0	4	3	4

Manchester United's Supremacy.

Thornley opened the score for City.

Whose ball? An altercation between Blair and Meredith.

Ross worked head and foot.

Turnbull's header made the game all square.

Roberts rose to the occasion.

The Athletic News caricatured United's early season victory.

MATCH VERDICT

"CITY CONQUERED". . ."UNITED WIN AFTER BEING GOAL BEHIND" reported "The Umpire" newspaper as the Reds recorded their fourth successive League win of the new season. Both sides were forced to make changes, the most significant selection being Harold Hardman (ex-Everton winger and a future United Chairman) on the wing with Meredith playing inside him. On 20 minutes, shortly after Smith had saved brilliantly from United forward Jimmy Turnbull, City took the lead. Billy Lot Jones hit a clever pass out to winger Webb who centred for Thornley to score with a shot that gave Moger no chance. City comfortably maintained their lead until five minutes from the interval when, following a stumble by Kelso, Wall raced away and his centre was deftly headed home by Jimmy Turnbull. It was frankly against the run of play in the second half when United scored a somewhat fortunate but crucial second goal. Smith and Turnbull collided as they converged on Meredith's centre and Halse was left free to tap the ball into the unguarded net.

Harold Halse - tapped the ball into the unguarded net for United's derby winner.

18

MANCHESTER UNITED 3
(Livingstone 2, Wall)

MANCHESTER CITY 1
(Conlin)

DATE	23rd January 1909
DIVISION	One
VENUE	Clayton
ATTENDANCE	40,000

Manchester United		Manchester City
Harry MOGER	1	Herbert BROOMFIELD
George STACEY	2	Tommy KELSO
Vince HAYES	3	Frank NORGROVE
Dick DUCKWORTH	4	James BUCHAN
Charlie ROBERTS	5	John WILKINSON
Alec DOWNIE	6	James BLAIR
Billy MEREDITH	7	George DORSETT
George LIVINGSTONE	8	Irvine THORNLEY
Jimmy TURNBULL	9	Tom HOLFORD
Sandy TURNBULL	10	David ROSS
George WALL	11	Jimmy CONLIN

BACKGROUND

The season was proving a struggle for City as their inconsistent form dragged them dangerously near the bottom of the table. Convincing victories against (Bury 6-1, Liverpool 3-1, and Bristol City 5-1) were not built upon. Goalscoring was not a problem, with Thornley bagging 13 and George Dorsett seven, but the defence were simply giving too many goals away. After their brilliant start to the season (not defeated until visiting Aston Villa in their eighth game) United had fallen away and returned some erratic performances to boot. They were often involved in high scoring games but not always in their favour. The two League games prior to the derby brought defeat, a 2-0 home reversal to Preston and a humiliating 5-0 drubbing at Middlesbrough. Morale was though slightly repaired by a 1-0 Cup victory over Brighton seven days before the derby.

George Livingstone – the ex-City favourite was on target twice for United to add to the Blues' misery.

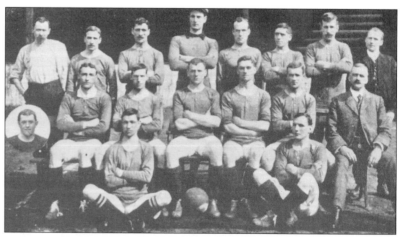

*The strong United squad of 1908-09 that won both derby matches and went on to lift the F.A. Cup, beating Bristol City 1-0 at the Crystal Palace. **Back:** F.Bacon (Trainer), Halse, Meredith, Moger, Picken, Wall, Stacey, Burgess. **Middle:** A.Turnbull (inset), J.Turnbull, Duckworth, Roberts, Bell, Hayes, E.Mangnall (Manager). **Front:** Livingstone, Downie.*

BEFORE THE GAME							
	P	W	D	L	F	A	Pts
UNITED	22	13	2	7	43	41	28
CITY	22	10	3	9	42	40	23

MATCH VERDICT

George Livingstone was the man who took the plaudits in this easy victory for United. It must have been a depressingly bitter spectacle for the City fans as Livingstone was yet another of their former favourites and one of three ex-Blues in the United line-up. The game was extremely one sided, with United virtually assured of victory after Livingstone had marked an electrifying debut with two goals inside the first quarter of an hour. The crowd, although large, showed surprisingly little of the traditional derby passion associated with the matches, but this possibly reflected the predictability and lop-sided nature of the current conflicts between the two local rivals.

The Athletic News of Monday, 25th January reported on Livingstone's remarkable debut as follows:-

"The name of Livingstone is handed down from generation to generation as an explorer. He was a Scotsman, and a fellow countryman of the same name is also following in his footsteps in the world of football. George T.Livingstone can tell of various discoveries he has made, for he has figured with Sunderland, Liverpool, Manchester City, Glasgow Rangers, and now he is exploring under the banner of Manchester United. And he did it to some purpose on his first appearance with his new club on Saturday in the return battle for the supremacy of Manchester. It is a singular coincidence that he should make his debut against his old club, and, by the way, no fewer than three of the famous City forwards were in the United forward line, while another, Booth, was playing the part of spectator, and I have no doubt that the fifth man William Gillespie, was anxiously awaiting the result across the Atlantic.

McMahon was also watching the game, and would doubtless like to have been participating therein. But to return to Livingstone, who, I may add, is, playing on Saturday, qualified for the next round of the English Cup Competition. He was readily recognised by the 35,000 spectators and he created such an impression that any who did not know him were soon enlightened. For a man to score the first couple of goals under such circumstances on the meeting of the Manchester giants is a feat to be talked of in years to come. He did not wait very long before he registered his first English League goal of the season - a quarter of an hour sufficed.

Roberts, however, deserves a great deal of credit for the points as he skipped along the ground over players' legs with the ball almost bound to his toes. It was a fine piece of individual play and Livingstone completed it by crashing the ball through a ruck of players into the net. The latest capture next improved on good work by Meredith. The Welshman's intentions were unknown to anyone but himself. Certainly the defence did not comprehend, and when he made his way from near goal in the centre to the corner flag the crowd were wondering. But there was method in the wily Welshman's apparent madness. He re-doubled and, passing back to his partner, Livingstone shot over the heads of the opposition and into the net. When United recorded a third goal in the second half the game had lost all interest. A splendidly placed corner by Meredith led up to the point, for the ball came over the heads of the other players to Wall on the fringe of the crowd, and he, without hesitation, immediately fired it into the net to the surprise of Broomfield.

Quite suddenly the City players thought that a goal to their credit would look more respectable and in the last few minutes they pressed so much that, following a galloping run by Dorsett, Conlin scored the City consolation after Ross had failed to gather the ball. "Put that down to Conlin" is the trite phrase to the Press gang or a dusty workman who never fails to trumpet the name of HIS hero whenever there is fog - or any doubt concerning the goal-getter. As the United have won both matches this season with their rivals they may rightly claim to be the champions of Manchester. I did not see the first match, but on Saturday's display there is no comparison whatever between the two. It is simply a case of the United an easy first. There was none of the excitement we used to have in the old Newton Heath and Ardwick days; in fact, I never saw a more subdued crowd for such a match. Whether due to the fact that the ultimate result was so palpable to the supporters of both sides, I cannot say, but there was little enthusiasm displayed.

The feature of the forward play was the fine combination of Meredith and Livingstone, who renewed their acquaintance. I have often remarked that Meredith has been particularly fortunate in his partners - first Finnerhan, then Ross and later Livingstone. They played together as in the old City days, and I need not pursue the matter further".

Tom Holford – an experienced half-back whose spell with City was part of a 26-year long League career.

AT THE SEASON'S END

UNITED: Finished 13th on 37 points
(the same as 9th placed Middlesbrough. However the Cup victory over Brighton was a good omen; they went on to win the F.A. Cup for the first time, beating Bristol City 1-0 in the Final)

CITY: Finished 19th on 34 points
Relegated to Division Two

19

MANCHESTER UNITED 2
(West, A.Turnbull)

MANCHESTER CITY 1
(Jones)

DATE	17th September 1910
DIVISION	One
VENUE	Old Trafford
ATTENDANCE	60,000

Manchester United		Manchester City
Harry MOGER	1	Jack LYALL
Oscar LINKSON	2	Tommy KELSO
George STACEY	3	Bert JACKSON
Dick DUCKWORTH	4	William BOTTOMLEY
Charlie ROBERTS	5	Bill EADIE
Alec BELL	6	Rowland CODLING
Billy MEREDITH	7	Joe DORSETT
Harold HALSE	8	David ROSS
Enoch WEST	9	Tom HOLFORD
Sandy TURNBULL	10	Billy Lot JONES
George WALL	11	Jimmy CONLIN

BACKGROUND

City returned to the First Division at the first attempt, finishing Champions one point ahead of Oldham in second place. City's first game back in the top flight was played at a refurbished Hyde Road. £3,000 had been spent covering the three open sides of the ground, providing shelter for 35,000 spectators. The Blues swamped Bury 5-1, with George Wynn scoring a hat-trick. Tom Holford scored City's goal in the 1-1 draw at Preston but the third game brought a disappointing 1-0 home defeat to Notts County.

The previous season had not brought the Reds a trophy (5th in the League) so the management made the close season purchase of Enoch "Knocker" West for £850 from Nottingham Forest. West was a robust and talented centre-forward with a century of League goals behind him at Forest. In theory this was a shrewd move by Mangnall and strengthened an already powerful attacking side. It certainly looked a good move as West scored in both opening fixtures, a 2-1 win at Woolwich Arsenal and a 3-2 home victory over Blackpool.

This was also to be a particularly significant derby match as it was the first to be played at United's superb new ground at Old Trafford, which had been opened earlier in the year.

BEFORE THE GAME							
	P	W	D	L	F	A	Pts
UNITED	3	2	0	1	6	5	4
CITY	3	1	1	1	6	3	3

UNITED'S FIRST GOAL.

Manchester United beat Manchester City by 2—1 at Old Trafford on Saturday. We reproduce above a striking snapshot of Lyall, the City goalkeeper, attempting to save the United's first goal.

Jack Lyall - saved City from a heavier defeat in this match with a string of brilliant saves.

MATCH VERDICT

A new derby attendance record was set at the fine new stadium at Old Trafford. In this record derby United made it one to remember by obtaining a deserved victory over the old enemy.

United showed their superiority and were two goals up in 37 minutes. After Holford had fouled Roberts, Duckworth's fierce free kick was parried by Lyall only for West to run in and put the Reds ahead. Duckworth again featured in the second goal. His perceptive pass sent Meredith away and his cross was rifled home by the deadly Turnbull. In an exciting second half City deservedly pulled a goal back when Linkson missed his kick and Billy Lot Jones jubilantly smashed the ball past Moger. United poured back on the attack but Lyall's brilliance ensured that the score remained as it was.

'The Umpire' newspaper of the day was present at Old Trafford for the first derby in the new stadium:

"When I reached Old Trafford yesterday and looked from the grandstand one of the United officials said to me "This is a football ground". Yes, Old Trafford is a football ground, and on one or two occasions I would like to have whispered in the ears of some of the players "This is a football ground". Maybe the referee whispered this to Holford, and judging by the expression on Sandy Turnbull's face as he lay down while Lot Jones took a penalty, Sandy must have thought it.

Old Trafford was a sight for the critics. I shall be told by some pessimistic ignoramus that the crowd was composed of partisans. So be it. I love a partisan. You can never accuse him of sitting on the fence or being a wobbler. You know him at once. He is neither deceitful nor two-faced. Open, clear, definite, you know just exactly where he stands, you can tell his team by the colour of his remarks.

But football crowds have their redeeming virtues and how patiently this big crowd waited. Was Job ever endowed with such colossal patience? I am not going to give you all the doings of the two clubs. Both have won the Cup, both have won promotion, but whilst Manchester United have won the League Championship, City can only offset this with a Second Division Championship. But what are championships when you come to Derby Day.

The first half was of a very even character. The game was fast, if not furious. The City attack was quick and full of energy, but the old story, lack of ballast in front of goal accounted for their forwards failing to score. United's attack was more spasmodic, yet it carried off the honours.

The two goals recorded in the first half were just charming, the honours in each case being divided amongst several players. Dick Duckworth was the first player to stamp his presence. He initiated the movements. In case of the first goal Holford bad-fouled Roberts. Duckworth took the free-kick, Lyall saved brilliantly, but before the 'keeper could clear,

West had the ball in the net. In the second goal Duckworth worked forward, just as if he were Meredith's partner, passed to the latter, who centred to Sandy Turnbull, and was delighted to see the latter flash it into the net with a shot that hit the underside of the bar. The lead was well-deserved if flattering, but the two goals were masterpieces in conception and execution.

That City were two goals behind was down to the indecision of the forwards and to Lot Jones' inability to score from a penalty given against Linkson for handling a centre by Conlin. Moger saved from the rebound as Jones hit the cross-bar and the defence cleared. This was a sad miss, for penalty kicks are meant to be scored from. At half-time the band, with thoughtful intelligence and with a real note of sympathy for the City team and its supporters, struck up the tune 'Somewhere the sun is shining' but for the first seven or eight minutes after the interval it looked as if the United would revel in it and City curse it. Yet in those minutes fortunes thrice smiled on the City; first Lyall saved in masterly fashion from Wall, and then West hit the crossbar, and Turnbull the far post with well-considered shots. Such is luck which at times hung like a heavy pall over the United, not only in attack but defence also, for Linkson missed his kick and let in Lot Jones who scored laughing at Moger, who was helpless. This was all the scoring, but only Lyall's brilliance saved the City from a heavier defeat.

The supporters of both teams may well be content with the result. It was a grand game full of interest and excitement right to the finish, and all things considered it was not over-weighted with foul tactics".

Harry Moger – the United goalkeeper saved the rebound after Billy Lot Jones hit the bar with a City penalty.

*A view of **Old Trafford** shortly after the stadium was opened on 19th February 1910.*

20

MANCHESTER CITY 1
(Jones)

MANCHESTER UNITED 1
(A.Turnbull)

DATE		21st January 1911
DIVISION		One
VENUE		Hyde Road
ATTENDANCE		40,000

Manchester City		Manchester United
Walter SMITH	1	Harry MOGER
Tommy KELSO	2	Arthur DONNELLY
John CHAPLIN	3	George STACEY
George DORSETT	4	Dick DUCKWORTH
Bill EADIE	5	Charlie ROBERTS
Tom HOLFORD	6	Alec BELL
George STEWART	7	Billy MEREDITH
David ROSS	8	Harold HALSE
John SMITH	9	Enoch WEST
Billy Lot JONES	10	Sandy TURNBULL
Joe DORSETT	11	George WALL

BACKGROUND

'Knocker' West was proving to be worth every penny of his transfer fee. He was also proving a big favourite of the United fans and was establishing a reputation as one of the "stars" of the period. West scored seven times in the nineteen games between derbies. Sandy Turnbull remained a bitter reminder to City fans of what might have been as he netted ten times. The Reds entered the game top of the table and in good form with two victories behind them over Nottingham Forest (4-2) and Blackpool in the Cup (2-1). City's season was turning into one of struggle and the Blues were saved in a number of games by the goalkeeping exploits of Walter Smith, who had replaced Lyall in the eighth game. Smith had the reputation of being one of the best 'keepers in the country and was to be the first in a long line of City greats in that position. Winning only six of the nineteen games between derbies City were in serious threat of returning to the Second Division. Hopes were raised by three victories before the derby, one in the Cup, but the Blues entered the game desperate for points against a team going for their second title in four years.

The **Manchester United** team that clinched the club's second League Championship in 1910-11. **Back:** Green, Halse, A. Nuttall, J. Nuttall, J. Broad. **Middle:** Bacon (Trainer), Meredith, Hodge, Stacey, Whalley, Holden, Moger, Stanford, A. Turnbull, E. Mangnall (Manager). **Front:** Homer, Connor, Roberts, West, Bell, Linkson. **Seated:** Aspinall, Sheldon, Donnelly.

George Stacey - "has not a superior at left-back" reported The Umpire newspaper.

BEFORE THE GAME							
	P	W	D	L	F	A	Pts
UNITED	23	15	2	6	42	25	32
CITY	23	7	4	12	27	35	18

MATCH VERDICT

United gained a point in a game many people thought they should have won. Brave City, reduced by injury to ten men for much of the match, fought doggedly but were indebted to another inspired display by goalkeeper Walter Smith. The game started well for the Blues when a clever move involving Stewart and Ross left Jones to convert an open goal. For a time City's celebrated half-backs Holford and Dorsett controlled the play and overshadowed their equally famous opposites of Duckworth, Roberts and Bell. However the Reds' pressure eventually told and, shortly before half-time, the old one-two brought the equaliser with Meredith's fine centre being headed in by Turnbull. The ten men put up a brave second half rearguard action and held out with the aid of many fine saves by Smith. The large crowd brought in healthy receipts of more than £1,000 showing what a popular fixture the derby had now become.

'The Athletic News' reported on the latest derby with an article headlined 'The Battle of Manchester':

"In the old days, when Manchester's two premier clubs were known as Newton Heath and Ardwick, the team whose headquarters are at Hyde Road invariably had the worst of the season's battles, and there has not been a great improvement since those days. From two matches during the current campaign, the United have annexed three points. The City, are to be complimented on the result of Saturday's game, which was attained under a very serious handicap, as throughout the second half they had to battle with four forwards. At the same time I must record my impression that United were the better and more skilful side. Their tactics were those of men at the head of their profession, and had they displayed the same keenness in the second half as they did in the first, they must surely have won.

Apparently they thought that it did not require so much exertion to overcome ten men as eleven, but they made a mistake. A team bereft of a unit often plays with more determination than with a full complement. It was only forward, however, where the United displayed any marked superiority, and I have seen their forwards more effective.

For instance, Meredith was not given the ball very often in the first half while Wall was similarly neglected in the second half; yet on one of the few occasions that Meredith mastered Holford he proved his value by leading up to the only goal for his side. This was near the interval, and he certainly outwitted the half-back, finishing with a centre almost from the goal-line. The Meredith-Turnbull combination was once again brought into play, for Turnbull neatly equalised from the centre.

Meredith came out in his true colours in the second half and gave the defenders many anxious moments. Wall was at his best in the first half, for Turnbull allowed him to rest after changing ends.

Turnbull is one of those players who seem to do as the spirit moves them. Apparently he is indifferent, but watch him closely and his seeming lack of energy is part of his programme, with intent to deceive the opposition. They forget he is playing, as it were, but he does not, and two fine shots of his in the last five minutes well deserved a goal. West, like Halse, is of the dashing order, but with less method than Halse. He is rightly named "Knocker". The City's centre-forward J.W.Smith, has yet to make his reputation. I hope he does so, but he will have to make considerable improvement on the form he displayed on Saturday. Joseph Dorsett put in some good work prior to leaving the field just before half-time, and he delivered one particular shot which nine times out of ten would have scored. Nor did Jones render him much assistance, for the Welshman was far too much amongst the half-backs, though after all it was Jones who scored the opening goal thirteen minutes from the start. Nor do I wish to see a better goal recorded. Stewart took the ball along, and, instead of centring, as the defenders anticipated, he merely tapped it to Ross, who skilfully drew out the defence ere crossing with the result that two City forwards had an open goal and Jones took the opportunity of giving his side the lead in a very clever manner.

The United's famous half-back line - Duckworth, Roberts and Bell were on view once again, but fine men though they were they were outshone by the powerful City division. There were none of the United side to compare with Holford and G.Dorsett. Holford, who seems to have no settled position faced the most dangerous outside-right in the country with a calmness which did him credit. Other players were indulging in horseplay, but Holford, who used to enjoy a rough and tumble affair, played the game and practically held Meredith in check in the first half, even if the old City player was more frisky afterwards.

But W.Smith was the man above all others on the City side. His goalkeeping in the first half was wonderful, and to his good work, more than anyone else's, is due the fact that City got a point. The United have two thumping full-backs in Donnelly and Stacey. The first time I saw Donnelly was with Heywood United two or three seasons ago. I thought then that he was a lad with a future. He has now 'arrived' and is likely to stay, while Stacey has not a superior as a left-back and his returns were fine.

The gate receipts were £1,052 - evidence of what would be at Hyde Road with a team going for the Championship. There was a good deal of crushing among the spectators, and several were carried away on the ambulance".

*Enoch 'Knocker' West –
a popular and regular
scorer in United's pre-war
days, he was eventually
banned for life in 1915 for
trying to 'fix' the result of
a United match with
Liverpool.*

AT THE SEASON'S END

UNITED: League Champions

P	W	D	L	F	A	Pts
38	22	8	8	72	40	52

CITY: Finished 17th on 31 points
(6 points more than Nottingham Forest in 20th place).

21

MANCHESTER CITY 0
MANCHESTER UNITED 0

DATE	2nd September 1911
DIVISION	One
VENUE	Hyde Road
ATTENDANCE	35,000

Manchester City		Manchester United
Walter SMITH	1	Hugh EDMONDS
Tommy KELSO	2	Leslie HOFTON
Frank NORGROVE	3	George STACEY
Robert DAVIES	4	Dick DUCKWORTH
Bill EADIE	5	Charlie ROBERTS
Tom HOLFORD	6	Alec BELL
Sidney HOAD	7	Billy MEREDITH
George WYNN	8	Harold HALSE
Irvine THORNLEY	9	Thomas HOMER
Billy Lot JONES	10	Sandy TURNBULL
Joe DORSETT	11	George WALL

BACKGROUND

The opening day of the new season was eagerly awaited in Manchester as the first fixture placed the local rivals against each other on the 2nd September. City made few changes to the side that had escaped relegation the previous season. Sidney Hoad was signed from Blackpool in May 1911, while Eli Fletcher came from Crewe at the same time. Again the outlook seemed one of struggle for City who were still feeling the effects of the disastrous happenings of the 1904-05 season.

Across the city the situation was totally the opposite. The Reds, having found success with two League Championships, the F.A. Cup and the Charity Shield, all within four years, were enjoying their first golden age. No team strengthening was deemed necessary and City fans would have noted the irony that two of the Reds' key men remained former Blues, Billy Meredith and Sandy Turnbull.

George Wynn – City's Welsh International inside forward was to enjoy his best ever season for the club in 1911-12 with 17 League goals, but he was unable to break the derby deadlock at Hyde Road. His goals however, ultimately saved City from relegation.

Walter Smith – unbeatable on the day, City's brilliant goalkeeper earned several ovations for outstanding saves.

BEFORE THE GAME
NO RECORD
FIRST MATCH OF THE NEW
1911-12 SEASON

MATCH VERDICT

A goalless start to the new season, but that fact was almost entirely due to the brilliance of City goalkeeper Walter Smith. The "Manchester Guardian" talked of him being "unbeatable" on the day. The game, played in heat wave conditions, proved frustrating for the Reds. The more they pressurised City and created chances the better Smith played. Hoad had a useful debut, but in general the City forwards were no threat.

As a guide for the season to come United looked as though they would once again be competing for prizes but City might find it a struggle.

The 'Manchester Guardian' reported on the opening day meeting:

"The meeting at Hyde Road of Manchester City and Manchester United on the opening day of the football season resulted in a division of points, as neither side could score a goal. The City forwards seldom developed strong attacking movement, but the visitors were only kept out by the remarkable goalkeeping of Walter Smith, who on the showing of the afternoon is still the one great player the City club can put in the field. The match, it may be said, lacked some of the importance which would have attached to it later in the season when the way the clubs are going in the League competition has been indicated, but there was the special interest for the crowd of noting the degree of skill shown by the recruits to the City team. The strength of the United eleven was a known quantity, and the problem of the afternoon centred upon the quality of the opposition which the home club could offer to the champions of last season. The game was contested in hot and almost windless weather, but the players, who turned out in capital condition, maintained a fair show of vigour throughout the match, and particularly in the second half, kept the spectators fully interested. There were about 35,000 people present, and the followers of the two clubs seemed to be in about equal force. The ground could have held a larger crowd, but the spectators on the popular sides of the playing piece were densely massed. The United won the toss, and City until the interval had to face the dazzling sun. There was little, however, to choose between the teams in the first half hour. Both sides worked well in midfield, and it was only near to goal that the United showed better tactics. The inaccurate passing of the City men spoiled many of their attacks, and only Wynn and Hoad seemed able to send the ball along. Hoad too failed to get fairly past Stacey, and he more often ran the ball into touch than swung in a useful centre. Despite this weakness Hoad pleased the crowd, and when he has settled down he may do very useful work for his new club.

The United forwards, and the half-backs too shot often and shot hard, but the efforts were not all well-directed, and when the ball did come to the goal Smith was always ready and safe in his clearances. Once he gathered the ball very cleverly from a screw-in by Homer. City made very few dangerous advances. Hoad only once in a while got in a shot, and the man who came nearest to scoring was Thornley, who struck the post when he crashed the ball in at short range.

After the interval the United forced the pace, and sharp attacks on the City goal were made ineffective by the remarkable judgement and agility of Smith who set the cheers echoing around the ground. Smith seemed unbeatable. He often left his goal, but every time he ran out he had calculated the position perfectly, and the only occasion on which he came to grief was when he collided with Homer and damaged himself sufficiently to need the attentions of the trainer. The accident occurred after a strenuous twenty minutes, and attackers and defenders, when they knew that the goalkeeper was not seriously hurt, stretched themselves on the grass to rest a minute, while even the referee was glad to borrow a wet sponge with which to bathe his hot face.

Try as the United men would in the closing stages of the game they could not get through. Meredith was fouled close in, and a goal seemed certain, but although for some reason the free kick was taken twice the danger was averted, and near the end Hoad varied matters by breaking away on his wing and putting in a long oblique shot which brought out Edmonds. City were fortunate perhaps, to get a point out of a game in which they had been overplayed, but Smith, after all, is a member of the side, and as he was unbeaten at the end the team got no more than the reward of his cleverness.

The first game of the season is hardly one to reveal the true strength of a side. City, however, gave the impression that they will win more games than they did last season. Hoad was often smart in snapping up the passes which Wynn put across to him, and against a back who gives him the least latitude he will prove a dangerous forward. Smith, of course, was the outstanding man of his side. The City supporters were delighted to find the goalkeeper as brilliant as at any time last season, and he had two or three ovations all to himself during the afternoon.

The United played with the confidence of a strong team, and but for Smith would easily have secured the two points. Hofton and Stacey defended soundly, and the half-backs were so lively and decisive that half the City passes were made ineffective. Roberts fed his forwards continually, his placing being beautifully done. Meredith was very closely watched by Holford, but often beat his man, and his centres gave the City defence many an anxious moment".

22

MANCHESTER UNITED 0
MANCHESTER CITY 0

DATE	30th December 1911
DIVISION	One
VENUE	Old Trafford
ATTENDANCE	50,000

Manchester United		Manchester City
Hugh EDMONDS	1	Walter SMITH
Oscar LINKSON	2	William HENRY
George STACEY	3	Eli FLETCHER
Dick DUCKWORTH	4	Valentine LAWRENCE
Charlie ROBERTS	5	Bill EADIE
Alec BELL	6	Tom HOLFORD
Billy MEREDITH	7	Sidney HOAD
Mick HAMILL	8	George WYNN
Enoch WEST	9	Alexander 'Sandy' YOUNG
Sandy TURNBULL	10	Billy Lot JONES
George WALL	11	Joe DORSETT

Alec Bell – Another of the famous United half-back line that for ten years was the nucleus of the Reds' first great side.

BACKGROUND

The season had started disastrously for City as the Blues recorded only one victory in the opening thirteen games and looked certainties for relegation. Manager Harry Newbould attempted to strengthen the team by signing Sandy Young for a large fee from Tottenham Hotspur. William Henry was also signed and a gradual improvement in the Blues' form was noted. In the six games before the derby four were won, with Notts County beaten twice and Young among the goalscorers in both matches.

United's season was again proving more successful than City's but had been a little disappointing in comparison with previous seasons. West, Halse and Sandy Turnbull were regular scorers for the Reds. "Knocker" West was the club's top scorer on twelve goals. The only notable signing for United during this period was Mick Hamill, an Irish inside forward later to play for City. The Reds' two games over Christmas saw a 1-0 home defeat by Bradford City and a 1-0 victory at Valley Parade.

BEFORE THE GAME							
	P	W	D	L	F	A	Pts
UNITED	19	9	5	5	29	22	23
CITY	19	5	5	9	25	33	15

MATCH VERDICT

A disappointing derby season with a second goalless match. The "Manchester Guardian" with the headline 'A GREAT CROWD AT OLD TRAFFORD' commented that 'the crowd was more remarkable than the match at Old Trafford'. The attendance was the largest seen at the ground since the replayed F.A. Cup Final (between Newcastle and Bradford City) in April. It was thought that a lot more than the 41,000 crowd figure was in the ground and that a figure of 50,000 might well have been more accurate. The fans' excitement seemed to be shared by both sides' forwards who were guilty of lamentable finishing. It proved to be a frustrating game for the crowd, of untidy and scrappy play. Dorsett and Hoad showed occasional danger on the wings for City. However the United half-back line seemed impenetrable with the great trio of Roberts, Bell and Duckworth unbeatable on the day. A draw was considered a fair result to a disappointing game but obviously this proved a useful point for City.

The "Manchester Guardian" had this to say on the disappointing draw:

"The crowd was more remarkable than the game at Old Trafford on Saturday. An exciting match had been expected and excitement was provided, but neither side played good football, and there were some lamentable failures in front of goal. The eagerness of the spectators spread among the players and seemed to put them off their game. Men who usually would have scored from the easy chances offered to them drove the ball into the crowd instead of the net, and the defence on either side had rocky moments.

The crowd was the largest seen on the ground since the replayed cup final in April. Half-an-hour before the start there were 35,000 people present, and when the teams came out, over 50,000 enthusiasts divided their cheers between the two elevens. There was all the spirit and boisterousness of a cup-tie and favours were freely worn. Even the striped umbrella rose above the crowd before the game began, and one got an idea of what a yell a goal would have produced by the deep roar of cheering which followed every player who made a good show of going through the opposing defence. The yell nearly came once. West headed the ball past Smith, but the referee's outstretched hand pointed towards the goal and not away from it. The exhultation was checked before it could fairly break, and the crowd, like the players, argued hotly as to whether or not West was off-side when Hamill made the pass which the United centre forward used.

There was little to choose between the sides. City were more often attacking in the first half, but the United made strenuous efforts in the last quarter of an hour, and Turnbull almost won the match when he met a fine centre from Meredith and headed right across the front of the goal. The crowd got its most exciting moments through slips by the defence which left a forward with a clear run for goal. The cheering, however, seemed to be too much for the men, and the finishing shot was usually of a type which called out a long-drawn "Oh" at the tail of the encouragements. Dorsett on the left wing for City won a way cleverly along the touch line on many occasions, but could neither centre nor shoot as he did in the match with Notts County. Hoad was fast and sometimes got the ball nicely placed for the inside men, but Jones could not shoot at all, Wynn was more often off the mark than on it, and Young was too closely shadowed by Roberts to get many real chances. Towards the end of the first half he did swerve through the defence, and shot hard from four yards range for Edmonds to save in remarkable fashion. Had the ball reached the net though, the point would not have counted as the whistle was blowing for a stoppage as Duckworth had been hurt. The City half-backs were moderately good. Eadie worked hard, and although he made mistakes, was quick to recover. The two backs sometimes miskicked, but they played very well indeed. Henry, at least, was invariably cool, and some of his clearances were remarkably good. Fletcher took a quarter of an hour to grasp the guile of Meredith, but afterwards he beat the great wing forward more often than Meredith beat him. Smith in goal was not severely tested.

One the United side, the half-back line was the best part of the team. Roberts made it almost impossible for Young to get a real opening, and he Duckworth and Bell also excelled in putting the ball out to the forwards. Duckworth could not catch Dorsett when Dorsett gave him the slip, but Bell held Hoad and Wynn rather well. Linkson played pluckily at full-back, although he found Dorsett too smart for him, and Stacey stopped many advances which might have been dangerous. The United backs were not however, so sound a pair on the play as Henry and Fletcher, and Edmonds had many anxious moments. The goalkeeper saved several shots very finely. Forward, the home team were weak until the closing stages of the match. Meredith was so troubled by Fletcher that his centres went sadly astray, Wall could not get the better of Henry, and the inside men were not seen to much advantage. The passing was poor and the shooting bad, almost worse than that of the City front line. The interest of the game lay in the rapid crossing of play from end to end and the continual spoiling which was seen when forwards seemed likely to go through. A draw was a fair result and a satisfactory one".

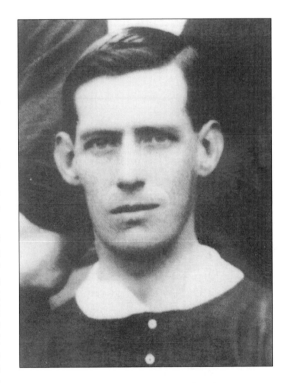

Dick Duckworth – part of United's outstanding trio of half-backs, he was one of the greatest players ever to wear a United shirt and his telepathic understanding with Meredith was at the root of many United goals during this era.

AT THE SEASON'S END

UNITED: Finished 13th on 37 points

CITY: Finished 15th on 35 points
(A remarkable recovery of 17 points from the last ten games finally avoided relegation)

23

MANCHESTER UNITED 0
MANCHESTER CITY 1
(Wynn)

DATE	7th September 1912
DIVISION	One
VENUE	Old Trafford
ATTENDANCE	40,000

Manchester United		Manchester City
Robert BEALE	1	Jim GOODCHILD
Oscar LINKSON	2	William HENRY
George STACEY	3	Eli FLETCHER
Dick DUCKWORTH	4	William BOTTOMLEY
Charlie ROBERTS	5	Bill EADIE
Alec BELL	6	Tom HOLFORD
Billy MEREDITH	7	Sidney HOAD
Mick HAMILL	8	George WYNN
Enoch WEST	9	George WEBB
Sandy TURNBULL	10	Billy Lot JONES
George WALL	11	Joe DORSETT

BACKGROUND

Both clubs retained virtually all their playing squads from the previous season. United were still relying on their successful Championship side built around Roberts, Meredith, Turnbull and West, although Halse had left for Aston Villa. City still had the likes of Fletcher, Eadie and Jones and had secured the services of amateur International George Webb from West Ham.

The really sensational news of the early season involved the proposed move of United's manager Ernest Mangnall to Manchester City! Nine years at the club, Mangnall had brought United up from Division Two, won the League twice, the Cup, the Charity Shield and made the Reds a power in the land. The double irony of the curt announcement in the Athletic News, that he was to take up the manager's position at Hyde Road, was that to a large degree his success with the Reds was due to his astute acquisition of the five banned Blues after the 1905 bribes scandal. City and United fans naturally wondered how his move would change the fortunes of the two clubs. United meanwhile, appointed J.J.Bentley to replace Mangnall, for whom this was his final match in charge of the Reds.

BEFORE THE GAME

	P	W	D	L	F	A	Pts
CITY	1	1	0	0	1	0	2
UNITED	1	0	1	0	0	0	1

*United's **Billy Meredith** and City's **Bill Eadie** shake hands before tossing up at the start of the match.*

Ernest Mangnall – his final match in charge of United before his shock move to neighbours City.

MATCH VERDICT

"PLUCKY BUT LUCKY". . ."City win with 10 men". . . reported "The Umpire".

Meredith was honoured with the captaincy on this his special day and the band welcomed him on to the pitch to the strains of "for he's a jolly good fellow". The bumper crowd ensured it was a good pay day for the "Welsh Wizard". The Umpire reported: "receipts of over £2,000, which is the best benefit ever accorded a Football League player".

In a poor game City took the plaudits by winning with ten men, as recent signing George Webb, injured early on, left the field shortly before half time. Four minutes from the break, City broke the defensive deadlock. Hoad's great run and shot hit the bar and Wynn smashed home the rebound to "terrific cheering from the City section of the crowd". City, with a stiff wind against them in the second half, fought a plucky rearguard action to defy United's forwards and record an historic first away victory in derby fixtures.

In what would perhaps now be considered rather unusual circumstances this was Ernest Mangnall's final match as United's manager, as on the Monday he was due to take charge at City, and become the only man to have managed both clubs. City were quite obviously hoping that he would bring them the success that had marked his illustrious career at United. It also reflected City's status and wealth that they were able to tempt the man away from their great rivals. Mangnall must have had curiously mixed feelings about this result as "United speeded their manager rejoicing with two points to his new club".

The Manchester United programme for the day carried this special tribute to beneficiary *Billy Meredith*.

OUR PORTRAIT GALLERY.

Immediately the announcement was made that the Directors of the Manchester United Club had set apart the home fixture with Manchester City for the benefit of William Meredith, it was instinctively felt that the occasion would become historic. That the countless admirers of our famous forward would embrace the opportunity of displaying in a practical manner their interest in their favourite was rightly assumed, as was the belief that the attendance and "gate" would constitute an easy record for matches of this kind. It is, of course, merely fitting that the holder of record achievements on the field of play should achieve a record at the turnstiles, and the speculation is not now merely one of how far the figures of other benefit matches will be left hopelessly in the rear, but by how much the Villa figures of February 4th, 1911, when 65,101 spectators contributed £2,464, will be beaten. There have been bigger "gates" at Old Trafford than the Villa one; for instance, the replayed Cup final between Bradford City and Newcastle United attracted 66,646 spectators, who paid £4,478, and the cash in the Rovers' match last season exceeded £3,100. But higher prices than those prevailing to-day were charged, and so no comparison can fairly be made between them and the present match.

William Meredith has occupied the lime-light for so long a period that it must come as a surprise to many to discover that he only reached his thirty-sixth year on the 28th of last July. Nearly half his years have been spent in the service of Manchester clubs, for he joined the City on October 27th, 1894, on which date he signalised his advent by scoring a fine goal against Newcastle United. Against the same club, on October 12th, 1907, or almost thirteen years afterwards, Meredith scored his two hundredth League goal, a total that has not been reached by any other wing forward, either of the present or past generation.

The most astonishing feature of Meredith is not so much what he has done, but what he is likely to do in the future. None dare be bold enough to set a limit to his career, and, judging by his display in the trial matches, he appears destined to fill the part of "the greatest outside right of his time" for many more years to come. It reads astonishing now to have on record that Meredith has taken part in 40 International matches, but a year hence one will be writing the figures as 43, and eventually the half-century will be passed if present indications are anything to go by.

Apart from his incomparable skill, Meredith will be best remembered for his perpetual freshness of manner. The hardest game fails to dull the edge of his supernormal keenness, nor can the most trying season diminish by one iota his infinite variety. He enters upon his latest game with the zest displayed in his first adventure, and he delights the spectators of this generation just as he did their fathers of the last. With a unanimity that is quite refreshing, his football contemporaries have acclaimed him the greatest touch-line player the game has ever known, and the man in the street, whose instincts are invariably sound, declares that "Meredith never had an equal," and this opinion will assuredly be endorsed by posterity. There are many stars, but only one sun.

Action from the match shows *Enoch 'Knocker' West* (grounded) screwing his shot wide of an open goal as City goalkeeper *Jim Goodchild* scrambles across.

24

MANCHESTER CITY 0
MANCHESTER UNITED 2
(West 2)

DATE	28th December 1912
DIVISION	One
VENUE	Hyde Road
ATTENDANCE	36,000

Manchester City		Manchester United
Jim GOODCHILD	1	Robert BEALE
William HENRY	2	James HODGE
Eli FLETCHER	3	George STACEY
William BOTTOMLEY	4	Dick DUCKWORTH
Bill EADIE	5	Charlie ROBERTS
Lionel WALL	6	Arthur WHALLEY
Sidney HOAD	7	Billy MEREDITH
Harry TAYLOR	8	Sandy TURNBULL
Tom HOLFORD	9	George ANDERSON
Billy Lot JONES	10	Enoch WEST
Joe DORSETT	11	George WALL

BACKGROUND

City's George Webb, injured in the previous derby, shocked the club later in the season by refusing to play. Webb, a strict amateur, was dismayed to find that money had changed hands between City and West Ham when the Blues obtained his services. Webb was reported to be so disgusted at this that he retired from the game. Sadly he died of consumption in 1915 at the early age of 28. City were having a reasonable season under new management with the most obvious sign of improvement being in a defence that gave away fewer goals. The Reds were somewhat inconsistent but retained a potent strike force. Eight different players had scored for the team including Anderson, Meredith, Turnbull and West. A close game seemed in prospect.

BEFORE THE GAME							
	P	W	D	L	F	A	Pts
CITY	19	11	2	6	25	18	24
UNITED	19	9	4	6	37	26	22

Jim Goodchild – City's goalkeeper was unable to prevent United sweeping to a convincing victory.

In Affectionate Remembrance of

POOR   OLD

MANCHESTER CITY F.C.

Boldly to the fray we went,
On honor, fame, and vict'ry bent;
But with sad hearts we came away,
For the match we'd lost to-day.

Our opponents they were far too good;
In fact we stood like logs of wood;
Our chance is past, our day is o'er,
At football we will play no more.

R. J. P.

AN INCIDENT IN THE BATTLE OF MANCHESTER.

*Pre-First World War derby action pictures are rare, but here City's **Billy Lot Jones** prepares to shoot as United's **Charlie Roberts** (left) shapes to tackle, but United goalkeeper **Rob Beale** (crouching right), saved the shot.*

MATCH VERDICT

"MANCHESTER UNITED MASTERFUL" were the headlines in The Athletic News. The newspaper was very definite in its appraisal of this game. For them there was only one team in it; "bad generalship, poor play and opponents with cunning brains and crafty feet, proved a combination far too strong for Manchester City". Enoch "Knocker" West showed he was still a forward to be feared and scored both the Reds' goals. West's skimming shot opened the scoring in thirteen minutes and ten minutes later he headed in Meredith's centre to effectively end the game as a contest. After this United controlled the play much as they pleased and ran out easy winners.

AT THE SEASON'S END

UNITED: Finished 4th on 46 points
(8 points behind Champions Sunderland)

CITY: Finished 6th on 44 points

Charlie Roberts - pictured here in 1912 when he was the Red's skipper and still a king-pin at centre-half.

25

MANCHESTER CITY 0
MANCHESTER UNITED 2
(Anderson 2)

DATE	6th December 1913
DIVISION	One
VENUE	Hyde Road
ATTENDANCE	40,000

Manchester City		Manchester United
Walter SMITH	1	Robert BEALE
William HENRY	2	James HODGE
Eli FLETCHER	3	George STACEY
Edwin HUGHES	4	Frank KNOWLES
Ted HANNEY	5	Arthur WHALLEY
James HINDMARSH	6	Mick HAMILL
James CUMMING	7	Billy MEREDITH
Harry TAYLOR	8	Sandy TURNBULL
Fred HOWARD	9	George ANDERSON
Tommy BROWELL	10	Enoch WEST
William WALLACE	11	George WALL

BACKGROUND

United had made an excellent start to the season and were up with the League leaders. From late September they went seven games undefeated. November marked only their second defeat, 3-1 at Cup-holders Aston Villa, but this prompted a dismal run of two consecutive defeats and a 3-3 home draw with Derby County seven days before this match.

City had quite simply made a disastrous start to the season and were down among the deadmen in the League table. In an attempt to bolster the side and stay in the First Division, a number of signings were made; Hanney, Hindmarsh and Cumming all made their debuts in some morale boosting victories leading up to the derby.

BEFORE THE GAME

	P	W	D	L	F	A	Pts
UNITED	14	9	1	4	28	15	19
CITY	14	3	5	6	17	21	11

Manchester United in 1913-14 **Back:** *Hodge, Gipps, Knowles, Beale, Stacey, Hamill, Whalley.* **Front:** *Meredith, Woodcock, Anderson, West, Wall.*

MATCH VERDICT

The game was played against a slightly sour background, as an article in the City programme referring to the possible transfer of Sheldon from City to United commented tersely; 'all negotiations with United now and for the future are closed'. This was no doubt a reflection of the club's still underlying feelings about United's almost wholesale acquisition of their former stars after the 1905 bribes scandal. The match was won in the first half. United, considered much the superior side, dominated the Blues and scored twice through the opportunism of Anderson. For once the reliable Walter Smith was considered to be at fault. Anderson first shot home from a rebound off a post, with Smith's attempted save being described as half-hearted, and the second was an easy tap into an empty net after Smith had hesitated and then dropped a cross. In the second half, with Whalley injured, United were reduced to ten men and were consequently restricted as an attacking force. They still, however, had little difficulty in subduing the very disappointing Blues.

"The Sunday Chronicle" reported on United's comfortable win as follows:

"Once more have Manchester City succumbed to the near and - I was almost saying dear - rivals from Old Trafford. Successive victories had put the City on good terms with themselves, their supporters were beginning to dream of glorious things in the future, but whilst I did not see those triumphs, I must say that the opposition must have been weak if the Hyde Road men played in anything like the style which characterised their efforts yesterday. More impotent work in front of goal it has not been my lot to witness for many a long day, and the City's forward problem is apparently no nearer to a settlement than it was at the beginning of the season. I cannot be accused of exaggeration when I say that the United did not cross the half-way line more than half a dozen times in the second half, and if Smith handled the ball more than three times after the interval I must be terribly mistaken.

Yet everything the City did ended in smoke as it were. They did all the attacking in the second half, principally because Arthur Whalley, the United centre half-back was carried off nine minutes after the restart with a twisted right knee never to return, and while one could not help but admire the heroic work of the Old Trafford defence, it almost passes comprehension that the City were unable to find the net.

Their forwards could not grumble for lack of opportunity: they could not complain of lack of support from the half-backs: they simply showed up a weakness which stood out in bold relief against anything else that took place in the match. This weakness was in the marksmanship of the whole line of forwards who simply could not control the ball for a final effort at close quarters, and who were beaten time and again because their work was more in the nature of a scramble than anything else.

Having said so much of the City forwards, I want to lay the blame for United's first-half goals at the feet of a portion of the defence. Anderson scored twice, and each time, Henry was, in my opinion, caught napping in the course of the points materialising. In the first place, he let West skip round him to centre for Anderson to whip the ball into the net at the second attempt, and in the second place, he was mixed up with a bad misunderstanding between himself and Smith which resulted in the goalkeeper losing the ball and Anderson rounding them both and scoring again.

Henry's display, particularly in the first half left a deal to be desired. His kicking was ill-timed, his tackling lacked judgement, and he only improved in the second half, apparently, because he had a disorganised wing to play against - Wall having gone to assist the half-backs when Whalley left the field. I think if he had left the ball to Smith in the second instance all would have been well, but who was looking after Anderson when all this was going on? Nobody.

There is no remedying such lapses as those and whilst United have to thank their opponents for such luck, some credit is due to Anderson, who proved himself a rare opportunist. In the first half, indeed, the United were much the superior eleven. There was more science about their methods; their forward movements were something more than the mere kick and rush business which the City indulged in after the interval, and there was no doubt about it that man for man they were the cleverer combination".

Arthur Whalley – the United centre-half was carried off with a twisted knee early in the second half, reducing the visitors to ten men for the remainder of the match.

Tommy Browell – one of the City forwards who had an off day. It was his first Manchester derby after signing from Everton for £1,780 in October of 1913, but he enjoyed better days at City, netting 139 League and Cup goals during ten seasons with the club.

26

MANCHESTER UNITED 0
MANCHESTER CITY 1
(Cumming)

DATE	11th April 1914
DIVISION	One
VENUE	Old Trafford
ATTENDANCE	36,000

Manchester United		Manchester City
Ezra ROYALS	1	Walter SMITH
Ed HUDSON	2	William HENRY
George STACEY	3	Eli FLETCHER
Frank KNOWLES	4	Edwin HUGHES
William 'Cocky' HUNTER	5	Ted HANNEY
Tommy GIPPS	6	James HINDMARSH
Billy MEREDITH	7	James CUMMING
George TRAVERS	8	George WYNN
George ANDERSON	9	Fred HOWARD
Enoch WEST	10	Tommy BROWELL
John THOMSON	11	Joe DORSETT

A NICE EASTER EGG.

[Stacey and Turnbull took their benefit at Old Trafford this afternoon, the occasion being the meeting of Manchester United and Manchester City in the return League engagement.]

BACKGROUND

City's season continued to be one of mixed fortunes. Only one win in six matches during December plunged them into serious relegation trouble. January however, brought a change in fortunes with the Blues winning all four matches. Again a bad run of results followed, only for City to record two consecutive victories before the derby. Tommy Browell, signed from Everton in October for the large fee of £1,780 was having an excellent first season, scoring eleven goals in 23 League matches.

The Reds' season meanwhile had turned into a disaster. In the eighteen games between derbies United won only four! This wretched form meant that a side, virtually settled early in the season, now made a whole series of changes. No less than 30 different players had been used by the Reds over the season .

In tandem with long-serving defender George Stacey the mercurial Sandy Turnbull had chosen this game against his old club as his testimonial - an obvious choice for one of Manchester's first real footballing stars. Sandy had been a great favourite with the Blues early in his career and was of course one of the major forces behind United's first golden age.

BEFORE THE GAME							
	P	W	D	L	F	A	Pts
CITY	34	12	7	15	44	49	31
UNITED	32	13	4	15	46	56	30

Edwin Hughes – the City half-back was one of a number of players on both sides who were to lose their peak footballing years to the War.

MATCH VERDICT

Turnbull, suffering from injury, was sadly not available for the game. However, he must have been more than pleased with the attendance which brought in receipts of £1,216. City still tended to have the greater support in Manchester despite United's dominance in these traditional fixtures, and their entry onto the pitch warranted the bigger cheer. In a close fought first half, Meredith showed he had lost none of his skill and was a constant danger to the Blues. Generally though, as "The Umpire" reported, there was precious little to enthuse over; the play was strenuous but lacking in the finer points. The scrappy game was settled 15 minutes from time when Cumming finished clinically after Dorsett had broken through the United defence.

Sandy Turnbull would never appear in another derby. Throughout a controversial career Turnbull had his share of troubles with the football authorities and ended it under a further cloud with a life ban for betting irregularities. Even more sadly, Turnbull, serving with the Manchester Regiment, was killed in the trenches at Arras in May 1917.

'The Last Straw' was the heading on "The Umpire"'s match report of the derby:

"From the point of view of attendance, Stacey and Turnbull's benefit match at Old Trafford proved an unqualified success, for the attendance must have exceeded 40,000, but the fact that the United were again beaten, and, worst of all, by their City rivals, should be distinctly unpalatable to themselves and their well-wishers.

It was easily to be observed which was the most popular team when the men entered the arena, for the cheer which greeted the United was faint as compared with that which heralded the appearance of the City. No doubt the poor progress made by the United during the later portion of the season has had much to do with the lack of enthusiasm, though, when it was seen they were more than holding their own, despite the fact that they were battling with a strong wind, it was plain to be observed they were not without friends. The wind seemed to bother City more than help them; anyhow, the kicks as a rule carried the ball beyond the forwards. The United on the other hand played with better method. Meredith was ever a source of trouble, and quite a number of corners were won by him, and placed with his usual exactitude, in the opening stages. On these occasions there was invariably a warm time in store for the City men, and Smith was kept occupied in dashing out or fisting from under the bar. Meanwhile, what few shots Royals had to deal with came from long range, though one, made by Hindmarsh was certainly laden with peril, the goalkeeper fielding this attempt very well. Anderson let slip a very fair chance of giving the home side the lead when he slipped the backs, but his shot passed just outside. If this was a narrow escape for the City, the United were equally fortunate, if not more so, immediately

afterwards, for Dorsett slipped past Hudson and was careering for goal when Knowles followed and foiled him. The concluding stages of the first half were indeed, crowded with exciting incidents. Howard had got practically beyond all opposition when he was fouled by Gipps who was injured in the process. Following a free kick for an infringement by Hanney on Travers, the City goal had a very narrow escape indeed. Once Smith dashed out and missed the ball, but he returned in time to spring among a crowd of opponents and punch the ball away. The defences had been quite too strong for the attacks, though the United had enjoyed rather the better of a game which had not been remarkable for its scientific methods.

With the wind to help them in the second half - it is, however, sometimes a hindrance - it was expected the United's prospects of winning were distinctly rosy. In the first minute or so Travers had a favourable opportunity, but he could not reach the ball which was probably helped forward by the wind. Almost immediately afterwards, Cumming was going through when he was fouled, though, instead of granting a free kick, I thought it would have been more to the point had the referee allowed the game to proceed. The City had their narrow escapes for Anderson was virtually through when Smith came to the rescue. On the whole, however, there was precious little to enthuse about, for if the play was strenuous, it was lacking in the finer points. The chance of the match so far came midway through the second half when, as Cumming centred, Howard tried to kick, but only sent the ball a few yards where it fell at the feet of Browell. The latter, with a delightful opening, kicked rashly and the ball sailed among the crowd at the back of the goal. In the next minute, Smith saved from Travers who had broken through. Then, however, came the goal which not only settled the issue, but had the effect of investing the closing stages with added interest. With thirty-two minutes gone by, Dorsett passed across and Cumming, taking steady aim, landed the ball into the far corner of the net. This was the prelude to a busy time for Smith who, amongst other efforts, kept out a great shot by Stacey from a free kick. The game was by now won and lost and neither side approached a score afterwards. The defences were undoubtedly the better part of the teams, the forwards being evidently handicapped by the gusty wind which can be very troublesome at Old Trafford. The United were not great marksmen, but I think there was not a better man in the line than Travers. He made a splendid partner for Meredith and was thrustful to a degree. In the light of what happened at Preston and Barnsley yesterday they can still afford to view the outlook with a certain amount of equanimity - but two points since New Year's Day!"

Sandy Turnbull – an always colourful character he enjoyed a bumper benefit against his old club.

AT THE SEASON'S END

CITY: Finished 13th on 36 points

UNITED: Finished 14th on 36 points
(City had better goal average).

27

MANCHESTER UNITED 0
MANCHESTER CITY 0

DATE	5th September 1914
DIVISION	One
VENUE	Old Trafford
ATTENDANCE	20,000

Manchester United		Manchester City
Robert BEALE	1	Walter SMITH
John HODGE	2	William HENRY
George STACEY	3	Eli FLETCHER
William 'Cocky' HUNTER	4	Edwin HUGHES
Patrick O'CONNELL	5	Ted HANNEY
Frank KNOWLES	6	James HINDMARSH
Billy MEREDITH	7	Sidney HOAD
George TRAVERS	8	Harry TAYLOR
Enoch WEST	9	Fred HOWARD
Wilf WOODCOCK	10	Horace BARNES
George WALL	11	Joe DORSETT

BACKGROUND

During the close season City made the headlines by signing Derby County's star forward Horace Barnes for a record-equalling fee of £2,500. Barnes had scored 25 goals the previous season but wanted to leave Derby because they had been relegated. Barnes quickly repaid some of the fee by scoring in the first game of the season, a 4-1 victory over Bradford City at Hyde Road. Consequently, City entered the derby full of confidence and ready to put one over the old enemy.

United made a disappointing start to the season. They were well beaten 3-1 by Oldham Athletic at Old Trafford, half-back O'Connell scoring on his debut. Far more momentous events were, however, looming fast on the horizon, as before the season had got underway the First World War had broken out. The new season though started as normal, and at this stage little thought was given to whether it should be suspended or not. At this time the call to the colours was purely voluntary, and team selection was not affected. Interestingly, City's directors were involved in a "notice to encourage their men", claiming that they would not stand in the way of any of their players who wanted to join the forces. The official notice commented that "If any professional in our pay wishes to serve his King we will do our best for his dependents provided we have any money taken at the gate".

Horace Barnes joined City for a record £2,500 fee from relegated Derby County in May 1914. This derby was only his second game for the club, but he was a striker with a deadly left foot shot and when linked with Tom Browell after the War, was a consistently high scorer during the early 1920's

BEFORE THE GAME							
	P	W	D	L	F	A	Pts
CITY	1	1	0	0	4	1	2
UNITED	1	0	0	1	1	3	0

Games players might have been frowned upon after war was declared, but much of the derby spirit of 'playing the game' was carried into the trenches amid the terrible slaughter. Note the football on the right of this contemporary illustration.

The newspapers of the day were full of calls for men to do their Duty and many had little sympathy with the players of games at such a time, but **Manchester City** took a lead by issuing a notice that they would not stand in the way of any player who wished to join up.

MATCH VERDICT

A disappointing goalless draw with few chances and little good play. Walter Smith again impressed with a confident display in the City goal. United were considered to have had the slight edge overall but there was little to cheer the partisan crowd. Perhaps the supporters thoughts were moving towards the much more serious conflict that was erupting across Europe.

A great pre-war forward with both City and United, **Sandy Turnbull** indulges in some cricketing horseplay during training. Sadly, Turnbull was to die in the trenches during a much greater game of life - the First World War.

28

MANCHESTER CITY 1
(Howard)

MANCHESTER UNITED 1
(West)

DATE	2nd January 1915	
DIVISION	One	
VENUE	Hyde Road	
ATTENDANCE	30,000	

Manchester City		Manchester United
Walter SMITH	1	Robert BEALE
William HENRY	2	John HODGE
Eli FLETCHER	3	George STACEY
James HINDMARSH	4	Tommy GIPPS
Ted HANNEY	5	Patrick O'CONNELL
John BRENNAN	6	Sam COOKSON
Joe DORSETT	7	Billy MEREDITH
Harry TAYLOR	8	Arthur POTTS
Fred HOWARD	9	George ANDERSON
Billy Lot JONES	10	Enoch WEST
Joe CARTWRIGHT	11	Joe NORTON

BACKGROUND

With the World War raging the Football League had been subject to a great deal of criticism for insisting that the League programme be completed. According to news reports City's players and officials agreed to give five per cent of their wages to a war fund set up by the Prince of Wales. It was believed that a number of other clubs, United included, were about to do the same.

On the football front the two teams were enjoying vastly different seasons.

For United it was a season of struggle with a root cause that the once great side was growing old together. Indeed, none of these players would turn out for United in another derby. The 2-1 home defeat by Bradford Park Avenue on New Year's Day left the club in relegation trouble, which presented quite a task for new manager John Robson who had only arrived at the club a week earlier from Brighton. City were having a good season and were proving a hard side to beat. Their success was based on an excellent defence built around their admirable goalkeeper Walter Smith. A 0-0 draw the day before the derby at high flying Oldham Athletic (now captained by former United legend, Charlie Roberts) kept City up with the Divisional leaders.

Bobby Beale – the United goalkeeper had no chance with the City equaliser.

BEFORE THE GAME							
	P	W	D	L	F	A	Pts
CITY	20	10	7	3	26	17	27
UNITED	19	3	6	10	22	34	12

MATCH VERDICT

Amidst a fast and furious start, with both goals under siege, City were awarded a penalty when Hodge handled, but Howard's spot kick was straight at Beale who stopped the ball and booted it up field to "terrific cheering". Meredith's wing play showed advancing age had dulled none of his old skills, and it was from his short corner that Gipps crossed for West to head the Reds into a half time lead. City started the second half strongly having a Jones goal ruled out for offside. Howard made up for his penalty gaffe by equalising for City, shooting firmly past Beale when the ball reached him from a corner. City made a big push for a second goal but the United defence withstood the pressure, with the derby stalwart George Stacey outstanding.

Sadly the first death at a derby was reported at this match when a certain William Broomfield, aged 56, of Milton Street, Hulme, collapsed in the main stand and died of heart failure before medical help could reach him.

"HONOURS EVEN - THE UNITED MAKE A DRAW" headlined "The Umpire", reporting on the final derby before the ever deepening Great War crisis led to the suspension of League football until 1919-20.

"The matches between the Manchester clubs always attract huge crowds, and though there has not been the same interest in the doings of the United this season, the meeting on the City ground drew together 30,000 people. Of course the home team is one of the best of the season, judging from their position in the League chart, so there is every reason why the match should prove such a big attraction.

The game opened fast and after Jones had been given offside in the first minute when he was almost through, Meredith got hold after a little tussle and shot for goal. Smith was unsighted, but Fletcher, standing on the line, kicked away a certain goal. Just after this Taylor shot out and then Meredith ran to the line and sent across a lovely centre, one of those reminiscent of his balmy days, but West headed wide. Beale was called on next and he saved a hot one from Howard. Both goals were visited rapidly and Anderson at one end and Howard at the other went close, but in one attack by the City, Hodge was adjudged to have handled the ball in the penalty area. Howard took the kick but sent straight at Beale who stopped the ball and then cleared, amid terrific cheering.

Both sides had chances, but they tried to work too close in before making a shot, with the result that they were dispossessed. This fault was most noticeable in the play of the United centre Anderson, and had it not been for this he might have scored twice over. The game was fast and good, but it was Beale who had the most work to do. He filled the picture at one period and made some clever saves, but though City had been having a good share of the game, the United were not slow. Meredith got hold in a favourable position as the result of a mis-head by Fletcher, and taking the ball in his stride sent across a lovely centre which Norton headed out. Then City came again and Taylor and Howard both tried hard to get in a shot and once Beale came out and saved just as Cartwright was getting up, and another time he dropped the ball nearly in his own net. Hanney stuck to Meredith extremely well but he was outwitted once and Gipps shot in forcing Smith to give a corner. Meredith sent this to Gipps who was standing well out and shooting well into goal had the pleasure of seeing West head into the net. Soon after, United had another chance but, the interval arrived with City a goal behind.

The second half saw City having most of the play, and Hodge gave a corner which was cleared. But still attacking Dorsett placed a cross and Jones forced the ball in the net but the cheering was premature, the referee giving Jones offside. However, the City maintained the pressure and a corner kick taken by Cartwright was touched to Howard and he shot hard between several legs into the net, Beale having no chance. The United improved in their play after this, and Meredith, Anderson and Norton progressed, only to see either Henry or Fletcher save. Then the City came again, Howard looking all over a scorer, but his shot was beautifully parried by Beale.

As the game reached the last quarter the City made strenuous efforts to secure the lead but they found both Stacey and Hodge doing their best. Meredith was held by Brennan and his efforts were nippd in the bud, but he was often watched by two or three players altogether. City tried further and then came an anxious time for the City goal, West spilling a chance in front only to see Beale knock the ball out. It was then returned by Meredith, but no-one was able to stop the ball, Norton being the last to miss the chance. Near the finish a nasty accident to Cookson upset the players and things were getting serious when the end arrived with a goal to each side".

Eli Fletcher – the City defender saved an almost certain goal from Meredith with a goal line clearance.

AT THE SEASON'S END

CITY: Finished 5th on 43 points
(3 points behind Champions Everton).

UNITED: Finished 18th on 30 points
(avoided relegation by 1 point).

BETWEEN THE WARS

The Yo-Yo Years
1919-1939

29

MANCHESTER CITY 3
(Taylor, Browell 2)

MANCHESTER UNITED 3
(Hodge, Spence, Hopkin)

DATE	11th October 1919
DIVISION	One
VENUE	Hyde Road
ATTENDANCE	32,000

Manchester City		Manchester United
Walter SMITH	1	Jack MEW
William HENRY	2	Charlie MOORE
Eli FLETCHER	3	Jack SILCOCK
Herbert TYLER	4	Arthur WHALLEY
Ted HANNEY	5	Jack GRIMWOOD
Frank KNOWLES	6	Tommy MEEHAN
Tommy BROAD	7	James HODGE
Herbert TAYLOR	8	Wilf WOODCOCK
Tommy BROWELL	9	Joe SPENCE
Richard CRAWSHAW	10	William TOMS
Bill MURPHY	11	Fred HOPKIN

BACKGROUND

The Football League programme resumed on 30th August 1919. City began the season with virtually the same players who had finished the 1914-15 season. The side was built around the experience of Walter Smith, Eli Fletcher, Tommy Browell, Horace Barnes and Ted Hanney. The only new player on the season's opening day was Tommy Broad, a signing from Bristol City in 1915. City's playing staff at this time was huge with many players making just one or two appearences over the season. City had high hopes for William "Spud" Murphy, signed in 1918, a player renowned for his stamina and speed. One other notable signing was that of the half-back Frank Knowles from United just five days before the derby. Knowles was an experienced player with 46 appearances for the Reds, scoring once at Bradford City. United by contrast, virtually rebuilt their team from the pre-war side. Jack Mew replaced Bobby Beale in goal. He had been signed from Marley Hill Colliery in 1910 and played regularly through the war years. Two of the stalwarts in defence were John Silcock and Charlie Moore. Moore was signed from Hednesford in 1919 whilst Silcock, a regular through the war, turned professional in 1918. The most significant signing though was Joe Spence. Spence was an extremely successful centre forward with amateur club Scotswood. In the years to come he would develop into one of United's greats. One player still with the club was Wilf Woodcock, who by the 1919-20 season had gained two England caps. Both sides made modest starts to the new season.

Manchester City line up in 1919 with players who appeared for them during the war years before League football resumed in 1919-20. Back: H. Tyler, A. Sorden, J. Goodchild, P. Fairclough, W. Newton, T. Johnson. Front: W. Meredith, H. Barnes, J. Brennan, T. Browell, J. Cartwright. Inset: T. Broad, E. Fletcher.

BEFORE THE GAME							
	P	W	D	L	F	A	Pts
UNITED	8	3	4	1	14	9	10
CITY	8	3	1	4	18	23	7

MANCHESTER DUEL.

Great Game Between the City and United.

SIX GOALS SHARED.

(By R.G.)

In the whole series of the meetings of the Manchester rivals none has provided more thrilling football than that which enthralled over 30,000 spectators at Hyde-road on Saturday. From first to last it was a great game, and the quality of the football was on as high a plane as the excitement.

Thrice the United had the lead and thrice they lost it, and twice within a minute each side scored. What more could anyone want! For their point the United were indebted

T. Meehan,   T. Browell,
Manchester United.   Manchester City.

first to Mew and secondly to the quickness of their forwards. Mew kept a wonderful goal, and it would be no exaggeration to say that he of all his team was the man who prevented the City from winning.

The home men were the cleverer team, and had considerably more of the play than the United. Some of their forward play was the perfection of skill allied with method, but in spite of two brilliant single-handed goals by Browell, they scarcely had the nippiness or the virility of the United quintette.

HOW THE GOALS CAME.

Within two minutes of the commencement Hodge gave the visitors the lead as the outcome of slight hesitancy on the part of Fletcher and Smith, and it was not until 34 minutes' later that Taylor equalised with a high shot that curled back from Mew's upstretched arm. This was the state of affairs at the interval, thanks in the main to Mew, who kept a wonderful goal.

Again in the second half the play went in favour of the City, but at the end of 21 minutes an egregious blunder by Smith in bouncing the ball in his goalmouth enabled Spence to equalise, only, however, for Browell to restore equality right from the restart.

Hanney had broken his nose in a collision with Toms and was off the field when both these goals were scored, but he came back to play better than ever.

A breakaway by Spence resulted in Hopkin putting the United ahead for the third time, five minutes from the finish, but once more Browell immediately made the scores level, as Murphy centred, and so the game ended.

Apart from Mew, the United defence was wonderfully quick and sound, and Grimwood, a South Shields youth, making his debut at centre half-back, in the absence of Hilditch, was one of the conspicuous successes of the match.

If they had not the skill of the home quintet, the forwards were remarkably quick on the ball, and in this respect none rendered his side greater service than Spence.

The City played a greatly improved game all round, and apart from Smith's mistake, the defence was most faultless. The rearrangement of the half-back line worked for the general good, Knowles making a very satisfactory debut, but the best part of the team was the forward division, where Browell scintillated, and where Taylor, Crawshaw, and Murphy distinguished themselves with some glorious football.

MATCH VERDICT

A classic derby with the non-stop excitement of end to end attacking football. City were considered slightly unlucky not to take the spoils but United's forwards and goalkeeper were reported as outstanding. After just two minutes Hodge nipped in between Smith and Fletcher to give the Reds the lead. Taylor's powerful shot levelled matters shortly before the interval. United controversially took the lead 21 minutes into the second half when Smith was dispossessed, while bouncing the ball in his area, by the quicksilver Spence who then rolled the ball into the empty net. The crowd had scarcely caught its breath as Browell shot home for City in a move direct from the kick off. The Reds thought victory was assured three minutes from time, as Spence cleverly made a goal for Hopkin, only for the Blues to again equalise direct from the re-start when Tommy Browell headed in Murphy's cross. Quite remarkably, the legendary Billy Meredith was still playing - and at the highest level. He missed the game due to International duty, scoring in Wales' 1-1 draw with England.

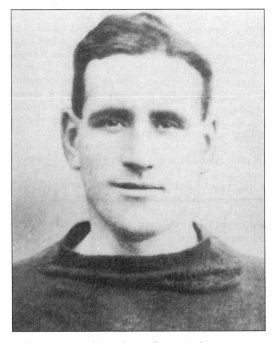

Jack Mew – United's regular goalkeeper in the years following the war, he made several fine saves to keep his team in the match.

30

MANCHESTER UNITED 1
(Spence)

MANCHESTER CITY 0

DATE	18th October 1919
DIVISION	One
VENUE	Old Trafford
ATTENDANCE	49,000

Manchester United		Manchester City
Jack MEW	1	Jim GOODCHILD
Charlie MOORE	2	William HENRY
Jack SILCOCK	3	Eli FLETCHER
Tommy MEEHAN	4	Herbert TYLER
Clarrie HILDITCH	5	Sidney SCOTT
Arthur WHALLEY	6	Frank KNOWLES
James HODGE	7	Tommy BROAD
Frank HODGES	8	Herbert TAYLOR
Joe SPENCE	9	Tommy BROWELL
Wilf WOODCOCK	10	Horace BARNES
Fred HOPKIN	11	Bill MURPHY

BACKGROUND

The matches immediately after the war were played on consecutive Saturdays. Therefore, significant events between fixtures were somewhat limited. In this instance the only thing worthy of note was that the last derby a week earlier had marked the final appearances for City of Walter Smith and Teddy Hanney. As City reorganised in mid-season to ease the burden of an excessive wage bill for a professional staff of 40 players, Hanney was later signed by Coventry for a remarkable £2,000 fee and Smith moved to Port Vale to complete a distinguished career. It was a busy week for the Blues, who also signed two new players T.Lamph and E.Goodwin from Leeds City who were in the process of being wound-up.

BEFORE THE GAME

	P	W	D	L	F	A	Pts
UNITED	9	3	5	1	17	12	11
CITY	9	3	2	4	21	26	8

*Rebuilding after the war **Manchester United's** staff had almost completely changed by the time of this team picture in 1919-20. **Back:** C. Moore, Mr G. Bedford, C. Hilditch, J. Mew, J. Silcock, A. Nealmer (Trainer), A. Whalley, F. Hodges, T. Meehan. **Front:** G. Bissett, J. Hodge, J. Spence, W. Toms, F. Hopkin.*

MATCH VERDICT

Almost 20,000 more fans gathered at Old Trafford than had been at Hyde Road seven days before, perhaps attracted by all the excitement and goals of the last fixture. The attendance was a new record for the ground, surpassing the 41,743 for the 1911 derby.

In the event the crowd was disappointed in a dour game with both defences well on top. The deadlock was finally broken nineteen minutes from the end with the decisive goal that sent the home fans away happy. Ironically the goal came from a defensive mistake by the experienced City defender and captain Eli Fletcher. It was he who lost possession to Hodge who centred for the unmarked Joe Spence to head into the corner of the net.

Eli Fletcher – City's long serving full-back and skipper was at fault for the goal which gave rivals United the points.

AT THE SEASON'S END

CITY: Finished 7th on 45 points

UNITED: Finished 12th on 40 points

COSTLY MISTAKE.

Gives United the Verdict in Manchester Derby.

50,000 SPECTATORS.

(By "THE ONLOOKER.")

Practically the only mistake Fletcher made in the game resulted in a goal that gave Manchester United two valuable points in their engagement with their rivals from Hyde-road.

It occurred after nineteen minutes play in the second half. Fletcher had time to clear, but he hesitated about passing back to Goodchild, and in the meantime was tackled by Hodge. The outside right got possession and centred to Spence, who was standing absolutely unmarked and he headed cleanly into the net.

It was not a great game by any means, and not containing anything like so many thrills as the previous week. The ground, however, was a spectacle, for there must have been fully 50,000 present, a record for a League game on this ground. The previous best was 41,743, on December 30, 1911, when Manchester City were also the visitors.

T. Lamph,
Manchester City's
new player.

The return of Hilditch to the half-back line strengthened this section of the team considerably, and all three played well. The backs, too, were sound, with Silcock slightly the superior. Mew had very little to do.

The forwards relied on long passing, and Woodcock and Hopkin were the better wing. Spence played a hard game in the centre, and Hodges at inside right exhibited some dainty touches, whilst Hodge was always useful.

Scott's Debut.

For City, Goodchild had no chance with the ball that scored and otherwise played his part well. Both Henry and Fletcher defended finely, despite the last-named's mistake. Scott gave quite a good display in Hanney's place at centre-half, but both Knowles and Tyler had the ball in the air too often.

Barnes worked hard amongst the forwards, and kept Murphy well plied with passes. Browell was too well watched. Taylor industrious, but on the slow side, and Broad erratic. He had plenty of chances in this game.

Play opened at a fast rate, but in the first twenty minutes neither goalkeeper was seriously troubled. Then Goodchild made a good save from a hurriedly-taken free kick by Whalley.

Generally, however, the defence was superior to the attack, and so we came to the second half, when Spence's goal livened up things considerably.

Twice Goodchild saved on the line and a free kick saved the situation. City made some brief attacks, but generally were well held, the United defence being on the alert to the end.

31

MANCHESTER UNITED 1
(Miller)

MANCHESTER CITY 1
(Barnes)

DATE	20th November 1920
DIVISION	One
VENUE	Old Trafford
ATTENDANCE	63,000

Manchester United		Manchester City
Jack MEW	1	Jim GOODCHILD
Charlie MOORE	2	Sam COOKSON
Jack SILCOCK	3	Eli FLETCHER
Thomas FORSTER	4	Fred FAYERS
Frank HARRIS	5	Max WOOSNAM
Tommy MEEHAN	6	Mick HAMILL
William HARRISON	7	Tommy BROAD
Tommy MILLER	8	Frank CARROLL
Henry LEONARD	9	Tommy BROWELL
George SAPSFORD	10	Horace BARNES
Fred HOPKIN	11	Bill MURPHY

BACKGROUND

United's season started inauspiciously and no points were acquired until the beginning of September when they drew at Bolton. Billy Meredith appeared in their opening games at the grand old age of 46. Although obviously not quite as swift as of old, he retained many of his natural skills and remained a great crowd favourite. Joe Spence had now established himself as the club's leading marksman. Top scorer the previous season with 14 goals from 32 games, he was again scoring regularly, despite injury restricting his appearances.

City had made quite a number of changes from the previous season. The most notable were the acquisition of two former Reds, Wilf Woodcock and Mick Hamill. Woodcock signed directly from United on 5th May 1920, having played 61 times for the Reds and scored 21 goals. Hamill, whilst playing for Belfast Celtic, was persuaded by Mr. Mangnall to join the Blues. Mangnall, the architect of so many great United successes before the War, was now shrewdly building the Blues into another strong side. A further important move had brought the young Sam Cookson to the club in 1918, from Macclesfield. Cookson was a small well built defender, often later described as the best uncapped full back of his time.

Manchester United in 1920-21. **Back:** J. Spence, T. Forster, J. Greenwood, C. Moore, J. Mew, J. Silcock, T. Meehan, E. Partridge. **Front:** W. Harrison, T. Miller, H. Leonard, G. Sapsford, F. Hopkin.

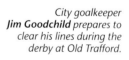

*City goalkeeper **Jim Goodchild** prepares to clear his lines during the derby at Old Trafford.*

BEFORE THE GAME

	P	W	D	L	F	A	Pts
CITY	14	7	2	5	22	22	16
UNITED	14	5	5	4	19	18	15

MATCH VERDICT

Another massive crowd showed just how popular this fixture was, and they were treated to a close entertaining contest. City looked the stronger early on, particularly along the right wing where Broad was a constant danger. Barnes was unlucky to see his early goal ruled out for offside. It was against the run of play therefore, when United took a first half lead, Miller neatly heading in Hopkin's corner kick. The Blues must have been rueful of their missed first half chances as United began to dominate the second period, only for City to break away and equalise. 'Spud' Murphy's clever play down the left allowed the City inside forward Horace Barnes to shoot cleanly past Mew.

Sam Cookson

Mick Hamill – a stylish wing-half, the former United man was now on City's books.

HALFBACKS COUNT

WHY GOALS WERE SCARCE AT OLD TRAFFORD.

A HUGE CROWD.

Manchester U. 1, Manchester C. 1.

If a referee had had to award a victory "on points" at Old Trafford on Saturday, the spoils would have gone to the visitors, but I do not think anyone could complain very much of a division.

There was a wonderful crowd, announced at 63,000, the receipts totalling £4,100, and enthusiasm ran high. It inspired the players, too, for, if the game was not of a classic character, it was certainly full of fire and life.

Not a man spared himself, and, at times, the pace was remarkable, while to the credit of all concerned, the match, strenuous though it was, provided an admirable example of sportsmanship and fair play.

I must be very lucky, for I have seen nothing of the baneful effects of bonuses which are said to have changed the whole character of the game. Saturday's was the fourth "Derby" I have witnessed this Autumn, and none has been "dirty."

The Weakness.

I have said that the football did not reach a particularly high standard, and this, I fancy, was partly due to the mediocre form of the half-back lines.

City's was the better, and Max Woosnam, if he had not yet the constructive skill of a M'Call, was the best of the lot. He pushed the ball well forward, nearly always along the ground, and usually to a colleague. What is more, he tackled soundly.

The others were not very successful in attack, their passing was indifferent, and they were lacking in initiative. They were not very satisfactory as forward supports, and, naturally, the men in front suffered. Meehan was the most virile and thrustful, but was inclined to wander.

I have emphasised these weaknesses—or what appeared weaknesses to me—because a really successful side is built up upon a half-back foundation, and, in this game, the foundation was lacking. The men were real triers, but fell short of the standard of polish and style expected of them.

In all the circumstances, it was not surprising that the honours were carried off by the defences. It is significant that Mew had far more chances to shine than did Goodchild, and he was not only sound and safe, but excellent in judgment and anticipation—a class keeper.

Fine Backs.

There was not a great deal to choose between the respective pairs of backs, who all played really well, collectively and individually. Moore and Cookson were perhaps more showy than their colleagues, but both Fletcher and Silcock displayed fine judgment and admirable tackling.

Forward, the City had the pull which most people anticipated. Better supported than their rivals, they were a more machine-like combination, though Browell was not so conspicuous as he often is. Carroll was cool and clever in mid-field, if lacking "devil," Barnes being much the most dangerous and thrustful of the five. Murphy has played better, and Broad's weakness was that he did not always, or indeed often, make the best of the advantage given him by his pace.

Mediocre Finishing.

The finish of the wing men generally was not brilliant; one could never be sure where they would land their centres, or whether they would get them in at all.

Harrison, at least in the second half, was much more successful than Hopkin, but was inclined to give himself too much to do against an old campaigner in Fletcher, who is a bit faster than some opponents seem to think.

The United wingers, however, have the excuse that they were not too well looked after. Sapsford was not prominent, and Miller was rather slow. And the inside forwards are only a little less important than the half-backs.

With all its flaws, however, the game was really interesting, and the defences had plenty to do in combatting the opposition, even if the latter did depend rather on dash and pace than subtlety.

The City had distinctly the better of the first half, though the United took the lead in good time and kept it until well on in the second half.

The Goals.

Many people thought the City really opened the scoring when Barnes' successful shot was negatived by offside. I am not questioning the decision—some did—when I say that the movement of Broad, Browell, and Barnes merited a goal.

The United's rushes forced a number of corners, and from one of these Miller headed a goal.

The United opened the second half at a great pace, but the City defence stood up to them, and, gradually, the game became level again.

The equaliser was the result of a dash and centre by Murphy. Browell got the ball and just managed to pull it down to the foot of Barnes, who placed it well out of the reach of Mew. **ADJUTANT.**

32 MANCHESTER CITY 3
(Barnes, Browell, Murphy)

MANCHESTER UNITED 0

DATE	27th November 1920
DIVISION	One
VENUE	Hyde Road
ATTENDANCE	40,000

Manchester City		Manchester United
Jim GOODCHILD	1	Jack MEW
Sam COOKSON	2	Charlie MOORE
Eli FLETCHER	3	Jack SILCOCK
Fred FAYERS	4	Frank HARRIS
Max WOOSNAM	5	Clarrie HILDITCH
Mick HAMILL	6	Tommy MEEHAN
Tommy BROAD	7	William HARRISON
Frank CARROLL	8	Tommy MILLER
Tommy BROWELL	9	Henry LEONARD
Horace BARNES	10	Joe SPENCE
Bill MURPHY	11	Fred HOPKIN

BACKGROUND

City were having serious problems with their ground at Hyde Road. The ground was not only rapidly becoming delapidated but was struggling to cope with the swelling crowds of 40,000 plus that accompanied City's growing success. There were very real fears for spectator safety and efforts got underway to search for alternative accommodation. United offered Old Trafford but the offer was declined. Then, just weeks prior to the November derbies the main stand at Hyde Road was burnt down. The City directors turned to United whose terms now included a demand for all receipts in excess of City's attendances for corresponding fixtures the previous season. City decided to soldier on at Hyde Road and improve the ground as much as they could in the circumstances. Within days of the fire, the old stand was replaced by a huge cinder embankment and usefully, this increased the ground capacity to 45,000. Changing and washing facilities, however, remained a problem and for this derby both teams had to use the nearby Galloway works.

City were unchanged from the previous week. United made two changes, strengthening the side with the recall of International half-back Clarrie Hilditch and forward Joe Spence.

Fred Fayers – the City man came close to handing United a goal when his clearance struck Sam Cookson and looped just over the crossbar.

Manchester City – a growing force in 1920-21 they finished the season unbeaten at home and runners-up in the League.

BEFORE THE GAME

	P	W	D	L	F	A	Pts
CITY	15	7	3	5	23	23	17
UNITED	15	5	6	4	20	19	16

MATCH VERDICT

A rousing victory for City whose forwards put on a dazzling display of attacking football. United's performance was recorded as being "too bad to be true", and they were outplayed throughout. Wingers Murphy and Broad had fine games, Horace Barnes was a constant danger but man of the match was City's International sports star Max Woosnam. He gave a cultured half-back display and according to reports was the 'finest player on view'.

City after a succession of attacks finally broke through on 22 minutes. Woosnam beat three men in a mazy dribble and then passed to Barnes, who drove his shot past Mew. United, under severe pressure, cracked again five minutes later. Woosnam sent Broad away down the wing and his cross was headed in by Browell. The game remained very one-sided and seven minutes into the second half Murphy, left unmarked in the penalty area, had no trouble in smashing the ball past Mew for the third City goal.

"The Empire News" with a headline trumpeting 'WOOSNAM THE MASTER' reported on City's splendid victory as follows:

"In all the meetings of the Manchester teams there has seldom been so one-sided a game as the one at Hyde Road yesterday.
Manchester City won by three clear goals. Had the margin been doubled it would not over-estimate the difference between them, for Manchester United were completely outplayed throughout.
In every department the Old Trafford team compared badly, but nowhere more than half-back. Fayers and Hamill both played really well, but Woosnam stood out by himself as the finest player on view.
He seemed to be always in the vicinity of the ball, and it was his work that paved the way to both the City's first two goals.
Goodchild had little to do, and Cookson and Fletcher had a fairly easy time. The forwards played dazzling football and Murphy was a veritable box of tricks. He repeatedly left the opposition standing, and on the other extreme Broad gave just about his best display since joining the club.
Barnes, too, was at his best and both Browell and Carroll acquitted themselves with distinct credit.
United's form was too bad to be true. Mew was not his usual good self, and got ruffled in the second half. Moore neither kicked nor tackled well, and Silcock was below form.
Owing to the races the crowd was hardly of the dimensions expected, though there would probably be 40,000 present. The gates closed before the kick-off but opened again, and there was room on the vast new terracing.
The club has really made an amazingly rapid recovery from the effects of the fire, and the ground will probably now hold more than it ever did.
City opened well and early on Murphy crashed the ball across the face of the goal. United came near scoring when Fayers, in stopping Spence, kicked the ball hard against Cookson, from whom it rebounded just over the bar.
But City were doing so much pressing that it came as no surprise when they scored after 22 minutes. Woosnam beat three opponents and passed to Barnes, who steadied himself and shot a beautiful goal.
The game was going all one way, and five minutes later Woosnam passed neatly to Broad, who closed in and centred for Browell to head into the net. Seven minutes after the interval the ball came across from the right, and Murphy found himself unmarked and promptly shot a third goal".

AT THE SEASON'S END

CITY: Finished 2nd on 54 points

UNITED: Finished 13th on 40 points

Max Woosnam – an archetypal amateur and top all-round sportsman he fitted in games for City around various other sporting and business commitments, but this was undoubtedly one of his finest games for the club.

*The burnt out remains of Manchester City's **Hyde Road** stand after it was destoyed by fire in early November 1920.*

33

MANCHESTER CITY 4
(Barnes 3 (1 pen), Warner)

MANCHESTER UNITED 1
(Spence)

DATE	22nd October 1921	
DIVISION	One	
VENUE	Hyde Road	
ATTENDANCE	20,000	

Manchester City		Manchester United
Tom BLAIR	1	Jack MEW
Sam COOKSON	2	Charles RADFORD
Eli FLETCHER	3	Frank BRETT
Sammy SHARP	4	Ray BENNION
Max WOOSNAM	5	Clarrie HILDITCH
Fred FAYERS	6	John SCOTT
Billy MEREDITH	7	George BISSETT
John WARNER	8	Arthur LOCHHEAD
Tommy BROWELL	9	Joe SPENCE
Horace BARNES	10	George SAPSFORD
Bill MURPHY	11	Ted PARTRIDGE

BACKGROUND

United's 5-0 hammering at Everton on the opening day of the season was a grim sign of things to come for the Reds. Disappointing defeats and a clutch of 0-0 draws reflected in telling fashion on a side in decline. Joe Spence though remained a potent force at centre-forward, and scored in each of United's three games leading up to the derby. The gentlemanly figure of Clarrie Hilditch, injured early in the season, was sorely missed by the United defence and there was general relief at his return to fitness shortly before the derby. The major development from the City camp during the pre-season was the news that their old favourite Billy Meredith had rejoined the club from United, in the capacity of player coach. Meredith had in fact played more than 100 games for the Blues during the war years, even though still registered with United. Now, following a row over wage payments, the grand old man of football crossed Manchester once again. City, still unbeaten at home for well over a year, had also appointed the charismatic Max Woosnam as Club skipper. Woosnam was quite a character; a "Wilsonian" figure he was an amateur who excelled at most sports. He won Olympic gold in tennis doubles at the 1920 Antwerp games, the Wimbledon doubles with R.Lycett in 1921, captained the British Davis Cup team in America (missing the start of the 1920-21 season!) as well as winning Cambridge Blues for football, golf, and tennis. He was also a useful cricketer. United fans needed no reminder of his talents, following his wonderful display in the previous derby at Hyde Road almost a year earlier.

BARNES' BIRTHDAY.

"Hat Trick" for Manchester City in United's Defeat.

Horace Barnes - the first derby hat-trick since 1894.

	P	W	D	L	F	A	Pts
BEFORE THE GAME							
CITY	10	5	2	3	13	14	12
UNITED	10	2	5	3	11	16	9

MATCH VERDICT

A crushing defeat for United as they received another thrashing from their local rivals. Although the Reds played the final minutes of the game with ten men, following an injury to Bissett, they were thoroughly outplayed by a far superior City side. Horace Barnes proved quite simply the man of the match with a spectacular birthday hat-trick. An inside forward of real class with a particularly powerful left foot, he was a constant thorn in United's flesh. Twice in the first half he shot powerfully home, and his second half penalty ensured the first derby hat-trick since Richard Smith's four goals for Newton Heath in the first ever derby back in November 1894. Joe Spence did pull back a consolation goal for United, but Warner's headed fourth goal put the match way beyond the Reds' capabilities.

"The Sunday Chronicle" reported on City's dominance of the match:

Bill 'Spud' Murphy - City's speedy left-winger.

"Manchester City gained a decisive victory over their neighbours the United in their first conflict of the season at Hyde Road, where the rain which practically fell throughout the afternoon, spoiled the game for the 20,000 spectators present.

The City were always the better team, and thoroughly deserved their victory, although some measure of sympathy must be extended to the United for the absence of Silcock.

It was in the rear division that the United were let down, for Brett was completely at sea, especially in the first half, and Radford was little better. The United after the change of ends were outmatched.

It did not affect the result in the least that Bissett had to leave the field ten minutes from the finish. It was a great day for Barnes from a scoring point of view, for he achieved the distinction of the hat-trick. He scored two in the first half and one from a penalty kick in the second.

Spence obtained the United's only point, and Warner headed the City's fourth goal. The City played very skilfully and at a great pace, and it was due to Mew that they did not win by a greater margin".

Ted Partridge – United's inside-left with a flair for making goals for others.

City's hat-trick hero **Horace Barnes** heads narrowly over the crossbar, while (inset) United goalkeeper **Jack Mew** gathers the ball.

34

MANCHESTER UNITED 3
(Spence 3)

MANCHESTER CITY 1
(Murphy)

DATE	29th October 1921	
DIVISION	One	
VENUE	Old Trafford	
ATTENDANCE	56,000	

Manchester United		Manchester City
Jack MEW	1	Tom BLAIR
Charles RADFORD	2	Sam COOKSON
Jack SILCOCK	3	Eli FLETCHER
Thomas FORSTER	4	Sammy SHARP
Clarrie HILDITCH	5	Max WOOSNAM
John SCOTT	6	Fred FAYERS
William HARRISON	7	Billy MEREDITH
Arthur LOCHHEAD	8	John WARNER
Joe SPENCE	9	Tommy BROWELL
George SAPSFORD	10	Horace BARNES
Ted PARTRIDGE	11	Bill MURPHY

BACKGROUND

United in a state of shock following the heavy defeat seven days previously, made three changes. Bissett had not recovered from injury and was replaced by Harrison, but the reliable Silcock returned in place of Brett, while Forster replaced Bennion in a defensive reshuffle. Even so, United entered the derby simply hoping for the best and out to avoid the humiliation of the previous weekend. A confident City were not surprisingly unchanged.

BEFORE THE GAME

	P	W	D	L	F	A	Pts
CITY	11	6	2	3	17	15	14
UNITED	11	2	5	4	12	20	9

SPENCE'S SPLASH.

"Hat Trick" in Meeting of City Rivals.

By R.Y.

Manchester United put paid to the account rendered by City by defeating them in the return game yesterday. There was a magnificent crowd, the "gate" being officially returned at 56,000.

Manchester United at the last moment played Harrison at outside right, and the City were unchanged. The afternoon was fine and clear, but a strong wind blew from goal to goal, handicapping the teams.

It was curious that both sides played better against the wind than with it.

Manchester United had the wind behind them in the first half, and at the half-way stage they led by two goals to one, which, considering the strength of the breeze, did not seem too great an advantage.

Manchester City were first to score, a splendid centre by Sharp leaving Barnes with the ball at close quarters.

His shot was finely saved by Mew with one hand, but the ball went to Murphy, who was close in, and had an easy task.

A minute later a fine drive by Spence, who throughout the game played finely, was beautifully saved under the bar by Blair, and immediately after this Spence equalised.

Three minutes from the interval, during an attack by the United forwards, the ball went to Spence, who was stood in the goalmouth right in front of Blair, and he scored easily, a claim for offside falling. In the second half the United were decidedly the better side, and after twenty-five minutes Spence put them further ahead. He was well covered as he received the ball, but by clever, strong footwork he literally forced himself into the goalmouth, and shot past Blair amid a remarkable demonstration of enthusiasm.

Two of the finest efforts made by the City in this half were furious, long shots by half-backs, namely, Fayers and Woosnam, but the City vanguard was repeatedly broken up by the half-backs in the last 45 minutes, and the visitors were well beaten in the end.

Considering his years, Meredith showed wonderful pace and quickness, and he was decidedly the best of the four outside wingmen. Spence, Sapsford, and Hilditch were four of the strong men of the game. Woosnam played well, but he had by no means his own way with Spence. Both Blair and Mew kept goal finely, and there was little wrong with the full back play considering the difficulties created by the wind.

Result:—Manchester United, 3; Manchester City, 1.

United goalkeeper **Jack Mew** claws the ball off the head of City forward **Horace Barnes** as United gained revenge for their defeat a week earlier.

The great match at Old Trafford as seen by the cartoonist of the 'Daily Dispatch'

MATCH VERDICT

After years of City proving the most popular team in Manchester, United were starting to pull the bigger derby crowds and the home support was pleasantly surprised to see the Reds exact a sweet revenge for the previous week's comprehensive defeat. Quite amazingly, a hat-trick was scored again, but this time it was United hero Joe Spence who took the honours.

The afternoon had started where matters ended the week before, with a confident City in control and quickly into the lead; Mew parried Barnes' fierce shot and Murphy fired in the rebound. However, two pieces of opportunism by Spence later in the half turned the match in United's favour. Ten minutes from the interval he scored from close in and, on the stroke of half time, was left unmarked in the area and easily put the Reds ahead. Confidence restored, United took the game to City and Spence wrapped it up 20 minutes from time when he burst through the City defence, beat three men, and crashed an unstoppable shot past Blair.

"The Sunday Chronicle" commented on the fine display from the veteran Meredith; his play showed "wonderful pace and quickness". He had become a football legend in his own lifetime. It should not be forgotten that he played in the very first derby in 1894 and virtually every other Manchester derby over the intervening 27 years, but at the age of 46, this was his final derby appearance, although incredibly, he had some further glory with City to come and played on until his 50th year.

Another era ending was that of United manager John Robson who resigned through ill-health two days after the match and was replaced by John Chapman.

Joe Spence - the United forward joined an exclusive club by becoming only the third player to net a derby hat-trick.

AT THE SEASON'S END

CITY: Finished 10th on 45 points

UNITED: Finished 22nd on 28 points
Relegated to Division Two
(United were 8 pts behind Everton in 20th place)

35

MANCHESTER CITY 1
(Cowan)

MANCHESTER UNITED 1
(Rennox)

DATE	12th September 1925
DIVISION	One
VENUE	Maine Road
ATTENDANCE	66,000

Manchester City		Manchester United
Jim MITCHELL	1	Alf STEWARD
Sam COOKSON	2	Charlie MOORE
Philip McCLOY	3	Jack SILCOCK
Sammy SHARP	4	Ray BENNION
Sam COWAN	5	Frank BARSON
Charlie PRINGLE	6	Frank MANN
Billy AUSTIN	7	Joe SPENCE
John WARNER	8	Thomas SMITH
Frank ROBERTS	9	Jimmy HANSON
Tom JOHNSON	10	Clatworthy 'Clat' RENNOX
George HICKS	11	Frank McPHERSON

BACKGROUND

United had spent three seasons in the Second Division and returned as runners-up to Leicester City. Some of the old faithfuls remained, notably Silcock and Spence, but inevitably team strengthening and transitions had occurred, in particular, with the acquisition of club captain Frank Barson. Signed in 1922 for the huge sum of £5,000, United promised Barson a pub if they were promoted within three years - and he just made it! A former blacksmith, Barson was an attacking centre-half of international standard but also carried a notorious reputation as a traditional 'hard man' who was quick to exact retribution if a team-mate was fouled. Another useful signing was Frank McPherson, a man with reputedly the hardest shot in football. The Reds made a quite promising start to the new campaign and had looked impressive in a 3-0 home victory against Aston Villa.

City's playing squad had changed considerably since the last derby, while manager Ernest Mangnall who had joined the Blues from United in September 1912 and played such a major role in the development of both clubs had left City in May 1924, and was replaced by David Ashworth. Meredith had also finally retired in 1924, bowing out in an FA Cup semi-final against Newcastle, although he retained a connection through his son-in-law Charlie Pringle who now played for the Blues. A number of fresh signings had been made; Frank Roberts for £3,400, Billy Austin for £2,000 and Philip McCloy for £3,000. City also had great hopes that Sam Cowan, a centre-half signed from Doncaster Rovers in December 1924 would develop into a quality player. City had moved to their magnificent purpose-built stadium at Maine Road in August 1923 and, with the derby imminent, its capacity was viewed at a possible 90,000!

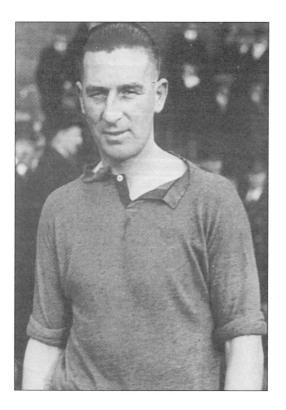

Frank Barson – United skipper and legendary 'hard man'.

BEFORE THE GAME							
	P	W	D	L	F	A	Pts
UNITED	4	1	1	2	5	4	3
CITY	3	1	0	2	3	4	2

MATCH VERDICT

The derby rivalry resumed in front of what was, at the time, City's record League gate. City were deemed the better side in what was a rousing contest. Local born 'keeper Alf Steward had an outstanding game keeping the lively City forwards at bay with a string of fine saves, before 'Clat' Rennox then went down to the other end and gave the Reds the lead with a smart shot.

Sam Cowan capped a wonderful display by scoring the equaliser with a powerful far post header from a left wing corner. It was a fitting reward for Cowan, who besides being the man of the match, looked to be a player the Blues could build a future around.

"The Athletic News" reported on the resumption of the derby match after a four year break:

"The first meeting of the Manchester rivals after a lapse of four years brought the City club the largest League gate they have ever enjoyed. It was not so great as that recorded at the Cup-tie with Cardiff City in March 1924, when 76,166 spectators paid for admission, but over 62,000 people passed through the turnstiles, and, with ticket-holders, the attendance was officially returned at nearly 66,000. It was a magnificent spectacle and a game fought in a splendid spirit. That the City did not defeat their rivals was due primarily to the brilliant goalkeeping of Steward, a Manchester-born player, to whose rich promise the Athletic News referred last Monday.

It was fitting that on the only occasion he was beaten the success fell to Samuel Cowan, for these players were the outstanding figures in the contest. Cowan's headwork was a feature of the match. More, he tackled with grim determination and effectiveness, and distributed the ball with discrimination and accuracy.

Cowan promises to be all that the City club expected when they brought him from Doncaster Rovers last season. He has all the physical requirements for a centre half-back, and, judging by his display in this match, he has the temperament for the big event. His equalising goal was a masterpiece in headwork and judgement".

Manchester City's magnificent new purpose-built ground at *Maine Road* pictured shortly after it was opened in 1923.

Sam Cowan who enjoyed an outstanding game heads in City's equaliser from an acute angle following a corner.

36

MANCHESTER UNITED 1
(Rennox)

MANCHESTER CITY 6
(Roberts 2, Austin 2, Johnson, Hicks)

	DATE	23rd January 1926
	DIVISION	One
	VENUE	Old Trafford
	ATTENDANCE	48,657

Manchester United		Manchester City
Alf STEWARD	1	Jim GOODCHILD
Tommy JONES	2	Sam COOKSON
Jack SILCOCK	3	Philip McCLOY
Ray BENNION	4	Clifford COUPLAND
Clarrie HILDITCH	5	Sam COWAN
Frank MANN	6	Charlie PRINGLE
Joe SPENCE	7	Billy AUSTIN
Christopher TAYLOR	8	Tommy BROWELL
Frank McPHERSON	9	Frank ROBERTS
Clat RENNOX	10	Tom JOHNSON
Henry THOMAS	11	George HICKS

The 1926 Manchester City line-up that trounced United at Old Trafford. The only Blues player missing here is Clifford Coupland.

BACKGROUND

United were in the process of re-establishing themselves as a First Division force. However, their form was inconsistent. Fine victories such as the 6-1 thrashing of Burnley were followed by surprise defeats such as a 5-0 drubbing at lowly Liverpool. Frank McPherson was proving a useful marksman and had scored twelve times in 19 League appearances before the derby.

City were also proving to be a highly unpredictable side with a potent strike force but a highly suspect defence. Tommy Browell remained the club's most dangerous forward, and he would have taken particular delight in scoring four times against his old club in the 4-4 draw with Everton in September. Typical of the erratic form which became something of a trademark were two games in October. Browell scored five times in an 8-3 thrashing of Burnley at Maine Road. Yet two days later when City travelled to Sheffield United they themselves were on the end of an 8-3 scoreline!. Serious trouble loomed and, following a run of defeats in November, manager David Ashworth, in charge for just over a year, resigned. City's board decided not to appoint a new manager immediately, and Chairman Albert Alexander Snr. took total charge of the team until the arrival of Peter Hodge when the season was almost over. City were at this stage a crisis club, desperate for League points and had just narrowly got through the 3rd round of the F.A. Cup, needing a replay to see off the Corinthians.

BEFORE THE GAME

	P	W	D	L	F	A	Pts
UNITED	24	12	4	8	43	35	28
CITY	26	6	8	12	59	70	20

MATCH VERDICT

In one of the most amazing results in derby history the form book, not for the first - or last time - was turned completely upside down. Underdogs City thrashed their neighbours by the largest victory margin in derby history and furthermore executed the operation in front of a disbelieving Old Trafford crowd. Although United had a couple of reserves on their right wing this was still a complete humiliation.

City's forwards showed speed and skill in giving the United defence a torrid opening. Justifiably the Blues took the lead on 18 minutes when Roberts headed in Austin's corner. Following a spell of sustained pressure, United's defence caved in, conceding two goals in the five minutes before half time. Austin, having an inspired game, fired into the unguarded net following a goalmouth scramble and then his clever chip was headed in by Roberts. United checked the Blue tide for half an hour in the second half only to capitulate again in the closing 15 minutes. Johnson headed in Hicks' centre as Steward completely missed the cross. Austin crashed in a fifth from close range and Roberts created the sixth for Hicks. There was really scant consolation for the Reds when Rennox scored from a goalmouth scramble shortly before the close. A glorious and memorable record-breaking victory for City, but sadly all too indicative of the inconsistent form which saw the Blues relegated yet also reach the FA Cup Final.

The "Empire News" reported on 'CITY'S SMASHING VICTORY':

In all their career Manchester United have seldom suffered a bigger humiliation than in the game with their local rivals at Old Trafford yesterday.

That they were overplayed admits no contradiction, and the big margin that Manchester City won by was thoroughly deserved.

From beginning to end United were playing second fiddle, and in the first half especially there was only one team in it. After the interval there was some improvement on the part of the Old Trafford men, but they were never convincing.

The form of City in the first half was a revelation to the crowd. They were much the speedier side and far better in positional play.

True, they were helped by a fairly strong wind, but even that was no excuse for some weak defence by the Old Trafford side, the wing half-backs especially being beaten over and over again.

Quite early on Austin hit the United crossbar, and this was in keeping with the run of the play, for United were constantly defending.

Johnson seemed a certain scorer, but Steward caught the ball like a juggler. He was, however, well beaten after eighteen minutes, when Roberts neatly deflected the ball into the net following a corner kick by Austin.

It was only on rare occasions that United came within striking distance of the City goal, and it was again hard lines on Austin to hit the crossbar when he had the goal at his mercy.

However, Austin had some compensation, when after 40 minutes, he had an empty goal to drive the ball through after Silcock had saved a seemingly hopeless situation.

Right on the interval Austin was allowed a clear course, and lifting the ball right into the jaws of the goal, saw Roberts turn it past the helpless Steward, giving City a three goals lead.

There was some scrambling play in the second half, though United did more frequently threaten danger.

Still the City attacks were more ominous, and inside 30 minutes after the interval Johnson headed a fourth after Steward had come out and missed a centre from Hicks.

With a terrific drive that struck Jones in transit and dazed him, Austin crashed home a fifth. He had previously had the ill-luck to strike the inside of the upright, only to see the ball come out again. In the last five minutes Hicks scored a sixth from close quarters after Roberts had provided him with the chance.

Two minutes from the end Rennox obtained United's only consolation in the midst of a goalmouth scrimmage. It was a game that will be long remembered at Old Trafford"

AT THE SEASON'S END

UNITED: Finished 9th on 44 points

CITY: Finished 21st on 35 points
Relegated to Division Two
(F.A. Cup finalists, losing 1-0 to Bolton W.)

Billy Austin - on target twice and hit the woodwork three times in City's 6-1 rout.

Charlie Pringle - the City half-back held United's Joe Spence in "such a vice that he has seldom seen so little of the ball".

*It was a busy day for United goalkeeper **Alf Steward** who here punches clear from a corner during the Reds' crushing 6-1 defeat.*

37

MANCHESTER CITY 2
(Roberts, Johnson)

MANCHESTER UNITED 2
(Wilson, Johnston)

DATE	1st September 1928	
DIVISION	One	
VENUE	Maine Road	
ATTENDANCE	61,007	

Manchester City		Manchester United
Bert GRAY	1	Alf STEWARD
John RIDLEY	2	Charlie MOORE
Philip McCLOY	3	Jack SILCOCK
Malcolm BARRASS	4	Ray BENNION
Sam COWAN	5	Frank MANN
Jimmy McMULLAN	6	Jack WILSON
Billy AUSTIN	7	Joe SPENCE
Bobby MARSHALL	8	James HANSON
Frank ROBERTS	9	William RAWLINGS
Tom JOHNSON	10	Billy JOHNSTON
Eric BROOK	11	David WILLIAMS

BACKGROUND

City had finished the 1927-28 season as Second Division Champions after the almost unparalleled agony of missing out on promotion the previous season to Portsmouth by five thousandths of a goal, despite winning their final match by an incredible 8-0. A number of new players had joined the Blues in between derbies. Malcolm Barrass joined the club from Sheffield Wednesday in 1926. In the same year Jimmy McMullan was signed from Partick Thistle for £4,700. By 1928 he was a regular Scottish International and indeed he captained the "Wembley Wizards" to their famous 5-1 victory over England. Eric Brook and Fred Tilson were both signed from Barnsley in 1928, the Blues paying £6,000 for the two entertaining forwards. Brook had a reputation for scoring amazing goals and he packed a fierce shot. Although only 5 feet 6 inches tall, he was a versatile player capable of operating in a number of positions, indeed he deputised in goal on three occasions. So City had returned to the First Division a stronger side ready and willing to do battle with the old enemy. A 4-1 defeat, at Birmingham in their opening fixture however, gave them food for thought.

United's changes had been minimal. Frank Barson had left to join Watford on a free transfer. Two players had been signed from neighbours Stockport County. Billy Johnston, an inside forward with an eye for goal, was bought for £3,000 and wing half Jack Wilson cost £500. The Reds made a steady start to the new season with two away draws.

The 1925 change in the offside law was now having some profound effects on the game. The law meant that instead of needing three opponents between himself and the goal line, an attacker needed only two. Previously full backs, working in tandem, were catching forwards offside so often the game had become increasingly boring and gates were falling. Now there were greater attacking possibilities, more attractive games and as Dixie Dean was proving, more goals, as defences struggled to come to terms with the change.

*United goalkeeper **Alf Steward** jumps to fist the ball clear under pressure from City forward **Tommy Johnson** who was on target for the Blues in the 2-2 draw.*

BEFORE THE GAME						
	P	W	D	L	F	A	Pts
UNITED	2	0	2	0	1	1	2
CITY	1	0	0	1	1	4	0

MATCH VERDICT

Ivan Sharpe's sermon in the "Athletic News" (reproduced here) was that United, and Silcock in particular, had not learned the lessons of the changes in the offside rule.

"The defender who exploits this out of date system will suffer severely", wrote Sharpe. It was Silcock's attempt to play the old offside trap that cost United the victory. Silcock, standing purposefully up the field, could only stand and watch as the ball was lobbed forward and Johnson raced away and scored. In a close contest, watched by another massive crowd, a draw was deemed a fair result. Roberts put the Blues ahead with a snap shot. Wilson's equaliser for the Reds was fortunate as his high centre from the touchline ended up in the net, Gray having made a mess of the attempted "tip over". Johnston put United into a half time lead with a good header from Spence's cross but then came the Reds' "offside folly".

John Silcock - a top quality long-serving left full-back for United, he was a fine exponent of the off-side trap, although he was caught out on this occasion.

Charlie Moore - a regular for United at right-back during the 1920's, he was a dependable defender who eventually topped 300 League games for the club.

HERE'S A SERMON

PREACHED IN SILENCE BY MANCHESTER CLUBS' PLAYERS.

OFF-SIDE FOLLY : : By Ivan Sharpe.

Manchester City 2   *Manchester United* 2

SOON after Bishop Welldon from his arm chair had told the world all that was wrong with football and had closed down with a totally unnecessary reminder that football "should exhibit the true spirit of honourable British sportsmanship," the players of the City and United Clubs of Manchester set before the public in the plainest possible fashion the simple truth.

That is that, considering the tension of modern football, the play is exceptionally good tempered and clean.

It is the old story, I suppose. One unhappy incident inspires the critics. One glint of flame—this time at Villa Park—is turned into a prairie fire. The tone of football is excellent. Football does not need to be told to "play the game."

The truer sermon was preached on Saturday at Maine-road where 60,000 odd frenzied folk urged the teams to extra effort, on a field as warm as a Turkish bath, and despite the ninety minutes of thrill and strain and continuous excitement, not one incident marred the match. That was a sermon worth noting. It was eloquent, silent preaching.

JUST FOLLY.

Now let us get on with the game. Two—two it ended, and, all told, this was not a bad result.

United were more purposeful in the first half, and were very unfortunate when an unsaveable drive by Spence struck the post. City stayed better, but in the second half missed chances. That was not United's fault. A point apiece, then, was a result at which the man who sees both sides could not really quibble.

But one set deserved to be beaten. I thought they "asked for it." This was United. How many times are we to say the off-side game does not pay—is folly?

Silcock is a splendid back, but he persists in off-side tactics. I don't condemn them from the sporting point of view; the forward now has protection enough. But the defender who exploits this out-of-date system will suffer severely sooner or later.

WIT AND NIP.

Arsenal threw away the Cup semi-final last season because Cope tried the old dodge to save his legs. Silcock is still playing with fire, and well though he performed in other respects he was responsible for City's equalising goal (through being too far forward), and if the home team had had inside forwards with quicker wits

he would have paid a heavier penalty. The whistle checked some attacks, but when Roberts wisely was refusing to interfere with play when in off-side positions in the second half sharper inside men than Marshall and Johnson would have jumped to it and romped away for goal with the openings offered.

Once and for all, the off-side game is folly! Time will bring home that fact to Manchester United.

It was a game of throbs and thrills. Roberts scored—a subtle move but a snap goal. Wilson equalised—a centre from the touch-line that Gray should have tipped over the bar. Johnston gave United the lead with a header after a capital attack and perfect Spence centre. Two—one at half-time. Then a long lob found Silcock stranded, and Johnson equalised.

Promptly the City took a grip of the game, and Roberts had more than one chance to win the match. But he was not the only offender in City's attack. The inside pair were poor, and Austin too timid before the interval. Brook shirked nothing, while Roberts was cute, though short of the nip and pace asked of the modern centre-forward.

Behind, I thought all was well, although Gray made one serious error and McCloy for a time sliced his clearances, for Cowan and M'Mullan by contrasting methods were always inspiring their forwards.

THE VERDICT.

Nor need United worry. Remember "the Day." Nerves also twitch on the field. The defence was solid, apart from Silcock's system, and the attack had more method than I saw in their play last season.

The pass back to the half-back occasionally was called into play by the inside pair, but better centre-forward play is required than Rawlings here revealed. Spence rarely does the wrong thing. Williams used his chances well. Hanson never gives in. Tries all. A star centre-forward would soon drive away the relegation fears of a season back (Rawlings was not in good health).

But we do not expect the finest football in such a clash. "The true spirit of honourable British sportsmanship" certainly is on trial. I leave the verdict with those who see football and those who watched this match.

Manchester City.—Gray; Ridley, McCloy; Barrass, Cowan, M'Mullan; Austin, Marshall, Roberts, Johnson, and Brook.

Manchester United.—Steward; Moore, Silcock; Bennion, Mann, Wilson; Spence, Hanson, Rawlings, Johnston, and Williams.

Referee: A. Josephs, South Shields.

38

MANCHESTER UNITED 1
(Rawlings)

MANCHESTER CITY 2
(Austin, Johnson)

	DATE	5th January 1929
	DIVISION	One
	VENUE	Old Trafford
	ATTENDANCE	42,555

Manchester United		Manchester City
Alf STEWARD	1	Lewis BARBER
Charlie MOORE	2	John RIDLEY
Jack SILCOCK	3	Philip McCLOY
Ray BENNION	4	Malcolm BARRASS
Charles SPENCER	5	Sam COWAN
Clarrie HILDITCH	6	Jimmy McMULLAN
Joe SPENCE	7	Billy AUSTIN
James HANSON	8	Bobby MARSHALL
William RAWLINGS	9	Frank ROBERTS
Harry ROWLEY	10	Tom JOHNSON
David WILLIAMS	11	Eric BROOK

BACKGROUND

City's form had been something of a struggle and as the derby approached they found themselves in the wrong half of the table. Defensively they remained suspect and were letting in too many goals. Goalkeeper Bert Gray, at fault in the last derby, soon found himself replaced by Lewis Barber. Barber had joined the Blues the previous summer from Halifax and from Christmas he had made the position his own.

United were faring even worse. Winning was a foreign habit. It had taken them seven games to record their first victory (beating Newcastle 5-0). Despite the size of that victory, goals were proving hard to come by. Heavy defeats in November and December left the club's position looking precarious. However hopes were raised in the game before the derby when they obtained a 2-2 draw with high flying Aston Villa.

BEFORE THE GAME							
	P	W	D	L	F	A	Pts
CITY	22	7	5	10	45	54	19
UNITED	23	4	9	10	32	47	17

MATCH VERDICT

A tense match of poor quality between sides that were worried about "that relegation feeling". The result left United with the greater worry. Commentary in the "Athletic News" referred to the ball being "like a hot thing to be got rid of as soon as received". As is always the case in contests of this nature, the quality of the football played was of a very poor standard, inhibited by doubt and anxiety. The scrappy game was settled in the second half. United took the lead with a goal by Rawlings that had looked "yards offside". Billy Austin equalised immediately from the only quality move of the match. As United unwisely settled back in defence during the closing minutes Tommy Johnson grabbed the winner for the Blues.

Tommy Johnson - the City forward's goal was just one of 38 strikes in 39 appearances during this season, a feat that is still a club record.

AT THE SEASON'S END
CITY: Finished 8th on 45 points
UNITED: Finished 12th on 41 points

RELEGATION FEELING.

No Chance for the Real Footballer in This Atmosphere.

BATTLE OF MANCHESTER: By IVAN SHARPE.

Manchester City 2   •Manchester United 1

Frank Roberts - the forward cost a massive £3,400 when signed by City from Bolton in 1922. He was now in his last season, and this was to be his final derby. Roberts goalscoring record however, was splendid with 130 League and Cup goals in 237 appearances when he left the club in the summer.

PERHAPS you remember "Big Bill" Morrison—"Big" Bill or Joe or Jimmy is a common term of the trade in football.

"Big Bill" played for Fulham—a towering Scottish centre half-back. Came the day when Tom T. Fitchie, the amateur International Scottish forward of twinkling toes, who played for Arsenal and Queen's Park, figured in front of him for Glossop.

Morrison was a grand defender, but his passes were punched. "The first I received," said Fitchie, "hit me in the middle of the back and I nocked me breathless. The second hit me on the head and knocked me out!"

In the first half of this hectic battle of Manchester, Austin, the City's outside right, received a pass from one of his half-backs. As was common this day he had to apply his head to the ball. The pass knocked him sick. For the second time in the match he had to go to the dressing-room.

A RED-HOT THING.

Ponder those words, and you have a fair sample of the standard of play served up in this relegation duel.

Twenty-two men in shorts, I pictured, running around the im of Hades. Clubs spoil it relegation. The ball, a red-hot thing to be got rid of as soon as received.

Twenty-two men running and kicking frantically. Do I exaggerate? I think not. Remember, this was a First Division match, and comes for judgment as first-class football, due allowance being demanded for "Derby" day.

Crazy, daisy footh! Ball lofted high or slashed down the field. Up and at 'em! calls from the crowd. Fancy an artist like McMullan being expected to shine in an affair of this kind.

Fancy expecting a sane result. A draw was the only fitting termination, since it was an affair of fury, not football. Yet it was not foul.

But you do not get a fitting result, because this helter-skelter play means fortuitous football and snap goals.

I thought United the more dangerous team and worthy of one if not two points. They got none. Their second half lead, taken through RAWLINGS—the goal, I thought, was clearly offside—was rubbed off in the closing minutes when AUSTIN made his first contribution of any consequence whatever by scoring a capital equaliser, and immediately JOHNSON snatched the other point out of the fires of Hades. United in these worrying closing moments making the mistake of adopting mainly a defensive attitude.

So City sneaked two very precious points and United had a right to bemoan their luck.

FOOTBALL A BAD SECOND.

What can one say by way of individual criticism of such a match?

There are known to be flaws in both teams, but the finest of men cannot show or touch first-class football in such a match. It was just one more case of tension over all.

Perhaps it is excusable on "Derby day." But modern football consists too largely of excitement first, football second —and sometimes "nowhere."

There was much puerile forward play. In this respect the City were streaky and decidedly frail on the wings. I could see only one forward of real class a-field and his name was Hanson.

But what can forwards do with the ball ever lunged too desperately and in the air? Spence and Williams centred well, but this was part of the lunging—long, "up and at 'em" centres, they were.

I saw no other forward who was able to beat down the hurly-burly. If defence is judged by powers of destruction, however, there were stars.

There is not much amiss with either defence on this showing. I liked both goalkeepers, and thought Moore the best back in the battle, with Ridley second. The half-back play was of the "stop them" character, and here Cowan earns chief commendation.

The great crowd revelled in the thrills. And there must have been 50,000 people making things hum. Hum? Hm! We shall never get football in this atmosphere. Football is holding and controlling the ball.

Manchester United—Steward; Moore, Silcock; Bennion, Spencer, Hilditch; Spence, Hanson, Rawlings, Rowley, and Williams.

Manchester City. — Barber; Ridley, M'Cloy; Barras, Cowan, M'Mullan; Austin, Marshall, Roberts, Johnson, and Brooks.

Referee: A. Josephs, South Shields.

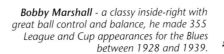

Bobby Marshall - a classy inside-right with great ball control and balance, he made 355 League and Cup appearances for the Blues between 1928 and 1939.

39

MANCHESTER UNITED 1
(Thomas)

MANCHESTER CITY 3
(Johnson, Marshall, Brook)

DATE	5th October 1929
DIVISION	One
VENUE	Old Trafford
ATTENDANCE	57,201

Manchester United		Manchester City
Alf STEWARD	1	Lewis BARBER
Charlie MOORE	2	John RIDLEY
Jack SILCOCK	3	William FELTON
Ray BENNION	4	Malcolm BARRASS
Charles SPENCER	5	Sam COWAN
Frank MANN	6	Geoff HEINEMANN
Joe SPENCE	7	Ernie TOSELAND
James HANSON	8	Bobby MARSHALL
Tom REID	9	Tom JOHNSON
Harry ROWLEY	10	Fred TILSON
Henry THOMAS	11	Eric BROOK

BACKGROUND

United's side was basically still the same as that which had won promotion in 1925. Steward, Moore, Bennion, Mann and Spence remained the backbone of the side. But it looked as though it might be another season of struggle for the Reds as they made an inauspicious start. The opening games were both 4-1 defeats by Newcastle and Leicester City. A slight rally in form was followed by a further two defeats by Liverpool and Derby County, and thus the Reds entered the derby fairly low in morale.

Ernie Toseland made his debut for City the previous season, replacing the outside right Billy Austin in the last three games and was to prove an outstanding addition. City had made a promising start to the new season. The second match showed their true potential when they beat a strong Arsenal side 3-1 in front of 50,000 at Maine Road.

BEFORE THE GAME

	P	W	D	L	F	A	Pts
CITY	7	4	1	2	17	13	9
UNITED	7	3	0	4	10	15	6

MATCH VERDICT

A comprehensive victory by the Blues, much the better side on the day, and worrying signs that United were once again a team in decline. The controversy of the match was the fact that the referee's time-keeping went awry and he unexpectedly finished the game two minutes early. This was particularly galling for City because as Mr Caswell blew his whistle, Tommy Johnson was running around Steward and placing the ball into an empty net, effectively robbing jubilant City supporters of a crushing 4-1 victory.

City's forwards were far too clever for a dithering Reds defence and the Blues always looked likely to score. However, they had to wait until the second half for the goals to come. As Moore tried to play his tried and trusted off-side ploy, Tommy Johnson got away and shot City in front. Marshall edged the Blues further ahead with a clever shot with the outside of his boot, but Thomas, the Reds' best forward briefly put United back in contention with a goal against the run of play. However, the emerging Brook settled the issue with a glorious shot on the run which settled in the corner of the net.

"A Minutes Muddle in the Battle of Manchester" reported Ivan Sharpe in the "Athletic News":

When Thomas C.F. Johnson was a boy he dreamed of playing for a First Division team, and like every youngster, of playing at centre-forward.

On his night of nights he was playing against his own club's deadly rivals, and over 100,000 eyes were rivetted upon him as he darted through the defence - "Go on Johnson!" - dodged this man and that man, drew out the goalkeeper, dribbled the ball round the other side's last hope and with the roars of the delighted populace acclaiming his performance, rolled the ball through the untenanted goal.

I have not asked him, but I know it's true, because every schoolboy gets those midnight, alone-I-did-it goals.

But isn't it a hard world? The once-in-a-lifetime goal dribbled around the goalkeeper on the aforesaid deadly rivals' very own ground all came true in this battle of Manchester, and the referee said the time had expired a moment before the ball had crossed the line!

And that's not all. Time had not expired. My watch and every watch around me - plus the carefully compiled record I invariably keep of the minutes of the passing show - definitely established that the referee was two and a half minutes too soon. And this is making no allowance whatever for lost time. The real result was 4-1, plus any further goals that might have been added in the missing minutes.

A very anxious City supporter asked me afterwards whether there was any danger that such a point could be used as a protest against the result of the match being allowed to stand. No! The referee is the one and only timekeeper. It is a question of fact (not of law), and the referee's decision being final there will be no replay.

Anyway, Johnson should have been a fairly happy man. He will be happier when, and if, his right foot becomes as lively as his left. Still, he has the credit of making the match come to life. It was going to pieces early in the second half when Moore thoughtlessly pulled up while appealing for off-side and Johnson - with his right foot - scored and set the game alight.

Quickly Marshall flicked the ball away from the goalkeeper's grasp with the outside of his foot - quite a Meredith touch - and got a glorious second goal; Thomas received his due reward by scoring for United, and Hanson could not keep sufficiently cool when he might have made the match all square. So shocked was Brook that the old Barnsley spirit flared up and sent him racing away from the defence to score - on the run - the knock-out goal. It all went to show again how much difference one goal makes to a match. Before this tonic it is all very noisy and exciting and just as unimpressive as an exhibition of First Division football.

'After Taking' as the advertisements say, the City

became a first class team and the forwards reached a standard more worthy of the reputation they are building up this season.

But how far did United's failings contribute to this great revival? I came away feeling that too many members of the home defence are showing signs of Time's wear and tear and could not stay the full distance.

The United seem to have serious problems looming up. Steward was sound enough, but the backs have slumped decisively; Bennion left his wing, Spencer had the ball too often in the air, and Mann wavered in defence.

The forwards lacked a leader, for Reid could not link or lead the line, and Spence was very poorly served. Thomas, who centred capitally, being quite the best man of a moderate attack. Obviously what it needs is a centre who can inspire the line. Probably the whole team will revive if the right man comes along. Is a player worth £10,000? It is at such times that one wonders what is the answer.

Manchester City in the first half seemed to have been flattered by their friends. People kept saying: "You can't judge them without McMullan". But McMullan was left to rest in peace between his influenza blankets. One goal made new men of them.

The secret of their success is fore and aft. The backs are solid and inspiring; the forwards are young, clever, incisive and decidedly dangerous when they strike the scent. Read the names backwards from outside left to outside right - and you have my order of merit.

That they do not always readily find their stride is due to the fact that the half-backs, as a line, do not 'feed' with the true First Division touch, but I thought Heinemann, the understudy, came through very well.

How curious, though, that the referee got in a muddle with his minutes on the day the clock goes back. He provided the last 'rows' of Summer."

Frank Mann - *a stalwart for United during the 1920's, he was now in his late thirties and certainly showing signs of 'Time's wear and tear'. A quick thinking football brain was no longer enough to see him through, and indeed, a month after this derby defeat he retired.*

Alf Steward - *United's regular goalkeeper during the 1920's, he was "sound enough" in this game despite being on the losing side. It was rather the story of his career at Old Trafford, where despite topping 300 League games, he never collected a major honour.*

40

MANCHESTER CITY 0
MANCHESTER UNITED 1
(Reid)

DATE	8th February 1930	
DIVISION	One	
VENUE	Maine Road	
ATTENDANCE	64,472	

Manchester City		Manchester United
Lewis BARBER	1	Alf STEWARD
William FELTON	2	Tom JONES
Philip McCLOY	3	Jack SILCOCK
Malcolm BARRASS	4	Ray BENNION
Sam COWAN	5	Clarrie HILDITCH
Jackie BRAY	6	Jack WILSON
Ernie TOSELAND	7	Joe SPENCE
Bobby MARSHALL	8	Thomas BOYLE
Tommy TAIT	9	Tom REID
Tom JOHNSON	10	Harry ROWLEY
Eric BROOK	11	George McLACHLAN

BACKGROUND

Probably the most influential figure in Manchester's footballing history made his debut for City between derby matches. Matt Busby's League bow came in City's 3-1 victory over Middlesbrough on 2nd November 1929. However, by the time this derby came around he was still not a regular and had made only one further appearance in the City line-up. City were having a good season, were well placed in the League and had lost only five of the 19 games in between derbies.

United had recovered somewhat from their disappointing start to the season. Some useful victories were accrued including a 1-0 defeat of Arsenal and a 5-0 trouncing of Newcastle. A 7-2 away defeat at Sheffield Wednesday reminded the side of their defensive fallibility. However the Reds entered the derby in a more confident frame of mind following the 4-2 defeat of West Ham, when the evergreen Joe Spence scored all four goals.

BEFORE THE GAME							
	P	W	D	L	F	A	Pts
CITY	27	14	6	7	64	49	34
UNITED	27	11	3	13	43	54	25

MATCH VERDICT

City disappointed their fans against a very moderate United side. The Blues showed little of the cohesion and understanding that had brought the 3-1 win at Old Trafford and made them such a respected side this season. The game was settled after just 15 minutes when Reid, described by Ivan Sharpe in the "Athletic News" as "a cumbersome chap and a dismal failure at centre forward", beat Barber with a shot from close range. The Reds were no doubt pleased to have gained revenge for the early season mauling at Old Trafford, but in reality this was a game of a very poor pedigree.

AT THE SEASON'S END

CITY: Finished 3rd on 47 points
(13 points behind Champions, Sheffield Wednesday)

UNITED: Finished 17th on 38 points
(Everton were bottom on 35 points)

Malcolm Barrass - a mainstay of the City team this season at wing-half, his performance was below par during the home derby defeat by United.

NOT TO-DAY!

The Battle of Manchester

*Manchester United .1 *Manchester City..0*

By IVAN SHARPE.

SIXTY - FIVE thousand people scurried in! Outside, a host of vendors of cough drops ("Make you roar like Carneral"), and other odds and ends couldn't tempt them. Not to-day 'No time Must get inside

Also outside the ground were posters " Can City Win the Cup?—by Ivan Sharpe.' I didn't put them there, but I can respond in half a dozen words: " Not if they play like this!"

It was good billing, if intelligent anticipation counts for anything, as there was no reference to the League Championship, despite the fact that James McMullan, the City's captain, has been telling the world for some time past that the club would do the ' double."

Unless there is a decided improvement on recent displays Manchester City will win neither. They have been beaten at home twice in a week, and by lowly teams like Everton and Manchester United. Of course, the successful invasion from Old Trafford was a bitter pill. Well, what's amiss?

MANCHESTER CITY SLUMP.

I have not regarded Manchester City as a great team.

The only side coming in that category in my experience this season is Sheffield Wednesday, who would set a problem to Newcastle United at their best.

But the City have been decidedly effective.

There has been little elaboration. All their work has been clear cut—progressive and penetrative. They seem to be going back because the reserve players recently introduced at back and wing half-back have not been good enough to maintain the blend

They may revive; I think they will. But there must be a return to their highest standard if they are to have a hope of getting to Wembley '

When I reflect on the moderate forward play pitted against them on Saturday, there is evidence at once of a decided slump in defence.

Reid, after getting the one goal of the game in the fifteenth minute, was such a cumbersome chap and dismal failure at centre-forward that one was not very surprised when he lobbed the ball over the bar from point-blank range after the interval.

Boyle was not much better, and Spence does not get on with it in the old Spence way, but fidgets and doubles back or too readily centres the ball. Really, therefore, the United had only two good forwards, and both were on the left wing, where, too Rowley promises much and has a way of fading out before the crowning move.

Moderate back play contributed to their victory, but staunch defensive play all round by the United really won the match. The half-backs excelled, if not artistic, while Steward and Silcock were magnificent Jones (playing with a limp) being also a very brave little back. These men are the real match winners.

Tom Reid - the United man was described in this match as a 'cumbersome chap and a dismal failure at centre-forward' but he scored the winning goal at Maine Road. In all he totalled 67 League and Cup goals in five seasons with the Reds between 1928-29 and 1932-33.

Sam Cowan -
City's sheet-anchor

41

MANCHESTER CITY 4
(Tait 2, Marshall 2)

MANCHESTER UNITED 1
(Spence)

DATE	4th October 1930
DIVISION	One
VENUE	Maine Road
ATTENDANCE	45,000

Manchester City		*Manchester United*
Lewis BARBER	1	Alf STEWARD
John RIDLEY	2	Tom JONES
William FELTON	3	Jack SILCOCK
Malcolm BARRASS	4	Clarrie HILDITCH
Sam COWAN	5	Hugh McLENAHAN
Jackie BRAY	6	Jack WILSON
Ernie TOSELAND	7	Joe SPENCE
Bobby MARSHALL	8	Arthur WARBURTON
Tommy TAIT	9	Tom REID
Jimmy McMULLAN	10	Harry ROWLEY
Eric BROOK	11	George McLACHLAN

Tommy Tait - two goals in City's crushing victory, but it was his goalscoring prowess the previous season which prompted the unpopular sale of Tommy Johnson to Everton.

BACKGROUND

The 1930-31 season was one of crisis as far as United were concerned both on and off the field. In their worst ever League start they had lost all their opening eight League games, an unhappy record that was to stretch to 12 consecutive reverses. The team had grown old together and financial difficulties meant little possibility of strengthening the side. Heavy defeats by Huddersfield Town (0-6) and Newcastle United (4-7) in front of Old Trafford crowds of 11,000 indicated just how bad things were. The supporters in their disgust at the plight of the club even attempted to organise a boycott of home matches. Thus United entered the derby in little short of total disarray.

Manchester football was at a low ebb, with City not doing much better than their neighbours. They had obtained only one victory, a 1-0 win over Leeds United, and fans at Maine Road were equally disgruntled with the management and showing of the team. They were, in particular, most critical of the previous season's sale of the club's record goalscorer Tommy Johnson to Everton.

BEFORE THE GAME							
	P	W	D	L	F	A	Pts
CITY	8	1	2	5	11	21	4
UNITED	8	0	0	8	10	34	0

MATCH VERDICT

United's dreadful start to the season continued as City made it nine defeats in a row. For United nothing seemed to be going right and during the match they lost no less than three players to injury, with full-back Tom Jones suffering a broken collar bone. Indeed, in these days before substitutes were permitted, City fared little better in this respect and in the closing minutes supporters suffered the farcical scene of nine men against eight. The expected protests by disgruntled United supporters failed to materialise; perhaps by the end total demoralisation had set in.

All this aside, the game was won in the first 30 minutes when the Reds were at full strength. After containing the City forwards for a short time the Reds' defence was twice cut to ribbons by moves of high quality. Tommy Tait and Bobby Marshall both getting on the end of flowing passing movements that the United defence was powerless to cut out. The state of United's desperation and poor planning was illustrated at the start of the second half. The Reds adopted the highly dubious tactic of leaving one back-stopper and pouring the rest forward in search of goals. The predictable response to this was that the unmarked City forwards counter-attacked and scored twice in ten minutes, again through Marshall and Tait. With McLenahan then stretchered off and the United defence in even further disarray the Blues looked capable of double figures. In fact City seemed to ease up - perhaps even in sympathy - and Spence pulled back a goal, but United finished the afternoon a sadly dejected club.

The ever acerbic pen of Ivan Sharpe in "The Athletic News" reported on United's defensive folly:

Manchester United have become the football which the Fates are kicking. I wonder what Mr Greenhough thought about it. Mr Greenhough, you must know, is the Hitler of the Manchester United Supporters' Club. He is carrying the banner and using the megaphone at the Supporters demonstrations against the United directors for failing to get new players and stop the rot.

Surely sorrow and sympathy must have crept into his hard heart on Saturday afternoon when the wooden-spoon holders he is so energetically prodding, first lost a full-back Jones with a broken collar-bone, then a centre half-back, McLenahan with a damaged ankle, and at one period near the end had only eight players on the field.

As the City had then lost their centre-forward Tait, owing to concussion, and temporarily Silcock (United) was laid out and Barrass (City) and Hilditch (United) were also in the trainer's hands, there was a time when the score in regard to players still standing read City 9 United 8.

Yes, five men were off the field at one time. Oh, and McMullan had to be helped off for a while in the first half. It was like visiting day at the hospital, the visitors being nearly 45,000 strong. And all this was entirely accidental; there wasn't a bit of bad temper in the whole match.

All this too, made the game farcical in the last half hour, but there are one or two important things to say, notwithstanding.

The first is complimentary. The match at the outset struck a far better note than one expected. This was no 'clashing of the cans' as it had been described in advance at one of those supporters' meetings. For Manchester United one can say that for however much they have been damned, they shaped at the start like quite a useful side. They were as good as their opponents - up to the goalmouth - and got there just as often.

When City then delivered a blow on the nose and another on the point, they were blows that no defence in the country could have side-stepped. Magnificent goals both - the first to Tait and the second to Marshall, and each the outcome of high-

class, clear-cut forward play. You can't blame United for that!

So stood the game at the end of half an hour. Then United's injuries and troubles began. They had played really well up to a point. Now they lapsed into serious tactical errors. When Jones went off, they called Wilson to left back and Rowley from inside left to left half. I suggest that this was wrong, because Rowley had been far and away their best forward. He was the man they could least spare from the attack.

'Wait a minute folks' those screenmen announce, 'you ain't heard nothin''. That is how I feel about the second half. For the United now changed their tactics. They sent Rowley into the forward line again. So far, so good. But they retained all three half-backs and adopted the one-back game with brave Silcock as the one back.

Under the present off-side law, this policy is simply suicidal. I went to this match, intending if at all possible, to give Manchester United a helping hand, so mercilessly, and in some cases unfairly, have they been condemned.

I am still anxious to play that part, and it is simply in their interests to state that they now presented Manchester City with two goals in ten minutes by this absurd one-back method of defence. The one-back game under the present off-side law is sheer folly. You may as well have no back at all - this would be better maybe, as then the off-side law would come to your aid.

As it was, Manchester City had only to make a wide pass drawing Silcock to the wing, and an inside pass when he got there, and the way to goal was clear for the inside forwards.

Ten minutes of this gave the City two easy goals. Marshall got the first because there was no other back to intervene, and Tait the second, this to the student, being a pathetic exposure of this defensive system.

How many goals the City would have got had not McLenahan then been carried off, leaving United with only nine men, the City forwards may care to estimate.

What actually happened was that the City obviously grew sympathetic and declined to rub it in, so that after Spence had headed a clever goal, the game became a drab runabout and everyone welcomed the end.

ONE BACK: NO BACK.
PROBLEMS OF MANCHESTER'S "DERBY."

Tommy Johnson - seen here in Everton colours, caused much unrest among City supporters when he departed to Goodison, yet it says something for the goalscoring expectations of fans during this period that they were upset that City managed only 75 goals in 1930-31!

42

MANCHESTER UNITED 1
(Spence)

MANCHESTER CITY 3
(Brook, Toseland, Halliday)

DATE	7th February 1931
DIVISION	One
VENUE	Old Trafford
ATTENDANCE	39,876

Manchester United		Manchester City
Alf STEWARD	1	Len LANGFORD
Jack MELLOR	2	John RIDLEY
William DALE	3	Laurie BARNETT
Ray BENNION	4	Matt BUSBY
Clarrie HILDITCH	5	Sam COWAN
George McLACHLAN	6	Jimmy McMULLAN
Joe SPENCE	7	Ernie TOSELAND
Arthur WARBURTON	8	Bobby MARSHALL
Tom REID	9	David HALLIDAY
Stanley GALLIMORE	10	Charlie ROBERTS
Sam HOPKINSON	11	Eric BROOK

BACKGROUND

City's previous derby win proved the stimulus for improved League form and they moved steadily up the table with a series of victories. Len Langford, purchased from Nottingham Forest, was now the regular goalkeeper, replacing Barber. Matt Busby, who had surplanted Malcolm Barrass earlier in the season, was set to play his first and last derby. How ironic with hindsight that Busby should play against United in one of their darkest hours.

United's season was by now little short of a complete relegation catastrophe. The first points and victory came in the 13th fixture, a 2-0 victory over Birmingham. However, with the defence leaking an average of three goals a game, defeats remained commonplace. By the derby fixture United already looked certainties to make the drop down into Division Two. Circumstances on the pitch, bad though they seemed, were mild in comparison to the growing financial plight of the club as United struggled to beat the national Depression and stay in business. Sliding towards the edge of the precipice on two fronts, United therefore entered the 42nd derby with many of the Manchester public clear this would be the last such popular local fixture for at least a season, but worse, speculating this might possibly be the final ever such meeting between the teams.

Clarrie Hilditch - a United stalwart since 1919, this was his final derby match in a career with the club that spanned more than 300 League games.

BEFORE THE GAME

	P	W	D	L	F	A	Pts
CITY	28	12	5	11	50	51	29
UNITED	28	4	4	20	36	86	12

Jimmy McMullan - a splendid passer and terrific tactician, the Scottish international was a key City player during this era, but United's relegation was to make this his last derby match.

MATCH VERDICT

City did the double over their crisis ridden neighbours who had the frustration of seeing the winning two goals arrive in the final ten minutes. The match illustrated the importance of wing forwards in the British game at this time. Indeed, the inimitable Ivan Sharpe was of the opinion they had become the most valuable members of any team - the "Bank of England men". Certainly they were at the forefront of this derby result, as trickery and sharp shooting played a part in all the goals. In line with the result it was City's Brook and Toseland who caught the eye.

In a lively opening City took the lead when Brook, receiving the ball from a free kick, picked his spot and fired an unstoppable shot past Steward. United clambered back into the game and Spence showed he had lost little of his natural ability when he cut in from the wing and shot past Langford. Despite City having all the play in the second half United looked likely to hang on until City cut loose to wrap up the points. Brook's delightful wing play finally proved too much for the tormented Reds' defence and it was from his pair of crosses that Toseland shot and Halliday headed City to their 14th derby victory. City were now just one victory behind the Reds.

AT THE SEASON'S END

CITY: Finished 8th on 46 points

UNITED: Finished 22nd on 22 points
Relegated to Division Two
(Leeds were 21st on 31 pts)

"BANK OF ENGLAND" MEN.

WING FORWARDS' VALUE CONFIRMED.

Manchester City...3 Manchester United 1
(Half-time 1—1.)

By IVAN SHARPE.

IF League football, or football of any grade for that matter, requires further evidence of the fact that *outside* forwards have become matchwinners, this game between the Manchester rivals supplied it.

Brook, Manchester City's outside left, got the first goal when following a free kick, he suddenly found himself all alone with no one save the helpless goalkeeper to say him nay. Perhaps this does not assist my contention.

But, directly after, Spence, Manchester United's outside right, obtained the equaliser. He did so by descending on goal and shooting—very accurately. Previously, too, Spence had struck the post.

In the second half Brook shot into the net again, but the point was disallowed. Then he provided the centres from which the City's second and third goals were scored in the last ten minutes.

May that the second goal fell to the outside right (Toseland). The other was headed home delightfully by Halliday, who, incidentally, had failed rather badly to profit by other scoring opportunities.

As the nearest bid for a goal by Manchester United after the interval came from Hopkinson, the home outside left, who had taken up a position in front of Langford, it will be seen that the wing forwards are no longer trudgers of the touch-line.

Let that fact sink in. In future wingmen are going to be "Bank of England" men: high-priced players in transfer transactions.

The outside man who cannot cut in and pass across goal or shoot cannot now properly do his job—unless he is an Alan Morton or a William Meredith in artistry on the wing.

The outside man who can cut in and doesn't need a "dressing down." Times have changed.

SMILING THROUGH.

It was superior forward play which gave Manchester City the victory over their neighbours, and on the wings the superiority was emphatic—partly because these men were better served.

Toseland boomed in the first half and Brook in the second. They had help from Marshall and, in lesser degree, from Halliday and Roberts, each of whom can make a dainty pass but Halliday had not the old power in the mid-field burst or around the goal.

Behind these forwards was a defence that gave a stern challenge to the United's anxious attacks. Cowan was a man and a half, and Ridley, seen through home glasses, was almost equally unneighbourly. What I liked about Ridley, too, was that although "bumped and bored" a bit he got up with a smile.

All told, however, Manchester City had little, if any, advantage over the United in half-back and full-back play, Bennion being in splendid form, McLachlan quite good, and Mellor a live right back.

I thought the losers' only real weakness in defence, in fact, was in the methods of Steward, the goalkeeper, in dealing with centres.

Leaving the losers' attack here is their real weakness.

If your centre-forward cannot quickly settle on the ball and control, pass, or shoot it, the line is sorely handicapped. That was the trouble of the First Division "bottom dogs" in this match: Reid was clumsy in method, and forward movements frequently broke down in the centre of the line—a vital spot.

When it is added that Gallimore, a clever little inside left, and Warburton, the outside right, are both frail in build and finishing power the lack of effectiveness in Manchester United's attack is laid bare.

On the wings, Spence and Hopkinson were useful—nothing more—so that the attack owed most of its advances to earnestness and endeavour rather than to the football skill and subtlety that lead defences astray and create scoring chances.

Matt Busby - his first and only derby as a City player

43

MANCHESTER UNITED 3
(Bamford, Manley, Bryant)

MANCHESTER CITY 2
(Bray, Heale)

DATE	12th September 1936
DIVISION	One
VENUE	Old Trafford
ATTENDANCE	68,796

Manchester United		Manchester City
Roy JOHN	1	Frank SWIFT
Hubert REDWOOD	2	Billy DALE
William ROUGHTON	3	Sam BARKAS
James BROWN	4	John PERCIVAL
George VOSE	5	Roy DONNELLY
Bill McKAY	6	Jackie BRAY
William BRYANT	7	Ernie TOSELAND
John WASSALL	8	Alec HERD
Tommy BAMFORD	9	Jimmy HEALE
George MUTCH	10	Peter DOHERTY
Tommy MANLEY	11	Eric BROOK

The Finest Team in Maine Road !

Manchester City

GOAL
BROOK

R-BACK
B.ROOK

L-BACK
BROOKIE

R-HALF
BROOK

C-HALF
ERIC

L-HALF
BROOK

O-RIGHT
VALENTINE'S
BROOK

I-RIGHT
DONNY
BROOK

CENTRE
BABBLIN'
BROOK

I-LEFT
BECHER'S
BROOK

O-LEFT
GORTON
BROOK

Referee: Great Big Stiff

MANCHESTER UNITED 3
Manchester City   1 } 2
One Lovely Present   1 }

The following Gentlemen were noticed amongst
the Spectators:- Swift, Barkas, Dale, Percival,
Donnelly, Bray, Doherty, Heale, Herd, Toseland

BACKGROUND

United were finally back in Division One after a gap of five seasons, which, most dramatically had seen the club salvaged from bankruptcy. The Club saviour was businessman James Gibson, who took over United's tangled financial affairs in December 1931 when the club were on the brink of financial ruin. Mr Gibson was now Chairman and Scott Duncan manager. United had endured some grim Second Division years, culminating in 1934, when they had to beat Millwall in the final game to avoid the drop to Division Three. This they managed and fortunes recovered rapidly enough during the following two seasons to enable the club to finish the 1935-36 season as Second Division Champions. The side was now much changed. Only Rowley, McLenahan and Mellor remaining from the old First Division days. Notable signings had included the two George's, Mutch and Vose. Mutch joined from Arbroath in the 1933-34 season and the powerful inside forward finished his first season top scorer with 18 goals. Vose arrived at the same time and was making a name as a hard-tackling defender. United made a moderate start to the new season, but looked a little vulnerable at the back - a fact illus-

Tommy Bamford - struck United's first goal as the derby contests resumed with the Reds' 3-2 win.

trated seven days before the City game at Derby County where Tommy Bamford scored three of United's four goals, only for the defence to concede five!

City were now clearly top dogs in Manchester football. Regularly placed in the upper half of the League table, they were also a great Cup side; beaten Semi Finalists in 1932, losing Finalists in 1933 and Winners over Portsmouth in 1934. Many now fancied the experienced and cultured Blues to capture their elusive first League Championship. Easily the better supported Manchester side during this period, they constantly set new attendance records; a massive 84,569 against Stoke in the Cup on 3rd March 1934 and 77,582 in the League against Arsenal on 23rd February 1935. City's good side of the early 1930's had developed into an excellent one with the addition of some more genuine City greats. The brilliant Frank Swift was regarded as one of the best goalkeepers in the country. Sam Barkas, the stylish left back was now an England International. Ex-Red Billy Dale filled the other full back berth. Alec Herd was an inside forward of exceptional quality. A club record fee of £10,000 to Blackpool brought City the "greatest player ever produced by Ireland", the legendary Peter Doherty, who was to finish the season with 30 League goals. All this linked to the likes of Eric Brook, Ernie Toseland and Fred Tilson at their best made up a quite formidable team. Breathtaking attacking displays against Leeds United (4-0) and West Bromwich Albion (6-2) showed the inherent quality this Blues side were to display throughout the season.

Peter Doherty (left) - a brilliant inside-forward with City he played a key role in their championship season.

Eric Brook (right) - City's exciting forward was considered by United followers to be the only Blues player in this match who was not left a spectator by the Reds' splendid victory.

game reached a crescendo after 65 minutes when Heale's header from Toseland's corner brought the Blues level. It could have gone either way after that, but with only nine minutes left Bamford's pass sent Bryant clear and his drive earned the Reds a famous victory.

BEFORE THE GAME

	P	W	D	L	F	A	Pts
CITY	4	2	1	1	11	5	5
UNITED	4	1	1	2	9	10	3

MATCH VERDICT

In mudbath conditions following many hours of Manchester rain United won a quite thrilling derby encounter. The Reds' direct 'up and at 'em' tactics proved more successful on the day than the more studied and skilful approach of the Blues. After 30 minutes, with the Blues' slick moves constantly floundering in the mud, the enthusiastic Reds raced into a two goal lead. Mutch and Manley created the first for Bamford to shoot into the net, and Manley was left completely unmarked to head the second from Bryant's clever cross. City hauled themselves back into the game with a controversial goal six minutes before the break. Doherty and Heale both looked comfortably offside as Bray's 30 yard shot found the net but the referee ruled they were not interfering with play and the goal stood, despite United's protests. City came on even stronger in the second half and the

GREAT GOALKEEPING IN "DERBY" DUEL

City Play the Wrong Type of Football

MANCHESTER UNITED 3   MANCHESTER CITY 2

MANCHESTER people waited five years for the thrills of this "Derby" game and no one can say that the waiting has been in vain. Thrills? Heavens, yes, almost every minute. And goalkeeping? De luxe, par excellence, splendid, magnificent, splendidly magnificent, magnificently splendid.

Both Swift and John were wonderful. On several occasions I have seen John when he didn't just altogether satisfy me, but yesterday he gave a display that could not be better, while Swift, at the other end, was busy doing the same thing.

If I say that I thought United just deserved to win I must also add that had the game ended in a draw no one could have grumbled. It was the activity of the whole team that won the game for United.

I, the ball didn't look like coming to them, they went after it and usually got it. Then they did what they thought best and did it as quickly as possible. Their play was not always polished but they had a definite object—to get to the goal and get the ball in the net, and it was the correct game under the conditions.

It had rained practically all the time from early morning and during most of the game, and although the ground could not be called soft it was absolutely squelching in most parts.

On such a ground City made the mistake of starting the game by playing studied football. It simply wouldn't work, and I was surprised that they kept it up so long.

Then they did follow United's example and play the open game to suit the conditions. Although United were two goals up by this time City were shaping so well that one looked forward to anything happening.

It did. Barkas went lame with a right leg injury and changed places with Brook and Bray got a gift of a goal for City. He shot a low ball from about 30 yards. From the press-box, both Doherty and Heale looked dead offside, almost hard up against John. Not only was the keeper's view obstructed but he was actually cramped for space and although he got his left hand down to the ball he could not stop it.

APPEALS DISMISSED

No doubt the referee was convinced that neither Heale nor Doherty interfered with the play.

Anyway, he gave a goal and summarily dismissed all appeals by the United players. And as the referee is the one man who can decide no more can be said.

That bit of luck was offset almost immediately however. Bray's goal was scored in the 43rd minute. Before half-time Herd was carried off with a leg injury. He didn't come back until five minutes of the second half had gone and then he limped at first outside right and then outside left. Barkas was going back to his own position and Brook playing a kind of

By LUKE SHARP

loose forward from the inside right position.

City engaged in some weird movements round about this time and I kept wondering when Heale and Doherty were going to change places. And I'm still wondering why City don't keep Bobbie Marshall at centre-half.

A word of commendation is due to Roughton, from Huddersfield Town, playing his first game for United. He was splendid throughout. Toseland had very little pull over him in pace.

Redwood, too, did very well indeed. This lad gives promise of becoming more than a merely useful back.

City's defence never settled at all. Had they done so a different tale might have had to be told.

EARLY GOAL

Manchester United are not a team of world beaters but they are all enthusiastic triers, and on yesterday's play can be looked to to meet with more success than failure.

About the goals! In six minutes United opened the score with a first class effort by Mutch and Manley for Bamford to drive the ball home.

The clock had ticked 31 minutes of play when Manley scored a second, a beautiful header this time from a peach of a centre by Bryant.

But why oh why, was Manley left so wide open to do as he pleased with the ball.

City's first goal came from Bray as I have described.

After twenty minutes in the second half ... ale equalised for City with a head ... from a corner by Toseland.

In c 36th minute Bryant gave United the le ad from a pass by Bamford. United's victory will do them more good than it will do City harm

Manchester United—John; Redwood, Roughton; Brown, Vose, McKay; Bryant, Wassall, Bamford, Mutch, Manley.

Manchester City—Swift; Dale, Barkas; Percival, Donnelly, Bray; Toseland, Herd, Heale, Doherty, Brook.

44

MANCHESTER CITY 1
(Herd)

MANCHESTER UNITED 0

DATE	9th January 1937
DIVISION	One
VENUE	Maine Road
ATTENDANCE	62,895

Manchester City		Manchester United
Frank SWIFT	1	Tommy BREEN
Billy DALE	2	Hubert REDWOOD
Sam BARKAS	3	William ROUGHTON
John PERCIVAL	4	James BROWN
Bobby MARSHALL	5	Walter WINTERBOTTOM
Jackie BRAY	6	Bert WHALLEY
Ernie TOSELAND	7	George MUTCH
Alec HERD	8	George VOSE
Fred TILSON	9	Harry ROWLEY
Peter DOHERTY	10	Bill McKAY
Eric BROOK	11	Tommy LANG

BACKGROUND

The period in between derbies was a mixed one for City. For such a talented team results were not quite up to expectations. Only seven points had been gathered out of a possible 18 immediately following the 3-2 derby defeat. The team was even slow handclapped at Maine Road and the future was not unduly promising. The turning point however, seemed to come in mid-November when Everton were thrashed 4-1. It was now a much more confident City side that put together a series of good results prior to the derby, culminating in the 3-1 beating of championship favourites Arsenal at Highbury.

United's season back in the big time was once again turning into another battle to avoid relegation. Despite some enthusiastic displays it already looked as if the task might be beyond them. Tommy Breen was now the regular 'keeper having been signed from Belfast Celtic. In common with the struggles of his team, Tommy suffered a gruelling debut at Leeds, where his first touch of the ball was to pick it out of the net. It was not a confident side that travelled across the City for the derby fixture but it was a side in desperate need of the points.

BEFORE THE GAME

	P	W	D	L	F	A	Pts
CITY	23	8	8	7	47	40	24
UNITED	24	6	6	12	37	51	18

Manchester City's 1936-37 Championship winning side. **Back:** T. Chorlton (Trainer), F. Jolly (Director), Dr. J. Holmes (Director), R. Smith (Chairman), A. Alexander (Vice-Chairman), W. Shaw (Director), H. Wood (Director), W. Wild (Secretary/Manager). **Middle:** J. Percival, W. Dale, A. Herd, S. Barkas (Captain), F. Tilson, P. Doherty, J. Bray. **Front:** E. Toseland, R. Marshall, F. Swift, E. Brook.

Alec Herd - the only goal of a dull derby match.

"Now, then, City!" ... "Now, then, United!" A section of the crowd at Maine-road this afternoon at the "Derby" match.

Frank Swift - a pillar of strength in goal.

MATCH VERDICT

In a rather colourless derby City gained the points but many felt United were unlucky. United however did not help themselves by playing centre-half Vose in the forward line, a tactical move which failed miserably. City were the more polished side but were still not at their best.

It was fitting that Alec Herd, considered the "best all round player on the pitch", scored the winner after half an hour. In an innocuous move Tilson set Brook free and his pass was stabbed into the net by the unmarked Herd. There were few clear cut opportunities after this as defences remained on top, although McKay was unlucky with a spectacular shot which hit the crossbar. Although the Reds came away empty handed they would have been pleased by an improved defensive display, where Breen and Winterbottom

took the eye. For Walter Winterbottom, a future England manager, this would prove to be his one and only derby. The derby victory was a most important result for City as it became part of a glorious unbeaten run that lasted to the end of the season and led to their first championship title.

AT THE SEASON'S END

CITY:
FIRST DIVISION CHAMPIONS

P	W	D	L	F	A	Pts
42	22	13	7	107	61	57

(3 points clear of second place)

UNITED: Finished 21st on 32 points
Relegated to Division Two
(2 points less than the 20th club)

Vose, brought into United's attack at the last minute, making a vain attempt to score, while Dale, Barkas, and Bray watch Swift punch the ball clear.

Manchester City in 1946-47. **Back:** Mr. A. Alexander (Vice-Chairman), L. Barnett (Trainer), J. Percival, B. Sproston, F. Swift, Mr. R. Smith (Chairman), E. Westwood, L. McDowall, A. Emptage, Mr. A. Jolly (Director). **Front:** M. Dunkley, A. Herd, A. Black, G. Smith, J. Hope,

Manchester United in 1946-47. **Back:** Warner, Walton, Collinson, Hanlon, McGlen, Cockburn. **Front:** Delaney, Morris, Rowley, Pearson, Mitten, Chilton.

BOOM YEARS

Busby Greats & Revie Plans 1946-1957

45

MANCHESTER CITY 0
MANCHESTER UNITED 0

DATE	20th September 1947	
DIVISION	One	
VENUE	Maine Road	
ATTENDANCE	78,000	

Manchester City		Manchester United
Alec THURLOW	1	Jack CROMPTON
Bert SPROSTON	2	John CAREY
Eric WESTWOOD	3	John ASTON
Bill WALSH	4	Jack WARNER
Joe FAGAN	5	Allenby CHILTON
Albert EMPTAGE	6	Bill McGLEN
Jackie WHARTON	7	Jimmy DELANEY
George SMITH	8	John MORRIS
Eddie McMORRAN	9	Jack ROWLEY
Tommy CAPEL	10	Stan PEARSON
Roy CLARKE	11	Charlie MITTEN

*Struck by German bombs in March 1941, **Old Trafford** was still in a state of disrepair and the United shared City's Maine Road ground.*

BACKGROUND

Over ten long years, punctuated by World War Two, had elapsed since the clubs last met in the League. The clubs had enjoyed differing fortunes in this period, although now found themselves thrown together in the most unusual of circumstances. United the 'yoyo' side of the 1930's had been promoted back to the First Division as runners-up at the end of the 1937/38 season, whilst almost unbelievably, City went the other way, relegated despite being the highest scorers in the Division, the season after being Champions. The following season 1938/39 saw the Reds finish 14th in the First Division and City fifth in the Second. The next campaign was however ended after three games following the declaration of War and the two clubs found themselves playing each other in the Northern War Leagues. It was during hostilities that a near critical blow hit Old Trafford. On the night of the 11th March 1941 Old Trafford suffered a direct hit by German bombs, resulting in major damage to the main stand and the pitch. At the end of the war, the ground was a long way from being fully repaired and it was City who came to their rivals' rescue.

United were allowed to use Maine Road for an annual rent of £5.000, plus a share of the gate receipts, whilst the Reds allowed City to play their reserve games at the Cliff. United now had a ground, but still no manager. At the club's Board meeting of 15th February 1945 it was announced that Matt Busby, the former City favourite, would leave Liverpool and become United's new Manager.

Managerial changes were also underway at City. Wilf Wild in charge since 1932, returned to secretarial duties and in November 1946 the former City skipper Sam Cowan was appointed manager. The first season after the war, 1946/47, saw Cowan bring City back up as Champions, as United, in Busby's initial season were League runners-up. However the City board were unhappy with Cowan's commuting pattern from his home in Sussex and rather surprisingly he was dismissed and Jock Thomson appointed in his place.

Matt Busby inherited the nucleus of an excellent side. Already at the club were the likes of Johnny Carey, Charlie Mitten, Johnny Morris, Jack Rowley and Stan Pearson.

However, Busby quickly showed some subtle positional changes and almost immediately imbued the side with a creative attacking philosophy. The hallmark of the team was the

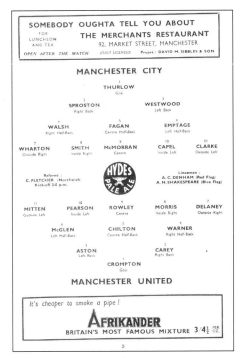

Team details as announced in City's programme.

excellence of their passing game and intelligent running off the ball. Thus far in the new season results had been mediocre, but United were now clearly very much a force to be reckoned with in the British game, perhaps for the first time since the fine championship side of 1911.

City had made a reasonable start back in the top echelon and based their hopes around a clutch of players recruited just before and after the war; Bert Sproston (signed from Tottenham in November 1938 for £10,000), Eric Westwood (a former amateur with United, signed November 1937), Joe Fagan (debut in January 1947), Les McDowall (signed from Sunderland for £7,000 plus in 1938) and Roy Clarke (joined at end of 1946/47 season from Cardiff).

BEFORE THE GAME

	P	W	D	L	F	A	Pts
CITY:	8	3	2	3	11	9	8
UNITED:	7	2	3	2	13	9	7

MATCH VERDICT:

The largest ever derby crowd drifted away from Maine Road after this encounter rather disappointed. Expectations at the recommencement of the derby contest were high, but unfortunately in a game of few chances the quality of the football left a lot to be desired.

A general criticism was the lack of creativity by the half-backs, particularly those wearing Red shirts; their play was considered too rushed and distribution inaccurate; perhaps all the players were a little over-excited by the promptings of the large crowd. City's defence had little trouble dealing with a series of rather predictable United attacks. Bert Sproston was outstanding in City's defence, not only with a number of clever interceptions but also his immaculate distribution of the ball. Joe Fagan (later of course to claim fame as Liverpool Manager) was rock solid at centre half.

United's performance fell below par, although they did have some mitigating circumstances, having been forced to reorganise the side following injury. Carey's sprained ankle early in the second half forced a reshuffle, but the nearest the game came to a goal was Crompton's fine save at the feet of Wharton late in the first half.

"The Daily Dispatch" under the headline 'Honours to Defences' reported on the resumption of the Manchester derby match.

"A crowd of 78,000 left Maine Road for home yesterday with no man able to boast to his neighbour about the result of of the Manchester 'Derby' game. Nor could anyone boast about the display of his favourite team.

Manchester City did not live up to their promise, and the United never displayed their true capabilities.

Both sides finished poorly, but the City were the more dangerous side before half-time, and one of the highlights of the game was Crompton's daring save at the feet of Wharton as the ball flashed across the United goalmouth.

Another highlight was the full-back display of City's Sproston. His interceptions in the first half particularly, were brilliant, although United made his task easier by slinging high passes towards Mitten.

United's lack of method in attack was surprising. Delaney was repeatedly beaten by Westwood, and although Rowley attempted one or two high power shots nowhere near the goalkeeper, he and his wingmen suffered through poor support. United's only plan seemed to be 'bang the ball upfield'. City made better use of the wingmen, but the wingmen did not always make the best use of the ball. Smith and Capel had some good moments against the hardworking Warner and McGlen, and the three City half-backs Walsh, Fagan and Emptage did well.

Perhaps it was over-excitement that produced so many inaccurate passes and so much hurried distribution of the ball.

There was one curious effect after 15 minutes of the second half, when Carey's sprained ankle caused a re-shuffle of the United side. Carey went to outside-right, Delaney to centre-forward, Rowley to inside-left and Pearson became left-half - and a good left-half.

Instead of faltering, United increased their pressure, although their general manoeuvring did not improve. Too many passes went to Carey who tried desperately to overcome his handicap, and Delaney shot wide after outpacing Fagan in one threatening raid. City's defence however, took most honour from this game".

Bert Sproston - outstanding in City's defence on derby day.

Bill McGlen - United's hardworking wing-half.

46

MANCHESTER UNITED 1
(Rowley)

MANCHESTER CITY 1
(Linacre)

		DATE	7th April 1948
		DIVISION	One
		VENUE	Maine Road
		ATTENDANCE	71,690

Manchester United		Manchester City
Jack CROMPTON	**1**	Alec THURLOW
John CAREY	**2**	Bert SPROSTON
John ASTON	**3**	Eric WESTWOOD
John ANDERSON	**4**	William MURRAY
Allenby CHILTON	**5**	Joe FAGAN
Thomas LOWRIE	**6**	Bill WALSH
Johnny HANLON	**7**	Jimmy MUNRO
John MORRIS	**8**	Andy BLACK
Ronnie BURKE	**9**	Billy LINACRE
Jack ROWLEY	**10**	Albert EMPTAGE
Charlie MITTEN	**11**	Roy CLARKE

BACKGROUND

After a rather unspectacular start to the season, the turning point came for United on the 25th October at Maine Road, when they beat Aston Villa 2-0. This proved to be the start of a 14 match unbeaten run which took them up the table and gave them an outside chance of taking the title. In addition to this the Reds were enjoying a great Cup run and had beaten five crack First Division teams to reach the F.A.Cup Final.

The balance of soccer power in Manchester was shifting from Blue to Red and this was clearly reflected in the attendances United were getting at their Maine Road 'home'. This derby gate would push United's aggregate League attendance to beyond the million mark, and they were averaging 54,643 over the 19 'home' games played. City by comparison were still averaging a tremendous 41,935 at Maine Road. Even so, many older City fans feel in retrospect that during this successful United period, City actually lost fans to the Reds and subsequently, when United returned to Old Trafford these missing fans were effectively gone forever.

Certainly City, who had boasted the greater support of the two Manchester clubs up to this point, would never recover this disparity in support, and over the next 43 years would only better United's crowds in just one season.

City had consolidated in a mid-table position and entered the derby in good form following three consecutive victories, but both teams had players missing because of injuries and international calls.

United's use of their rivals Maine Road ground for this 'home' derby was the subject of amusing cartoon comment.

BEFORE THE GAME							
	P	W	D	L	F	A	Pts
UNITED:	37	17	13	7	71	43	47
CITY:	36	15	9	12	49	38	39

MATCH VERDICT

End of season staleness and pre-Wembley nerves were forgotten in a typically hard fought derby. United started well and quickly had the City defence backpeddling. The Reds were unlucky early on as Thurlow, looking a little shaky, failed to hold Rowley's high diagonal kick and Morris, following in, headed against the bar. The Blues hit back and opened the scoring with a splendid goal made by Roy Clarke's skilful wing play. Gathering the ball on the halfway line, Clarke avoided Carey's challenge and set off on a mazy run towards the right flank. Exchanging passes with Munro, he got close to the by-line and pulled back the perfect centre. The City forwards were lining up and Billy Linacre easily converted. United stormed back and within quarter of an hour they were level. City's defence looked most unsettled under the almost constant pressure, and when Mitten floated in a harmless centre, Fagan, in a rush to clear the ball, completely missed his kick, leaving Rowley, standing directly behind him, the simple task of tapping in the ball. The second half was almost all United, but sterling defensive work particularly by full-backs Sproston and Westwood, and inspired keeping by Thurlow, allowed the Blues to secure a well earned point.

AT THE SEASON'S END

UNITED: Finished 2nd on 52 points
(7 points behind Arsenal
F. A. Cup Winners, beating Blackpool 4-2)

CITY: Finished 10th on 42 points

*City's **Roy Clarke** centres the ball as United skipper **Johnny Carey** tries to cover.*

Joe Fagan - City's defender was caught out for the United goal.

Eric Westwood - City's solid full-back was just one of many players of this era whose peak footballing years had been lost to the war.

*Manchester United in 1948 - runners-up in the League and FA Cup Winners. **Back:** Johnny Carey (Captain), John Anderson, Jack Crompton, Allenby Chilton, Henry Cockburn, John Aston. **Front:** Jimmy Delaney, Johnny Morris, Jack Rowley, Stan Pearson, Charlie Mitten.*

47

MANCHESTER CITY 0
MANCHESTER UNITED 0

DATE	11th September 1948
DIVISION	One
VENUE	Maine Road
ATTENDANCE	64,502

Manchester City		Manchester United
Frank SWIFT	1	Jack CROMPTON
Eric WILLIAMS	2	John CAREY
Eric WESTWOOD	3	John ASTON
Joe FAGAN	4	Henry COCKBURN
Les McDOWALL	5	Allenby CHILTON
Bill WALSH	6	Bill McGLEN
Jack OAKES	7	Jimmy DELANEY
Andy BLACK	8	John MORRIS
Verdi GODWIN	9	Jack ROWLEY
Billy LINACRE	10	Stan PEARSON
Roy CLARKE	11	Charlie MITTEN

BACKGROUND

Matt Busby considered his Cup winning side did not need any strengthening as United started the season one of the hot favourites for more honours. The club had been feted with a further award at the end of the previous season, by the election of Club Captain Johnny Carey as the Footballer of the Year. Carey epitomised the class and quality of United's football at this time. An International for both Eire and Northern Ireland, his standing in the game was reflected in his selection to captain the Rest of Europe against Great Britain in 1947. However, the fancied Reds had made an indifferent kick-off to the new season, suffering two home defeats at the hands of Derby County and Blackpool, but the famous five forward line of Delaney, Morris, Rowley, Pearson and Mitten still looked highly dangerous and already averaged two goals a game.

Like United, City had made no major team changes in the summer. The legendary Frank Swift was still in goal, although he had announced that this would be his last full season. Frank wanted to go out at 'the top'. The fact he captained England in May to the exciting 4-0 defeat of Italy in Turin, reflected the giant man's lofty standing in the game. City had also made an uncertain start to the new season. Defeat at Burnley was followed by conceding a goal just seven seconds into their first home game against Preston. However, City showed themselves to be a skilful and determined side and won the game against Preston 3-2. Andy Black netted the winner at Birmingham three days before the derby to put City above United in the League table.

Andy Black - City's inside forward scored the winner at Birmingham three days before the derby, but was unable to break the deadlock at Maine Road.

Johnny Morris - part of Manchester United's famous five forward line, he was unlucky not to break the deadlock when his shot struck a post.

BEFORE THE GAME							
	P	W	D	L	F	A	Pts
CITY:	6	3	1	2	9	7	7
UNITED:	6	3	0	3	14	10	6

MANCHESTER UNITED DRAW

Anderson Missed

By an Old International

Manchester City 0, Manchester United 0

Manchester City drew with Manchester United 0—0 at Moss Side on Saturday, and it is difficult to avoid the feeling that Manchester United stirred up trouble for themselves when they omitted Anderson. The part that Anderson played in his side's success last season is still fresh in the memory. His drive, his thrust, his opportunism near goal, and, in particular, his instinctive understanding of Morris's requirements were powerful assets; and it was not until these qualities were put at the disposal of his colleagues part way through the season that the team became the smooth-running, beautifully balanced, free-scoring combination which won the F.A. Cup. Now, presumably, because Anderson has played one or two bad games in first-class company, while McGlen has done well in the Central League, Anderson is rested, McGlen introduced, and a delicate balance and rhythm destroyed.

It is true that Manchester City played a strong defensive game in which Westwood rose far above—and McDowall fell somewhat below—his general level of competence. Other things, however, were troubling United besides the keen tackling, the quick anticipation, and the zest of the City players. McGlen did everything that a willing, fearless footballer could to block City's progress and to disorganise their attack, but he requires not a little polishing yet before he can be slipped into the United side without impairing something of its efficiency. Here, indeed, was an example of how fidgety the outlook of leading clubs can become. A few games lost, a temporary loss of form, and changes must, it seems, inevitably be made, and the unsettlement of a fine side begins.

Saturday's game, if not the best that either side can produce, was agreeably packed with incident—Rowley's remarkable free-kick, for instance, a veritable monster of pace; Morris's grimace as his shot struck a post; Swift's fine save where post and crossbar meet; Oakes's two violent shots, which marked a welcome addition to City's shooting power; the all-round excellence of Walsh; and Godwin's pluck and persistence for one so small and slight. Chilton, too, maintained his steady progress, helped as he was by the skill and tenacity of Cockburn, Aston, and Carey. But best of all, perhaps, was City's welcome return to first principles and the air of contentment and relish with which their remodelled forward line now goes to work. Soon Manchester will be envied again, not merely for the blessings of its rainfall but as the home of two first-class teams. Teams:

MANCHESTER CITY.—Swift: Williams, Westwood: Fagan, McDowall, Walsh: Oakes, Black, Godwin, Linacre, Clarke.

MANCHESTER UNITED.—Crompton: Carey, Aston: Cockburn, Chilton, McGlen: Delaney, Morris, Rowley, Pearson, Mitten.

Les McDowall - it was to be the last derby for City's versatile defender and half-back who was signed from Sunderland for more than £7,000 in 1938.

MATCH VERDICT

A goalless draw was the outcome of a close contest at Moss Side. However, there was a lot of incident to excite the large crowd and suggest that both sides might reasonably anticipate fair seasons, although for United, the Cup holders, this was a rather disjointed performance.

Anderson's omission seemed to leave the side unbalanced. The Reds' forwards had few clear cut opportunities and were denied by either the brilliance of Swift or the misfortune of hitting the woodwork. Rowley's cannon-ball free kick almost opened the scoring and Morris was unlucky to see a shot hit the post, but as the game progressed Swift began to look unbeatable.

City, as a combination looked the more likely team, but made few clear cut chances. Westwood and Walsh had excellent games in the defence, and Oakes went close with two fierce shots. Don Davies the Manchester Guardian's 'old international', who covered so many derbies during this period, concluded that Manchester would soon be envied as the home of two first class teams.

Johnny Carey - the United skipper entered the new season as the 1948 'Footballer of the Year'.

48

MANCHESTER UNITED 0
MANCHESTER CITY 0

DATE	22nd January 1949
DIVISION	One
VENUE	Maine Road
ATTENDANCE	66,485

Manchester United		Manchester City
Jack CROMPTON	1	Frank SWIFT
John CAREY	2	Bert SPROSTON
John ASTON	3	Eric WESTWOOD
Henry COCKBURN	4	Bill WALSH
Allenby CHILTON	5	Joe FAGAN
Bill McGLEN	6	Albert EMPTAGE
Jimmy DELANEY	7	Billy LINACRE
John MORRIS	8	Johnny HART
Jack ROWLEY	9	Andy BLACK
Stan PEARSON	10	George SMITH
Charlie MITTEN	11	Roy CLARKE

BACKGROUND

Frank Swift, who had announced his intention to retire at the end of the season, on occasions gave way to Alec Thurlow who was being groomed for the goalkeeping position. Thurlow had played in the first derby after the war, but had appeared infrequently ever since then. Despite turning out in a game three weeks before the derby, he again failed to hold down his place as Swift returned between the posts. City were struggling to find consistency during this period. Their best run of results was an unbeaten eight game spell between 20th November and New Years Day, although only three of these games were victories. A 1-0 defeat at home to Charlton prior to the derby was a disappointment to the City faithful.

Whilst City were concerned about the imminent departure of Frank Swift, United still had the reliable Jack Crompton in goal and he was part of a defence that had now tightened up on its early season generosity. Between derbies, United were only beaten twice and had moved steadily up the table. The Reds also received the go ahead from the Ministry of Works to step up repairs to the Old Trafford ground, in a bid to re-open the following season. In December 1948 City had given United formal notice to quit the Maine Road ground, and this was the last occasion it was used as the Reds 'home' ground in a derby match. United's final game before the derby proved a record-breaker. The attendance for the match against Arsenal on 17th January 1948 was an incredible 82,950. This was not only the largest attendance for a United home game, but also a record for any League match in the country. United won the game 2-0 with goals from Mitten and Burke.

City goalkeeper **Frank Swift**, plunges to keep out a shot from **Jack Rowley** as Blues' **Joe Fagan** clears from the lurking **Stan Pearson**.

BEFORE THE GAME						
	P	W	D	L	F	A	Pts
UNITED:	25	12	8	5	51	26	32
CITY:	26	9	10	7	36	37	28

IT COULDN'T HAPPEN AT EPSOM — BUT THE LAST FOUR 'DERBYS' AT MAINE ROAD HAVE ALL RESULTED IN 'DEAD HEATS'

A SUGGESTION FOR THE NEXT CLASH

STOP EVERYTHING BETWEEN THE CORNER-FLAGS

MAYBE A CHANGE OF NAMES & COLOURS MIGHT HELP

OR BETTER STILL — LIMIT THE GATE TO 22 PLAYERS —

AND LET THE SUPPORTERS FIGHT IT OUT!

MATCH VERDICT

Football was still enjoying a marvellous 'boom' period after the war, with record attendances. The Maine Road gates opened at 1pm to hundreds of waiting school children and by two o'clock the ground was already half-full. Unfortunately the large crowd witnessed another goalless game, the first time a derby season had produced no goals at all in either match.

United created most of the attacking ideas but were denied by an outstanding display of goal-keeping from Swift. The match was billed as his derby swansong - although as circumstances later transpired it was not his final derby - but this performance would be remembered for many a day. Mitten's terrific shot early on had 'goal' written all over it, but Swift diving to his right tipped it round the post.

Miraculous was the only appropriate adjective to describe his series of point-blank saves as Stan Pearson, Morris and Rowley were also denied. City did have their moments and ironically, could have won it following a mistake by United 'keeper Jack Crompton. After Westwood had raced half the length of the field, his shot-cum-centre was fumbled by Crompton and, with the goalkeeper prostrate, Smith and Linacre closed in to score. However, Johnny Carey appeared from nowhere to hack the ball into the crowd and preserve United a point.

Albert Emptage - a regular wing-half for City in these immediate post-war years.

George Smith - City's forward was denied by Carey's clearance as he closed in to score. Smith lost a hand in World War Two, but it never proved a handicap playing football, and it was reported he often used his 'stump' to prod players out of the way!

AT THE SEASON'S END

UNITED: Finished 2nd on 53 points
(League Runners up on goal average, 5pts behind Portsmouth)

CITY: Finished 7th on 45 points

49

MANCHESTER UNITED 2
(Pearson 2)

MANCHESTER CITY 1
(Munro)

DATE	3rd September 1949	
DIVISION	One	
VENUE	Old Trafford	
ATTENDANCE	47,706	

Manchester United		Manchester City
Jack CROMPTON	1	Frank SWIFT
John CAREY	2	Eric WILLIAMS
John ASTON	3	Eric WESTWOOD
Jack WARNER	4	Bill WALSH
Sammy LYNN	5	Joe FAGAN
Henry COCKBURN	6	Albert EMPTAGE
Jimmy DELANEY	7	Billy LINACRE
Stan PEARSON	8	Jimmy MUNRO
Jack ROWLEY	9	George SMITH
Ted BUCKLE	10	Andy BLACK
Charlie MITTEN	11	Jack OAKES

Welcome Home! *Old Trafford was still scarred by bombs, but the club and its supporters were glad to be back at last.*

Stan Pearson shapes to shoot in the shadow of the chimneys that surrounded Old Trafford. He netted both goals in United's 2-1 win over their rivals.

BACKGROUND

As planned, the great Frank Swift had retired during the close season, at the age of 35. Unfortunately, his intended replacement Alec Thurlow was taken seriously ill and had gone to Norfolk to convalesce. Sadly, Thurlow was to die in 1956 at the early age of 34. The Blues were caught without a goalkeeper and in desperation, spent a considerable time persuading Swift to reverse his decision and come out of retirement. Swift eventually agreed on condition that the comeback would only last until the time when the club found a replacement. Swift played in the opening 3-3 draw with Aston Villa, a game in which George Smith made two of the goals. Smith played despite the unusual handicap of having his right arm amputated from the wrist down, following a war injury. City gained their first victory of the season, by beating Portsmouth 1-0 in the last game prior to the derby.

United had at last returned 'home', and they celebrated this on 23rd August 1949 by beating Bolton 3-0, before 41,748. In a confident start to the season the Reds were unbeaten, with Rowley, Pearson and Mitten once again amongst the scorers. Jack Rowley, top scorer the previous season with 20 goals was now in his prime and was one of the most feared centre-forwards in the country. The Reds entered the derby then in confident mood, looking for their first win at Old Trafford over their local rivals since 1936.

BEFORE THE GAME							
	P	W	D	L	F	A	Pts
UNITED:	4	3	1	0	7	2	7
CITY:	4	1	2	1	6	7	4

MATCH VERDICT

The derby returned to a 'battle-scarred' Old Trafford, and it was a dramatic and incident-filled game that broke the recent sequence of draws between the teams.

City had the better of the first half as their defence was able to neutralise the lively United forwards. Fagan's battle royal with Rowley caught the eye, a contest in which the gutsy City player took the honours. Deservedly the Blues snatched the lead in 34 minutes when Munro's shot from outside the area beat the diving Crompton. Early in the second half City cursed their luck as Black's header struck the bar. A goal at that point would have put the game beyond the Reds. As it was City looked likely winners until the final quarter of an hour when the game was turned on its head. Firstly, Pearson scrambled the equaliser in rather dubious circumstances following a goal-mouth melee, but the goal stood, a decision which so enraged Frank Swift that he chased after the referee to register his protest. To compound the agony, there was a further cruel twist near the finish as City, in front for so long, were beaten by a goal splendidly conceived and executed by Stan Pearson.

However, the excitement was still not over and with two minutes remaining passions boiled over and Cockburn and Linacre were dramatically sent off, following a 'dispute' near the touchline. Cockburn's dismissal was all the more sensational as he always had a gentlemanly reputation during his career. Don Davies assessed his performance before the dismissal as one of 'scrupulous fairness and sustained brilliance'. Other commentators claimed the referee had little option and the players had to 'slowly trudge across the green acres and down the tunnel while nearly 50,000 silently watched'.

The Manchester Guardian reported on 'A Sad End After Much Fine Play':

"'Don't never prophesy unless you know' was Josh Billing's sage counsel. How many of us spread comfortably round Old Trafford's battle-scarred perimeter in Saturday's sunshine, and there enjoying first, some very old fashioned song tunes from a very up-to-date Grenadier Guards band, and then the fast exchanges of a real 'Derby' match between Manchester United and Manchester City would have dared suggest beforehand that the quality of football would be so good; that an end would be made at last to the monotonous sequence of draws; that City would hold a one goal lead for the best part of an hour and then slump feebly into defeat fifteen minutes from time?

And who, knowing Cockburn and his high standing in the football world as an international player of unblemished repute, and having seen him as recently as Saturday enthral a crowd for 88 minutes with a half-back display of scrupulous fairness and sustained brilliance, would have imagined that the same player barely two minutes from time, would be ordered with Linacre to quit the scene which his presence hitherto had so greatly enriched.

A dispute had occurred which gave the referee no option but to order the players concerned to their dressing-rooms. There, no doubt, a wealth of good counsel and the rapid evaporation of spleen would tend to make plain to both the wisdom of the FA's ruling that no player, under whatsoever provocation, may take the law into his own hands. Rough justice sometimes, but on the whole it pays.

The pity is that there was so much in the match

Manchester City in 1949-50. *Back:* Joe Fagan, Albert Emptage, Eric Williams, Ronnie Powell, Bill Walsh, George Smith, Jack Rigby. *Front:* Billy Linacre, Jimmy Munro, Eric Westwood, Andy Black, Roy Clarke.

worth remembering. The back play throughout was superb, and here perhaps United had their strongest pull, having two masters like Carey and Aston to offset Westwood and his less gifted partner Williams. Fagan stood out among the City half-backs, and his strong opposition to Rowley, coupled with Munro's snap goal in the thirty-fourth minute seemed likely at one time to settle the match in City's favour.

Perhaps if Black's header which struck the United crossbar had been a shade lower - but that is another story. Swift saw to it that the dubious nature of United's first goal, attributed to Pearson, was brought to the referee's notice. He could not have chased him more excitedly if he had seen the Armada coming up Stretford Road, but he had no fault to find with Pearson's second effort, a little gem of the neatest and most expert contrivance. Lynn and Warner like Walsh and Emptage had few mistakes to grieve about, though all were outmatched and outshone by the calm mastery and penetrative insight of Cockburn".

Manchester United in 1949-50. *Back:* T. Curry (Trainer), Allenby Chilton, Jack Warner, Jack Crompton, Henry Cockburn, John Aston, Matt Busby (Manager). *Front:* Jimmy Delaney, Tommy Bogan, Johnny Carey, Jack Rowley, Stan Pearson, Charlie Mitten.

50

MANCHESTER CITY 1
(Black)

MANCHESTER UNITED 2
(Delaney, Pearson)

DATE	31st December 1949	
DIVISION	One	
VENUE	Maine Road	
ATTENDANCE	63,704	

Manchester City		Manchester United
Bert TRAUTMANN	1	John FEEHAN
Ernie PHILLIPS	2	John CAREY
Eric WESTWOOD	3	John ASTON
Ray GILL	4	Jack WARNER
Joe FAGAN	5	Allenby CHILTON
Bill WALSH	6	Bill McGLEN
Jimmy MUNRO	7	Jimmy DELANEY
Andy BLACK	8	Tommy BOGAN
Bobby TURNBULL	9	Jack ROWLEY
Jimmy ALISON	10	Stan PEARSON
Roy CLARKE	11	Charlie MITTEN

BACKGROUND

Between derbies United were dogged by inconsistent form and the established side underwent some changes. Tommy Bogan, a Scottish International half-back was signed from Preston and for a mid-season spell the regular goalkeeper became Irishman John Ignatious Feehan. Five points were taken from the three games before the derby and United entered the game at Maine Road as favourites. For City the season was turning into one of struggle. Frank Swift had finally retired and Ronnie Powell had taken over to fill the gap. During this period the City management uncovered a German goalkeeper playing for St.Helen's Town. His name was Bert Trautmann and on the 2nd November 1949 City signed the blond giant. This was a bold move by the club. The war had only ended four years previously and there was still much anti-German feeling about. According to Trautmann's 1956 autobiography City received hundreds of letters protesting about the signing and threatening a boycott of the Club. Season tickets were sent back and there were even reports of fights between spectators. The newspapers loved the 'story'. They often aired the views of anti-Trautmann supporters and reported on the 'unpatriotic' news daily. Despite all of this Trautmann quickly won a place in the side and was warmly welcomed by club captain Eric Westwood - who fought at Normandy - with the words; "there's no war in the dressing-room, we welcome you as any other member of staff." For Bert Trautmann this would prove to be the first derby of many.

However, the Blues were not picking up enough points in the League and a home defeat to Huddersfield prior to the meeting with United saw nervous glances cast over their shoulder at the dreaded drop.

Jack Rowley - United's powerful centre-forward scored only once in derby matches but still hit 208 goals in 422 League and Cup games during a dozen seasons with the club.

Jimmy Delaney - hit United's equaliser with a smart shot from Bogan's fine through pass.

BEFORE THE GAME							
	P	W	D	L	F	A	Pts
UNITED	24	11	9	4	40	20	31
CITY	24	5	7	12	22	42	17

MATCH VERDICT

The keen nature of derby rivalry was reflected in this contest. Unfancied City nearly pulled off the surprise of the day, but it was United who eventually took the points and entered the new decade in good heart. As in September, City took the lead and were unlucky based on their first half performance not to win. During this period the Reds' defence was constantly under pressure, John Aston had a particularly torrid time trying to mark 'deputy' winger Munro. Inside ten minutes the Blues were ahead, as Clarke's high centre caught the Red defence flat-footed and Andy Black rammed a shot high into the net. Shortly after Black's header from Clarke's centre appeared to put City two goals ahead, but for no obvious reason the goal was disallowed. This proved a turning point, for in the second half United's famed passing game began to tear holes in the City defence. Delaney equalised with a smart shot from Bogan's defence-splitting pass, and at the death it was Stan Pearson again who took the glory, smashing in the loose ball after Trautmann had brilliantly parried Delaney's goal-bound shot.

UNITED: Finished 4th on 50 points
(3 points behind Champions Portsmouth)

CITY: Finished 21st on 29 points
Relegated to Division Two

*City's decision to sign **Bert Trautmann** attracted a number of sensational stories in the tabloid press headlined like this one, claiming the club were acting in an unpatriotic fashion.*

There was a warm enough greeting at Maine Road for Trautmann who gets a lift here from City players Westwood, Westcott, Rigby, Branagan and Hannaway.

*Despite all the adverse publicity surrounding **Bert Trautmann's** arrival, the blond German giant was made more than welcome by the City players. Here he is wished well by his illustrious predecessor - the great City goalkeeper **Frank Swift** (above).*

51

MANCHESTER CITY 1
(Hart)

MANCHESTER UNITED 2
(Berry, McShane)

DATE	15th September 1951
DIVISION	One
VENUE	Maine Road
ATTENDANCE	52,571

Manchester City		Manchester United
Bert TRAUTMANN	1	Reg ALLEN
Ernie PHILLIPS	2	John CAREY
Jack HANNAWAY	3	Bill REDMAN
Roy PAUL	4	Don GIBSON
Jack RIGBY	5	Allenby CHILTON
Frank McCOURT	6	Henry COCKBURN
Jimmy MEADOWS	7	Johnny BERRY
Johnny HART	8	Stan PEARSON
John WILLIAMSON	9	Lol CASSIDY
Dennis WESTCOTT	10	John DOWNIE
Roy CLARKE	11	Harry McSHANE

Allen keeps the Blues at bay

Though they lost two points, Manchester City fans must take off their hats to goalkeeper Reg Allen, of Manchester United. Time and again the home forwards stormed the United goal, but in Allen they met a " stone wall " . . . until the 64th minute. And then inside right Hart completely beat the " barrier " and full-back Carey could only watch in dismay as Chilton made a wild sweep with his hand in an attempt to stop the equaliser.

Here is one of the many daring saves by Allen, who swoops down at the feet of Hart to take the ball safely ☛

BACKGROUND

The 1950/51 season had seen the Manchester Clubs both finish second in their respective divisions. United collected their fourth League runners-up spot in five years while the Blues shook off the shock of relegation and returned to the top flight at the first attempt.

City were attempting to form the backbone of a strong side that would stay and prosper in the First Division. Quality acquisitions were made including Roy Paul, signed from Swansea for £25,000 in 1950 and Jimmy Meadows purchased from Southport in 1951. In goal, Bert Trautmann had won the fans over with some outstanding displays.

The Club had made an uncertain start to the new season gaining only a draw in the opening three games. However, spirits were raised by the 3-1 away win at Derby prior to the match with United.

The United side had undergone some change since the last derby. Jimmy Delaney, Busby's first signing had now joined Aberdeen. Long serving Charlie Mitten had shocked the Club by going off to South America to try his luck in the reputedly highly paid world of Colombian football. On his return a season later in 1950, he was transfer-listed by United and eventually moved on to Fulham. Meanwhile Busby made one or two astute signings. Reg Allen was considered one of the top goalkeepers in the League when bought from Queen's Park Rangers in June 1950 for £11,000. John Berry, a flying winger with a fine shot, cost £25,000 from Birmingham City, while Harry McShane was also signed from neighbours Bolton Wanderers in 1950.

United made a confident start to the new season, suffering only one defeat - at Bolton - and they entered the derby clear favourites.

BEFORE THE GAME

	P	W	D	L	F	A	Pts
UNITED	8	5	2	1	22	12	12
CITY	7	2	2	3	9	12	6

*Manchester City in September 1951. **Back:** Ernie Phillips, Jack Rigby, Roy Paul, Bert Trautmann, Frank McCourt, Jack Hannaway, Billy Spurdle. **Front:** Jimmy Meadows, Johnny Hart, John Williamson, Roy Clarke.*

MATCH VERDICT

In what became a repeat of a somewhat predictable scenario in recent derbies, City had all the play and threatened United with a hiding only to lose the game in the final few minutes.

City seemed highly motivated by the resumption of local rivalry and in the first minute the United penalty area resembled The Alamo as the Reds struggled to repel a mass of Blue shirts. Usually cool defenders seemed un-nerved and only Allen's bravery kept the Blues out. The siege was lifted temporarily as Gibson put Berry away. Hannaway failed to hold the little winger and with Trautmann leaving an inviting gap between himself and the post, Berry shot United into a ninth minute lead. Undaunted City returned to the attack and pounded the Red defence for the rest of the half, however they found Allen in superlative form, leaving his line with gusto and showing particularly safe handling. Deservedly City equalised nine minutes into the second half. Westcott, impressive on the left wing, found Meadows with a long ball, took the return ball and interchanged passes with Hart who shot past Allen. Williamson and Clarke all fired over the bar as City went for the win. A reflection of City's superiority was that United's 77th minute corner was their first of the game. Ironically, at this point the Blues began to tire and United made some dangerous raids. From a harmless-looking centre from Pearson, Cassidy stepped over the ball and McShane, charging in at speed, crashed the ball past Trautmann.

Allen goes down again, and Meadows, the City outside right, almost crashes over the goalkeeper.

52

MANCHESTER UNITED 1
(Carey)

MANCHESTER CITY 1
(McCourt)

DATE	19th January 1952
DIVISION	One
VENUE	Old Trafford
ATTENDANCE	54,245

Manchester United		Manchester City
Reg ALLEN	1	Bert TRAUTMANN
Tommy McNULTY	2	Ken BRANAGAN
Roger BYRNE	3	Jack HANNAWAY
John CAREY	4	Billy SPURDLE
Allenby CHILTON	5	Jack RIGBY
Henry COCKBURN	6	Frank McCOURT
Johnny BERRY	7	Johnny HART
Stan PEARSON	8	Don REVIE
John ASTON	9	Jimmy MEADOWS
John DOWNIE	10	Ivor BROADIS
Jack ROWLEY	11	Roy CLARKE

United Superior, But City Hold Out

BACKGROUND

The Reds had a good spell in between derbies, losing only five out of eighteen games which placed United up with reigning champions Tottenham Hotspur and Arsenal challenging for the title. Matt Busby's revolutionary youth policy was beginning to pay dividends and Roger Byrne had now established himself in the first team.

Seven days before the derby United were stunned by elimination from the F.A.Cup by Second Division Hull City. The Yorkshire club had beaten the Reds 2-0 at Old Trafford, so it was a chastened United outfit who faced the old enemy.

City had a good spell of form between derbies and also became the First Division's big spenders. In a bold bid to reinforce the side with quality players the Blues twice broke their transfer record. On 5th October £25,000 was spent on talented Ivor Broadis of Sunderland. Ivor had a big reputation in the game and was renowned for his speed, creative ability and fierce shot.

The transfer paid immediate dividends as City went to high-flying Spurs and won 2-1. Less than two weeks later the same sum was invested in the purchase of Don Revie from Hull. Revie, later to become Leeds United and England manager, was a clever inside forward with a reputation for having his own clear views on the game. City, like United, found themselves out of the Cup following a replayed defeat at Wolves.

BEFORE THE GAME							
	P	W	D	L	F	A	Pts
UNITED	27	14	7	6	58	39	35
CITY	27	12	5	10	45	40	29

A most significant moment in Manchester City's history as talented midfielder Don Revie signs from Hull City for £25,000 in October 1951. Pictured with Revie are his wife Elsie, City manager Les McDowall (left) and Director Walter Smith.

MATCH VERDICT

In an exciting match United had the lion's share of the game but City frustrated them and shared the points. City's half-backs Spurdle and McCourt impressed early on with their clever distribution and indeed from their promptings City should have scored on five minutes but Revie missed the chance in front of an open goal. However, it was United who began to look the more dangerous side and Rowley and Pearson both went close before the interval.

City shocked the home crowd by taking the lead with a spectacular goal on 50 minutes. Hart's corner kick was headed out by Cockburn, straight to McCourt, whose fierce volley went in via the upright. United now forced a hectic pace and were unlucky when Branagan appeared to handle Rowley's shot in the penalty area, but the referee waved play on. Immediately Berry returned the ball into the box and Carey's shot went through a ruck of players and into the net. City were now under severe pressure. Downie appeared to have won it as his shot beat Trautmann, only for Rigby to pop up and clear off the line as the Blues held out in a hectic finish.

Johnny Berry - the talented winger who set up the Reds equaliser in this game had arrived from Birmingham City at the start of the season for £25,000. He was, with Roger Byrne, the start of United's rebuilding programme towards further glory.

Manchester United in 1951-52. After four runners-up spots in five years, the club were League Champions for a third time. It was the peak of achievement for Matt Busby's first great United side, as many players were now approaching the end of their top class careers. *Back:* John Downie, Jack Rowley, John Aston, Reg Allen, Allenby Chilton, Roger Byrne, Stan Pearson. *Front:* Johnny Berry, Johnny Carey, Henry Cockburn, Tommy McNulty.

AT THE SEASON'S END

UNITED:
FIRST DIVISION CHAMPIONS

	P	W	D	L	F	A	Pts
	42	23	11	8	95	52	57

CITY: Finished 15th on 39 points

53 MANCHESTER CITY 2
(Clarke, Broadis)

MANCHESTER UNITED 1
(Downie)

DATE	30th August 1952	
DIVISION	One	
VENUE	Maine Road	
ATTENDANCE	56,140	

Manchester City		Manchester United
Bert TRAUTMANN	1	Jack CROMPTON
Ken BRANAGAN	2	Tommy McNULTY
Eric WESTWOOD	3	John ASTON
Roy PAUL	4	John CAREY
Jack RIGBY	5	Allenby CHILTON
Billy SPURDLE	6	Henry COCKBURN
Jimmy MEADOWS	7	Johnny BERRY
Don REVIE	8	John DOWNIE
Bill SOWDEN	9	Jack ROWLEY
Ivor BROADIS	10	Stan PEARSON
Roy CLARKE	11	Roger BYRNE

BACKGROUND

City had made a poor start to the new season - no points and only one goal. Fred Smith epitomised the Club's early problems up front. Newly signed from Sheffield United in May, he had scored City's only goal so far, but following the second game was immediately discarded and sold in September to Grimsby Town. In his place City put their hopes in reserve centre-forward Billy Sowden. Billy had actually been signed back in 1949 from Greenwood Victoria, but following a 1-0 home defeat by Tottenham Hotspur, found himself called up for a derby debut.

United, the defending League champions, had started the season with victory, beating Chelsea 2-0 and a 2-1 defeat at the hands of Arsenal. However, the side were not surprisingly once again amongst the favourites to win silverware and entered the derby slight favourites.

BEFORE THE GAME

	P	W	D	L	F	A	Pts
UNITED	2	1	0	1	3	2	2
CITY	2	0	0	2	1	3	0

*Another brilliant save by **Bert Trautmann** keeps United at bay in front of a packed Maine Road derby crowd in August 1952.*

Ivor Broadis - outstanding pieces of skill and a superb goal to steer City to a memorable victory over their old rivals.

MATCH VERDICT

"Manchester City gave their loyal and long suffering supporters that experience for which they have watched and prayed these last five years" was how the Manchester Guardian reported on City's first derby victory in the last nine contests.

In a classic match full of attacking, entertaining football, City fully warranted the victory over their illustrious neighbours. It was a result which left Carey 'chastened', Pearson 'humbled' and Rowley 'subdued'. City produced a great team effort based around a brilliant performance by Ivor Broadis. The home crowd were also delighted with a highly promising derby debut by an unknown local centre-forward Sowden, who gave the experienced Chilton a most uncomfortable afternoon.

City defied the recent form book and simply outclassed United for the opening hour of the match. Spurdle was outstanding at left half-back, intelligent in his reading of the game and a constant source of creativity for the City forwards. An indication of Broadis' brilliance was the extent to which his marker, the experienced and usually imperturbable Carey, was unsettled. It was two pieces of outstanding skill by Broadis that settled the match in City's favour. Firstly he split United's defence wide open with a delightful through ball which left Clarke with just the goalkeeper to beat - which he duly did. The second was a goal with all the hallmarks of class. In a crowded goalmouth, Broadis trapped the loose ball, and crashed an unstoppable half volley past the startled Crompton. Downie's spectacular shot beat Trautmann to ensure an exciting final fifteen minutes, during which United went on all-out attack but City's brilliant goalkeeper kept them at bay.

Roy Clarke - ran onto a delightful through pass from Broadis to shoot City into the lead.

United's **Stan Pearson** challenges City's **Eric Westwood** during the Blues early season win at Maine Road.

54   MANCHESTER UNITED 1
(Pearson)

MANCHESTER CITY 1
(Broadis)

DATE	3rd January 1953
DIVISION	One
VENUE	Old Trafford
ATTENDANCE	47,883

Manchester United		Manchester City
Ray WOOD	1	Bert TRAUTMANN
John ASTON	2	Ken BRANAGAN
Roger BYRNE	3	Eric WESTWOOD
John CAREY	4	Don REVIE
Allenby CHILTON	5	Dave EWING
Jeff WHITEFOOT	6	Roy PAUL
Johnny BERRY	7	Jimmy MEADOWS
John DOHERTY	8	Johnny HART
Eddie LEWIS	9	John WILLIAMSON
Stan PEARSON	10	Ivor BROADIS
David PEGG	11	Bob CUNLIFFE

David Pegg - a star of the young United side that were to win the FA Youth Cup this season, he had made his League debut only a month earlier. A lively 17-year-old he was just one of the Reds' remarkable crop of up and coming stars.

BACKGROUND

In October the Manchester public had the uncomfortably unfamiliar scene of both their favourites occupying the last two positions in the First Division table. For Champions United this represented a minor crisis, and the first real set back during Busby's management. Busby refused to panic and positively chose this moment to begin the gradual introduction of the club's younger players, who had been receiving rave reviews for their performances in the reserves. One such player who made his debut during this period was David Pegg, a fast winger with a good shot. In this particular derby, Whitefoot, Doherty and Lewis represented the youthful Reds and joined the now established Roger Byrne. The infusion of youth had the desired effect and galvanised the Reds who began to climb the table. They entered the derby unbeaten in six games.

City's form had been erratic with heavy defeats such as a 7-3 drubbing by Wolverhampton Wanderers coming in November, the same month as a 5-1 win over high-flying Charlton Athletic. The Blues had assembled some skilful players, but were giving so many goals away, a relegation struggle seemed imminent. City's last game before the derby was a soul destroying 6-2 defeat away at Preston which left the club languishing in the bottom two on derby day. The Blues decided this was the moment to stiffen that leaky defence, and gave a derby day debut to a raw-boned centre-half called Dave Ewing who they had signed from Luncarty Juniors in 1949.

BEFORE THE GAME							
	P	W	D	L	F	A	Pts
UNITED	24	11	5	8	38	37	27
CITY	23	5	4	14	36	52	14

MATCH VERDICT

In a match of poor quality, the goals and points were shared. Generally City were considered to have had the better of a scrappy affair. In Ivor Broadis they had the one player able to perform to a much higher standard than the generally mediocre level of play from those around him, and his skilful control constantly created danger for the United defenders. United looked what they were, a side in transition, with youngsters

Pegg, Doherty and Lewis rarely able to get into the game.

City started well with a series of dangerous attacks and it was against the run of play when United scored within ten minutes from one of the few quality moves in the match. Carey carried the ball out of defence and with a long raking pass found Lewis. His deft touch rolled the ball into the path of Pearson who resisted Paul's lunge, raced forward and shot past Trautmann with venomous power. The frozen pitch made conditions underfoot difficult but City must have rued a series of missed chances. Williamson lashed a shot high and wide when clear in front of goal. Cunliffe headed over when it seemed easier to score and Hart sliced badly wide when Broadis put him clean through. Justice was however, done on the hour, when Broadis netted in a goalmouth scramble. United attempted to mount a late rally but City's defence looked secure as Ewing enjoyed an impressive first match.

'The Manchester Guardian' reported the match as follows:

"Manchester United and Manchester City met at Old Trafford on Saturday for Manchester's second local derby match of the season. The day was fine, the sun shone, excitement ran high as Mr W.R. Crickmer tactfully appealed to the spectators to pack themselves more and still more like sardines all round the terraces, and everything pointed to a great occasion. But after ninety minutes exertion the players shook hands warmly and took their leave, having shared the goals (one each), the points (one each), the bonus (£1 each), and likewise the responsibility for a display of football which was but a drab and featureless substitute for the real thing.

Many spectators had shaken hands and taken their leave long before the players did, and their faces as they passed told of minds fixed already on good fires, warm slippers, hot tea and toasted muffins. For those who remained the one abiding comfort seemed to be that no player had got seriously hurt and that anyhow, the Cup-ties are due to begin next week.

The odd thing was that City began the match with the flourish and sparkle of a Mozartian overture, and it is no exaggeration to say that if at the end of five minutes play they had been three goals up none of the rapt spectators would have been at all surprised. Broadis was the moving spirit at first, and the way he drifted in and out among the red shirts, dodging here and passing there, boded good for neither Aston nor Carey. In fact, during those few harrowing minutes when City were on top and Broadis schemed ideal openings for Hart and Williamson which neither could accept, United's defenders wore the anxious looks of members of a beleaguered garrison surprised by a sudden attack, but not quite sure from which direction the attack was coming. Then, as often happens in football, having barely escaped by the skin of their teeth from a drastic hammering themselves, they were able to sit back and take a welcome breather and watch their own forwards move upfield and pierce the City defence at the first time of asking and with a marked economy of effort.

That Carey and Pearson should be associated with this, one of the few good tactical moves of the match, was only to be expected. What pleased the home supporters more was the mature touch young Lewis added to the move. Many a veteran player would have been proud to gather Carey's well-conceived long-carrying pass, smooth it out, and roll it sweetly for Pearson to pick up in his stride as sweetly as Lewis did. Pearson's response was just the sort to encourage a youngster to persevere in these intelligent ways. Pearson darted forward with the ball at his toe, was pushed off the ball by Paul, recovered and ran on to leave Trautmann helpless with a blistering shot from close range. This all occurred in or about the tenth minute and from that point until Broadis rushed through a scrambled sort of equaliser for City some fifty minutes later, play fell away visibly both in quality and temper.

It seemed as though the playing conditions were too tricky for all but the tried experts to master. A lively ball on a frozen ground can create technical difficulties far outside the scope of infant prodigies or 'Johnny Raws' any time, and it was the mistakes of these youngsters on Saturday that did most to upset the general rhythm.

It was inexperience, for instance, that caused Williamson to lash so wildly at a bouncing ball and waste a golden chance only seven yards away from United's goal. Pearson would have probably tried a 'stun shot'. It was inexperience too that caused Cunliffe to crouch and head Williamson's centre upwards and over the bar when he should have risen to his full height and nodded the ball downwards. The fault that caused Hart to slice so badly when he let drive at Broadis' through pass was possibly a slight wobble of the ball on an uneven patch at the precise moment when the shot was taken. If all, or any of these chances had been converted it seems fairly certain that City would have won. They were certainly enjoying a slight tactical advantage before the close. United were hampered by the fact that of their three youngsters only Lewis seemed able to make his presence felt, and even he seemed to lack speed. Whitefoot had a disappointing match. Pegg did little and Doherty never caught up with the affair at all. For City, Ewing, a reserve centre-half, attracted some interest. He is big enough, and he is certainly game enough, but that he is good enough remains to be proved".

Roger Byrne - fast becoming an established and reliable fixture at full-back in Matt Busby's rebuilding plans.

Jimmy Meadows - City's versatile utility player appeared in seven different positions during his spell at Maine Road during the early 1950's.

AT THE SEASON'S END

UNITED: Finished 8th on 46 points

CITY: Finished 20th on 35 points
(1 point more than relegated Stoke City)

55

MANCHESTER CITY 2
(Hart, Revie)

MANCHESTER UNITED 0

DATE	5th September 1953
DIVISION	One
VENUE	Maine Road
ATTENDANCE	53,097

Manchester City		Manchester United
Bert TRAUTMANN	1	Ray WOOD
Ken BRANAGAN	2	John ASTON
Roy LITTLE	3	Roger BYRNE
Don REVIE	4	Jeff WHITEFOOT
Dave EWING	5	Allenby CHILTON
Roy PAUL	6	Henry COCKBURN
Harry ANDERS	7	Johnny BERRY
Johnny HART	8	Dennis VIOLLET
Ken WHITEFIELD	9	Tommy TAYLOR
Billy SPURDLE	10	Stan PEARSON
Roy CLARKE	11	Jack ROWLEY

BACKGROUND

It was a disastrous start to the new season for both Manchester clubs. With only one win to show between them, both were down at the wrong end of the table by derby day. City's only victory had been a dramatic 5-4 victory over Sunderland at Roker Park. However, four defeats had left the Maine Road faithful muttering their discontent. City were still a wealthy club, with some fine individual players and excellent support that had averaged between 35,000 and 40,000 since the war. However the club's performances on the field during that period left a lot to be desired. The fans were further puzzled by the de-selection of Ivor Broadis, arguably City's best player in recent seasons.

Sensationally in derby week the Manchester Evening Chronicle reported on its front page 'City to transfer Broadis.' Manager Les McDowall commented; "Following a heart to heart talk between the player and myself, it will be in the best interests of the club and player to part."

United without a League win were certainly going through a period of transition. Their forward line for the derby exemplified this. Pearson and Rowley remained of the 'old guard' while the young blood was represented by Dennis Viollet and Tommy Taylor. Signed the previous March from Barnsley for £29,999 - to avoid burdening him with a £30,000 tag! - Taylor had proved himself to be a brave intelligent forward of immense talent and promise with a keen eye for goal. With Johnny Carey now the manager at Blackburn the captaincy passed on to big Allenby Chilton, a regular stalwart for the past seven seasons and now playing some of the best football of his career. United therefore entered the derby looking for a victory over the old enemy that would perhaps prove a catalyst for the club to begin an ascent from their currently embarrassing position.

Don Revie - 'calmness personified' as he scored his first and only League derby goal to clinch City's fine victory.

Billy Spurdle - an influential player for City in several positions during the early 1950's.

BEFORE THE GAME							
	P	W	D	L	F	A	Pts
UNITED	5	0	3	2	7	11	3
CITY	5	1	0	4	5	14	2

MATCH VERDICT

United's poor start to the season continued and this defeat not only dumped them to a lowest ever League position under Busby's rule but had the press screeching about their inadequacies. The Daily Dispatch talked of 'United's worst forward line in 20 years'. Alf Clarke writing in the Manchester Evening Chronicle exclaimed; 'the level of passing by United was their worst ever'. All this rather seemed to detract from what was a solid and most conclusive victory by City.

The first half belonged in the main to City as their light forwards always played the more fluent football and created the clearer chances.

United's front line however, showed a complete lack of understanding. Viollet appeared very nervous and Pearson lacking in match practice. Tommy Taylor proved the only real threat and Trautmann's brilliant save from Taylor's fierce shot on the run, right on the stroke of half time, proved a turning point. In the second half City ran out easy winners. Hart atoned for a first half miss by neatly beating Wood and Don Revie was calmness personified scoring his first derby goal.

For manager Les McDowall victory over the old enemy brought some much needed relief and a degree of vindication for his controversial omission of Broadis. But as the Evening Chronicle surmised; 'City's half-backs and full-backs should have passed a vote of thanks to the United men for being such friendly neighbours'.

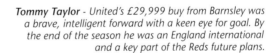

Manchester United in 1953-54. A team in transition as Matt Busby started to introduce his talented youngsters. **Back:** *Roger Byrne, Bill Foulkes, Jack Crompton, Jackie Blanchflower, Jack Rowley, Duncan Edwards.* **Front:** *Dennis Viollet, Johnny Berry, Allenby Chilton, Jeff Whitefoot, Tommy Taylor.*

Tommy Taylor - United's £29,999 buy from Barnsley was a brave, intelligent forward with a keen eye for goal. By the end of the season he was an England international and a key part of the Reds future plans.

Johnny Hart - atoned for a first half miss by neatly beating United goalkeeper Ray Wood for City's opening goal.

56

MANCHESTER UNITED 1
(Berry)

MANCHESTER CITY 1
(McAdams)

DATE	16th January 1954
DIVISION	One
VENUE	Old Trafford
ATTENDANCE	46,379

Manchester United		Manchester City
Ray WOOD	1	Bert TRAUTMANN
Bill FOULKES	2	Ken BRANAGAN
Roger BYRNE	3	Jimmy MEADOWS
Jeff WHITEFOOT	4	John McTAVISH
Allenby CHILTON	5	Dave EWING
Duncan EDWARDS	6	Roy PAUL
Johnny BERRY	7	Paddy FAGAN
Jackie BLANCHFLOWER	8	Johnny HART
Tommy TAYLOR	9	Billy McADAMS
Dennis VIOLLET	10	Don REVIE
David PEGG	11	Roy CLARKE

BACKGROUND

United were struggling desperately without a victory in eight games and only five points to their name when they went to Middlesbrough on 16th September. A 4-1 victory at Ayresome Park proved a turning point in the season and sparked a much improved run of nine more victories in the next seventeen games that enabled the Reds to climb the table. During this period more of the 'Busby Babes' joined the first team. Bill Foulkes now established himself at full-back and Jackie Blanchflower and Dennis Viollet became regulars in the side. Also at this time the legendary Duncan Edwards became a member of the first team and began to astound the public with some prodigious performances of power and skill. The previous April he had been United's youngest ever debutant when he played against Cardiff City at the tender age of 16 years 185 days. He was now set for his derby debut. Following a disappointing Cup exit (beaten 5-3 at Burnley) Busby caused some consternation in the local press by dropping 'gunner' Rowley for the derby match.

The Blues remained in the wrong half of the table throughout this period. Manager Les McDowall made numerous changes to the team with only Trautmann, Branagan and Ewing being ever-presents at the time of the derby. One man beginning to make a name for himself was Billy McAdams. He had joined City from the Irish League Club, Distillery, on 6th December 1953. On 2nd January he made a scoring debut in the 2-1 defeat of Sunderland. In the Cup game that followed he scored a hat-trick in the 5-2 away win at Bradford, and so entered the derby with the Blues' fans hoping his scoring streak would continue against the 'old enemy'.

Roy Paul - City's versatile wing-half who combined his natural skills with good honest endeavour. They were qualities that would help him lead City to successive FA Cup Finals in 1955 and 1956.

BEFORE THE GAME							
	P	W	D	L	F	A	Pts
UNITED	26	10	10	6	48	36	30
CITY	26	8	6	12	35	50	22

MATCH VERDICT

Another close derby contest. United had most of the play but were unable to make their superiority tell. As it was, Berry's first half goal seemed to have won the match for the Reds, only for City to snatch a dramatic last minute equaliser. Busby's controversial omission of old favourite Rowley brought some criticism. The Sunday Chronicle opined; 'it is one thing to go so far with promising youngsters, but it is quite another to go too far.' Certainly the promise of Pegg, Viollet and Blanchflower did not blossom in the inevitably intense derby atmosphere. As far as Duncan Edwards was concerned though, the statement 'boys among men' certainly did not apply, and he showed a maturity and quality beyond his years. United were much the better side in the first half and Trautmann had to make a series of daring saves. However, he was powerless to stop Berry's firm shot putting the Reds in front. The ever dangerous Taylor twice went close to increasing the lead and Ewing had a difficult time, as his somewhat rustic tackling annoyed the home crowd, who proceeded to barrack him. Yet, with all apparently lost, Meadows dispossessed Berry and set Clarke free down the left wing. With Foulkes in his wake, the winger cut in to beat Chilton and squared the ball for McAdams who shot cleanly past Wood to maintain his fine scoring record.

AT THE SEASON'S END

UNITED: Finished 4th on 48 points

CITY: Finished 17th on 37 points

Billy McAdams - his equaliser at Old Trafford was part of a remarkable start to a City career which brought five goals in his first three games.

Rowley the man United needed

By EDGAR TURNER

Manchester United ... 1   Manchester City ... 1

IT'S not often that the wisdom of that Soccer sage, Matt Busby, may be doubted. But I do so now. I think he was wrong in dropping Jack Rowley—that if "The Gunner" had been in the side yesterday, United would easily have won the Manchester "derby."

It's one thing to go so far with promising youngsters, but it is quite another to go too far. I couldn't altogether blame young Pegg, who took Rowley's place on the left wing, for he received only the same sort of service from his inside man, Viollet, that Rowley received a week ago in the Cup-tie at Burnley.

Viollet is not yet a first-class inside forward, though he is among the stand-bys for England's Intermediate team which plays in Italy this week.

And the game goes for Blanchflower, at inside right. They're good young speculations, it is true, but they've suddenly come to a full-stop in probably the most difficult positions in any team.

A much better move probably would be to put Rowley at inside left. Great effort though Taylor made, it looked as though he could have done with someone with experience at his side yesterday.

Clarke's Great Pass

No doubt that Taylor, with his darting, narrow-hipped efficiency, put United into a position from which they ought to have securely buckled up the issue.

But apart from Berry, who scored in the first half, there was no one else in the forward line to crash in more telling blows to secure the victory which United really deserved.

Moreover, if Aston is fit again, then he ought to go in at right back. Foulkes hasn't impressed me at all these last two weeks. City outside left, Clarke, had matters virtually his own way in the first half.

To Clarke must go the greatest credit for City's surprise equaliser a few minutes from the end.

Meadows pulled down a ball almost off the nose of Berry and gave a pass to his left winger, who took the ball up the field and then beat Chilton as the centre half tried to cover up for Foulkes.

Clarke could have finished with a blinding shot which might also have finished up in the crowd at the back of the goal. But he wisely put the ball square for McAdams to score his fifth goal in three first-team appearances.

United played rather more crisply than City, whose right wing triangle of Hart, Fagan and McTavish were never really in the game.

Ewing Barracked

And Revie, whose main idea seemed to be one of icy deployment, looked as though he had less heart for inside left than the role of right half, which he covets.

Meadows had his name taken, but the most-booed man on the ground was that blustering centre half, Ewing, who would be a great player if only he could find skill to match his enthsiasm. He means no harm.

A word for Edwards. And Byrne. And Paul—and one in capital letters for that king of goalkeepers, Trautmann. One save of his from a flying header by Taylor was something out of another world.

Judging from what he writes on page 10, it looks as though it won't be long before he leaves us. That will be a sad day. If anyone hasn't seen this German, then they should do so before it's too late.

Duncan Edwards - a youngster with all the makings of a great player, he displayed skills beyond his years in his first Manchester derby match.

57

MANCHESTER CITY 3
(McAdams, Fagan, Hart)

MANCHESTER UNITED 2
(Taylor, Blanchflower)

DATE	25th September 1954
DIVISION	One
VENUE	Maine Road
ATTENDANCE	54,105

Manchester City		*Manchester United*
Bert TRAUTMANN	1	Ray WOOD
Jimmy MEADOWS	2	Bill FOULKES
Roy LITTLE	3	Roger BYRNE
Ken BARNES	4	Don GIBSON
Dave EWING	5	Allenby CHILTON
Roy PAUL	6	Duncan EDWARDS
Paddy FAGAN	7	Johnny BERRY
Billy McADAMS	8	Jackie BLANCHFLOWER
Don REVIE	9	Tommy TAYLOR
Johnny HART	10	Dennis VIOLLET
Roy CLARKE	11	Jack ROWLEY

BACKGROUND

City's opening game of the new season resulted in a gloomy 5-0 beating at Preston. Yet surprisingly, by mid-September the Blues were contesting at the top of the table with their red shirted Manchester rivals. Many put the transformation down to Manager Les McDowall and his introduction of the revolutionary 'Revie Plan'. McDowall simply showed he was a keen student of the game and became one of the first men to digest the lesson the Hungarians had taught the national side the year before. The Hungarians had of course, inflicted England's first home defeat by continental opposition. The Magyars thrashed them 5-1 and introduced the concept of the 'withdrawn' centre-forward. In the City formation Don Revie played this role in a deep lying position close to the midfield and away from the centre-half expected to mark him. This allowed Revie a free-ranging role to join with the wing halves in orchestrating moves and allowed other forwards to move in and out of the forward gap he had left behind. Thus far it had bemused a number of opponents and brought the Blues some very promising results.

For United many of the 'Busby Babes' were now established first-teamers. Foulkes, Byrne, White-foot, Edwards, Blanchflower, Webster and Viollet were all part of an exciting line-up that seemed to have the potential to win almost anything. However, it was Jack Rowley, starting his final campaign for the Reds, who got United's first goal of the season. Despite losing that first game, United set off on a purple patch of form and entered the derby unbeaten in their previous eight matches.

BEFORE THE GAME							
	P	W	D	L	F	A	Pts
UNITED	9	6	2	1	20	11	14
CITY	9	5	2	2	15	14	12

MATCH VERDICT

An outstanding derby, brimful of creative attacking football brought a glorious victory for City and the revolutionary Revie plan. City, with Revie operating in his withdrawn centre-forward position quickly strung together some impressive passing movements that had both the full-backs and goalkeeper looking rather vulnerable. City's opening goal epitomised the 'plan', which demanded swift running off the ball and clever changes of conventional positions. With Revie withdrawn, Hart dashed to the vacant space on the right and was met by a perfectly weighted pass from Barnes. Hart quickly played a one-two with Fagan who had come in-field from the wing and centred at once into the middle where McAdams headed powerfully past the bemused Wood. With hardly twenty minutes gone United were again run-ragged and found themselves two goals down. Following more clever running off the ball, McAdams found himself in the clear and his fierce shot beat Wood but cannoned off the post. As the City fans cursed their luck, little Paddy Fagan raced in and rocketed the rebound into the net. United battled to get back into the game and following a goal-mouth scramble Taylor prodded the ball in. There was no denying the Blues though and another slick passing movement carved the United defence open and from McAdams' final ball Hart, running into the space where Revie would have been, shot high into the roof of the net. Blanchflower's goal set up a grandstand finish where the Reds twice hit the woodwork but the victory on the day went to City's slick teamwork which triumphed over United's youthful individualism.

City goalkeeper **Bert Trautmann** makes a spectacular dive as a shot from **Jack Rowley** passes just outside the post. Looking relieved in the background is City's right half-back **Ken Barnes**.

MANCHESTER CITY'S SUCCESS

A Fine Test of Contrasting Styles

BY AN OLD INTERNATIONAL

Manchester City 3, Manchester United 2

High among the pleasures of Association football are the "Derby Days"; and on Saturday, at Moss' Side, Manchester City gained a piquant Football League victory over their close neighbours and rivals Manchester United by 3-2. As a result these two splendid teams are now racing neck and neck at the heels of West Bromwich Albion. Could there be any surer guarantee that football excitement in Manchester is likely now to remain at fever heat until the cup-ties start, and then perhaps boil over?

The significant thing about City's victory is that the shock of a serious reverse at Cardiff the week previous was not allowed to weaken City's faith in the new strategy which they have adopted this season and which is giving such widespread pleasure. It is a strategy which shows off to perfection the strength and maturity of Paul among his younger defenders, and which gives full scope to the inspired wanderings of Revie. City have staked their all on pure football and they are proving that football pays. What is more, by one of those delicious strokes of irony which play round the uncertainties of sport, the City's forwards helped themselves to three goals, and narrowly missed scoring as many more—without taking into account hot claims for an odd penalty or so—against a defence the three least masterful members of which were to be chosen later in the day as England's bulwark against Ireland. Most ironical of all, of course, was the outstanding figure, in United's defence, the iron man, Chilton, the veteran who generously does three men's work to cover up the immaturity of his youthful prodigies, never gets chosen.

Points for Argument

The fast exchanges of this match; its fierce ebb and flow; the bouts of great football that led to some goals; the strings of blunders that led to others; the short sharp flare-up of fraying tempers; the strain of shabby tackles; the protruding necks that prevented goals at the last agonising split second; the splendour of United's last despairing rally; and the steadiness with which City rode the storm —these and a host of other debatable topics will prove a godsend to the local barbers for weeks to come. The City supporters will argue that the prize in any football contest should go to the team which employs the cleverer technique and relies on the more measured, more logical approach-play, not to mention the more utilitarian aspect of converting chances as they arise. United supporters, in answer, will ask their City friends to forget who won the match ("Dash it all, it's time you won something") and reckon up on which side had the greater number of positive scoring chances. And the City supporters, if they are honest, and willing to survey the question magnanimously as from the lofty standpoint of victors, may admit, by and large, and with certain reservations as regards penalties, that United had been to a limited extent, and in certain respects, a trifle unlucky.

Perhaps the two City players who have improved most under the new dispensation are Hart and Meadows. Hart, in particular, approaches his task nowadays with a freshness, a liveliness, an enthusiasm, and a resource which are pleasing to see. Revie's frequent withdrawals from City's line of attack undoubtedly give Hart more room to manoeuvre, more scope to employ his own wits, and he is developing a rare judgment in the art of turning up in the right spot at the right time. This was beautifully exemplified on Saturday when City scored their first goal—the finest of the match. As the ball rolled shuttle-wise between Barnes and Paul, Hart dashed across to an open space on the right wing, whither Paul followed him with a perfect pass. Without pause Hart fed Fagan daintily, then glided smoothly into position to receive the return pass. Came a perfect centre—again from Hart,— a bold leap and shattering header by McAdams, and a shout arose sufficient to lift the slates off all the roofs in Moss Side as England's defence-to-be fell for the first time.

City's next goal, scored by Fagan, had alternate layers of good and bad luck about it, like streaky bacon. It was bad luck indeed when McAdams's fierce, low shot from the left struck a post—or was it somebody's leg?—and rolled to Fagan; but good luck beyond doubt when Fagan's smashing first-timer cannoned off somebody's ribs and passed hopelessly wide of Woods. City's third goal went, appropriately enough, to one of the most deserving, Hart: it followed a hard, high shot from McAdams's perfect pass.

Teamwork v. Individualism

The match gave students of football a heaven-sent opportunity to compare the merits of two contrasting styles. City, the winners, were content to rely on smooth, ordered teamwork and a patient, logical build-up as the best means to secure goals, whereas United, though no less able to indulge in effective combination at will, seemed somehow drawn by youthful exuberance and perhaps the challenge of the occasion into heroic individual efforts that came so frequently to nought. Nevertheless there was something mightily impressive about Blanchflower's abundant energy, crowned, as usual, by a good goal (if Paul's contributory negligence is forgotten), and about the remarkable speed with which Viollet covered the ground. Though Taylor scored United's first goal, a rather scrambled affair that caught several City players blundering and Trautmann diving the wrong way, it was Viollet who remained throughout the greatest potential danger. If Viollet, like Edwards, would only learn to vary his manoeuvres a little, and combine with his wingman more often; and if Edwards would take Paul as a model of how to distribute passes evenly and how to vary the point of attack, what a force in the land these youngsters would be.

Meanwhile, no United supporter who was present on Saturday and who saw Blanchflower's magnificent header graze one post and Taylor's beautiful shot well-nigh uproot the other; who saw Trautmann barely able to scramble Rowley's lovely, low shot round one post for a corner and then nearly break his back pushing Ewing's gross mis-header over the bar for another; and who saw Meadows and Little stick out their heads and necks like gargoyles to head away shots that had the goalkeeper hopelessly beaten—no such supporter but would maintain, while the breath remained in his body, that the better team lost. Teams:

MANCHESTER CITY.—Trautmann; Meadows, Little; Barnes, Ewing, Paul Fagan, McAdams, Revie, Hart, Clarke.

MANCHESTER UNITED.—Wood; Foulkes, Byrne; Gibson, Chilton, Edwards; Berry, Blanchflower, Taylor, Viollet, Rowley.

A corner and a crushing! **Dave Ewing**, City's centre-half falls on United's inside-left **Dennis Viollet** as he makes a timely interception for a corner. Watching the ball to safety is City's full-back **Jimmy Meadows**.

58

MANCHESTER UNITED 0
MANCHESTER CITY 5
(Hart, Fagan 2, Hayes 2)

DATE	12th February 1955
DIVISION	One
VENUE	Old Trafford
ATTENDANCE	47,914

Manchester United		Manchester City
Ray WOOD	1	Bert TRAUTMANN
Bill FOULKES	2	Jimmy MEADOWS
Roger BYRNE	3	Roy LITTLE
Don GIBSON	4	Ken BARNES
Allenby CHILTON	5	Dave EWING
Jeff WHITEFOOT	6	Roy PAUL
Johnny BERRY	7	Paddy FAGAN
Jackie BLANCHFLOWER	8	Joe HAYES
Colin WEBSTER	9	Don REVIE
Duncan EDWARDS	10	Johnny HART
David PEGG	11	Roy CLARKE

BACKGROUND

Following their great victory over United in September, City beat Everton 1-0 with a goal from Welsh International Roy Clarke, but from this lofty pinnacle of League form the season fell away a little, with City's unpredictable nature coming to the fore. An excellent 3-1 away win at mighty Blackpool was followed by a 5-1 defeat at home to Charlton. However, the Revie plan continued to prosper and its success meant the Blues were enjoying their best season since 1949. Certainly the 'plan' seemed to have totally foxed the Reds as two weeks before this derby City knocked United out of the FA Cup.

The 'Busby Babes' were the talk of the football world and large crowds flocked to see them play. A crowd of 55,966 saw United beat Chelsea 6-5 at Stamford Bridge, while on Merseyside, 63,021 saw Everton win 4-2 and Aston Villa had their highest attendance of the season - 48,718 - when United visited Villa Park. Although occasionally sustaining defeat, the public were excited by the skills and attacking instincts of the Babes and their potential seemed limitless.

Despite the plaudits, United were still having trouble with the old enemy as the recent Cup exit proved.

COCK O' THE WALK

City's **Roy Clarke** crashes a tremendous shot beyond United goalkeeper **Ray Wood** but the outside-left's effort was ruled out by a hairline offside decision.

Paddy Fagan - two goals in City's crushing victory.

	P	W	D	L	F	A	Pts
BEFORE THE GAME							
UNITED	27	14	5	8	59	47	33
CITY	28	13	6	9	52	50	32

Revie plan still has them baffled

THREE times Manchester United have met Manchester City this season—and three times they have bitten the dust—or snow, ice and mud. And each succeeding time in terms of goals that beating has been worse.

First League meeting at Maine Road saw City win 3—2: a fortnight ago in the Cup City won 2—0 at home; yesterday they slipped over to Old Trafford and went nap—without reply.

Yet if there was a team which might be expected to have found the answer to the Revie plan—if such there be—it was United. But it seems the more they play against it the more baffling they find it.

Counter-plan

After yesterday's game I asked United skipper, Allen Chilton, what plan, if any, United had decided on to stop Revie. Said Allen: " We decided to ignore it. Revie roams so much from midfield and wing to wing that putting one man on him to mark him only results in upsetting the balance of your own side.

" So we decided to play an all-out attacking game ourselves and by sheer pressure offset the Revie plan. Our plan nearly succeeded in the first half when, for the last 20 minutes, we had City defending desperately and with luck might have had three goals.

"But it wasn't our day, and when City got their second goal after half-time they played us out of the game."

Fair enough, Allen. But now that he'd had a third ration of the Revie plan I asked him if he'd any new ideas about how to stop it.

Said Chilton—" Yes. I still think the best way is to let Don roam and let me as deep as he wants—but I think the answer is to mark closely the two inside forwards and stop them making use of the passes Revie sends through."

Must wait

We will have to wait until next season to see the Chilton theory in practice—but there was no doubting City's supremacy yesterday.

On a pitch frozen down one side and thawed on the other City took command for the first 20 minutes and went ahead with a goal which would have adorned the erudite books which Mr. Walter Winterbottom has compiled on coaching and Soccer strategy for the F.A.

Then it was United's turn until the interval. More by sheer enthusiasm than cultured football, they rampaged round the City goal. Dominating Duncan Edwards ranged along the whole battlefront from left wing to right wing.

He shot, he headed, he inspired and was always in the thick of it—but the thick of it was the City defence, which packed the goal with a solidity which must have been sickening to United.

City had their luck, of course, but fortune favours the brave and these were stout - hearted defenders, indeed.

I can say little new about the City display. It was the same teamwork which has baffled so many sides this season. Ken Barnes had another brilliant attacking wing half game and Revie enjoyed the freedom of Old Trafford in the same greedy way that he enjoys the freedom of Maine Road.

Ewing's best

In that torrid 20-minute spell before half-time full-backs Meadows and Little positioned themselves brilliantly and Ewing hit his highest spot this season.

Paul had a quieter game than usual, but what there was of it was of the usual vintage.

Edwards—who seems to be able to play well no matter how foreign the position—and Whitefoot were the United stars. Twice in the first half Whitefoot went within an ace of scoring, so effectively was he backing up his attack.

In the first half Fagg did well on the sunny side of the street, but suffered like the rest later, on going that was distinctly dodgy.

Chilton tried valiantly to rouse his flagging forces in the second half—but if 11 men couldn't stop Revie and the boys, what chance had one?

Both teams deserve the highest praise for a thriller on a pitch which never gave any expectations of entertainment. But this was City's day—as the result in the records will testify for posterity.

Arthur Walmsley

MATCH VERDICT

City, clearly the Champions of Manchester this season, beat United for a third time, and just to rub it in, this Old Trafford victory equalled the margin of City's emphatic win in 1926. On a cold winter's day, with the pitch frozen down one side and thawed out on the other, the Revie plan worked to perfection and United were trounced.

City's first goal on fifteen minutes was a perfect execution of the plan and Edgar Turner writing in the 'Sunday Chronicle' described it as one of the most finely constructed goals he had ever seen. Paul's throw in on the left flank in City's own half found Revie in the deep lying position. The ball was quickly switched between Hart, Clarke and back to Revie, whose final pass swung the ball to the far right where Hayes' quick fire centre was met by the on-rushing Hart, who fired past Wood. The Reds' defence gawped in open-mouthed bemusement. Stung by this, United spent the rest of the half besieging the City goal and could count themselves a little unlucky to go in at half time behind. However, after a brief second half rally by United the classy Blues began the demolition proper of their rivals. On 58 minutes clever interpassing between Clarke, Hart and Revie left Paddy Fagan in the clear and his firm shot ended the game as a contest. The Blues poured forward now and, following another Revie inspired move, Joe Hayes blasted City's third goal. The fourth again epitomised the essence of the plan as Hart and Hayes raced through into the gap left by Revie and, with Chilton in no-man's-land, Hayes reached Clarke's pass and swept the ball past Wood. With United's defence dissolving into increasing disarray, Fagan completed the rout by scoring a fifth and final goal.

AT THE SEASON'S END

UNITED: Finished 5th on 47 points
(1 point behind runners up Wolves)

CITY: Finished 7th on 46 points
(F.A. Cup Finalists, losing 3-1 to Newcastle)

Joe Hayes makes it 4-0 to City as he hammers a pass from **Roy Clarke** past United goalkeeper **Ray Wood** for his second goal of the game.

Hayes · Chilton · Hart · Wood

59

MANCHESTER CITY 1
(Hayes)

MANCHESTER UNITED 0

DATE		3rd September 1955
DIVISION		One
VENUE		Maine Road
ATTENDANCE		59,192

Manchester City		Manchester United
Bert TRAUTMANN	1	Ray WOOD
Ken BRANAGAN	2	Bill FOULKES
Roy LITTLE	3	Roger BYRNE
Ken BARNES	4	Jeff WHITEFOOT
Dave EWING	5	Mark JONES
Roy PAUL	6	Freddie GOODWIN
Billy SPURDLE	7	Colin WEBSTER
Joe HAYES	8	Jackie BLANCHFLOWER
Don REVIE	9	Eddie LEWIS
Bobby JOHNSTONE	10	Duncan EDWARDS
Paddy FAGAN	11	Albert SCANLON

BACKGROUND

City, buoyed up by the promise of the previous season, crashed badly in their second League fixture, thrashed 7-2 by Wolverhampton Wanderers at Molineux. A pair of 2-2 home draws, to Aston Villa and the Arsenal, were all they had to show by derby day and pre-season confidence had taken a battering. City's major change in personnel was the introduction of Scottish International Bobby Johnstone who had replaced broken leg victim Johnny Hart in the forward line. Johnstone, bought from Hibernian in March 1955 for £22,000, had scored City's only goal in the F.A. Cup Final defeat by Newcastle in May, and had proved himself a popular and skilful inside-forward, who in August had represented Great Britain against the Rest of Europe.

At United the last of the great 1948 side had left the club. Jack Rowley joined Plymouth as player-manager and his place in the side went to Albert Scanlon, the nephew of former favourite Charlie Mitten. Busby's young team entered the derby unbeaten as, following two draws, United had seen off West Bromwich Albion at home and Tottenham Hotspur away. Duncan Edwards had again displayed his all-round ability by scoring both the goals at White Hart Lane.

BEFORE THE GAME							
	P	W	D	L	F	A	Pts
UNITED	4	2	2	0	9	6	6
CITY	3	0	2	1	6	11	2

● Bert Trautmann gets there first and punches a fine centre from the head of Webster, United outside right.

Joe Hayes - on target with City's winning goal. He made quite a habit of scoring against United and was to finish his career as City's joint top scorer in derby meetings between the clubs.

MATCH VERDICT

Once again City came up trumps. Without a League victory, and with the whole of England talking about the Busby Babes, it was the Blues who stole the local glory and once again put one over their old rivals.

In a closely-contested opening half hour both sides had chances from attacking movements. Bobby Johnstone looked a particularly lively character as he chased after dangerous through-balls from Revie and Branagan. Duncan Edwards, operating at inside-left for the injured Viollet, was twice frustrated by brilliant saves from Trautmann, who once again looked in outstanding derby form.

On the half hour, City's measured football paid off when they scored what proved to be the winner. Branagan, moving up from full back, sent a long pass directly to the head of the diminutive Johnstone who nodded the ball to Joe Hayes, and his shot beat Ray Wood.

In a flurry of attacking football United strived hard for an equaliser before the break, but their efforts seemed to tire them out and as the second half progressed City controlled much of the play. However, in the final minutes of the match, Edwards' fierce shot seemed certain to bring an equaliser only for Trautmann to once again pull off one of his memorable saves.

TRAUTMANN'S GREAT SAVES

Manchester United Attack Frustrated

BY AN OLD INTERNATIONAL

Manchester City 1, Manchester United 0

A colourful, sun-kissed crowd, 50,000 strong, saw Manchester City patiently forge ahead of their lusty young rivals of Manchester United in the Football League match at Moss Side and pass the winning post with much more in hand than the score 1-0 would suggest.

Play broke evenly in the first fifteen minutes with Branagan, right back for City, showing himself an apt pupil of Revie in the art of driving alluring long passes through the likeliest of gaps in United's defences, and Johnstone, inside left, pursuing them with all the avidity of a frisky young terrier chasing a stone. United's approach play, too, was beautiful to watch. As against West Bromwich a week before, so here, too, they passed and repassed the ball with a fluency and a rhythm so smooth and continuous that one could almost imagine M. Busby training his young charges to play by metronome, with short crisp passes marking every beat. To add to United's rosy prospects of victory in this period was the thrustfulness of Edwards as substitute inside left for the injured Viollet—a hint of positional versatility which may yet place this active young man among the Careys and the Crabtrees of the game.

Then a curious thing happened. Barnes, City's gaunt and spidery right wing half-back, a precision worker as a rule, suddenly lost all control of his passing and began to feed friend and foe alike; while Paul, his captain, on the other flank, an artist whose play usually is marked by its shrewdness, decided to drive across his own crowded penalty area perhaps the two most ill-conceived passes of his career. The red shirts pounced upon these chances like hungry vultures. Lewis caught one a terrific wallop but with a slicing effect which curled it away into the side netting, while Scanlon, after a brilliant dribble,

wasted the other by shooting hurriedly when a square pass would have been more to the purpose. A little later when more foolish dithering gave Scanlon scope to race away and centre to Edwards closing in on the right, a terrific volley, dead on the mark, pointed to the one decisive factor which was to tip the scales in City's favour—the superb goalkeeping of Trautmann.

Edwards stood, hands on hips, a picture of open-mouthed frustration, as Trautmann rose like a bird and fastened his talons, so to speak, round the whirling ball. He stood thus many times, and with him his despairing colleagues Lewis and Webster, as Trautmann proved time and again that he was equal to the sternest tests these youngsters could contrive. Meanwhile they were to have the chastening experience of watching Johnstone nod a beautiful long ball from Branagan over to Hayes and of watching Hayes give an answering nod and steer the ball well wide of Wood's groping arms for what was to prove the only goal of the match. This happened on the half-hour, and the fury with which United strove to recover lost ground between then and the interval told on them severely in the second half.

City slowly fastened a grip on them as implacable as the closing of a vice, and Revie's scheming, Johnstone's enthusiasm, and Branagan's liveliness found full scope. Even so Edwards contrived to make one last low venomous thrust which would have beaten nine goalkeepers out of ten and purloined a belated equaliser. But no: Trautmann. Not the greatest of present-day goalkeepers. In certain moods, like Swift, he appears unbeatable. At the same time note should be taken of Wood's vastly improved form for United in this match. His great save against Fagan was itself worth the price of admission and served to keep the issue open until the very last kick. Teams:

MANCHESTER CITY.—Trautmann; Branagan, Little; Barnes, Ewing, Paul; Spurdle, Hayes, Revie, Johnstone, Fagan.

MANCHESTER UNITED.—Wood; Foulkes, Byrne; Whitefoot, Jones, Goodwin; Webster, Blanchflower, Lewis, Edwards, Scanlon.

Brilliant Johnstone

It's a goal! No it isn't! This set the fans arguing at Maine Road yesterday. The ball is bustled in by City outside right, Spurdle. United goalkeeper Wood seems to be balancing it on his arm. Johnstone holds up his hands. Foulkes watches. The referee says: "No goal!"

Bobby Johnstone, pictured here trotting out at Maine Road for his first Manchester derby match, was a £22,000 buy from Hibernian the previous March and also scored in City's FA Cup Final defeat by Newcastle Utd. in May.

60

MANCHESTER UNITED 2
(Taylor, Viollet)

MANCHESTER CITY 1
(Dyson)

DATE	31st December 1955
DIVISION	One
VENUE	Old Trafford
ATTENDANCE	60,956

Manchester United		Manchester City
Ray WOOD	1	Bert TRAUTMANN
Bill FOULKES	2	Bill LEIVERS
Roger BYRNE	3	Roy LITTLE
Eddie COLMAN	4	Ken BARNES
Mark JONES	5	Dave EWING
Duncan EDWARDS	6	Roy PAUL
Johnny BERRY	7	Billy SPURDLE
John DOHERTY	8	Joe HAYES
Tommy TAYLOR	9	Bobby JOHNSTONE
Dennis VIOLLET	10	Jack DYSON
David PEGG	11	Roy CLARKE

BACKGROUND

By the time of the second derby of the season on New Year's Eve 1955, the Reds were still undefeated at home, a proud record they were to keep throughout the season. It was this strong home form that kept the team at the top and challenging for the title. In fact, United headed the table at the end of October, but following a couple of poor results lost top spot until 3rd December. The conveyor belt of young talent continued to roll and on the 12th November Eddie 'snake-hips' Colman made his debut.

Colman had captained United's F.A. Youth Cup winning side of 1955, the third successive year the club had won the trophy. The traditional back-to-back Christmas fixtures did though cause the Reds some embarrassment. On Boxing Day United beat Charlton 5-1 at Old Trafford and yet they lost 3-0 to the Londoners the following day.

Over at Moss Side, City's inconsistency had limited their League progress. Throughout October and November the Blues lost six out of nine games, but by the time of the derby had overcome their bad patch and were unbeaten in the last six matches. One City man who made his debut at this time and would play a prominent role in this derby was Jack Dyson.

One of the old breed of footballer-cricketers, he played in the summer for Lancashire County Cricket Club. Dyson had made a bright start for City, scoring on his debut, and had bagged another three goals by the time of the derby. Bill Leivers, bought from Chesterfield for £10,500 in November 1953, was now established at right back. City entered the derby in confident mood following a victory over Bolton with goals from Clarke and Paul.

MANCHESTER'S SPIRITED DUEL
Two Hard-Earned Points for United

BEFORE THE GAME

	P	W	D	L	F	A	Pts
UNITED	25	13	6	6	51	37	32
CITY:	23	8	8	7	42	41	24

MATCH VERDICT

Amid remarkable scenes, a reported 80,000 fans attempted to get into this game but the gates were locked with 60,956 of them inside. The local populace who had arrived early showed good judgement, because this was an excellent match, full of good football. City looked slightly the better side in a fiercely competitive first half, their measured thoughtful football threatening to once again teach the 'Babes' a lesson. City's defence displayed great composure, with captain Roy Paul outstanding. United's forwards tended to be often caught out, ambitiously attempting to take on one man too many. Indeed, it was City that went in at the break one goal up. United's defenders were all ball-watching as Leivers' long pass up field found the unmarked Dyson who quickly pulled the ball down and calmly swept it past Wood. As the second half progressed United's efforts took on an air of desperation, but a Ray Wood punt upfield, previously a wasteful distribution, suddenly changed the course of the game as the wind floated it over the unlucky Ewing. Taylor, cleverly anticipating the situation, raced onto the bouncing ball and volleyed past Trautmann.

United now scented victory and, following a spell of pressure on the City goal, Pegg's fiercely driven corner was deftly headed in by Viollet. Now it was City's turn for desperate attack, but their luck was out as Clarke's powerful shot hit the crossbar and United held on to win.

Manchester City - FA Cup Winners in 1955-56. **Back:** W. Griffiths (Secretary), A. Douglas, R. Smith, W. Smith, F. Jolly, E. Gill (Directors). **Middle:** L. Barnett (Trainer), Ken Barnes, Bill Leivers, Bert Trautmann, Dave Ewing, Roy Little, Les McDowall (Manager). **Front:** Bobby Johnstone, Joe Hayes, Roy Paul, Don Revie, Jack Dyson, Roy Clarke.

Manchester United in 1955-56. League Champions with a side whose average age was only 22. **Back:** Eddie Colman, Billy Whelan, Mark Jones, Ray Wood, Ian Greaves, Duncan Edwards. **Front:** Johnny Berry, Roger Byrne, Dennis Viollet, Tommy Taylor, David Pegg.

AT THE SEASON'S END

UNITED:
FIRST DIVISION CHAMPIONS

P	W	D	L	F	A	Pts
42	25	10	7	83	51	60

CITY: Finished 4th on 46 points
(F.A. Cup Winners, beating Birmingham 3-1)

Bert Trautmann plunges out to gather a centre from United's **Johnny Berry**, but it is the 'rock-like' **Roy Paul** who clears the ball out for a corner.

61

MANCHESTER UNITED 2
(Viollet, Whelan)

MANCHESTER CITY 0

DATE	22nd September 1956
DIVISION	One
VENUE	Old Trafford
ATTENDANCE	53,515

Manchester United		Manchester City
Ray WOOD	1	Jack SAVAGE
Bill FOULKES	2	Bill LEIVERS
Roger BYRNE	3	Jack HANNAWAY
Eddie COLMAN	4	Ken BARNES
Mark JONES	5	Dave EWING
Duncan EDWARDS	6	Roy PAUL
Johnny BERRY	7	Billy SPURDLE
Billy WHELAN	8	Bill McADAMS
Tommy TAYLOR	9	Don REVIE
Dennis VIOLLET	10	Jack DYSON
David PEGG	11	Roy CLARKE

BACKGROUND

The League Champions made an excellent start to the defence of their title and entered the derby unbeaten. United had taken the revolutionary step, against the wishes of the F.A., of becoming the first English club to enter the European Cup. On the 12th September they had played their first European tie against Anderlecht of Belgium and won 2-0 with goals from Taylor and Viollet. This match was sandwiched between a 1-1 draw at Newcastle and a 4-1 home win over Sheffield Wednesday - the last match before meeting City. United's youthful side picked up very few injuries and Busby had been able to select the same side in every League game.

City's season started ominously with a 5-1 defeat at Wolves. For this early part of the season the Blues were without Bert Trautmann who had sustained a broken neck in the F.A. Cup Final victory the previous May. Trautmann, the reigning Footballer of the Year, and always a key performer in derby matches was likely to be sorely missed. George Thompson initially replaced him, but City quickly turned to the 6 ft 4 ins Jack Savage who had been signed from Halifax in November 1953. City, with essentially their Cup-winning side intact, were unable to make a League breakthrough.

With only two victories, against Leeds and Sunderland, the Blues approached a meeting against the 'Busby Babes' with some degree of trepidation.

*United's **Dennis Viollet** (left) and **Tommy Taylor** (right) cause confusion in the City defence.*

BEFORE THE GAME							
	P	W	D	L	F	A	Pts
UNITED	8	6	2	0	21	10	14
CITY	9	2	2	5	12	18	6

MATCH VERDICT

In a rather one-sided derby United ran out comfortable winners. Indeed, if it were not for the heroics of Savage in the City goal the margin of victory would have been much greater.

Throughout the first half City were second to the ball and seemed generally out of sorts and largely unable, as on previous occasions, to unnerve the 'Babes'.

United, without playing at their best, were able to dictate the play and set up a series of dangerous attacks. Eddie Colman was again outstanding, as his superb ball control and tenacious tackling constantly caught the eye. The first goal seemed merely a question of time and, following more United pressure, it duly arrived. Berry raced clear on the United right and, with the City defence caught flat-footed, pulled a cunning ball back into the middle where Viollet, arriving at speed, struck an unstoppable shot past Savage. Shortly after this, the game was effectively ended as a contest, as the Blues gave away a soft second goal. This time it was a harmless looking centre from the right which, unaccountably, the defence allowed to roll right across the penalty area to the unmarked Billy Whelan who had the relatively simple task of slotting the ball into the net. City, unusually for them, not only lacked any ideas, but also seemed short of real fire or passion for the derby contest, and finished up looking a well beaten side.

*An unmarked **Billy Whelan** steers United's second goal past City goalkeeper **Jack Savage** and full-back **Bill Leivers** on the line.*

*City's **Jack Dyson** gets away from United's **Bill Foulkes** and **Mark Jones** during a Blues' attack.*

Jack Savage - a fine game in the City goal to keep United from running riot.

*Eddie Colman (grounded) narrowly misses for United. Watching anxiously are City's **Bill Leivers** (on the line), United's **Tommy Taylor**, City 'keeper **Jack Savage** and defender **Dave Ewing**.*

62

MANCHESTER CITY 2
(Clarke, Hayes)

MANCHESTER UNITED 4
(Whelan, Taylor, Viollet, Edwards)

DATE	2nd February 1957	
DIVISION	One	
VENUE	Maine Road	
ATTENDANCE	63,872	

Manchester City		Manchester United
Bert TRAUTMANN	1	Ray WOOD
Bill LEIVERS	2	Bill FOULKES
Roy LITTLE	3	Roger BYRNE
Ken BARNES	4	Eddie COLMAN
Dave EWING	5	Mark JONES
Roy PAUL	6	Duncan EDWARDS
Paddy FAGAN	7	Johnny BERRY
Joe HAYES	8	Billy WHELAN
Bobby JOHNSTONE	9	Tommy TAYLOR
Jack DYSON	10	Dennis VIOLLET
Roy CLARKE	11	David PEGG

Duncan Edwards - the king-pin of United's great young side, he powered in the fourth goal to seal a seasonal derby 'double' for the Reds.

BACKGROUND

City's season had deteriorated following the last derby defeat and a 7-3 hammering at Arsenal in October left the Club in crisis. City were now struggling near the bottom of the table but a mid-season run of six games without defeat improved the picture. During this period two major events affected the first team. In November Don Revie, tactical architect of City's 1956 Cup Final win, was transferred to Sunderland for £24,000. Revie had made 177 appearances for the Blues and had been Footballer of the Year in 1955. Then on the 15th December the charismatic Bert Trautmann finally returned to the side following his broken neck. Although far from fully fit, his confidence grew during the game, but the result, a 3-2 defeat by high-flying Wolves, saw Les McDowall criticised in the Press for bringing him back too soon. The final game before the derby at least proved Trautmann's fitness as Charlton were hammered 5-1.

This season's derby was not United's initial visit to their neighbours ground at Maine Road, as the Reds' first game after the September derby was an exhilarating 10-0 victory over Anderlecht in the second leg European Cup tie, and they also met City there for the Charity Shield during October. The match was switched as United had no flood-lights at the time, making Maine Road the first English ground to stage a European match. City however, would have a further eleven year wait to appear in a tie themselves. On the Wednesday following this February derby United were due to play Bilbao in a second leg European Cup tie - again at Maine Road. In what proved to be one of their great European results, the Reds dragged back a two goal deficit to win through. United were therefore maintaining excellent progress on three fronts; in the League, (where they were to be champions again), the European Cup (beaten semi-finalists), and the F.A. Cup (beaten finalists). In the fixture prior to the derby United had thumped Wrexham 5-0 in the F.A. Cup fourth round. United were without doubt already one of the great teams, yet were still approaching the peak of their powers.

BEFORE THE GAME

	P	W	D	L	F	A	Pts
UNITED	26	18	4	4	67	37	40
CITY	27	9	5	13	50	55	23

MATCH VERDICT

In a cup-tie like atmosphere the Manchester public were treated to six goals and could easily have enjoyed another six given the wonderful display of attacking football served up by both sides. The dramatic pattern was set from the very first minute when Barnes and Fagan opened up the Reds' defence and the ball fell to Dyson only a couple of feet from the goal line. Unfortunately for City, Dyson's wild swing at the ball only catapulted himself into the net and United miraculously escaped. It proved a most expensive miss as, minutes later, Leivers slipped leaving Whelan in the clear and he stroked the ball past Trautmann. City roared back and equalised on 12 minutes when Clarke's fierce shot flew past Wood. Either side might have scored again amid the waves of attack and counter-attack. However, it was United who got the vital break. As the ball was centred in from the right, Taylor's downward header from six yards took a vicious bounce off the greasy surface and skidded through Traut-

mann's legs into the net. United now sensed the game was theirs, and Taylor's deft through-ball sent Viollet dashing away from the defence to fire the ball past Trautmann. Edwards thumped a characteristic fourth goal but following Jones' mistake, Hayes pulled one back for the battling Blues.

Manchester United in 1956-57. League Champions again and FA Cup runners-up. **Back:** *Webster, McGuinness, Blanchflower, Doherty, Coleman.* **Middle:** *Curry (Trainer), Foulkes, Charlton, Goodwin, Wood, Whelan, Jones, Edwards, Inglis (Assistant Trainer).* **Front:** *Viollet, Berry, Busby (Manager), Byrne, Murphy (Assistant Manager), Taylor, Pegg.*

AT THE SEASON'S END

UNITED:
FIRST DIVISION CHAMPIONS

P	W	D	L	F	A	Pts
42	28	8	6	103	54	64

(United also F.A. Cup Finalists, losing 2-1 to Aston Villa)

CITY: Finished 18th on 35 points

T. Taylor

J. Blanchflower

R. Wood

D. Edwards

Football's most famous 'babes'

Without any doubt these youngsters were, up to the time of the Munich crash, all set to become some of the world's best-known Soccer stars. League Champions, F.A. Cup Finalists, European Cup semi-finalists—all in one season, 1956-57.

R. Byrne

J. Berry

B. Foulkes

M. Jones

C. Webster

D. Pegg

F. Goodwin

W. McGuinness

R. Charlton

W. Whelan

D. Viollet

J. Doherty

E. Colman

UNITED'S TRAGEDY & RE-BIRTH

City's Slide
1957-1963

63

MANCHESTER UNITED 4
(Edwards, Berry, Viollet, Taylor)

MANCHESTER CITY 1
(Barnes)

DATE	31st August 1957
DIVISION	One
VENUE	Old Trafford
ATTENDANCE	63,103

Manchester United		Manchester City
Ray WOOD	1	Bert TRAUTMANN
Bill FOULKES	2	Bill LEIVERS
Roger BYRNE	3	Roy LITTLE
Eddie COLMAN	4	Ken BARNES
Jackie BLANCHFLOWER	5	Dave EWING
Duncan EDWARDS	6	Roy WARHURST
Johnny BERRY	7	Colin BARLOW
Billy WHELAN	8	Joe HAYES
Tommy TAYLOR	9	Bobby JOHNSTONE
Dennis VIOLLET	10	Bill McADAMS
David PEGG	11	Roy CLARKE

BACKGROUND

City hoped their only game played prior to the derby might prove a pointer towards a more successful season. The Blues had beaten Chelsea 3-2 at Stamford Bridge with goals from Hayes, McAdams and debutant Colin Barlow. Skipper Roy Paul had now left the Blues to manage Worcester City, and in his place, City purchased Roy Warhurst from Birmingham City.

United, after their near miss for the historic League and Cup 'double' the season before, had their sights set on going for all the prizes again. They had certainly made a most impressive start to the new season. Leicester City and Everton were both swept aside 3-0. Liam 'Billy' Whelan was now an established member of Busby's young side, and his cultured imaginative play added another facet to what was becoming a team blessed with a multiplicity of talents. He also displayed a keen eye for goal, scoring a hat-trick in that opening game at Leicester. The wealth and depth of talent Busby had now assembled was reflected in the keen competition for places that existed between players. One example of this was Jackie Blanchflower's selection at centre-half in preference to Mark Jones.

BEFORE THE GAME

	P	W	D	L	F	A	Pts
UNITED	2	2	0	0	6	0	4
CITY	1	1	0	0	3	2	2

Manchester United - pictured here at the end of the previous season in April 1957. This however was exactly the formidable line-up which turned out against City in August 1957 at Old Trafford. Back: Johnny Berry, Dennis Viollet, Ray Wood, Roger Byrne, Bill Foulkes, Duncan Edwards. Front: David Pegg, Billy Whelan, Tommy Taylor, Jackie Blanchflower, Eddie Colman.

MATCH VERDICT

United overwhelmed City with an awesome display of attacking football. The Blues were simply no match for a side that quite simply looked capable of winning just about anything or everything. Standing out, even above the general excellence that surrounded them, were two towering performances by talented pair Tommy Taylor and Duncan Edwards.

From the outset United's forward line, bolstered by Edwards and Colman at half-back, hemmed the Blues back in desperate defence. Edwards was now such a footballing colossus that his mere presence on the ball appeared to spread immediate anxiety in the opposition ranks. Significantly, it was the mighty Edwards who swopped passes with Whelan, advanced on the City goal, and with one swipe of the left boot put the Reds in front. Waves of United attacks forced the hard-pressed City defence to concede yet another corner, and from Pegg's accurate kick little Johnny Berry appeared from nowhere to head into the net. As City sought to gain some defensive respite by pushing forward, Colman intercepted the ball and his superlative forty yard pass beyond the City defence set Viollet racing free, and the United forward finished with aplomb. It was a fitting reward for Taylor, following a wonderful display at centre-forward, that he was on hand to stroke home the fourth goal when Trautmann parried Pegg's shot. Barnes' sweetly struck drive, from a cleverly worked free-kick proved meagre consolation on a day when United looked in-vincible. Scarcely could the Reds' faithful have imagined, as they cheered their heroes from the field, that for no less than nine members of Busby's gifted young side this would be their final derby appearance at Old Trafford.

"The Manchester Guardian" headlined their report 'LEAGUE CHAMPIONS AT THEIR BEST' and commented on a 'Feast of splendid attacking play':

"A huge crowd (63,103), a fine, still day for football, a pitch like velvet, five splendid goals - four to the United, one to the City - and an exhibition of football that tickled the palate and never palled from the first kick to the last - such was our portion at Old Trafford on Saturday.

There is no doubt that Manchester United's decision last season to enter the European Cup is beginning to pay dividends, regarding the competition as not merely a money-spinner, but as an educational medium of the highest value. Not since the Anderlecht massacre at Moss Side last autumn has a Manchester crowd been treated to such a feast of smooth, resourceful attacking play as was the case on Saturday. The four goals scored by Edwards, Berry, Viollet and Taylor in turn, and the gem scored by Barnes for the other side, were all perfect specimens of the art of goalscoring.

Not for months has Taylor seemed so confident, so masterful. His headwork and positional sense have never been in question, but he now seems to be paying more attention to footcraft, and the result should be devastating. In this game he played Ewing as skilfully and elusively as a mature player, and the City captain, good natured fellow that he is, left the field at the close smiling ruefully, a sadder and we imagine, a much slimmer man. Alongside Taylor, Viollet and Whelan flitted to and fro, pressing here, probing there, changing and interchanging positions with a certitude

that seemed to spring as much from intuition or from second sight as from ingrained knowledge of each others tricks. Out on the wings Berry and Pegg were both speedy, both waspish, and a sore trial to the City's hard working and resolute backs Little and Leivers. Without adequate support from their wing half-backs Edwards and Colman it is doubtful whether the United's forward line could have given City's defenders the hammering which they did. In the opinion of some judges, Edwards' performance was just about the best of his career. His goal against the City was a typical opportunist stroke, and followed a delightful piece of interplay with Whelan. It was soon followed by a second from Berry which had the crowd roaring. He thrust his head at a corner from Pegg exactly as a tortoise pokes its head from its shell and the result was a projectile akin to a violent shot.

Colman too had his moments, though he was not as uniformly successful as Edwards. For one thing, he has not his bulk and big assemblance, and on Saturday he was guilty of repeatedly being dispossessed by opponents creeping up from behind and nipping the ball off his toes. But if Colman had done nothing else - which is far from the truth - he earned his bonus with the pass which cut the City line in two and sped Viollet away on a 40-yard scoring errand. Taylor's final goal for United was lovingly and easefully stroked home after Pegg's violent shot had almost severed Trautmann's hands at the wrists, during that late period when United seemed to be toying with what was obviously a leg-weary and disconsolate opposition.

Yet, if any outraged City supporter grips you by the coat lapels and swears that if City's so-and-so forwards hadn't been a set of peg-legs they could have drawn the match or possibly won it, don't spurn him as a lunatic. The plain facts are that in the sixteenth minute McAdams gave Clarke a scoring chance on a plate. Result? A wild whizz-bang into the crowd. In the twenty-first minute Edwards faltered momentarily and in a fit of abstraction, rolled a back-pass to Clarke instead of to Wood. Result? A flurry of arms and legs in front of United's goal until McAdams eased the tension by aiming a shot at the half-time scoreboard. Barnes' beautiful goal followed from a slyly taken free-kick and then two dogged efforts by Hayes.

The last opening fell to Barlow, but his preference for violence as against placing sent another opportunity to the scrap heap. It was a sad day for the City as a whole, and a positive torture for their defenders. Leivers, Little, Barnes, Ewing and Warhurst fought gamely enough, but gameness was not enough.

Two lost points. Are City becoming so obsessed with offside tactics and neglecting the important consideration of defending in depth? If so, Viollet's breakthrough should give them food for thought. And is Fagan of such low value these days that his shooting would not have been useful on Saturday? - assuming of course, that he is not injured".

Duncan Edwards - *a towering performance.*

Ken Barnes - *a gem of a goal as City were outclassed.*

Tommy Taylor - *so confident, so masterful.*

Roy Little - *fought gamely in the City defence.*

64

MANCHESTER CITY 2
(Hayes, Foulkes og)

MANCHESTER UNITED 2
(Viollet, Charlton)

DATE	28th December 1957
DIVISION	One
VENUE	Maine Road
ATTENDANCE	70,493

Manchester City		Manchester United
Bert TRAUTMANN	1	Harry GREGG
Bill LEIVERS	2	Bill FOULKES
Roy LITTLE	3	Roger BYRNE
Ken BARNES	4	Eddie COLMAN
Dave EWING	5	Mark JONES
Roy WARHURST	6	Duncan EDWARDS
Colin BARLOW	7	Kenny MORGANS
Alan KIRKMAN	8	Bobby CHARLTON
Bobby JOHNSTONE	9	Colin WEBSTER
Joe HAYES	10	Dennis VIOLLET
Paddy FAGAN	11	Albert SCANLON

Bert Trautmann - yet another fine display of goalkeeping in a derby match from City's brave, blond giant.

Colin Webster - A versatile and committed player for United despite never being a regular choice.

BACKGROUND

City's season continued in its own inimitable style, with the Blues always entertaining, but frustratingly unpredictable. Above all, they were simply conceding too many goals. Indeed, they were to end the campaign as the first team to score and concede 100 goals in a season. The game at West Bromwich Albion on 21st September encapsulated their problems. After an hour of the game City trailed 3-2 and were still in contention, yet a further 30 minutes saw Albion overwhelm the Blues 9-2 to register their record win of the century! Always an innovative tactician, McDowall unveiled during this period the revolutionary idea of playing with just four defenders at the back. It appeared to pay immediate dividends, as City's form improved and they progressed into the upper half of the division, and warmed up for the derby by beating Burnley 4-1 on Boxing Day.

Despite their excellent start to the season, United found opposition to their bid for a title hat-trick became tougher at every turn. Strong rivals Wolves won 3-1 at Molineux, and Portsmouth, Spurs and Chelsea all enjoyed the relatively unfamiliar feeling of beating United on their own ground. Busby showed he was quite prepared to make further changes, and yet more youngsters were drafted into the side. This put matters back on a more even keel and kept the club in contention for honours. Bobby Charlton, who had made his debut in October 1956, was now an established member of the line-up and was set to make the first of his record number of derby appearances for United. Albert Scanlon and Kenny Morgans on the wings were also to make their derby debuts. Harry Gregg had arrived from Doncaster for a record goalkeeper's fee of £23,000 to replace the injured Wood, and the Reds were also maintaining fine progress in the European Cup with a forthcoming quarter-final tie against Red Star Belgrade. Tragically, within weeks all these hopes would be dashed on an airfield runway near Munich.

BEFORE THE GAME

	P	W	D	L	F	A	Pts
UNITED	24	13	4	7	58	38	30
CITY	24	14	1	9	64	59	29

MATCH VERDICT

Goalkeeping played a key role in the outcome of this derby. Trautmann was at his peerless best to deny United's hungry young forward line, but Gregg suffered a less decisive afternoon and some of his antics had the Reds' supporters' hearts in their mouths. United opened in threatening style, and Trautmann twice thwarted Edwards and Scanlon in the first few minutes. He was though, powerless to stop United taking a 6th minute lead, as clever interplay between Colman and Webster created an opening for Viollet who made no mistake with his shot. City displayed great spirit by levelling almost straight from the kick-off. Johnstone's punt forward soared over a hesitant United defence and determined Joe Hayes got on the end of it to flick the ball past Gregg. After 20 minutes United re-gained the advantage when Charlton marked his derby debut with a goal. He collected a pass from Webster and, in what would soon be recognisable as typical fashion, struck a clean, powerful shot past Trautmann. With the Reds on top, only the City 'keeper's agility kept them in the game, but with 25 minutes remaining Trautmann's gallant efforts were rewarded as City snatched a dramatic equaliser. Barlow skated away from Byrne on the right flank, and his low cross into the area caught Gregg in no mans land. Foulkes charged in to clear his lines, but with a trio of City men also converging on the ball the defender only succeeded in guiding it into his own net.

AT THE SEASON'S END

CITY: Finished 5th on 49 points

UNITED: Finished 9th on 43 points
(F.A. Cup Finalists, losing 2-0 to Bolton W.)

Eddie Colman - an almost instinctive understanding with Duncan Edwards in the United team. Just 21-years-old he was one of the Reds' genuine jewels.

TRAUTMANN SHOWS GREGG A THING OR TWO

Honours even in Manchester duel

BY AN OLD INTERNATIONAL

Manchester C. 2, Manchester U. 2

Before a vast crowd estimated at 65,000, and in ideal weather for football, the long awaited tussle between those neighbours and close rivals, Manchester City and Manchester United, produced an entertaining contest in pleasantly contrasted styles and resulted in a 2-2 draw.

On the whole the result was a fair one for if Manchester United, at least for an hour, had a smoother, more precise, more engaging method, Manchester City certainly had the advantage in goalkeeping. Apart from one or two indiscretions in his disposal of the ball after making hurried saves, Trautmann was at his magnificent best, and showed such a mastery of the art of positioning as to make the impetuous Gregg at the other end seem in dire need of tutoring.

The timing of the goals in the first half and the general run of play kept the supporters of both camps in a constant teeter of excitement besides demonstrating the wealth of forward talent at Manchester United's disposal. Not many clubs in England could discard four international players as good as Berry, Taylor, Whelan, and Pegg and yet produce an alternative forward line able to dovetail and combine and press home attacks as smoothly and incisively as this one did. Twice within the first five minutes Trautmann's agility alone, expressed in the form of two graceful swallow dives, prevented Edwards and Scanlon from drawing first blood. And it was no surprise when, in the sixth minute, Viollet, the only survivor of a once glorious attack, responded perfectly to beautiful service from Colman and Webster and eluded Trautmann with a scoring shot which kissed the post as it passed through.

Counter-attack

What did surprise everyone was the speed and nature of City's counter-stroke. Almost from the restart Johnstone, lying deep, punted a long, high ball downfield with a carry well beyond United's defenders. Hayes went after it, gazing upwards, like a boy chasing a runaway kite, and as the ball touched the ground he managed to trap it and flick it sideways past Gregg, who was fielding somewhere near the penalty spot. Though Hayes stumbled heavily he quickly recovered and saw the ball bouncing slowly towards the goal. He straight away helped it in. That equaliser came as manna to the City supporters, not only as a reward for the enterprise of one of the game's best triers, Hayes, but also as an assurance that United were not going to settle the issue, as they threatened to do, too soon. Yet within eight minutes of Hayes's success and after Webster had wasted a model chance from Morgans, Charlton emphasised his team's ascendancy hereabouts by collecting a pass from Webster and scoring again.

The next half-hour until the interval ran strongly in United's favour. A strong defensive cordon consisting of Edwards, Byrne, Jones, and Foulkes lay well downfield and kept a watchful eye on City's four would-be goal poachers, thus leaving Colman with the whole of the midfield, as it seemed, as his personal preserve. There he shadowed Johnstone, intercepted passes meant for the little Scot, and then, with a twist of his chubby little body (a feint that rarely fails), wormed his way forward, and rolled all manner of seductive passes to Charlton, Viollet, and Webster.

During this period, too, Scanlon got the measure of Leivers and a stream of menacing centres from Scanlon's wing hurtled across the City goal. From two of these Morgans with greater determination in jutting forward his head, might have taken two valuable goals. But from Trautmann's point of view there was excitement enough, especially from the restless feet of Charlton—Rowley's true successor as a perfect kicker of the ball.

The most City had been able to offer in reply to United's delightful approach work had been some exquisite interplay by their attacking wing halves, Barnes and Warhurst, and one glorious shot by Fagan which narrowly missed the goal from which Gregg was again a notable absentee. And when after the interval United promptly took up the initiative again, with Colman preparing gleefully to administer the medicine as before and Charlton, Viollet, and Webster vying with each other as probes, resignation in the City camp became almost as plainly marked on the field as on the terraces. But in this match, which had given us a little of everything, we might have guessed that catastrophe was lurking somewhere in the wings merely waiting for the opportune moment at which to strike. In the sixty-fifth minute that moment arrived and it was against United that catastrophe struck.

Inadvertent equaliser

The shock and disruptive effect of Foulkes's inadvertent equalising goal for City will haunt him for the rest of his days. Small blame to Foulkes. He had seen Barlow break through on the right, show Byrne a clean pair of heels, and whip a fast, low centre past Gregg, who had left his goal with what seemed more haste than judgment. As Foulkes raced back, perhaps a little panicky, he was conscious of Fagan and Hayes closing in from the left and Kirkman hurrying up behind him, all intent on a rolling ball and a yawning goal in front of them. Foulkes had to act and act quickly. He did. But his attempt to hoist the ball into the crowd misfired. Instead it flew off his toe-end into the net.

The effect on City was extraordinary. While Trautmann continued to defend like a man possessed, Barnes and Warhurst put up a dogged fight in midfield, while Hayes and his fellow-poachers strove hard to prove that what was lacking in method could easily be made up in fire and enthusiasm. In fact, if Barlow had lobbed a twisting ball into another unguarded goal instead of into the crowd, City could have won a last-minute victory.

MANCHESTER CITY.—Trautmann; Leivers, Little; Barnes, Ewing, Warhurst; Barlow, Kirkman, Johnstone, Hayes, Fagan.

MANCHESTER UNITED.—Gregg, Foulkes, Byrne, Colman, Jones, Edwards; Morgans, Charlton, Webster, Viollet, Scanlon.

*City's **Bert Trautmann** pulls off another save closely watched by **Roy Warhurst** and United's **Dennis Viollet**.*

65

MANCHESTER CITY 1
(Hayes)

MANCHESTER UNITED 1
(Charlton pen)

DATE	27th September 1958
DIVISION	One
VENUE	Maine Road
ATTENDANCE	62,812

Manchester City		Manchester United
Bert TRAUTMANN	1	Harry GREGG
Bill LEIVERS	2	Bill FOULKES
Cliff SEAR	3	Ian GREAVES
Roy CHEETHAM	4	Freddie GOODWIN
Dave EWING	5	Ron COPE
Ken BARNES	6	Wilf McGUINNESS
Paddy FAGAN	7	Dennis VIOLLET
Colin BARLOW	8	Albert QUIXALL
George HANNAH	9	Colin WEBSTER
Joe HAYES	10	Bobby CHARLTON
Ray SAMBROOK	11	Albert SCANLON

Gregg saved this Taylorless United

*City's **Joe Hayes** gets in a shot on goal despite the close attentions of United full-back **Bill Foulkes**. The shot beat the advancing **Harry Gregg** but passed just wide of the goal.*

BACKGROUND

United were not expected to be in a position to challenge for honours following the shattering experiences suffered at Munich. On 6th February 1958 the aeroplane carrying the United players and officials home from a European tie in Belgrade crashed during attempted take-off at Munich.

The crash virtually obliterated the whole of the young 'Busby Babes' side which had looked destined to dominate English football for many years to come. The following players all died in the crash; Roger Byrne, Geoff Bent, Eddie Colman, Mark Jones, David Pegg, Tommy Taylor and Billy Whelan. Duncan Edwards, perhaps the key player of them all, died of his injuries 15 days later. Johnny Berry and Jackie Blanchflower survived, but never played again. Also killed in the disaster were; Walter Crickmer (Club Secretary and a former manager), and Trainers Tom Curry and Bert Whalley.

Also among the fatalities were a number of journalists, many of whom had regularly reported on derby matches: Alf Clarke, Don Davies, George Follows, Tom Jackson, Archie Ledbrooke, Henry Rose and Eric Thompson. City's great goalkeeper Frank Swift, working as a journalist was also killed, along with two crew members and two supporters. The City of Manchester and indeed the whole country, was devastated. Somehow United managed to fulfil their fixtures and carried forward on a wave of sympathy, even appeared in the previous season's FA Cup Final.

The United team selected for the opening League game of this new season at Chelsea - who were beaten 5-2 - was obviously very different from that which played in the last derby nine months earlier. The teamsheet read; Gregg, Foulkes (captain), Greaves, Goodwin, Cope, McGuinness, Dawson, Taylor, Viollet, Charlton and Scanlon.

Despite the enormous gaps created by the Munich tragedy, it was a reflection of the club's deep investment in youth that only Ernie Taylor had been bought, for £8,000 from Blackpool. Again watched by massive crowds, the Reds made a good start to the new season with the highlight to date a 6-1 thrashing of Blackburn Rovers, in front of 65,187 at Old Trafford on 6th September. But Matt Busby, whose indomitable spirit had helped him overcome the terrible physical and psychological blows of Munich, decided the team needed strengthening further and, shortly before the derby, broke the British transfer record by signing Sheffield Wednesday's 'golden boy' Albert Quixall for £45,000.

The Blues had also opened the new season in promising style, attracting healthy gates of around 40,000. They began with a 4-3 success at Burnley with Hayes and Johnstone sharing the goals. The opening victory, however, proved a false dawn and City failed to win again before the derby. Defeats became a more commonplace event and a 4-1 battering at Arsenal highlighted the team's short-comings. To bolster the side George Hannah, a skilful hardworking inside-forward, was signed from Lincoln City for £20,000.

Despite all the normal new season footballing activity, the return of the Manchester derby was still a poignant moment. There was of course the usual intense rivalry for much needed League points, but it was also a meeting between many friends who had offered help and comfort to their fellow citizens in the darkest hours of need.

BEFORE THE GAME

	P	W	D	L	F	A	Pts
UNITED	9	4	3	2	25	13	11
CITY	9	1	3	5	14	27	5

MATCH VERDICT

City were unlucky not to gather both points in this game. They looked the more fluid side and if Gregg had not saved Barnes' penalty ten minutes from time they would have got the win. Perhaps understandably, United looked somewhat disjointed and Quixall soon realised the pressures of being an expensive import, with both the crowd and journalists putting him under rather too much critical appraisal.

City were, however, up against it right from the outset, as with only three minutes gone 17-year-old Cheetham, playing his first game of the season, scythed Bobby Charlton's legs from under him inside the area. Charlton picked himself up and drove the penalty kick into the net. Five minutes later Sambrook found the United net and was convinced he had brought the Blues level but, mysteriously, the linesman called the referee back from the middle and the goal was ruled out. With Hannah prompting intelligently City remained on top and Gregg had to be very alert to keep them at bay. Eight minutes from half-time City finally broke through and equalised as Hayes atoned for earlier misses and drove the ball past Gregg. The second half was a closer affair of fewer chances, although Gregg made a couple of daring saves at the feet of the City forwards. Gregg then capped a wonderful performance by diving to his right to save Barnes' firmly struck penalty and so frustrate the City fans' hopes of derby victory.

Albert Quixall - United's British record £45,000 buy from Sheffield Wednesday shortly before the derby at Maine Road.

Bobby Charlton - successful from the penalty spot after being brought down by Roy Cheetham.

66

MANCHESTER UNITED 4
(Goodwin, Bradley 2, Scanlon)

MANCHESTER CITY 1
(Johnstone)

DATE		14th February 1959
DIVISION		One
VENUE		Old Trafford
ATTENDANCE		59,604

Manchester United		Manchester City
Harry GREGG	1	Bert TRAUTMANN
Ian GREAVES	2	Bill LEIVERS
Joe CAROLAN	3	Ken BRANAGAN
Freddie GOODWIN	4	Ken BARNES
Ron COPE	5	John McTAVISH
Wilf McGUINNESS	6	Ron PHOENIX
Warren BRADLEY	7	Ray SAMBROOK
Albert QUIXALL	8	Colin BARLOW
Dennis VIOLLET	9	Bobby JOHNSTONE
Bobby CHARLTON	10	Joe HAYES
Albert SCANLON	11	Dennis FIDLER

BACKGROUND

City, themselves in a period of transition, found League points hard to come by and continued to struggle in the lower reaches of the division. On a good day City looked capable of beating anybody as the 5-1 November thrashing of Chelsea and Tottenham testified. Unfortunately such form was not maintained, but a hard fought point gained at high flying Arsenal in the game before the derby put the Blues in better heart.

United appeared to lose form after the derby with only three points gained from eight matches. Warren Bradley, a school-teacher winger, made his debut in a 6-3 defeat at Bolton in November, replacing Kenny Morgans, and remained in the side up to the derby. Joe Carolan also made his debut at this time, keeping out Ian Greaves. United remained unbeaten in the ten games after the Bolton reverse and entered the derby as favourites.

BEFORE THE GAME

	P	W	D	L	F	A	Pts
UNITED	28	14	6	8	67	50	34
CITY	27	7	7	13	42	62	21

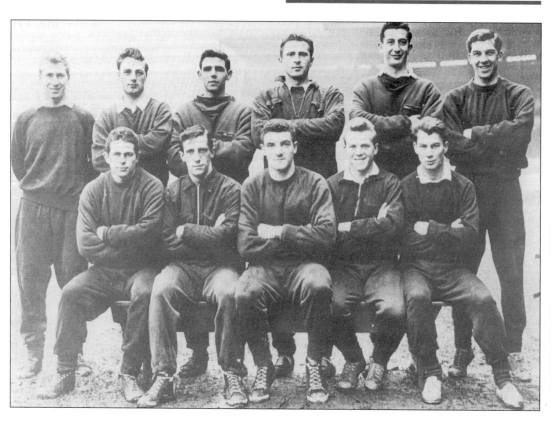

Manchester United in 1958-59. Despite the gaps created by the ravages of the Munich tragedy, the Reds still finished as League runners-up.
Back: *Bobby Charlton, Albert Scanlon, Joe Carolan, Harry Gregg, Freddie Goodwin, Ron Cope.*
Front: *Wilf McGuinness, Dennis Viollet, Bill Foulkes, Albert Quixall, Kenny Morgans.*

MATCH VERDICT

United made it 21 out of a possible 22 League points from the last 11 games with this title boosting derby victory. Freddie Goodwin took the post match plaudits. The lanky United right-half had an excellent match and inspired United to a decisive victory, something which seemed most unlikely at half-time.

It was the relegation-threatened Blues who had the best of a competitive first half. City's more direct methods coupled with the enterprise and subtlety of their best player, Bobby Johnstone, were factors which at the time seemed certain to reward the Blues with at least a point. It was Johnstone who gave the Blues a tenth minute lead when his snap shot beat Gregg. Branagan, Phoenix and Barnes all caught the eye as United sweated in front of the 60,000 crowd to get back on level terms. Matt Busby's half-time talk seemed to lift the Reds and the early minutes of the second half saw the City goal under siege. The Blues wilted beneath the pressure and in a decisive 25 minute period conceded a calamitous four goals.

Goodwin, who had been prompting the forwards with some delightful passes, moved forward to take Viollet's pass and his carefully angled shot brought the Reds level. With the Blues barely able to re-assemble their lines United immediately returned to the attack and, following a goalmouth melee when the ball struck a post, Bradley was on hand to tap the re-bound into the net. With the City defence in visible disarray Albert Scanlon cut in from his wing and left Trautmann helpless with a scorching 20 yarder. Nine minutes later the rout was complete as Goodwin again caught the City defence napping with a long through-ball which allowed the unmarked Bradley to jink around Trautmann and net United's fourth.

AT THE SEASON'S END

UNITED: Finished 2nd on 55 points
(6 points behind Champions Wolves)

CITY: Finished 20th on 31 points
(Avoided relegation by 1 point)

Goodwin inspired United to great revival

Ken Branagan (right) - a solid first half display from the stalwart City full-back who was now approaching the end of his Maine Road career.

Freddie Goodwin (far right)- his passing was the inspiration behind United's fine derby recovery.

67

MANCHESTER CITY 3
(Hayes 2, Hannah)

MANCHESTER UNITED 0

DATE	19th September 1959
DIVISION	One
VENUE	Maine Road
ATTENDANCE	58,300

Manchester City		Manchester United
Bert TRAUTMANN	1	Harry GREGG
Bill LEIVERS	2	Bill FOULKES
Cliff SEAR	3	Joe CAROLAN
Roy CHEETHAM	4	Shay BRENNAN
John McTAVISH	5	Ron COPE
Ken BARNES	6	Wilf McGUINNESS
Colin BARLOW	7	Warren BRADLEY
George HANNAH	8	Albert QUIXALL
Bill McADAMS	9	Dennis VIOLLET
Joe HAYES	10	Bobby CHARLTON
Clive COLBRIDGE	11	Albert SCANLON

BACKGROUND

City fans were cheered by an opening day victory over Nottingham Forest, and nearly 40,000 crowded into Maine Road for the game clearly hoping for a better season than the last which had seen the Blues narrowly avoid the drop. The Club had made some modest investments to strengthen the playing staff. Winger Clive Colbridge cost £10,000 from Crewe while Andy Kerr arrived from Partick Thistle. Unfortunately City gained only two more victories by derby day and were once again struggling. A 2-1 home defeat by Luton Town prior to the derby did not augur well for the Blues. Bill McAdams though retained a good touch in front of goal and by the derby had hit six goals in six games.

United's were guilty of early season inconsistency, beaten at Old Trafford by Chelsea but later going to Stamford Bridge and beating the 'Pensioners' 6-3. Certainly the Reds had a potent forward line with Bradley, Charlton, Quixall and particularly Viollet among the goals. A heavy 5-1 defeat by Tottenham Hotspur seven days before the derby was however, something of a blow to morale and no doubt gave Matt Busby much to ponder upon.

BEFORE THE GAME

	P	W	D	L	F	A	Pts
UNITED	8	3	2	3	21	17	8
CITY	8	3	0	5	15	20	6

Bert Trautmann and *Ken Barnes* can't stop this shot from United's *Dennis Viollet*, but City's *Bill Leivers* cleared the ball off the line.

City 'keeper *Bert Trautmann* misses this corner from United's *Albert Scanlon*, but he recovered to save on the line.

MATCH VERDICT

In what was considered really something of a 'turn up' City surprised their fans and sunk the old enemy without trace. It was a compact team performance by the Blues; the defence was steady throughout, Barnes was immaculate at half-back and in Hayes and McAdams up front they had a pairing which worried the United defence all afternoon. Hayes, obviously stung after being 'dropped' in midweek, started the game like a man inspired and had the Maine Road faithful rubbing their eyes in disbelief as little Joe scored twice for the Blues inside eleven minutes.

Firstly, with the United defence slow to clear their lines following a City attack, a cross was pumped back into the penalty area where Hayes beat Foulkes to the loose ball and rifled it past Gregg. Shortly after, United's defence generously left Hayes free in acres of space and his shot defeated Gregg's attempts to save. Stunned, United tried to climb back into the game but their moves were devoid of any real penetration. United's usually threatening wing-men, Bradley and Scanlon, were snuffed out by Leivers and Sear. When Viollet, who was kept significantly quiet by McTavish, finally shook off his marker to beat the diving Trautmann, Leivers popped up to clear off the line.

City maintained control and scored a third goal 20 minutes from time. Hayes, enjoying a field day, was again left unmarked and this time advanced on Gregg before squaring to the impressive Hannah who slotted the ball past the 'keeper and into the net.

*Not even a full length dive by United goalkeeper **Harry Gregg** (pictured above) can prevent a drive by **Joe Hayes** putting City 2-0 up after 11 minutes.*

*United's **Joe Carolan** and City's **Colin Barlow** challenge for the ball.*

*Despite a last ditch tackle from United's **Bill Foulkes**, City's **Joe Hayes** fires the Blues into an 8th minute lead. The other United players are **Ron Cope** (left) and **Wilf McGuinness** (right).*

68

MANCHESTER UNITED 0
MANCHESTER CITY 0

DATE	6th February 1960
DIVISION	One
VENUE	Old Trafford
ATTENDANCE	59,450

Manchester United		Manchester City
Harry GREGG	1	Bert TRAUTMANN
Bill FOULKES	2	Ken BRANAGAN
Joe CAROLAN	3	Cliff SEAR
Maurice SETTERS	4	Ken BARNES
Ron COPE	5	John McTAVISH
Shay BRENNAN	6	Alan OAKES
Warren BRADLEY	7	Ray SAMBROOK
Albert QUIXALL	8	George HANNAH
Dennis VIOLLET	9	Bill McADAMS
Bobby CHARLTON	10	Joe HAYES
Albert SCANLON	11	Clive COLBRIDGE

BACKGROUND

United remained in the top half of the table but inconsistency hindered their chances of really challenging for honours. A good win such as the 5-1 away thrashing of Nottingham Forest was all too often followed by a bad defeat such as a 7-3 hammering at Newcastle and, generally speaking, the defence seemed to have a fallible look about it. Goalkeeping was one area of concern and duties were shared between young David Gaskell and Harry Gregg. In an attempt to stiffen the defence Busby signed the tough tackling young England wing-half, Maurice Setters, from West Bromwich Albion for £30,000, and the derby was to be only his third game for the Reds.

The September derby victory at Maine Road gave City the impetus for a good run of League form. Four more consecutive victories placed the Blues in a title-chasing position.

However, in all too familiar fashion City's 4-3 defeat at Burnley started a run of eight games without a victory, a run that plunged the club into the wrong half of the table. Around the new year City arrested the slide with 4-0 and 4-1 victories over Everton and Sheffield Wednesday respectively, but two defeats prior to the derby had once again dampened spirits. In the Sheffield game the 17-year-old Alan Oakes made his second appearance of the season, kept his place and was now set to record the first of his 24 derby appearances.

City's **Joe Hayes** holds off the challenge from United 'keeper **Harry Gregg** and defender **Maurice Setters,** but his shot went just wide.

United's **Dennis Viollet** heads narrowly over the bar watched by City's **Cliff Sear** (left) and **John McTavish.**

BEFORE THE GAME							
	P	W	D	L	F	A	Pts
UNITED	27	11	5	11	65	57	27
CITY	27	11	2	14	59	59	24

MATCH VERDICT

A drab goalless draw ushered in the new decade. United disappointed their large following with a performance that lacked any real class, whereas unpredictable City took what few honours were available through gritty hard work. In an undistinguished first half, an element of farce surrounded the nearest either side came to a goal.

Hannah, scheming intelligently, spotted a gaping hole in the United defence and centred into the middle where Cope, desperately back-peddling, headed the ball past the advancing Gregg and against his own post. New boy Maurice Setters showed an early appreciation of the intensity involved in these local contests, but the referee took exception his excesses and both he and Cope entered the notebook.

The game might have been won by either side in the second half, with Bradley and Hayes both guilty of bad misses, while Bobby Charlton had clearly left his shooting boots back in the dressing-room. His blast late in the game at a yawning goal, threatened to dismantle the half-time scoreboard and prompted much laughter in the crowd massed behind the net, and began an exit for the match buses long before the welcome final whistle.

AT THE SEASON'S END

UNITED: Finished 7th on 45 points

CITY: Finished 15th on 37 points

Manchester City 1959-60. **Back:** *Roy Cheetham, John McTavish, Cliff Sears, Bert Trautmann, Ken Barnes, Ken Branagan.* **Front:** *Colin Barlow, George Hannah, Bill McAdams, Joe Hayes, Paddy Fagan.*

Manchester United 1959-60. **Back:** *Brennan, Cope, Greaves, Goodwin, Gregg, Shiels, Foulkes, Carolan.* **Front:** *Bradley, McGuinness, Viollet, Quixall, Charlton, Scanlon.* **Inset:** *Setters.*

United's **Dennis Viollet** *attempts to escape the attentions of City goalkeeper* **Bert Trautmann** *and* **John McTavish** *while* **Ken Barnes** *watches anxiously in the background.*

69

MANCHESTER UNITED 5
(Dawson 3, Charlton 2)

MANCHESTER CITY 1
(Barlow)

DATE	31st December 1960	
DIVISION	One	
VENUE	Old Trafford	
ATTENDANCE	61,213	

Manchester United		Manchester City
Harry GREGG	1	Bert TRAUTMANN
Shay BRENNAN	2	Barrie BETTS
Noel CANTWELL	3	Cliff SEAR
Maurice SETTERS	4	Ken BARNES
Bill FOULKES	5	Jackie PLENDERLEITH
Jimmy NICHOLSON	6	David SHAWCROSS
Albert QUIXALL	7	Colin BARLOW
Nobby STILES	8	George HANNAH
Alex DAWSON	9	Gerry BAKER
Mark PEARSON	10	Denis LAW
Bobby CHARLTON	11	Joe HAYES

Alex Dawson - enjoying his best season for United, he became the first player to hit a derby hat-trick since Joe Spence in 1921.

BACKGROUND

City had broken the British transfer record the previous March to sign Denis Law for £55,000 from Huddersfield Town. Rated as one of the greatest young prospects in the country, this would be the first of Law's many derby matches. The quicksilver Scot soon showed the qualities that would ultimately make him a Manchester folk hero, and had roared into the new season with ten goals in the opening 19 games. The defence had been strengthened by the acquisition of Barrie Betts from Stockport County and Jackie Plenderleith from Hibernian. Betts, recently recovered from a career-threatening back injury, was appointed club captain. Spurred by Law's goals, the Blues made a very useful start to the new season, unbeaten in the opening six games. Indeed, the first derby of the season should have been at Maine Road on 29th August, when Law also scored, but the game was abandoned in heavy rain with the score level at 2-2. Unfortunately all this initial promise was followed by a dip in form and some disappointing results. In an attempt to add further to the club's goalscoring potential Gerry Baker (brother of Joe) was signed from St.Mirren and duly obliged twice in the 3-2 defeat of Fulham a week before the meeting with United.

United were not enjoying the best of campaigns. Regular changes in personnel were a reflection on a series of inconsistent performances. A particularly cruel blow came in November when talented winger Johnny Giles broke his leg at Birmingham. Eire International Noel Cantwell joined the club in November, signed from West Ham for £30,000. On their day the side looked full of goals as a 6-0 thrashing of Chelsea in the match leading up to the derby clearly showed. Alex Dawson, United's bullish centre-forward, had also fired the Blues a warning by scoring a hat-trick in that match.

BEFORE THE GAME						
	P	W	D	L	F	A	Pts
UNITED	23	9	4	10	45	44	22
CITY	22	8	4	10	43	49	20

Denis Law - City's record signing from Huddersfield Town the previous March was a golden prospect. This was his first derby match, and City's Ken Barnes is seen here welcoming him to Maine Road.

MATCH VERDICT

The old year was rung out with United's greatest ever aggregate derby victory. In front of another capacity crowd and in wet muddy conditions City's light-weight game was blown aside by the more direct Reds. It was a match where some reputations were enhanced but others tarnished. The brilliant Bert Trautmann who, in recent times had virtually single-handed kept the Blues in the First Division, had an afternoon to forget. Maurice Setters was acclaimed Man of the Match, both for the enthusiastic promptings of his forwards and blotting out of City's 'golden boy' Denis Law, who had an undistinguished game trying to 'do too much in too many places'.

The game set off at a cracking pace with three goals inside 20 minutes. Quixall's corner, a result of United's first attack, was headed across the area by Dawson to Charlton who sent a fierce left foot shot past the motionless but possibly unsighted Trautmann. City hit back with some neat combination play and Barnes was inches away with a shot that beat Gregg. Deservedly the Blues then equalised as Barnes' cleverly flighted free kick found Hayes whose fierce header was parried by Gregg, but Barlow, following-in, made no mistake. The City fans' cheers were however, short-lived as three minutes later, Quixall's centre was inexplicably missed by Trautmann and Dawson, positioned beyond the 'keeper, headed into an empty net. City battled back but goals either side of half-time saw the end of their hopes. Charlton's well-directed corner was met by a rampaging Dawson whose header rocketed into the net with Trautmann unable to move. Four minutes into the new half Charlton gathered a pass from Nicholson 18 yards out and fired in a low shot which Trautmann appeared to have covered, but to the Blues dismay the ball entered the net. Alex

Dawson, who had earlier scorned some easy chances, finally moved on to Pearson's clever pass and shot wide of Trautmann to become the first player to score a derby hat-trick since United's Joe Spence in 1921.

Noel Cantwell - United's experienced buy from West Ham United in November for £30,000.

Strictly speaking the game at Old Trafford was not the first derby match of the season. The teams had already met at Maine Road on 29th August but referee Arthur Ellis, seen here surrounded by players from both sides, abandoned the game because of torrential rain.

70

MANCHESTER CITY 1
(Wagstaffe)

MANCHESTER UNITED 3
(Dawson, Charlton, Pearson)

DATE	4th March 1961
DIVISION	One
VENUE	Maine Road
ATTENDANCE	50,479

Manchester City		Manchester United
Steve FLEET	1	Harry GREGG
Bill LEIVERS	2	Shay BRENNAN
Barrie BETTS	3	Noel CANTWELL
David SHAWCROSS	4	Maurice SETTERS
Jackie PLENDERLEITH	5	Bill FOULKES
Alan OAKES	6	Nobby STILES
Clive COLBRIDGE	7	Ian MOIR
George HANNAH	8	Albert QUIXALL
Colin BARLOW	9	Alex DAWSON
Denis LAW	10	Mark PEARSON
David WAGSTAFFE	11	Bobby CHARLTON

BACKGROUND

Despite their convincing derby victory at the turn of the year, United were not enjoying a good season. Inconsistency continued to dog them in the League; high flying Tottenham Hotspur were beaten 2-0 but the Reds were thrashed 6-0 by Leicester City. The Cup had seemed a possible salvation as they battled through to a Fourth round tie with Sheffield Wednesday in February. However, in the replay at Old Trafford United received one of their heaviest ever defeats, subsiding 7-2. It was a morale-sapping defeat and still keenly felt a month later.

City's fortunes in the F.A.Cup had also made national headlines between derbies. In their Fourth round tie at Luton, City came back from two goals down to lead 6-2 after 69 minutes with Denis Law scoring all their goals. Cruelly at this juncture the referee abandoned the match due to the appalling weather conditions and ironically, City lost the replay 3-1. There was little compensation in the club's League form either, with a meagre four points from the past six matches.

BEFORE THE GAME							
	P	W	D	L	F	A	Pts
UNITED	30	12	5	13	59	58	29
CITY	28	9	6	13	57	66	24

Jackie Plenderleith - the City man was outsmarted by Bobby Charlton for United's second goal.

Colin Barlow - *involved in the build-up to City's goal.*

DAVID WAGSTAFFE

MATCH VERDICT

It was another derby packed with incident as United did the double over their neighbours from Moss Side. In a controversial match which contained rather more passion than class, the League's top referee Arthur Ellis had his hands full and made a number of decisions which enraged the crowd. City started the better side with some skilful football that pinned the Reds back on the defensive. On 18 minutes the game exploded as United took a debatable lead.

Barrie Betts - hit the crossbar with a penalty that should have put City back in the game.

Maurice Setters - United's powerful, hard-tackling wing-half of the early 1960's.

As the Reds attacked down the right the ball was hoisted into the middle where Dawson, Plenderleith and Fleet all went up and challenged for it. The United centre-forward appeared to punch the ball into the net, but much to the chagrin of both the City players and fans, Mr. Ellis allowed the goal to stand. Three minutes later the United players were equally incensed as the referee appeared to compensate and awarded the Blues a penalty after Colbridge went down under Pearson's innocuous challenge. However, the City fans' cheers were soon drowned out as Betts drove the resulting kick against the crossbar and, just eight minutes later, United went into a 2-0 lead. Charlton, moving in-field, held off two City defenders and hooked the ball over Plenderleith's head before shooting firmly past Fleet who was making his one and only derby appearance during a ten year City career as Trautmann's understudy. It was the goal of the match.

City looked rather dejected, and moved Law to a central striking role at the start of the second half but it seemed to make little difference. However, on the hour, David Wagstaffe, City's best forward, put the Blues back into the game. Leivers' clearance found Barlow on the right wing and following a one-two with Hannah, the little winger's cross to the far post was converted by Wagstaffe. But it was United who retained control and five minutes later Dawson's persistence created a chance for Pearson who scored easily.

AT THE SEASON'S END

UNITED: Finished 7th on 45 points

CITY: Finished 13th on 37 points

71

MANCHESTER UNITED 3
(Stiles, Viollet, Ewing og)

MANCHESTER CITY 2
(Stiles og, Kennedy)

DATE	23rd September 1961
DIVISION	One
VENUE	Old Trafford
ATTENDANCE	55,933

Manchester United		Manchester City
Harry GREGG	1	Bert TRAUTMANN
Shay BRENNAN	2	Barrie BETTS
Tony DUNNE	3	Cliff SEAR
Nobby STILES	4	Bobby KENNEDY
Bill FOULKES	5	Dave EWING
Maurice SETTERS	6	Alan OAKES
Albert QUIXALL	7	Ray SAMBROOK
Dennis VIOLLET	8	Peter DOBING
David HERD	9	Gerry BAKER
Mark PEARSON	10	Joe HAYES
Bobby CHARLTON	11	David WAGSTAFFE

BACKGROUND

David Herd, son of the former City favourite Alec Herd, joined United in the close season for £40,000 from Arsenal. Top scorer for the Gunners in every season between 1958 and 1961, he looked to be another astute purchase by Busby. Nobby Stiles had now established a first team berth for himself and, at this stage in his career, was very much an attacking wing-half with an eye for goal. With only one defeat at Chelsea, the Reds entered the derby in great heart.

Disappointed by City's struggles to stay in the First Division, Denis Law had left in July to join Italian Club Torino for a massive fee of £125,000. The Blues had made a handsome profit on the talented young forward, but needed to spend some of the available cash to reinforce the side. The elegant Peter Dobing came from Blackburn and the powerful Bobby Kennedy signed from Kilmarnock. The disappointments of the last few seasons had started to affect the Blues attendances, with the 1961 average dipping below 30,000 for the first time since the 1930's. However, the Blues made a rip-roaring start to the new season and by the beginning of September were top of the League following four straight wins. It was not to last though, and three defeats in the next five games deflated a lot of the early optimism in the camp.

Cliff Sear - City's stylish left-back was a regular during the early 1960's.

*United forward **Dennis Viollet** follows up his delicate lob over **Bert Trautmann** and despite a desperate chase back, City skipper **Barrie Betts** can do nothing to prevent the Reds taking a 2-0 lead.*

BEFORE THE GAME							
	P	W	D	L	F	A	Pts
UNITED	8	5	2	1	17	10	12
CITY	9	6	0	3	19	17	12

MATCH VERDICT

The 71st derby was another match full of incident and excitement but little of this was the direct result of any great skill displayed on either side. It was much more due to the bouts of nerves and anxiety that seemed to grip a number of players on the day. United started well enough and, roared on by the enthusiastic crowd, quickly took a commanding two goal lead. Stiles in particular caught the eye on the United left with some timely tackles and imaginative distribution to his forwards. Indeed, it was Stiles who opened the scoring. Moving up in support of his forwards, the little man received a pass from Quixall and beat Trautmann with an excellent shot from an acute angle. Ten minutes later, with the City defence under yet more pressure, Ewing's back-header only succeeded in presenting Viollet with the ball and his clever lob put the Reds two goals up. The match was played at a hectic pace with mistakes, tough challenges and angry gestures littering the action. Indeed, it was just such a scenario which brought City's first goal. A clever passing move down the left between Dobing and Baker threatened danger but as Stiles scuttled across to intercept, his hasty attempted clearance sliced past a bewildered Gregg into the net. The City fans then roared their approval as Bobby Kennedy scored a dramatic equaliser shortly before half-time. Collecting the ball some 30 yards out, he looked up, took precise aim and thundered a shot past Gregg into the roof of the net. However, the catalogue of errors continued and the next slip five minutes after the interval proved decisive. Viollet's speculative shot was harmless enough until Ewing, attempting to head clear, only succeeded in angling the ball into his own net.

STILES SETS MANCHESTER UNITED A FINE EXAMPLE

City recover but lose in the end

By Harold Mather

Manchester U. 3, Manchester C. 2

Sporting encounters between neighbouring clubs invariably are keenly looked forward to by the supporters of both of the teams concerned. Unfortunately when they come to pass they often fizzle out like a damp squib. Manchester United's home Football League match with their neighbours from Moss Side, who eventually were beaten 3-2, was not quite as bad as that —but nevertheless it lacked much in the matter of skill.

Indeed, skilful though most of the players obviously are individually, it was as if they were overawed with the thought that this match might be considered by many to be one for the championship of the city. The result was that teamwork, planned moves, and the ability quickly to improvise if something went wrong frequently were lacking. Not surprisingly, as a consequence, three of the five goals scored came as the outcome of mistakes rather than of good football and, though certainly not without its excitement, the match proved of little worth as a guide towards the future prospects of either side.

Stumbling block

The United deserved their victory, for in spite of being handicapped first by an injury to Herd then later by one to Setters they always looked just the better equipped at half back and forward. Indeed, in Stiles United had a wing half who not only proved a stumbling block to many of City's raids on the left but was adept in feeding his forwards with through passes into carefully selected open spaces. Regrettably for his side, such passes, like similar ones made at times by Setters and Foulkes, rarely were put to the best advantage, for the roamings of Charlton and Quixall seemed to hinder rather than help towards good teamwork when on attack.

City, whose defence often was too square and therefore prone to the quick attack mounted from through passes, did remarkably well considering that they were two goals down after only 14 minutes. Their recovery owed much to Sambrook and Dobing, whose combined thrust often was too much for Dunne, and to Kennedy who not only scored a fine goal but was the cause of many United attacks petering out. Both goalkeepers improved after uncertain starts, and Baker ferreted hard and often successfully as City's centre forward though even he possibly still it wondering how he managed to miskick and so lose the chance of equalising after Gregg could only parry a shot from Dobing in the game's last minute.

United took the lead soon after the start when, from a fine pass by Quixall, Stiles beat Trautmann with a strong shot from an acute angle. This, of course, got United all on the right foot and for a time City must have been aware of it as attack after attack was mounted against them. However it was a mistake by Ewing which led to United's second goal, for in making a back header he succeeded only in giving Viollet the chance to lob the ball past Trautmann.

Missed bouncing ball

Far from this proving to be the point from which United took command, City suddenly hit back hard—and again the goal came from a mistake. This time Stiles, trying to clear from a good, combined attack by Dobing and Baker, turned the ball past the helpless Gregg. Soon afterwards Ewing missed a high bouncing ball and almost let in Viollet and, at the other end Gregg, unsighted, did well to save a good shot from Dobing. Hereabouts a heavy drizzle which persisted until well after half time, in and tended to make the ball difficult to control. But Kennedy had no trouble in controlling when, from all of 35 yards out on City's right, he beat Gregg with a brilliant drive.

So, all still was to play for after the interval. All, that is, until, after five minutes, the luckless Ewing, down on his knees, saw the ball speed past his own goalkeeper off his head as he attempted to clear a shot by Viollet. So United led 3-2; they maintained this lead to the end, but most of the play is best forgotten. It contained little skill and too much of frayed tempers.

MANCHESTER UNITED.—Gregg, Brennan, Dunne, Stiles, Foulkes, Setters, cont. Quixall, Viollet, Herd, Pearson, Charlton.

MANCHESTER CITY.—Trautmann, Betts, sub. Sear, Kennedy, Ewing, Oakes, Sambrook, Dobing, Baker, Hayes, Wagstaffe.

Referee: A. W. Luty (London).

Nobby Stiles - United's bristling wing-half scored at both ends in the Reds 3-2 success.

BOB KENNEDY

United star Bobby Charlton in action during the Reds 3-2 win over City at Old Trafford in September 1961

S. COWAN

FOOTBALL - R. DONNELLY. MANCHESTER CITY

CARRERAS CIGARETTES

E. HINE
MANCHESTER U. (2ND DIV.)

WILLS'S CIGARETTES

G. MUTCH (MANCHESTER UNITED)

There have been various series of cards down the years featuring players from both Manchester United and Manchester City.

OGDEN'S CIGARETTES.

C. PRINGLE,
MANCHESTER CITY.

FOOTBALL - W. PORTER, MANCHESTER UNITED

FOOTBALL - MANCHESTER CITY PLAYERS

S. TILSON

A former Welsh miner Roy Paul was a tough-tackling wing-half with Manchester City during the 1950's and captained the Blues to victory in the 1956 FA Cup Final. He played in a total of 13 League and Cup derby matches against the Reds.

A stylish attacking left-back, Roger Byrne followed in the great tradition of Manchester United captain's. An England international he succeeded Johnny Carey as skipper and led the magnificent 'Busby Babes' team to consecutive League titles in 1956 and 1957, as well as an FA Cup Final. He played in 15 League and Cup derby matches, but was tragically one of those who perished in the Munich crash.

ROGER BYRNE
Manchester United
and England

City star Don Revie was Footballer of the Year in 1955 and was the inspiration behind the famous 'Revie Plan' tactics employed by the Blues during their successful period in the mid-fifties. City reached successive F.A. Cup finals in 1955 and 1956 largely based on Revie's role as a deep lying centre-forward, and on the second occasion lifted the trophy, beating Birmingham City 3-1.

The extrovert Albert Quixall joined Manchester United from Sheffield Wednesday for a record British fee of £45,000 in the wake of the Munich disaster. He took time to settle, but eventually linked well with Bobby Charlton and Dennis Viollet. He won an FA Cup medal in 1963 and played in eight derby matches against the 'old enemy'.

A fan's eye view of Maine Road before the start of the derby on 30th September 1967 in front of a crowd of nearly 63,000.

Manchester City's all conquering team of the late 1960's: Back: George Heslop, Alan Oakes, Mike Doyle, Ken Mulhearn, Tommy Booth, Harry Dowd, Stan Bowles, Arthur Mann, Glyn Pardoe, Tony Coleman. Front: Dave Connor, Bobby Owen, Colin Bell, Tony Book (Capt.), Francis Lee, Mike Summerbee, Neil Young.

Arguably United's greatest ever player, George Best swerves away from City full-back Glyn Pardoe during the Reds 2-1 win at Maine Road on 30/9/67.

A pause in the derby action during the same match gives City's Mike Summerbee the opportunity to exchange a few words with United's Pat Crerand and Tony Dunne.

City's marvellously talented midfielder Colin Bell turns on the power in an effort to break away from the terrier-like attentions of United's gritty little England international Nobby Stiles.

United's David Sadler stretches out a boot to deny City star Mike Summerbee.

United's George Best shows City defender Glyn Pardoe a clean pair of heels down the right flank.

Colin Bell of Manchester City and England was a supreme athlete who moved with enormous grace and ease and yet possessed the tremendous stamina of a long-distance runner. Coupled with his terrific skills, constant enthusiasm for the game and the keenest of eye's for goal, he was undoubtedly a thoroughbred, and stands as one of the most influential players of his era during the late 1960's and early 1970's.

George Best of Manchester United and Northern Ireland was one of the greatest players the game has ever produced. "If ever there was a football genius, Best was that player" said Sir Matt Busby who persuaded the teenager his future lay at Old Trafford. "He had more ways of beating an opponent than any other player I have seen. The number of his gifts was unique and he made people gasp and

The man who scored the winner at Old Trafford in that match was Mike Summerbee, a key performer in City's string of successes during the late 1960's and early 1970's.

Colin Bell jinks away from a tackle by United full-back Shay Brennan and the defensive attentions of Bill Foulkes as City attack during their 1-0 win at Old Trafford on 8th March 1969

The meeting at Maine Road on 6th November 1971 was one of the most thrilling derbies on record, finishing 3-3 after [...]-2 early in the second half. Here City's Francis Lee - a master at winning penalties as well as netting them - crashes his [...] nto the net past Alex Stepney to pull the score back to 1-2.

City arms are raised in jubilation as Mike Summerbee (No.7 left) wheels away after hitting a last minute equaliser in the [...] Maine Road in November 1971.

United break up a City attack early in the second half after the Reds had taken a two goal lead in the Maine Road derby of November 1971. An exciting match finished 3-3.

City's Wyn Davies, signed from Newcastle at the start of the 1971-72 season gets up above United's Steve James during the November

Charlton tries a shot watched by Brian Kidd and City trio Willie Donachie, Rodney Marsh and Tony Book.

Charlton looks on pensively as United's Steve James passes the ball forward.

City's Denis Law is engulfed by distressed supporters as the crowd invade the Old Trafford pitch following his instinctively back-heeled goal after 82 minutes. Law's strike gave the Blues a 1-0 win and condemned his old club United to the Second Division. The match, played on 27th April 1974 was eventually abandoned, but the League ruled that the result should stand. Law commented afterwards: "I have seldom felt so depressed in my life. After 19 years of giving everything I had to score goals, I finally scored one which I almost wish I hadn't".

The front covers of the United and City programmes for season 1962-63 which saw both clubs struggling to avoid relegation. City won the September derby at Old Trafford 3-2 but in May drew 1-1 at Maine Road - a critical result which led to the Blues relegation days later.

72

MANCHESTER CITY 0
MANCHESTER UNITED 2
(Chisnall, Herd)

DATE	10th February 1962	
DIVISION	One	
VENUE	Maine Road	
ATTENDANCE	49,959	

Manchester City		Manchester United
Bert TRAUTMANN	1	David GASKELL
Bobby McDONALD	2	Shay BRENNAN
Cliff SEAR	3	Tony DUNNE
Roy CHEETHAM	4	Nobby STILES
Bill LEIVERS	5	Maurice SETTERS
Bobby KENNEDY	6	Jimmy NICHOLSON
Neil YOUNG	7	Phil CHISNALL
George HANNAH	8	Johnny GILES
Peter DOBING	9	David HERD
Joe HAYES	10	Nobby LAWTON
David WAGSTAFFE	11	Bobby CHARLTON

City's **Roy Cheetham.**

BACKGROUND

After a splendid table-topping start, the season had turned upside down for City, and on 13th January things hit rock bottom as a 6-3 defeat by Burnley dumped them at the foot of the table.

One crumb of comfort was that 17-year-old discovery Neil Young had now established a regular place on the wing where he showed pace and a very keen eye for goal. Peter Dobing was the Blues' top scorer with twelve goals prior to the derby, and his efforts, combined with Young's contributions, enabled the team to pick up some valuable points and climb the table. Morale was raised shortly before the derby with two excellent wins over Bolton Wanderers and Arsenal and the City fans had fingers crossed that United would make up the hat-trick.

United's season had also gradually soured. The September victory against City was in fact the last until the 9th December when Fulham were beaten 3-0, ending an unhappy run of ten League games without a win. Former derby hero Alex Dawson was allowed to leave the club during this period, joining Preston North End for £20,000.

In common with City, United enjoyed something of a recovery prior to the derby, winning four of their last seven games. David Gaskell, having replaced Gregg in goal during November, was now first choice, while 19-year-old Phil Chisnall was showing some degree of promise at inside-forward.

BEFORE THE GAME							
	P	W	D	L	F	A	Pts
UNITED	26	10	5	11	45	51	25
CITY	27	10	3	14	50	61	23

MATCH VERDICT

The match was a disappointing spectacle for the City fans as the Blues gave a dispirited performance in a one-sided derby. The Reds opened brightly and Johnny Giles caught the eye on the wing. Twice he cut in, and only the sharp reflexes of Trautmann thwarted his goal-bound shots. The popular German goalkeeper was once again in magnificent derby form and kept the Blues in the game with a string of daring saves. City's forwards by comparison looked both light-weight and in rather diffident mood. They were quite unable to worry a United defence dominated by Setters, and although Young and Wagstaffe looked lively enough at times on the City wings, all too often they endeavoured to take on one man too many. It was therefore scant surprise when United took the lead ten minutes from half-time. City's defensive marking was entirely absent as United built quickly on the right and, when the ball arrived in the middle, the unmarked Chisnall gave Trautmann no chance. The goal seemed to completely knock the stuffing out of the Blues and, most unusually for these contests, there was little evidence of a typically frenzied fight back. United dictated the pace and looked more than capable of winning the match much as they pleased. So it proved, as on 68 minutes David Herd wrapped it all up for the Reds. The City defence was yet again absent without leave as Herd galloped on to a through ball and as Trautmann advanced off his line, Herd rattled in the sort of thundering drive which became his trademark.

Johnny Giles - outstanding on the United left flank.

Bert Trautmann - *fine saves by the City 'keeper kept his team in the match*

AT THE SEASON'S END

CITY: Finished 12th on 41 points

UNITED: Finished 15th on 39 points

David Herd - galloped through to score with a powerful drive.

Manchester United's supremacy never in doubt

City's defence again woefully weak

BY ERIC TODD

Manchester C. 0, Manchester Utd. 2

There was no evidence of tribal warfare or ancient feud at Moss Side on Saturday when Manchester United defeated Manchester City 2-0. If United, accompanied by Mr Norman Evans, had dropped in for a cup of tea or a chat over the garden wall, the whole affair could not have been more neighbourly or more frightfully respectable.

This should not lead to the assumption that one advocates rough play or strong-arm tactics or, alternatively, that one resents the lack of them, but on occasions like this the rivals surely might at least look as though they hated the sight of each other. To be perfectly fair, however, one can report that Gaskell once found it necessary to protest to Mr Taylor, an admirable referee, incidentally, that some of the spectators were getting him—he had no such complaints about the City forwards—and near the end, Stiles was almost denuded in a minor and seemingly unintentional skirmish with Wagstaffe of all people. Otherwise everything was peaceful and formal "Derby" game? Nothing like one.

Giles effective

The absence of Foulkes because of injury caused considerable readjustments in United's team which lost some of its recent sweet flowing rhythm in consequence. Herd, restored to health, took things quietly for three quarters of the match, and Stiles while effective, appeared less happy than he has been in the forward line, but so long as Giles was scheming and raiding, United looked much the better side. Certainly there never was any likelihood of their losing and seldom any danger of their conceding as much as a goal. Dunne and Brennan again were in excellent form and with Foulkes back in the side, United will give Sheffield Wednesday plenty to think about in the FA Cup match at Old Trafford. The pity of it was City could not put them in the mood to tackle that sterner task.

But City themselves were in one of those dilatory, congested moods that are the despair of their most loyal supporters. The shortcomings in the inside forward and wing half positions are painful enough as it is, but the weaknesses are enhanced by the absence of liaison between the two departments. For too long City,

unlike United, have tried to get by on individual talent, and it will not do. Wagstaffe and Young, prolific in promise, are having to learn the hard way, and it was significant that when they did decide to pass the ball it was as often as not, to each other and nobody else. Leivers and Sear worked hard and of course there was Trautmann. Imagination is taxed to its limits to consider the depths to which City might have sunk in recent years if it had not been for their goalkeeper. Their severest critics say that City need new directors, a new manager, five new players, and a marksman. If they could find a captain like Paul half their worries would be over.

Two brilliant saves gave Giles and Charlton early notice that Trautmann was on the alert. Then Trautmann stopped another tremendous drive by Giles and although the ball slipped through his hands, it went wide of a post. Hayes rightly was applauded for holding back when Gaskell dived to save, but he, like Hannah, carried courtesy too far in subsequent attacks, and prospects of a goal to City remained doubtful. In the thirty-fourth minute Chisnall took advantage of some deplorable covering by the City defence, and United took the lead. Another remarkable save by Trautmann prevented Lawton increasing it in the very next minute. City's retaliation was negligible until a left foot shot by Hannah nearly crept past Gaskell a few minutes before half-time.

Leivers attacks

A few minutes after the restart, Dobing swung a boot casually at a perfect centre from Young, and deserved all he got—nothing. Much better looking was a shot by the same player, and Stiles did well to head the ball away at the risk of concussion or worse. City won a few corners and Leivers came up to add height and weight to the home assault—why City do not try and find a centre forward with those physical attributes is a mystery—but Setters always seemed to reach the ball before anyone else. United thus rode easily on their lead and in the sixty-eighth minute Herd raced away and scored their second goal. It was spectacular and well taken, but once again, one could ask, where was the City defence? Ah, where indeed!

MANCHESTER CITY—Trautmann; MacDonald, Sear; Cheetham, Leivers, Kennedy; Young, Hannah, Dobing, Hayes, Wagstaffe.

MANCHESTER UNITED—Gaskell; Brennan, Dunne; Stiles, Setters, Nicholson; Chisnall, Quixall, Herd, Lawton, Charlton.

Referee: J. K. Taylor (Wolverhampton).

73

MANCHESTER UNITED 2
(Law 2)

MANCHESTER CITY 3
(Dobing pen, Hayes, Harley)

DATE	15th September 1962	
DIVISION	One	
VENUE	Old Trafford	
ATTENDANCE	49,193	

Manchester United		Manchester City
David GASKELL	1	Bert TRAUTMANN
Shay BRENNAN	2	Barrie BETTS
Tony DUNNE	3	Cliff SEAR
Nobby STILES	4	Bobby KENNEDY
Bill FOULKES	5	Bill LEIVERS
Jimmy NICHOLSON	6	Graham CHADWICK
Johnny GILES	7	Neil YOUNG
Nobby LAWTON	8	Peter DOBING
David HERD	9	Alex HARLEY
Denis LAW	10	Joe HAYES
Noel CANTWELL	11	David WAGSTAFFE

Manchester City triumph with last-minute goal

Law leads an unavailing revival

BACKGROUND

City made the most traumatic possible start to the new season, annihilated 8-1 at Wolverhampton Wanderers. Within seven days the Blues plunged into the transfer market, securing forward Alex Harley from Third Lanark for £18,000. He quickly displayed a return on the investment by scoring both goals in City's first victory, a defeat of Ipswich Town on 5th September.

However, it was defensive reinforcements that appeared a much more pressing requirement as the Blues suffered several disappointing defeats culminating in a 6-1 home crushing by West Ham. That match witnessed the barely credible scene of the affable Bert Trautmann being ordered off after kicking the ball at the referee following the fifth goal.

Across at Old Trafford the man making all the headlines was ex-Blue Denis Law. Following a dispute with his Italian club Torino the Scottish International had been brought back to Manchester as a Red, with Matt Busby forking out the British record fee of £115,000. As with City, Law's United debut was marked by a goal but that proved his only strike prior to the derby, and United's form was still highly inconsistent. An impressive 3-1 victory at Arsenal for example was quickly followed by a 1-0 home defeat to Everton.

However, a recent 3-0 defeat of Bolton Wanderers showed the side's capabilities and the Reds entered the derby clear favourites.

BEFORE THE GAME

	P	W	D	L	F	A	Pts
UNITED	8	3	1	4	11	11	7
CITY	8	1	2	5	9	27	4

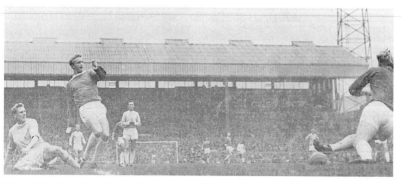

*Former Blue **Denis Law** holds off a challenge from City full-back **Cliff Sear** and fires a shot past **Bert Trautmann**, but on this occasion the ball also went wide of the goal. Law was on target twice in the match.*

MATCH VERDICT

Given that City had not managed to win at Old Trafford in the last seven attempts and had also made such an atrocious start to the season, a Blues victory was perhaps predictable! Tradition had shown how dear old City were often at their most dangerous when written off and in an exciting derby encounter it was the men from Old Trafford who left the field with red faces.

The Blues shocked the old enemy by racing into a two goal lead inside 25 minutes. The first seemed more than a touch fortuitous as Foulkes, challenged by Harley, appeared to handle the ball accidently as he fell to the ground. Referee Mr. Tirebuck interpreted things differently and pointed to the spot. Dobing blasted the penalty into the centre of the net with Gaskell diving away to his right. Six minutes later Hayes scored one of the very finest goals of his distinguished career. The Blues gained possession on the right wing and Harley's clever pass inside set Dobing racing clear. His high centre into the penalty area reached Hayes at shoulder height and the forward showed delightful skills as in one motion he caressed the ball down and swept an unerring shot past Gaskell.

Stung by the unlikely circumstances, United started the second period in dynamic fashion and the instigator of their spirited revival was none other than Denis Law. Just three minutes into the half his reaction to Cantwell's imaginative back-heel was faster than anybody else's and, in a flash, the ball was buried in the net. With the tempo increased, Law crashed a further shot against the bar only for City to race to the other end where Dobing also struck the woodwork. The Scot though was not to be denied and as Trautmann fumbled Giles' centre Law pounced and United were level. In an exciting finale there was miss and counter-miss until City won it with literally the last kick of the match. Kennedy's long ball out of defence bounced menacingly towards the United penalty area. Foulkes and Harley raced after it, but the City man arrived first and shot past Gaskell.

Jimmy Nicholson - versatile cover for the likes of Nobby Stiles and Maurice Setters, this was his third derby match for United.

Alex Harley - hit City's dramatic last minute winner.

74

MANCHESTER CITY 1
(Harley)

MANCHESTER UNITED 1
(Quixall pen)

DATE	15th May 1963	
DIVISION	One	
VENUE	Maine Road	
ATTENDANCE	52,424	

Manchester City		Manchester United
Harry DOWD	1	David GASKELL
Bobby KENNEDY	2	Tony DUNNE
Cliff SEAR	3	Noel CANTWELL
Alan OAKES	4	Pat CRERAND
Bill LEIVERS	5	Bill FOULKES
Matt GRAY	6	Nobby STILES
Neil YOUNG	7	Albert QUIXALL
Peter DOBING	8	Johnny GILES
Alex HARLEY	9	David HERD
Joe HAYES	10	Denis LAW
David WAGSTAFFE	11	Bobby CHARLTON

KEEPER THROWS AWAY POINT IN TOUGH DUEL

City's hopes are raised as early as the 9th minute as Alex Harley thumps a low shot beyond diving United 'keeper David Gaskell to put the Blues 1-0 ahead.

BACKGROUND

This was arguably the most important League derby to date in the long history of meetings between the two clubs. Following disastrous League seasons both teams were in grave danger of relegation and, with so few games left, the points at stake were absolutely vital. City, with only a difficult away trip at West Ham to come, needed both points to edge above the Reds in the table and leave their old rivals in the mire, while United, beaten five days earlier by fellow strugglers Birmingham, were also in dire straits. However, they did have a game in hand on the Blues (away at Nottingham Forest), and, with already-relegated Leyton Orient due to visit Old Trafford for the final home fixture, looked to have the easier finish, but with current form having little bearing in tense matches like these, nothing could be taken for granted.

Indeed, United were in serious danger of suffering the novel experience of appearing in the F.A. Cup Final and being relegated in the same season, as City had done in 1926. The Reds had already won through to Wembley and were due to play Leicester City in ten days time.

The 1962-63 winter was the worst since 1947 and the big freeze had caused a massive backlog of fixtures. During this period the Reds' League form never matched their Cup exploits and a meagre eight points were collected from 15 games, plummeting the Club down the table, and engineering this relegation cliff-hanger at Maine Road. In personnel terms United had purchased the classy, if fiery, Pat Crerand from Celtic in February in an effort to arrest the slide and he was due to make his derby debut.

Relegation had long looked a certainty for the unhappy Blues. Amid the many postponements because of bad weather City did however, remain unbeaten - albeit for only three matches - from December through to March. In recent years City had become experts at escaping the big drop, and many fans placed their faith in yet another Houdini act. However, the fixture backlog piled

JOY: Quixall saves United *GLOOM: City relegation blow*

Dowd penalty tragedy

on the agony and as defeat became common-place once again, the situation looked extremely grim. Alex Harley's Third Lanark colleague, Matt Gray, was signed in March and Harry Dowd, now the club's first choice goalkeeper, had replaced the legendary Bert Trautmann.

The Blues' hopes were raised four days before the derby, as Harley's goal defeated high-flying Spurs. The City faithful wondered if salvation might be at hand as derby victory here could leave the 'other lot' staring down into the Second Division.

Manchester United 1962-63. **Back:** *Setters, Nicholson, Gaskell, Brennan, Pearson, Cantwell.* **Middle:** *Foulkes, McMillan, Dunne, Stiles, Lawton.* **Front:** *Giles, Quixall, Herd, Law, Charlton.*

MATCH VERDICT

It was an understandably ill-tempered but dramatic derby of destiny which left the Blues claiming they were robbed of a crucial victory. Certainly amid all the tension the Blues were the better side, creating far more chances and showing the better combination, but Fate served up a cruel finale to one of their best performances of the season.

The gates were locked well before the kick-off with thousands still outside. City were quickly into their stride, playing confident purposeful football, and with United barely settled raced into a ninth minute lead. Following a slip by Charlton in the City half, the ball was swept out to Hayes who quickly fed Dobing and his sweet through-ball put Harley in the clear. The Scot admirably kept his cool and rifled a right foot shot beyond Gaskell into the corner of the net. United, edgy and apparently completely unable to put any telling moves together, were indebted to several good saves by Gaskell and some timely interceptions from Stiles which kept the deficit to a single goal. Both though were powerless on the half hour, as the home crowd roared in appreciation when Harley's splendid drive seemed to have given the Blues a vital second goal. But the crowd's joy turned to dismay as the referee disallowed the 'goal' on a hair's breadth off-side decision. Tempers that had bubbled throughout the half reached boiling point shortly before the break when Crerand and Wagstaffe were both booked following an ugly confrontation.

It was to emerge later in the Press that the affray did not end there and as the players had left the field for half time, it was reported Wagstaffe had been 'laid out' in the tunnel by an unnamed United man!

The players displayed rather more restraint in the second half but the Blues remained well on top. Man of the Match Alex Harley was again desperately close to the vital second goal as his header from Young's centre was hustled clear. As the minutes ticked away United seemed to have little idea of how to extricate themselves from such a worrying predicament, yet, with only four minutes remaining, utter disaster befell the Blues. Wagstaffe, 30 yards from his own goal, inexplicably attempted a suicidal backpass. Denis Law, innocuous all evening, suddenly saw his chance and closed in on Dowd to tussle for the ball. As Dowd dived at the forward's feet, Law fell and the ball ran out of play. To the goalkeeper's horror the referee pointed to the spot. Albert Quixall stepped up and, with many United players looking the other way, calmly slotted the penalty past Dowd.

Law commented afterwards: "It was a penalty; the goalkeeper had hold of my legs - but I would never have scored! I was going away from the goal and had lost the ball. It was a lucky break for us". Dowd counter-claimed: "It was never a penalty; I scooped the ball away from Denis' feet and sent it out of play. I can't remember holding his feet but I did get a kick on the head. I may then have caught hold of him, but the ball was out of play by then, and I'm sure the linesman was signalling for a corner." No matter, the incident entered the annals of Manchester football history as one of the most controversial and decisive derby match moments.

Alan Oakes - maturing rapidly in the City side following the introduction of Matt Gray.

*A Daily Mail cartoonist's view of the great Sixties tug-o'-war for the League title between United manager **Matt Busby** and City boss **Joe Mercer**.*

*It was a starkly contrasting end to the 1962/63 season for United and City. Here former Blue **Denis Law** celebrates the Reds' 1963 F.A. Cup win over Leicester City, with colleagues **David Herd** (left) and **Maurice Setters**. Days earlier Law had virtually condemned City to relegation when he won United - who were also in danger of the drop - a penalty minutes from the end of a tense drawn derby at Maine Road. Eleven years later his goal for City at Old Trafford would in turn push United into Division Two.*

THE SIXTIES

Manchester: Football Capital 1966-1971

75

MANCHESTER UNITED 1
(Law)

MANCHESTER CITY 0

DATE		17th September 1966
DIVISION		One
VENUE		Old Trafford
ATTENDANCE		62,085

Manchester United		Manchester City
Alex STEPNEY	1	Harry DOWD
Shay BRENNAN	2	Tony BOOK
Tony DUNNE	3	Bobby KENNEDY *
Pat CRERAND	4	Stan HORNE
Bill FOULKES	5	George HESLOP
Nobby STILES	6	Alan OAKES
George BEST	7	Dave CONNOR
Denis LAW	8	Colin BELL
David SADLER	9	Mike SUMMERBEE
Bobby CHARLTON	10	Glyn PARDOE
John ASTON	11	Neil YOUNG
Noel CANTWELL	12	Mike DOYLE (3)

VOLUME XXVIII No. 4   17th September, 1966

MATT BUSBY TALKING

If I say that my personal disappointment in our own failure to carry off an honour last season was tempered by Manchester City's success in achieving promotion, I hope I will not be misunderstood!

For, having played for City for some years between the wars, I have always had considerable affection for the Maine Road club with whom I won one of my most prized possessions—an F.A. Cup winners' medal in 1934.

In addition, of course, the winning of the Second Division Championship gave this great city not one but two First Division teams. It also stirred up considerable interest among football fans at a time when "gates" were falling in so many soccer centres.

And, naturally, promotion sees the resumption of these twice-a-season "derby" games, matches which in themselves capture the imagination of all football fans in the city.

In welcoming the City Directors, Officials, Players and their Supporters to Old Trafford this afternoon, I would also like to take this opportunity of, firstly, congratulating them on their return to the top sphere and, secondly, of wishing them well in the months ahead.

On a personal level once again, it will be very gratifying to greet their manager, Joe Mercer, a friend of many years standing, on his first visit here as City's manager.

Mr. Mercer did much last season to revive City's playing fortunes and I have little doubt his enthusiasm and ability will stand them in good stead in the future.

Now on with the game. I hope the supporters of both clubs will give their particular favourites a big welcome and the right kind of vocal encouragement in a game which, I feel sure, will prove most entertaining to spectators and players alike.

BACKGROUND

England had just won the 1966 World Cup helped in no little way by United's Bobby Charlton and Nobby Stiles. The Beatles were leading the World through the Swinging Sixties and City had rejoined United in the First Division to begin a glorious period when Manchester football would dominate both the English and European scene.

After three years in the Division Two doldrums City had been rejuvenated by the new management regime of Joe Mercer and Malcolm Allison. Long-serving manager Les McDowall had left and team changes since the disastrous 1963 relegation season had been widespread resulting in the club winning promotion in the duo's first season in charge. Dowd, Pardoe, Young and Oakes were now regulars in the team, and had been joined by a host of astute signings; George Heslop came from Everton for £25,000, Mike Summerbee from Swindon for £35,000 and, later in the promotion season, Colin Bell from Bury for £45,000. The only summer signing in 1966 was to prove simply inspirational as 30-year-old Tony Book came from Plymouth for £17,000. With the vastly experienced Johnny Crossan as team captain the Blues made a promising start to the new campaign back in the top flight. Following an opening day draw at Southampton, City delighted their fans by defeating reigning Champions Liverpool 2-1 in the first home game. Victory over Sunderland the following weekend had the Blues up with the early season leaders, but three defeats and a draw followed, leaving the Blues in less confident mood to take on their old foes who had enjoyed much success since their last fateful May meeting at Maine Road.

Lifting the 1963 FA Cup had proved a turning point for Matt Busby's new United. Wembley success had been followed by the Championship in 1965, a runners-up spot and three F.A. Cup semi-Final appearances. With virtually the same squad of players, Busby had, much against the odds, developed another great side to succeed his beloved 'Babes'. Principals were however unchanged, as this was again a side renowned for its flair and attacking capabilities. United were once more the nation's best supported team, and as the crowds flocked to see them play home and away, capacity attendances were commonplace.

One player new to this famous fixture was an immensely gifted young Irishman called George Best. Already a player of world class potential, the phenomenally talented young man from Belfast was grabbing regular headlines for his impudent brilliance. On his finest days he was simply impossible to mark, a quality which made this United forward line a most formidable force indeed. Best was amongst the scorers as the Reds opened the season with a goal feast, defeating West Bromwich Albion 5-3. By derby day Denis Law - now 'the King' of Old Trafford - was United's top scorer with seven goals. Law was now approaching the peak of his playing career as part of a dazzling front line, but Matt Busby was more concerned about the goals being conceded and indeed several points had been dropped due to defensive frailty. He moved to solve the problem on the Tuesday before the derby by purchasing Alex Stepney from Chelsea for £55,000 despite the fact the player had only joined Tommy Docherty at Stamford Bridge a few months earlier. The goalkeeper immediately ousted David Gaskell and was to prove another masterly buy by Busby.

Denis Law leaves City's *Harry Dowd*, *Alan Oakes* and *Tony Book* trailing as he slots in United's winning goal.

BEFORE THE GAME

	P	W	D	L	F	A	Pts
UNITED	7	4	0	3	15	14	8
CITY	7	2	2	3	8	13	6

MATCH VERDICT

Denis Law, who played such an important role in the last derby back in May 1963, was again the central character as derby rivalry resumed after a three year gap. In front of a massive crowd it was a bubbling game packed with all the usual passion and commitment associated with the fixture, although it did lack a little of the creativity that sets aside the truly great match. United had most of the ideas but their finishing left much to be desired. City were all hustle and bustle - new Coach Malcolm Allison was a great believer in the positive qualities of aggression - but a forward line including the withdrawn Connor and Pardoe offered little threat.

After a hectic opening spell with United doing the bulk of the attacking, the game exploded on 15 minutes. United won a free kick near the City penalty area which was taken by Law. His direct shot rebounded off the City 'wall' and Law, following up missed with a wild hack at the loose ball and then collided with the group of players who had constituted the wall. A flurry of fists and elbows ensued, with Law at the centre of it all. Oakes, who had initially squared up to the fiery Scot walked away and Mike Summerbee stepped in to calm things down. Perhaps surprisingly, referee Jack Taylor took no action and the game restarted. Six minutes later 'the King', as the Stretford end had nicknamed Law, showed the more healthy side of his game and netted what proved to be the winning goal. It was taken in a style the forward had stamped as his own. On the edge of

the City penalty area Law passed to Aston, darted forward quickly to receive the return, dribbled round the grounded Dowd and calmly side-footed the ball into the net, right arm spearing skywards in salute.

Doyle became the first derby substitute when he replaced Kennedy at the start of the second half, but he could not stop Aston's snap shot bouncing back into play off the underside of the bar. Summerbee went closest for City when his shot flashed across the face of the goal, but other than this, Stepney had a very quiet debut game. It was only the guile of the City defenders, particularly Book, Heslop and Oakes that kept the deficit down as United ran out easy winners.

A panel from a Manchester United programme advertising the prices for this forthcoming all ticket derby. Seat prices started at six shillings (the equivalent of just 30p!)

Manchester City in 1965-66 at the start of their promotion season. **Back:** Gomersall, Bacuzzi, Cheetham, Dowd, Doyle, Kennedy, Oakes, Clay. **Front:** Young, Pardoe, Murray, Crossan, Connor, Ogley.

<table>
<tr><td>76</td><td>**MANCHESTER CITY 1**
(Stiles og)
MANCHESTER UNITED 1
(Foulkes)</td></tr>
</table>

DATE	21st January 1967
DIVISION	One
VENUE	Maine Road
ATTENDANCE	62,983

Manchester City		Manchester United
Alan OGLEY	**1**	Alex STEPNEY
Tony BOOK	**2**	Tony DUNNE
Glyn PARDOE	**3**	Bobby NOBLE
Stan HORNE	**4**	Pat CRERAND
George HESLOP	**5**	Bill FOULKES
Alan OAKES	**6**	Nobby STILES
Mike SUMMERBEE	**7**	Jim RYAN
Dave CONNOR	**8**	Bobby CHARLTON
Colin BELL	**9**	David SADLER
Mike DOYLE	**10**	David HERD
Neil YOUNG	**11**	George BEST
Johnny CROSSAN	**12**	Shay BRENNAN

BACKGROUND

Following their September victory United had hit a rich vein of form with only three defeats sustained in a move back up the table to once more challenge for the title. Stepney's acquisition had tightened up the defence while the tigerish Nobby Stiles was due to return for the derby following suspension. The forward line remained the most potent in the country. By this, the 26th League match of the season, Law was top-scorer with 15 goals but his partner, the under-rated David Herd had bagged 14. Their fans made the trek across to Moss Side looking forward to two points against neighbours who were once again finding trouble consolidating their position in the top flight.

City's bright start to the season was long forgotten and their fans were once again haunted by the spectre of relegation. The redeployment of Tony Book as a sweeper was a useful ploy, but before Christmas, City lost what many critics regarded as their best player when the competitive Mike Summerbee was suspended following a sending off at Newcastle. Dreadful form over the New Year saw the club plunge down the table and left the Blues in real need of the points by derby day. An air of controversy followed the club at this time, particularly through the effervescent comments and actions of the high profile Allison. By the time of the derby Allison had managed to get himself banned from the dug-out for excessive touchline coaching. To make matters worse club skipper Johnny Crossan was not pleased by his omission from this vital game and was due to deliver Joe Mercer a transfer request on the Monday.

BEFORE THE GAME

	P	W	D	L	F	A	Pts
UNITED	25	16	3	6	50	33	35
CITY	24	7	6	11	23	34	20

Stiles returns and delights both friend and foe

*Dismay on the faces of City defenders **Glyn Pardoe**, **Stan Horne**, **Mike Doyle**, **George Heslop** and **Alan Oakes** as United's **Bill Foulkes** (over Heslop's right shoulder) heads in Jim Ryan's 75th minute corner to put United in front.*

Manchester United 1966-67. League Champions for a 7th time.
Back: *Les Olive (Secretary), Noel Cantwell, David Sadler, David Herd, Bill Foulkes, Jim Ryan, Jack Crompton (Trainer), Jimmy Murphy (Assistant Manager).*
Middle: *W. Young (Director), L. Edwards (Chairman), David Gaskell, Shay Brennan, Bobby Charlton, John Aston, Pat Crerand, Alex Stepney, J. Gibson (Vice-Chairman), D. Haroun (Director).*
Front: *John Fitzpatrick, Nobby Stiles, Tony Dunne, Matt Busby (Manager), Denis Law, George Best, Bobby Noble.*

MATCH VERDICT

An exciting match played in atrocious conditions resulted in a share of the spoils. City's gutsy performance warranted the much needed point, although they did leave it late. The Blues generally had the better of the first half. Bell took the eye with some clever decoy play that reminded many of the great Peter Doherty of old. However, it was the City goalkeeper Ogley who had to make the more vital early saves. Best seemed to have set Herd clear, but with the ball running away from him Ogley dived to smother. On the stroke of half time, an instinctive save again defied Herd, who had another headed effort ruled out from a corner because of a foul on the goalkeeper.

Meanwhile, Stiles, roundly booed for his every touch by the City fans, scarcely put a foot wrong in a well-marshalled United defence. With 15 minutes remaining the match looked destined for a goalless draw when United suddenly scored. It came, not from one of the feared forwards, but from 'Mr.Dependable' Bill Foulkes. Loping forward for Ryan's corner kick he out-jumped the City defenders and floated a header into the net. A gloomy air of resignation descended on Maine Road as the Blues pushed forward in desperate search of an equaliser. But then, when all seemed lost with only a minute remaining, the hardworking Bell pulled a teasing cross into the United penalty area. Stiles was again quick to spot the danger and raced in to clear but only succeeded in heading a spectacular own goal past Stepney.

In injury time the City fans thought an unlikely victory might be theirs as Doyle closed in with the goal at his mercy, only for Stiles to sweep across at the last second and clear the ball to safety.

AT THE SEASON'S END

UNITED:
FIRST DIVISION CHAMPIONS

	P	W	D	L	F	A	Pts
	42	24	12	6	84	45	60

CITY: Finished 15th on 39 points

Friendly rivals? **George Best** *and* **Mike Summerbee** *prepare for another derby 'duel'.*

*United's **David Sadler** is in the thick of the goalmouth derby action as seven players challenge for the ball.*

77

MANCHESTER CITY 1
(Bell)

MANCHESTER UNITED 2
(Charlton 2)

DATE	30th September 1967
DIVISION	One
VENUE	Maine Road
ATTENDANCE	62,942

Manchester City		Manchester United
Ken MULHEARN	1	Alex STEPNEY
Tony BOOK	2	Tony DUNNE
Glyn PARDOE	3	Francis BURNS
Mike DOYLE	4	Pat CRERAND
George HESLOP	5	Bill FOULKES *
Alan OAKES	6	Nobby STILES
Stan BOWLES	7	George BEST
Colin BELL	8	David SADLER
Mike SUMMERBEE	9	Bobby CHARLTON
Neil YOUNG *	10	Denis LAW
Tony COLEMAN	11	Brian KIDD
Stan HORNE (10)	12	John ASTON (5)

BACKGROUND

The reigning League champions United opened the season disappointingly, losing 3-1 at Everton. A young Brian Kidd made his debut in this match and by the time of the derby had scored twice. Although the Everton game was the Reds' only defeat to date, they had drawn several games they looked capable of winning. By derby day, United's best form appeared to be returning and they had looked particularly impressive in the 3-1 defeat of Spurs in the game before the trip to Maine Road.

City made a worrying start with only one point from their opening three games, but the fans need not have fretted as they then reeled off five straight wins to move positively up the League table. The confident Blues looked a side full of goals, and capable of playing fast, fluent attacking football. Colin Bell was the club's leading scorer and a young man named Stan Bowles made a scoring debut on 16th September - his only outing before the derby fixture. Despite a reversal at Arsenal prior to the big day, many City fans felt this was the game where at last the team would show their re-emergence as a genuine football power with a victory over the old enemy.

BEFORE THE GAME

	P	W	D	L	F	A	Pts
CITY	9	5	1	3	18	11	11
UNITED	8	3	4	1	13	10	10

*City centre-half **George Heslop** wins a battle with United's **Nobby Stiles**.*

*United substitute **John Aston** vaults over City's **Glyn Pardoe** during the Reds 2-1 win.*

Bobby Charlton dances one of his famous victory jigs as *Denis Law* (10) and *George Best* (7) salute the Reds' winner.

Colin Bell (out of picture) fires City into a 5th minute lead.

MATCH VERDICT

This was a game when the more recent sequence of Red derby supremacy seemed likely to be overturned. City opened with all the confidence in the world, were rewarded with a goal, and even looked capable of handing out a hiding to the Old Trafford stars. Yet by half-time the strut in City's step seemed to have slipped away and the masters from Old Trafford, using all their experience, had set up a memorable victory.

City's right flank of Bell, Doyle and Bowles was a constant source of danger to United. Indeed, after only five minutes City's goal by Bell originated from just this source, as he took Doyle's short pass in his stride and hit a low firm shot past Stepney. Twice thereafter 'Nijinski' (as Malcolm Allison was to nickname him after the famous thoroughbred racehorse) hit a pair of superb goalbound shots, only for Stepney to make equally brilliant saves. It was all going so well that it came as rather a nasty surprise to the home crowd when Bobby Charlton engineered a one-two on the edge of the City area and rifled the equaliser. City returned to the fray with renewed vigour but ten minutes from half-time they were undone again with what proved to be the winning goal. Doyle's hesitation in possession on the edge of the box proved fatal as Charlton quickly moved in, robbed him and swept the ball past the advancing Mulhearn.

In the second half City had lost their stylish poise and the play was characterised by a more attritional battle. The United defence came under much less pressure and the Reds held on to take the points which moved them above City in the table. For the City players and crowd it was a sorry tale of what might have been.

*United goalkeeper **Alex Stepney** saves a fine shot from City's **Colin Bell**.*

78

MANCHESTER UNITED 1
(Best)

MANCHESTER CITY 3
(Bell, Heslop, Lee pen.)

DATE	27th March 1968
DIVISION	One
VENUE	Old Trafford
ATTENDANCE	63,004

Manchester United		*Manchester City*
Alex STEPNEY	**1**	Ken MULHEARN
Shay BRENNAN	**2**	Tony BOOK
Francis BURNS	**3**	Glyn PARDOE
Pat CRERAND	**4**	Mike DOYLE
David SADLER	**5**	George HESLOP
Nobby STILES	**6**	Alan OAKES
John FITZPATRICK	**7**	Francis LEE
Denis LAW	**8**	Colin BELL *
Bobby CHARLTON	**9**	Mike SUMMERBEE
George BEST	**10**	Neil YOUNG
David HERD *	**11**	Tony COLEMAN
John ASTON (11)	**12**	Dave CONNOR (8)

The night City found their true level

AND THIS IS WHERE IT'S TAKEN THEM

BACKGROUND

Less than a fortnight after the late September derby defeat Joe Mercer went out and purchased forward Francis Lee from Bolton for £60,000. This key buy of the bustling 23 year old proved a turning point as the Blues put together an impressive run of form. The 6-0 drubbing of Leicester City in November showed the attacking potential the side now possessed. Lee proved excellent value, scoring 14 goals in the 21 games leading up to the derby. A 3-2 defeat at West Bromwich Albion on Boxing Day ended a bright run of eleven games undefeated. The Blues did not, however, let this deter them and, following the 5-1 thrashing of Fulham at Maine Road on 16th March, City went top of the division. A defeat by Leeds then knocked the Blues off top spot, making it even more essential for them to pick up the points at Old Trafford.

United's League form had gathered pace and they had in turn moved to the top of the table through a series of extremely good results. United were also pursuing Matt Busby's dream of European Cup success and by the time of the derby had reached the semi-final stage and were due to play Real Madrid. Some critics felt United's dual aspirations must have a cost and that they might fall between the two stools of English and European competitions. An example of this danger was United's 3-0 defeat at modest Coventry City following a gruelling midweek European quarter-final game in Poland with Gornik. However, United's squad looked both good enough and deep enough as they dispatched a strong Nottingham Forest side 3-0 in the final match before the derby. On their own ground United were the favourites and a win would not only give them a coveted 'double' over their close rivals, but more importantly, could open up a vital four point gap.

BEFORE THE GAME							
	P	W	D	L	F	A	Pts
UNITED	32	19	7	6	63	38	45
CITY	32	19	5	8	69	36	43

Man of the Match **Colin Bell** *blasts City's equaliser past a startled* **Alex Stepney** *in the United goal.*

*The decisive goal on a remarkable night for City arrives from an unlikely source as defender **George Heslop** (left) heads past United 'keeper **Alex Stepney**. Looking on anxiously are United's **David Sadler** and City's **Francis Lee**, **Mike Summerbee** and **Mike Doyle**.*

MATCH VERDICT

In one of the most famous and important derbies ever played City surprised all the pundits by beating the League favourites on their own ground and not only that, destroyed them with a brand of football United believed was their sole preserve.

What an amazing night it was for the Blues. Few of their fans in the capacity crowd could have anticipated what was to come as with only 38 seconds gone George Best's twinkling trickery completely foxed Tony Book and the Irish wizard shot past Mulhearn. The United aristocrats seemed set for a feast, and poor old City looked ripe for yet another beating by their old rivals. However, after a hesitant ten minutes it was the Blues, particularly through their midfield, who began to dictate the flow of the game. The man who changed the course of the contest around with a scintillating display of skill and stamina was Colin Bell. With Doyle winning some important tackles in the midfield and the willing Bell covering acres of ground, the United defence came under severe pressure and City deservedly forced an equaliser. Appropriately, it was Bell who initiated the right-wing move which brought the goal and he ran yards to reach the final pass and blast an unstoppable shot past Stepney.

United, busy repelling the rampant Blues, were totally unable to put their own game together and eventually the pressure told as City gained a decisive second goal. Following yet more attacking skills by the Blues down the right flank, the ball was curled into the middle from Tony Coleman's free-kick and centre-half George Heslop, who had never scored a League goal for City, rose above all the other defenders to send a firm downward header past a groping Stepney and into the net. Despite some frantic attacks by United, which saw Law go very close, there was little doubt that this was to be City's night. As United mounted a last desperate bid to salvage a point, Bell exploited the available space and raced clear. An elusive shadow all night to the United defence, Bell was hauled down in the area by Burns and up stepped Francis Lee to crash home the penalty in decisive fashion.

There were many quotes afterwards from those

involved in such a thrilling match, but perhaps the most telling comment came from the delighted City fan leaving Old Trafford who said: "for the first time in my life I'm dying to get to work tomorrow!".

Certainly the match proved a watershed derby. The balance of power in Manchester football was shifting. Little could the United fans have realised as their team sat on top of the table with a European triumph beckoning, that the club would before long enter a dispiriting stage in its history, and would win just one of the next 13 derby League matches. City on the other hand, were poised to enter a period of remarkable achievements and success.

The following day's newspapers were universal in their praise for City's outstanding performance. In the 'Daily Mail' Ronald Crowther wrote:

"The balance of power which has kept Manchester United perched so long beyond the reach of their poor relations from Maine Road took a violent swing in this drama-packed derby.
For magnificent Manchester City, who came from behind after a shock start that would have shattered the nerves of many sides, outplayed, outfought and out-manoeuvred the team who carry England's hopes in the European Cup.
With two points so richly deserved, if only for the relentless power of their non-stop running, they leap-frogged on goal average over United to second place in the table, and made it a three club deadlock at the top. Leeds, Manchester City and United are all on 45 points... a situation to set Manchester soccer fans tingling!"

AT THE SEASON'S END

CITY: League Champions

P	W	D	L	F	A	Pts
42	26	6	10	86	43	58

UNITED: Finished 2nd on 56 points
European Champions Cup Winners, beating Benfica 4-1 at Wembley

79

MANCHESTER CITY 0
MANCHESTER UNITED 0

DATE	17th August 1968
DIVISION	One
VENUE	Maine Road
ATTENDANCE	63,052

Manchester City		Manchester United
Ken MULHEARN	1	Alex STEPNEY
Bobby KENNEDY	2	Frank KOPEL
Glyn PARDOE	3	Tony DUNNE
Mike DOYLE	4	John FITZPATRICK
George HESLOP	5	David SADLER
Alan OAKES	6	Nobby STILES
Francis LEE	7	George BEST
Colin BELL	8	Alan GOWLING
Mike SUMMERBEE	9	Bobby CHARLTON
Bobby OWEN	10	Brian KIDD
Neil YOUNG	11	John ASTON *
Tony COLEMAN	12	Francis BURNS (11)

DEFENSIVE UNITED SHOW THEIR FEAR OF CITY

BACKGROUND

Manchester was, by 1968, the soccer capital of England with the League Champions and the European Cup winners both coming from the proud metropolis. The two clubs would now play in this season's European Cup competition, and ever-confident Malcolm Allison boasted that the Blues would 'scare Europe to death'. City had started the season impressively, hammering West Bromwich Albion 6-1 in the Charity Shield with new £35,000 signing Bobby Owen scoring twice. However, an opening League defeat at Liverpool showed that retaining the title was not going to be easy, but a 3-2 home win over Wolves left the Blues in good heart for the first important derby of the season.

For Matt Busby the European triumph had been the fulfilment of a lifelong dream and a fitting tribute to the memory of all those young men killed at Munich. Now the task at hand was how to maintain such a lofty position and also to resist the challenge of the Champions from the other side of Manchester.

The United squad, however, remained much the same as the one which had been highly successful for the last five seasons. Certainly it still looked a strong enough side as they beat a talented Everton team 2-1 in the opening League fixture. However, a more sobering experience was a 3-1 midweek defeat at West Bromwich Albion.

BEFORE THE GAME							
	P	W	D	L	F	A	Pts
CITY	2	1	0	1	4	4	2
UNITED	2	1	0	1	3	4	2

*A grimace from City's **Colin Bell** as another crunching tackle comes flying in from United's **John Fitzpatrick** who was specifically deployed to mark the midfielder.*

City defender **George Heslop** leaps to head the ball clear watched by **Colin Bell**.

George Best, whose turn and shot against the bar was a highlight of the match, chases for the ball with City's **Glyn Pardoe** and **Alan Oakes**.

MATCH VERDICT

It was another big crowd but an utterly dour match at Maine Road, with critics suggesting that perhaps United's defensive line-up and performance reflected a fear of their rejuvenated neighbours.

Not that City would have been overly pleased with their own performance as, in a typically competitive first half, the Blues were too often involved in petty skirmishes at the expense of the naturally creative side of their game. Fitzpatrick, brought in specifically to mark the elusive Bell, raised a few eyebrows with some robust tackling and both he and the volatile Summerbee were summarily booked.

In a close second half Bell's boundless energy created space for City, but few clear chances resulted. However, it was the star at the other end who, 15 minutes from time, nearly won the game for United. George Best had cut a very isolated figure up front throughout the second period as United's lone forward, but he suddenly received the ball in the City penalty area. With his back to goal the Irishman controlled and, in one movement, swivelled to leave Mulhearn helpless with a fierce shot against the crossbar. It proved a fleeting moment of genius to savour in an otherwise bland encounter.

Top of the tree! United skipper **Bobby Charlton** and City's captain **Tony Book** show off the European Cup and League Championship. Never had the two Manchester clubs been simultaneously at such a peak of their powers.

80

MANCHESTER UNITED 0
MANCHESTER CITY 1
(Summerbee)

DATE	8th March 1969
DIVISION	One
VENUE	Old Trafford
ATTENDANCE	63,388

Manchester United		Manchester City
Alex STEPNEY	1	Harry DOWD
Shay BRENNAN	2	Tony BOOK
John FITZPATRICK	3	Glyn PARDOE
Pat CRERAND	4	Mike DOYLE
Bill FOULKES	5	Tommy BOOTH
Nobby STILES	6	Alan OAKES
Willie MORGAN	7	Mike SUMMERBEE
Brian KIDD	8	Colin BELL
Bobby CHARLTON	9	Francis LEE *
David SADLER	10	Neil YOUNG
George BEST	11	Tony COLEMAN
John ASTON	12	Bobby OWEN (9)

BACKGROUND

United's season was not going particularly well by this stage, and a little team-strengthening was perhaps somewhat overdue. A 4-0 home thrashing by Chelsea merely underlined the growing shortcomings in certain departments. Willie Morgan the skilful Burnley winger was purchased for £90,000. Something of a George Best look-a-like, he had taken a little time to settle but by the derby date was in the line-up. Morgan was to prove one of Matt Busby's last signings as the maestro announced this would be his final season and he felt a younger man should take the reins in the summer. Defence of the European Cup now remained United's only hope of a trophy for this season, but hopes were high on that front as the Reds had reached the semi-final stage where they were due to play A.C.Milan of Italy.

Inconsistency dogged the Blues in their efforts to retain the League title. Attractive victories such as a 4-1 demolition of Chelsea were followed by several disappointing setbacks including a 2-1 defeat at Burnley in the match before the derby. Allison's early season boast about City's impact in Europe also came home to roost as City made an embarrassing first round European Cup exit to the unknown Fenerbahce of Turkey. By January Joe Mercer conceded City could not manage to win the League again and the F.A.Cup remained the only hope of glory. By derby day this objective was well advanced as City were in the semi-finals and were due to meet Everton, United's conquerors in the quarter-finals.

	BEFORE THE GAME						
	P	W	D	L	F	A	Pts
CITY	28	8	9	11	49	40	25
UNITED	28	8	9	11	33	39	25

*Watched by **George Best**, United's **Brian Kidd** powers in a header despite a challenge from City's **Glyn Pardoe**.*

MATCH VERDICT

United might have cursed their bad luck, but City showed all the composure and qualities necessary to remain top dogs in Manchester. In a cautious opening little was given away, although United went close to edging in front on 26 minutes.

Dowd's poor goal-kick went directly to Best, who needed no second invitation. The quick-thinking forward accelerated past Book and, as Dowd raced off his line, chipped the ball over the goalkeeper only to see it bounce against the crossbar and rebound to safety. City duly heeded the warning and responded by taking the lead some 13 minutes later. With United pressed forward in attack, Doyle dispossessed Crerand and his long ball forward was smartly controlled by Summerbee who lost Fitzpatrick and lobbed the ball over the advancing goalkeeper. Stepney, in a frantic scramble to recover his position, managed to get back and scoop the ball off the line but Summerbee followed up and gleefully hit the ball into the roof of the net. City now took control and Coleman caught the eye with a series of tricky runs and telling crosses. Young was most unlucky as his piledriver of a shot completely defeated Stepney but crashed against a post. United rallied in the final 15 minutes and subjected City to some considerable pressure. Charlton looked certain to conjure up the equaliser in front of an inviting net, but his shot struck a City player and although Kidd rattled the loose ball against a post, it proved too little, too late.

City substitute **Bobby Owen** lets fly at goal as United defender **Shay Brennan** attempts to block the shot.

A near miss for City as goalscorer **Mike Summerbee** moves for the loose ball watched by **Mike Doyle** (City), **Nobby Stiles** (United) and **Tommy Booth** (City).

AT THE SEASON'S END

UNITED: Finished 11th on 42 points

CITY: Finished 13th on 40 points
(F.A. Cup Winners, beating Leicester City 1-0)

UNITED REVIEW

Winners of the European Champion Clubs Cup Competition 1968
SEASON 1968·1969 · No 22

THE OFFICIAL PROGRAMME OF MANCHESTER UNITED FOOTBALL CLUB LIMITED

MANCHESTER UNITED
VERSUS
MANCHESTER CITY
MARCH 8th 1969 · KICK-OFF 3·00 p.m.

PRICE NINEPENCE

81

MANCHESTER CITY 4
(Young, Bell 2, Sadler og)

MANCHESTER UNITED 0

DATE	15th November 1969
DIVISION	One
VENUE	Maine Road
ATTENDANCE	63,013

Manchester City		Manchester United
Joe CORRIGAN	1	Alex STEPNEY
Tony BOOK	2	Shay BRENNAN
Glyn PARDOE	3	Tony DUNNE
Mike DOYLE	4	Francis BURNS
Tommy BOOTH	5	Ian URE
Alan OAKES	6	David SADLER
Mike SUMMERBEE	7	Carlo SARTORI *
Colin BELL	8	George BEST
Francis LEE	9	Bobby CHARLTON
Neil YOUNG	10	Denis LAW
Ian BOWYER	11	John ASTON
Dave CONNOR	12	Brian KIDD (7)

BACKGROUND

United promoted Sir Matt Busby's successor from within. Wilf McGuinness, a former 'Busby Babe' and already serving in a coaching capacity at the club, was appointed team manager, although Busby remained in a general manager's capacity. The season opened miserably, with United unable to win any of their opening six matches.

Former Scottish International centre-half Ian Ure was signed from Arsenal for £80,000. The craggy stopper seemed to strengthen the defence and a better run of of only two defeats in the next 12 games enabled the Reds to climb the table. United were also hopeful of a good run in the League Cup and a creditable 0-0 draw at Brian Clough's Derby County promised a semi-final date with City if the Reds won the replay.

City, by contrast, made a resounding start to the new season hammering Sheffield Wednesday 4-1. Goalkeeper Joe Corrigan was now first choice and, despite the occasional spectacular mistake, the 21-year-old had finally emerged from the shadow of Mulhearn. This was to be the first of his record breaking 26 derbies. Despite their emphatic first game victory, City's early form was in truth disappointingly inconsistent. However, a seven match unbeaten run prior to the derby revealed more of the side's true capabilities. The Blues were also making pleasing progress in their second excursion into Europe following the disappointments of the previous season. In the last match three days before the derby S.K.Lierse were beaten 3-0 in a second round Cup Winners' Cup tie.

BEFORE THE GAME							
	P	W	D	L	F	A	Pts
CITY:	18	9	5	4	28	17	23
UNITED	19	7	7	5	29	27	21

United's **Bobby Charlton** *slots the ball into an empty net watched by* **Glyn Pardoe**, **Joe Corrigan**, **Mike Doyle** *and* **Tony Book**. *Pardoe's raised arm gives an early indication that the 'goal' was about to be ruled out for an infringement.*

MATCH VERDICT

City were the masters in this comprehensive massacre of the old enemy. In what was quite simply a very one-sided game, City's impressive teamwork, with Bell outstanding, outclassed United in virtually every department.

Ironically, in what proved to be United's only real scoring opportunity, they almost took a first minute lead. Aston's wing play created an opening for Law but a chance the quicksilver Scot might well have dispatched a year earlier escaped his outstretched boot. That was the end of United as an attacking force, and the remainder of the half was spent in desperate defence endeavouring to resist wave after wave of City attacks. Bell's constant running both on and off the ball was a frequent source of irritation, not to mention the powerful forward play of the menacing Summerbee and Lee. Surprisingly, it took 38 minutes for City's superiority to register on the scoreboard, when the elegant Young curved a wicked shot past Stepney to secure the Blues an interval lead. More though was to follow as Colin Bell escaped his marker Burns early in the second half and crowned a fluent move by driving the ball unerringly into the net. United's defence now wilted and, following another Bell-inspired move, conceded an own goal when Sadler, under pressure from Bowyer and Lee, turned a cross past Stepney from close range. The rout was completed one minute from time with the United defence in total disarray as Bell arrived at the far post to slide the ball over the line. City left the field to a standing ovation, United to an eerie silence from the area populated by their disconsolate supporters.

'Attack must take the blame for this flop' shouted the headline in the Manchester Evening News over the report by regular Reds' reporter David Meek.

"Once upon a time Manchester City used to go weak at the knees at the thought of playing Manchester United. Malcolm Allison once said he couldn't get his players to go out and inspect the pitch at Old Trafford because they were frightened of the Stretford End reception.
But 'Svengali' Allison has clearly not been wasting his time, for the boot now seems to be well and truly on the other foot. United's forwards froze, hapless and helpless, with City dictating the pattern of the game and emerging superior in all departments"

It's smiles all round for City, but not for unhappy United man *David Sadler* whose own goal had just put the Blues into a 3-0 lead.

In a desperate effort to clear from City's *Ian Bowyer* and *Francis Lee*, United's *David Sadler* (No.6), fires the ball past his own goalkeeper *Alex Stepney* to put the Blues 3-0 ahead.

82

MANCHESTER UNITED 1
(Kidd)

MANCHESTER CITY 2
(Lee pen, Doyle)

DATE	28th March 1970	
DIVISION	One	
VENUE	Old Trafford	
ATTENDANCE	60,286	

Manchester United		Manchester City
Alex STEPNEY	1	Joe CORRIGAN
Paul EDWARDS	2	Tony BOOK
Tony DUNNE	3	Arthur MANN
Pat CRERAND	4	Mike DOYLE
David SADLER	5	Tommy BOOTH
Francis BURNS	6	Alan OAKES
Willie MORGAN	7	Derek JEFFRIES
Carlo SARTORI *	8	Ian BOWYER
Bobby CHARLTON	9	Francis LEE
Brian KIDD	10	Neil YOUNG
George BEST	11	Glyn PARDOE
Denis LAW (8)	12	Tony TOWERS

City's Joe Mercer and Malcolm Allison had plenty to smile about as the Blues became top dogs in Manchester,

BACKGROUND

City's disappointing League record was more than compensated for by the club's Cup exploits, as the Blues enjoyed a golden period in their history.

Following the semi-final defeat of United (see Cup section) the Blues had gone on to lift the League Cup at Wembley in the first season that all 92 League clubs had participated in the competition. City beat West Bromwich Albion in the Final 2-1 after extra time, with goals by Doyle and Pardoe. The Blues had also reached the semi-final of the European Cup-Winners' Cup, and were due to meet Schalke 04 in the first leg of the semi-final just four days after this derby match. In stark contrast, City's three League games prior to their visit to United were defeats, with a televised 5-1 home reverse against West Ham particularly embarrassing for Corrigan, who punted the ball upfield and was beaten by an instant long range volley as he trotted blithely back towards his goal.

It was though developing into a disappointingly frustrating season for United, who, following several years of League supremacy were not even in contention for the title. Possible salvation in the League Cup competition came to grief before Christmas time with defeat by City. Now, just two days before the derby, the season was effectively over as they lost a second replay to Leeds United in the F.A. Cup Semi-Final. George Best remained the side's one world class player as he showed in an earlier Cup game at Northampton Town when he scored six of the Reds' eight goals.

BEFORE THE GAME							
	P	W	D	L	F	A	Pts
UNITED	35	12	15	8	51	48	39
CITY	36	13	10	13	48	43	36

MATCH VERDICT

This fifth and final meeting of the season was yet further proof that City were Manchester's top team. The match proved a sad one indeed for David Sadler. The classy defender had recently celebrated his call-up to Alf Ramsey's Mexico World Cup 28 but this day he had a match to forget. He certainly appeared the guilty man on nine minutes when City took the lead. Sadler was slow to assess the pace of a pass from Charlton across the greasy surface and, as Young nipped in to collect

Brian Kidd who got on the scoresheet for United tries a header watched by *Mike Doyle* (left) but the effort was saved.

(far left) A grounded *Bobby Charlton* gets in a shot, but City's *Alan Oakes* and Mike Doyle looked unconcerned.

(left) *Brian Kidd* shields the ball from *Tommy Booth* but he could not prevent City completing the 'double' with a 2-1 win.

and rounded United 'keeper Alex Stepney, he was brought crashing down and the City fans roared for a penalty. Lee, with a long deliberate run-up, struck the spot-kick into the net via the bar. Just seven minutes later it was the turn of the United fans to cheer as yet another error brought the equaliser. Corrigan's clumsy attempt to gather Morgan's low cross only resulted in the ball squirming under his body and rolling on towards Kidd who made no mistake from a couple of feet.

Following a good spell by United another mistake by Sadler brought about their downfall and this time there was no reprieve. Young's innocuous centre threatened little danger as Sadler moved in to clear but his complete mis-kick allowed a grateful Doyle to sweep the ball past Stepney. As United's frustration grew Law came on for what was now becoming a regular 30 minutes as substitute, but somehow his appearance and obvious confusion as to which position to play epitomised United's growing despair.

AT THE SEASON'S END

UNITED: Finished 8th on 45 points

CITY: Finished 10th on 43 points
(League Cup Winners, beating W.B.A. 2-1. European Cup Winners' Cup winners, beating Gornik 2-1 to become the first English side to win a domestic and European trophy in the same season).

United pay for Sadler errors

Man. United 1, Man. City 2   *By BOB GREAVES*

ALL-MANCHESTER clashes, when they happen twice a season, arer eal events, engendering a sense of occasion and drama. Personal rivalries outweigh all else, every facet tends to be exaggerated—a foot wrong by a player can take six months or more to put right.

But when these clashes happen five times a season they fall into the almost commonplace.

All this particular episode proved was that City, with three wins to United's one—the other meeting was drawn—are firmly and fairly the better this season. But as fortunes sway it could all be so different in a year's time, though that is little consolation this morning to United. For them it was ironical that a disappointing week in a disappointing season being rounded off so unproductively by their closest rivals. e-yrh

This defeat just about ends the slim hopes of entry into Europe through the Fairs Cup. City, however, faced with a tough job on Wednesday in Germany against Schalke in the first leg of the Cup Winners' Cup, enjoyed victory after three successive League defeats came at what could prove a vital psychological moment.

Cold and greasy conditions and incessant rain, hardly helped to wards attractive football, but they cannot be blamed for the two fatal errors by Sadler—he's usually so sure and composed — which helped to bring City both their goals. His display only days after being named as one of the 28 players for Mexico, was hardly in character.

He delayed moving towards a ball from Charlton in the ninth minute, apparently misjudging both its pace and the closeness of Young, who shrewdly nipped in for a clear run to goal. Young rounded Stepney, and the keeper had little alternative but to bring him down. Lee took the penalty kick, and although he sent Stepney the wrong way, the ball hit the underside of the bar before going in.

United equalised when Corrigan made an inept drop onto a low cross from Morgan (16 minutes). He never looked like controlling the ball as it oozed under his arms and rolled to Kidd, standing two yards from goal. Kidd had only to pop it in.

Law not sure

Sadler's second mistake came when he miskicked entirely at Young's chip and Doyle gratefully swept the ball past Stepney.

United missed the recent infusion of bite in the guise of Stiles —out with a thigh strain a legacy of Thursday night's tussle with Leeds. Best went close a couple of times but although he is not quite the extra-special threat that he was, recent doubts about his ability are surely over-emphasised.

Law came on for what is now his almost customary half hour appearance, always at the expense of Sartori, but seems unsure of his role as a part time player.

City, despite being without Heslop, Bell and Summerbee, can feel far more satisfied. They were well served by Oakes, Young, Lee, Book and Doyle, as well as young Jeffries and Bowyer. And at least they still have Europe.

Man. Utd.: Stepney, Edwards, Dunne, Crerand, Sadler, Burns, Morgan, Sartori, Charlton, Kidd, Best. Sub.: Law. Man. City: Corrigan, Book, Mann, Doyle, Booth, Oakes, Jeffries, Bowyer, Lee, Young, Pardoe.

Referee: R. B. Kirkpatrick (Leicester).

83

MANCHESTER UNITED 1
(Kidd)

MANCHESTER CITY 4
(Doyle, Lee 3)

DATE		12th December 1970
DIVISION		One
VENUE		Old Trafford
ATTENDANCE		52,636

Manchester United		Manchester City
Jimmy RIMMER	1	Joe CORRIGAN
Willie WATSON	2	Tony BOOK
Tony DUNNE	3	Glyn PARDOE *
John FITZPATRICK	4	Mike DOYLE
Steve JAMES	5	Tommy BOOTH
Nobby STILES	6	Alan OAKES
Denis LAW *	7	Mike SUMMERBEE
George BEST	8	Colin BELL
Bobby CHARLTON	9	Francis LEE
Brian KIDD	10	Neil YOUNG
John ASTON	11	Derek JEFFRIES
Carlo SARTORI (7)	12	Arthur MANN (3)

BACKGROUND

City were now established as one of the most attractive and successful clubs in the country. They could claim, with fair justification, to be superior over neighbours who for so long had been the masters. At this point in time however, a fierce boardroom wrangle erupted over control of the club with a business consortium attempting a take over. As is often the case, these affairs attracted lurid headlines and, with Allison supporting the syndicate, an instability was set in motion which would ultimately lead to the break up of City's all-conquering management team. Perhaps not surprisingly, all the confusion appeared to affect matters on the field and, following a promising start to the season, the club were also badly hit by injuries, and had shown poor form in the two matches leading into the derby as they were beaten by high flying Leeds United and Arsenal.

Wilf McGuinness' second season at United opened modestly, as one point from the first three games was followed by a slight improvement of eight points from the next five. One change McGuinness had decided upon was the promotion of the reserve goalkeeper Jimmy Rimmer, but otherwise the side remained much the same as before. The improved form was not though maintained, and by the time of the derby the club had slipped into the wrong half of the table. Wembley however, seemed a real prospect as United had again reached the League Cup semifinal and with the further boost of a kindly looking draw, were due to play Third Division Aston Villa on the following Wednesday. A victory looked more than likely.

Injuries forced many changes on City this season. Here **Derek Jeffries** takes on United's **John Aston** in the 4-1 win at Old Trafford.

BEFORE THE GAME							
	P	W	D	L	F	A	Pts
CITY	19	8	6	5	23	17	22
UNITED	20	5	8	7	22	27	18

MATCH VERDICT

United were humiliated in front of their own fans as City handed out one of the heaviest derby beatings to confirm their status as the top team in Manchester football. Francis Lee, so often a thorn in United's flesh, once again showed what an excellent finisher he was and how much he loved performing in the limelight these games always afforded. Alan Oakes, the City veteran who had played most of his career in the shadow of the Reds, also had an outstanding game in a first class City showing. The only sad moment for the Blues was a seriously broken leg sustained by Glyn Pardoe in an accidental collision with George Best. The fracture trapped an artery and a swift operation was needed to save the City full-back's leg.

City, with their midfield totally dominant, created all the chances as they cut United's defence to ribbons and raced into an unassailable 4-0 lead. Mike Doyle, who came from a 'true Blue' family and never made any secret of his distaste for the Red opposition, took particular pleasure in scoring once again on United's pitch.

But it was the dynamic Lee who was simply unstoppable on the day. A pocket-battleship of a player, he ran rings round his markers and rattled in a quick-fire hat-trick, the first treble in these fixtures since United's Alex Dawson ten years earlier. Kidd's late goal was of no consolation to a United side who left the field in a thoroughly demoralised state.

*Delight for hat-trick hero **Francis Lee** who is congratulated by City team-mate **Alan Oakes**, while United's dejected defender **Nobby Stiles** slumps to his knees. The Manchester Evening News also paid tribute to Lee's superb treble. "He cruelly exposed the youthful and immature Steve James and took his goals in superlative manner, the last being his best with a delightful header into the top corner of the net."*

*An anxious **Alan Oakes** and other City players give desperate signals to the bench for a stretcher as **Glyn Pardoe** (grounded in agony right) clutches his leg which proved to be severely broken following a tackle with United's **George Best**.*

84

MANCHESTER CITY 3
(Hill, Lee, Mellor)

MANCHESTER UNITED 4
(Charlton, Law, Best 2)

DATE	5th May 1971
DIVISION	One
VENUE	Maine Road
ATTENDANCE	43,636

Manchester City		Manchester United
Ron HEALEY	1	Alex STEPNEY
Tony BOOK	2	Tommy O'NEIL
Dave CONNOR	3	Francis BURNS
Tony TOWERS	4	Pat CRERAND
George HESLOP	5	Steve JAMES
Willie DONACHIE	6	David SADLER
Steve CARTER	7	Denis LAW
Ian MELLOR	8	Alan GOWLING
Francis LEE	9	Bobby CHARLTON
Neil YOUNG	10	Brian KIDD
Freddie HILL	11	George BEST
Ian BOWYER	12	Carlo SARTORI

BACKGROUND

It took just three more games after the last derby to seal Wilf McGuinness' fate. On 28th December he was 'relieved of his duties' and Matt Busby returned as caretaker-manager for the rest of the season. The deep disappointment of defeat in the League Cup semi-final by Aston Villa had proved the final straw for the board, although the unlucky McGuinness could have fairly claimed he was not given long to make his mark, or indeed, a lot of resources. Busby called on all his old skills and years of experience to restore team confidence, and a series of victories allowed the Club to climb away from relegation worries into the top half of the table.

City's League form had disappointed, and a talented squad appeared to be under-achieving. Injuries were one major reason for this and the ongoing boardroom ructions were another. The take-over appeared to have polarised around the consortium group and its advocation of Allison for manager - a position he always coveted - and the old guard of Chairman Albert Alexander who clearly wanted Mercer kept in total charge. Acting as a peacemaker between the two disputing factions, a certain Peter Swales was co-opted onto the board. The club's one hope of a trophy disappeared shortly before the derby when Chelsea defeated them in the semi-final of the European Cup Winners' Cup and shattered hopes of retaining both the trophy and a foothold in Europe.

MANCHESTER CITY
VERSUS
MANCHESTER UNITED
LEAGUE DIVISION ONE
WEDNESDAY
5th MAY 1971
Kick-off 7-45 p.m.

NEWS 5p

THE AGONY of goalkeeper Ron Healey after he dropped the ball into the net to give Chelsea victory in that second leg battle. *Picture: Daily Express*

BEFORE THE GAME

	P	W	D	L	F	A	Pts
CITY	41	12	17	12	44	38	41
UNITED	41	15	11	15	61	63	41

Freddie Hill - a goal in City's gallant fightback for the £12,000 buy from Halifax.

Smiles all round as 'This is Your Life' compere **Eamon Andrews** catches **Sir Matt Busby** with the famous red book before the end of season derby at Maine Road. City manager **Joe Mercer**, a guest during Sir Matt's previous appearance on the programme in 1958 looks equally delighted. Incidentally, Joe himself had also been a subject on the show in March 1970 - with Sir Matt as his guest!

Ron Healey - the City goalkeeper was beaten four times in this friendly end-of-season goal romp.

George Best - on target twice as United's famous trio all got on the scoresheet to mark Busby's special night.

MATCH VERDICT

The headlines were made off the field in this 84th derby. The rather meaningless if entertaining match was, in effect, played as a tribute to Sir Matt Busby. It was a case of "Sir Matt Busby, This is Your Life...again" as Eamon Andrews and his famous red book surprised the old maestro, the players and the crowd by appearing on the pitch just before the game was due to start. It was delightful and appropriate timing surely much appreciated by Sir Matt who had such wonderful memories of his association with both United and City spanning nearly half a century.

The conviviality continued with Joe Mercer announcing that Busby was 'the greatest manager Britain had ever known' and with players exchanging handshakes and pleasantries there was almost an air of the testimonial about proceedings. Even the absence of the ultra-competitive Doyle from the City line-up seemed more than a little appropriate! Similarly, the game lacked a real competitive edge but there was much entertaining attractive football to appreciate. On this, Busby's night, it was totally appropriate that the famous trinity of Law, Charlton and Best scored the United goals in rapier thrusts through a static defence. City, stung by being three behind at half time, made quite a spirited fight of it as they fought back with goals from Lee, Mellor and Hill. However, on Sir Matt's special day, few really begrudged United the fourth and winning goal.

'A GOALDEN FAREWELL' was the headline in the Manchester Evening News as David Meek reported on 'the friendliest derby for years':

"It was ideal for the end of season and as a final flourish for the departure of Sir Matt Busby as team boss of Manchester United.

For this was the highest scoring derby for 45 years and it was full of attacking football from both teams.

It was too half-paced with too high a ratio of mistakes to be a classic, but as entertainment it left something to bridge the close season.

And it put into practice all that United's Sir Matt has tried to instil into his various teams... his belief in a creative, attacking philosophy.

Bobby Charlton, Denis Law and George Best all showed their flair and finish to have Manchester City three goals down at the interval.

But of course, Joe Mercer is not a defensive minded manager either and sent his youthful, inexperienced side out for a do-or-die fling.

And what a fling, with Freddie Hill coming into his own and scoring just after the interval. He was followed by Francis Lee and Ian Mellor, but George Best had by this time headed the outstanding goal of the game to leave the Reds with a 4-3 win. If it were not the end of season one might question United's defence against a patched up City side and also hope that the Reds won't build too much on goals that did come a trifle easily.

But that is to quibble. Sufficient that this was fine fare to ride us through the summer."

CHOPPING & CHANGING

Passion is never in short supply during Manchester derby matches. Here tempers boil over after a foul by United's Tommy O'Neil (No.2) on City's Francis Lee (No.10) at Maine Road in November 1972.

Two stars of the Seventies, United's Steve Coppell and City's Dennis Tueart tussle for possession during the 2-2 draw at Maine Road on 27th September 1975.

United's Jimmy Greenhoff takes on City's Mike Doyle as Willie Donachie chases back to cover during the Reds 3-1 win at Old Trafford in March 1977.

City's Mike Doyle (No.4) makes his point to Kenny Clements who is tightly marked by United's Stewart Houston. To the left are City's Joe Royle and United's Stuart Pearson who both scored for their respective teams as the Reds won 3-1 in March 1977.

City trio Brian Kidd, Gary Owen and Mike Channon look on as United's Sammy McIlroy (No.11) and Gordon McQueen (No.5) clear the danger during the Reds 1-0 victory in September 1978.

City's Gary Owen challenges United defender Gordon McQueen during the Reds 1-0 win in September 1978.

Expensive talent on show as Ray Wilkins, United's £850,000 buy from Chelsea skips round City's Steve Daley (a £1.4 million buy from Wolves) and Tommy Caton. The Blues won the match in November 1979 at Maine Road 2-0.

MATCH RESULT

MANCHESTER UNITED...1   MANCHESTER CITY...0
Thomas

MANCHESTER UNITED
Old Trafford,
Manchester.

In the 180th Anniversary year of the
Liverpool & Manchester Railway

City's Tommy Caton clears the danger as United favourite Steve Coppell puts in a challenge.

The front cover of United's commemorative programme for the 100th derby meeting in March 1980.

United goalkeeper Gary Bailey makes a safe catch watched closely by Dave Bennett (No. 10) and Gordon McQueen (No. 5) during a 2-2 draw in September 1980.

City's Dave Bennett shields the ball from United defender Martin Buchan during the 2-2 draw at Old Trafford in September 1980.

United's Ashley Grimes and City's Paul Power move in to challenge for the ball in the 2-2 draw in September 1980.

Signed from W.B.A. by his former boss Ron Atkinson for a then record fee of £1.8 million, Bryan Robson made his debut in the October 1981 derby. Here he challenges City's Martin O'Neill during the 0-0 draw at Maine Road in October 1981.

City goalkeeper Joe Corrigan saves this effort in October 1981 from United's Ray Wilkins as Blues full-back Ray Ranson chases back to cover during the 0-0 draw.

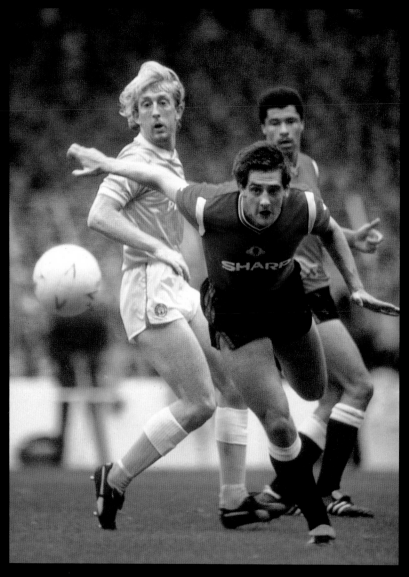

(above) Mark Hughes can find no way through this time as City's Mick McCarthy wins an aerial duel during United's 3-0 win at Maine Road in September 1985.

(left) United's Graeme Hogg keeps the ball away from City's Mark Lillis during the Reds 3-0 win at Maine Road in September 1985.

United defender Arthur Albiston celebrates with team-mate Graeme Hogg after Albiston scored in the Reds 3-0 win at Maine Road in September 1985.

*Sheer delight for David White and Ian Bishop, whose headed goal put City into
a 3-0 lead during the Blues crushing 5-1 win at Maine Road in September 1989.*

...respect with a spectacularly volleyed goal during the Reds heavy 5-1 defeat at Maine Road in September 1989.

Derby match tensions bubble over for United's Danny Wallace after his shirt is ripped during match at Maine Road in September 1989.

City's David White and United's Danny Wallace tangle for possession during the September '89 derby at Maine Road.

MATCH RESULT

MAN. UNITED 1   MAN. CITY 1
Blackmore   Brightwell

MANCHESTER
UNITED F.C.
OLD TRAFFORD
MANCHESTER
M16 0RA

A postal first day cover to commemorate the 100th First Division meeting between United and City.

United's Brian McClair caps a tremendous Reds recovery during the derby at Maine Road in October 1990 with the final equaliser in an exciting 3-3 draw.

City full-back Neil Pointon and United's Clayton Blackmore in derby action at Maine Road in October 1990.

City's Mark Ward holds off a challenge from United's Paul Ince and Neil Webb during the thrilling 3-3 draw at Maine Road in October 1990.

A great display of derby determination from City's Ray Ranson and United's Lou Macari during the 100th League match between the clubs on 22nd March 1980. United won the match at Old Trafford 1-0.

85

MANCHESTER CITY 3
(Lee pen, Bell, Summerbee)

MANCHESTER UNITED 3
(McIlroy, Kidd, Gowling)

DATE	6th November 1971	
DIVISION	One	
VENUE	Maine Road	
ATTENDANCE	63,326	

Manchester City		Manchester United
Joe CORRIGAN	1	Alex STEPNEY
Tony BOOK	2	Tommy O'NEIL
Willie DONACHIE	3	Tony DUNNE *
Mike DOYLE	4	Alan GOWLING
Tommy BOOTH	5	Steve JAMES
Alan OAKES	6	David SADLER
Mike SUMMERBEE	7	Willie MORGAN
Colin BELL	8	Brian KIDD
Wyn DAVIES	9	Bobby CHARLTON
Francis LEE	10	Sammy McILROY
Ian MELLOR	11	George BEST
Neil YOUNG	12	John ASTON (3)

*Backs to the wall for City as United's **Bobby Charlton** lets fly from a free-kick. **Brian Kidd** (left) and **Alan Gowling** (trying to distract the defenders) were both on the scoresheet in the classic 3-3 draw.*

BACKGROUND

United had appointed Frank O'Farrell of Leicester City as their new manager in the summer. He made no immediate moves to change personnel and the squad that opened the season was a familiar one. At first every move made by the genial Irishman came off as the Reds made a storming start to the new campaign. In what seemed an inspirational move, Gowling converted to a midfield role, while Law, Charlton and Best looked back to their very best form. Forced to play their first two home games at neutral venues, the penalty for the previous season's crowd troubles, this proved little handicap and the team roared to the top of the table with only two defeats in 15 games.

In derby week however, United were troubled by an injury to Law and a young Sammy McIlroy was put on stand-by for a sensational debut.

The Blues made a particularly astute summer signing when they picked up Wyn Davies, one of the best headers of a ball in Britain, for £60,000 from Newcastle United. This allowed City a wider variety of attacking options. With Malcolm Allison now installed as team manager and Joe Mercer as general manager, the men from Maine Road had also made a good start to the new season and were tucked in behind the leaders. Francis Lee was proving a prolific scorer with already a high proportion of his goals from penalties, more often than not gained by offences against himself. Lee's almost telepathic understanding of the boundaries of the penalty area and his rather convincing falls in the box soon accorded him the wry Chinese sounding nickname, 'Lee Won Pen'. Certainly there was much at stake as the teams prepared for this derby match.

BEFORE THE GAME

	P	W	D	L	F	A	Pts
UNITED	15	10	3	2	29	14	23
CITY	15	8	4	3	25	13	20

UNLUCKY CITY?

Yes BLUES WILL FOREVER CLAIM IT WAS ROBBERY ON BALANCE OF PLAY

No UNITED CAME BACK OFF THE ROPES TO HAND OUT A SCORING LESSON

MATCH VERDICT

In one of the great derbies more than 63,000 fans thrilled to an all-action display of attacking football that epitomised all that was good about Manchester football. There was no doubt about which man deserved the headlines, as 17-year-old Sammy McIlroy, pulled out of a morning reserve match, took the plaudits.

The action literally never stopped in, to use the cliche, a delightful feast of end-to-end football. City started impressively and United were virtually pinned back in their own half during the opening 20 minutes. With Stepney in outstanding form, United managed to weather the storm and by shortly after the interval had in fact stolen a two goal lead. Firstly Best, on a dazzling run, cut in from the right flank and was poised in a possible shooting position when McIlroy nipped onto the ball and showed no nerves at all as he slotted it between Oakes and Book and to the left of Corrigan. United fans, who had suffered such despair in recent years from this fixture, could not contain themselves shortly after the break as the Reds took what seemed a crucial two goal lead. Again a dangerous move on the United right saw the ball delivered at the far post and, as Corrigan scrambled to clear, Kidd steered it into the net.

The game though now took another sharp turn as, with United looking to impose total control, City immediately hit back. As the Blues poured forward there was a scramble in the United penalty area and, as a City man went down, the referee awarded the penalty. Despite United protests Lee powered the kick into the roof of the net. In a trice, unbelievably, City were level. With the United defence uncertain, Lee turned provider as he played a delightful through ball to Bell who galloped clear of the United back-line and, as he rounded Stepney and rolled the ball into the vacant net, it was the turn of the City fans to raise the roof.

With the match now bubbling to a crescendo, referee Ray Tinkler annoyed the home crowd by ruling out a Davies header as City pressed forward in search of the winner which would crown a remarkable recovery. But United were far from disheartened and with City pushing up they broke rapidly via Best, and when the ball was worked through to substitute Aston his shot rocketed past Corrigan into the net with the aid of a deflection off Gowling.

Back came City, and with just a minute remaining they looked to have salvaged a point as Summerbee's ferocious shot arrowed towards the top corner - only for Stepney to catapult across his goal and turn the ball round the post. With the fans out of their seats, the flag-kick floated across, but this time Stepney could only flap at the ball which rolled invitingly for Summerbee who drove it into the roof of the net and capped off one of the classic derbies.

*Seventeen-year-old **Sammy McIlroy** marked a tremendous debut by opening the scoring with this calmly taken shot wide of City goalkeeper **Joe Corrigan**.*

*City's **Mike Summerbee** and United's **George Best** chase for possession. Summerbee all controlled speed and aggression played one of his finest games and came up with City's late equaliser to round off the 3-3 thriller.*

*The aerial power of City's **Wyn Davies** is too much for United's Steve James in this attack, watched by **Bobby Charlton**, **Brian Kidd** and **Alan Gowling**.*

86

MANCHESTER UNITED 1
(Buchan)

MANCHESTER CITY 3
(Lee 2, Marsh)

DATE	12th April 1972
DIVISION	One
VENUE	Old Trafford
ATTENDANCE	56,362

Manchester United		Manchester City
John CONNAUGHTON	1	Ron HEALEY
Tommy O'NEIL	2	Tony BOOK
Tony DUNNE	3	Willie DONACHIE
Martin BUCHAN	4	Mike DOYLE *
Steve JAMES	5	Tommy BOOTH
David SADLER	6	Alan OAKES
George BEST	7	Mike SUMMERBEE
Alan GOWLING *	8	Colin BELL
Bobby CHARLTON	9	Wyn DAVIES
Brian KIDD	10	Francis LEE
Ian STOREY-MOORE	11	Tony TOWERS
Denis LAW (8)	12	Rodney MARSH (4)

BELL RINGS UP AN OMEN FOR TITLE

BACKGROUND

City were by now mounting a strong challenge for the title. Lee's hat-trick in the 5-2 beating of Wolverhampton Wanderers at the end of January had put the Blues two points clear at the top of the table. Shortly after this Allison made what at the time was a controversial move to sign the richly talented but unpredictable Rodney Marsh from Queen's Park Rangers for £200,000. The transfer of such a footballing maverick might almost have been construed as a calculated move by Allison to build on City's recent superiority over United. A genuine entertainer like Marsh would surely bring in the crowds and prove a thrilling counter-attraction to United's George Best. However, there were many mutterings about the dangers of changing a winning combination at this stage of the season. Most unfortunately for Marsh his first four games coincided with a 'blip' in the Blues' good form with only one victory obtained, and by the time of the derby City had slipped off top spot. Marsh had also been dropped down to a substitute role and City were in desperate need of the points to maintain their challenge.

United's season had collapsed quite dramatically. At the beginning of December the Reds had been clear at the top of the table and the title seemed a real prospect in O'Farrell's first season. But from this point United unbelievably, went two months and seven games without picking up a point in an all too spectacular descent. By March United were out of championship contention, but in an attempt to bolster a flagging squad O'Farrell now purchased the classy young defender Martin Buchan from Aberdeen and paid £200,000 for the exciting Nottingham Forest winger Ian Storey-Moore, just as it appeared he had signed for Midlands neighbours Derby County.

*United's **George Best** tries a flying header, but this effort just shaved the woodwork.*

Colin Bell - an outstanding contribution to City's fine victory

BEFORE THE GAME							
	P	W	D	L	F	A	Pts
CITY:	38	21	10	7	70	41	52
UNITED	37	17	9	11	62	53	43

MATCH VERDICT

An important victory for the Blues that resurrected their title aspirations. In a sterile and often rugged first half dominated by a packed midfield, United's four-four-two formation reflected a lack of confidence and ambition.

City seemed to have gained the initiative when, on the hour, United scored, as Buchan, easily United's best player, beat Healey with a crisp shot. This galvanised City who were level within a minute. Donachie, who had an impressive game at left-back, galloped down the wing and his high centre was expertly back-headed into the net by that ace poacher Lee whose goal made him the highest City scorer in a season since Tommy Johnson in 1929.

With the home crowd silenced it was City who now raised the tempo and within five minutes a harassed United surrendered a free kick which proved to be most costly. Summerbee swung the centre into the penalty area, Man of the Match Bell headed down, and Lee once again swept the ball in for his 32nd goal of the season. Allison then introduced his expensive substitute, and by so doing, effectively settled the match.

The tireless Bell displayed fantastic reflexes to dispossess Buchan and rolled the ball perfectly into the path of Marsh, whose exquisitely cool finish brought the City bench and Allison dancing onto the pitch. "Magic, pure magic!" purred a delighted Allison afterwards.

AT THE SEASON'S END

CITY: Finished 4th on 57 points
(same points as Leeds United in 2nd place and 1 point behind champions Derby County)

UNITED: Finished 8th on 48 points

Martin Buchan holds off the challange of City's Tommy Booth to fire United into a 1-0 lead on the hour.

The little Big Shot lifts City

*City's dance of delight as two-goal **Francis Lee** congratulates substitute **Rodney Marsh** on netting the Blues third at Old Trafford.*

87

MANCHESTER CITY 3
(Bell 2, Buchan og)

MANCHESTER UNITED 0

DATE	18th November 1972
DIVISION	One
VENUE	Maine Road
ATTENDANCE	52,050

Manchester City		Manchester United
Joe CORRIGAN	1	Alex STEPNEY
Tony BOOK	2	Tommy O'NEIL
Willie DONACHIE	3	Tony DUNNE
Mike DOYLE	4	Willie MORGAN *
Colin BARRETT	5	David SADLER
Derek JEFFRIES	6	Martin BUCHAN
Mike SUMMERBEE	7	George BEST
Colin BELL	8	Ted MacDOUGALL
Rodney MARSH	9	Bobby CHARLTON
Francis LEE	10	Wyn DAVIES
Tony TOWERS	11	Ian STOREY-MOORE
Frank CARRODUS	12	Brian KIDD (4)

BACKGROUND

Genial Joe Mercer, the man who had guided City through such successful years left the club for Coventry City in the summer, and Malcolm Allison assumed total charge of managerial affairs, but it was not ultimately destined to last long. His side started well enough with an impressive victory over Aston Villa in the Charity Shield, but this proved a false dawn and, after the Blues lost five of the opening six games, the club was anchored at the bottom of the table. By late October the Blues' form had picked up sufficiently for them to enter the derby unbeaten in four games, which included a 4-0 home win over Derby County and an impressive 3-2 victory at Everton on the Saturday prior to the meeting at Maine Road.

United had made a miserable start to the new season. Three straight defeats were followed by a meagre four points from the next six games, leaving the Reds also down at the bottom of the table. In mid-September there had been the rarity of a transfer between the Manchester clubs when Allison allowed Wyn Davies to move to Old Trafford for £60,000. Davies scored a debut goal in the season's first win, - a home game against Derby County who were beaten 3-0. O'Farrell, now under some pressure himself, went to the Third Division and paid a record fee of £220,000 to Bournemouth for the prolific goalscorer Ted MacDougall. The new striker had scored twice in the six games prior to the derby, one of them in a morale-boosting 2-0 defeat of Liverpool. United were hoping this improvement would be maintained at Maine Road.

BEFORE THE GAME							
	P	W	D	L	F	A	Pts
CITY	17	7	2	8	25	27	16
UNITED	17	3	6	8	16	23	12

*City's young defensive stars **Derek Jeffries** (No.6) and **Colin Barrett** challenge United forwards **Ted MacDougall** (No.8) and recent former Blue **Wyn Davies**.*

Shame on you both

MANCHESTER'S two world famous football clubs should be thoroughly ashamed of themselves today after the derby that heaped disgrace on British football.

If City take any pride in the 3—0 victory which they salvaged from this Soccer garbage they will be guilty of an unprincipled approach to the game.

All the chronic ills that beset English Soccer were crystalised in a disgusting first-half of snarling savagery. There were flying fists, disgraceful tackles, dissent that demanded more drastic measures by the referee, and filthy chants from fans from both camps. What sort of a way is all this to win for the game the affection of school-boys, to whom well-motivated City officials gave free tickets?

Without attempt to apportion the blame, United manager Frank O'Farrell had good reason to say there was too much intimidation, too much cheating and too much nastiness.

City and United were a disgrace

And while too many fouls went unpunished and too few were punished severely enough, City were the more belligerent force in the first half.

The attitude of their captain, Colin Bell, to referee John Homewood was clearly intimidatory, and his second booking of the season for dissent seemed long overdue when it happened.

The nastiness brimmed over in the astonishing 24th minute when, after a reckless tackle by Tommy O'Neil the full-back disappeared under the flailing fists of Francis Lee.

Annoyed

'It annoyed me when he hurt me badly with the kick that immobilised my knee,' said the England forward.

But Lee seemed none the worse for the experience after a brief absence from the game. With a stricter referee, his absence might have been much longer.

Probably the most grace-less sights in the first half were those of famous City forwards grubbing like scavengers for cheap penal-ties and free kicks.

Flashpoint again! **Colin Barrett** and veteran **Tony Book** prepare to intervene as City goalkeeper **Joe Corrigan** rounds on United striker **Ted MacDougall** during a derby match littered with ill-feeling and rash challenges.

MATCH VERDICT

In a game of poor vintage, constantly marred by flashes of ill-temper and torrid tackles, the Blues proved far too strong for a disorganised United side. Where possible, City were the more fluent team with the talents of Bell, Lee and Marsh outstanding in attack, while the youthful Barrett and Jeffries were impressive in defence. United, looking particularly nervous at the back, cracked after just seven minutes and from this point it became an afternoon of toil for the Reds.

There seemed no danger to United as a City attack fizzled out with a harmless high centre but as Stepney and full-back Tony Dunne both went for the ball the goalkeeper ended up present-ing City skipper Bell with the simplest of goals from a few yards. From this moment on, the com-bative City midfield were first to every fifty-fifty ball and only some doughty defending by Buchan kept the Blues from immediately increasing their lead.

In an attempt to climb back into the game Unit-ed showed more initiative at the outset of the second half and recent former Blue Wyn Davies was unlucky to see a header cleared off the line by Barrett. However, this was indicative of the rub of the green on the day and, with a final flourish, City banished their neighbours. The impressive Bell was once again United's executioner. Fatally left alone in space, he rifled a fierce shot past Step-ney and in the final moments of the match it was his shot that was comically diverted by Buchan past the helpless Stepney to leave United a well beaten team.

Alex Stepney's blunder leaves United's defence stranded as City's *Colin Bell* slots the Blues into a 7th minute lead.

88

MANCHESTER UNITED 0
MANCHESTER CITY 0

DATE	21st April 1973
DIVISION	One
VENUE	Old Trafford
ATTENDANCE	61,676

Manchester United		Manchester City
Alex STEPNEY	1	Ron HEALEY
Tony YOUNG	2	Tony BOOK
Steve JAMES *	3	Willie DONACHIE
George GRAHAM	4	Mike DOYLE
Jim HOLTON	5	Tommy BOOTH
Martin BUCHAN	6	Alan OAKES
Willie MORGAN	7	Mike SUMMERBEE
Brian KIDD	8	Colin BELL
Bobby CHARLTON	9	Rodney MARSH
Lou MACARI	10	Francis LEE
Mick MARTIN	11	Tony TOWERS
Trevor ANDERSON (3)	12	Derek JEFFRIES

BACKGROUND

Frank O'Farrell's short tenure as United manager came to an end on 16th December following a humiliating 5-0 defeat at Crystal Palace, and with relegation a real prospect. The ebullient Tommy Docherty was appointed manager and the club was turned inside-out with a rapid turnover of players. As was often the case with the popular 'Doc' the club took on a very high profile and was headline news as the Press recorded the infusion of a number of Scottish players including the likes of George Graham, Alex Forsyth, Jim Holton and Lou Macari. By the time of the derby Docherty's surgery had effectively succeeded in repelling the threat of relegation.

City's season had not been a happy one either. An apparently talented squad were unable to put any kind of significant run together and languished in the lower half of the table. There would however, be no derby contest between the two highest of profile Manchester managers as, following a row over the sale of Ian Mellor to Norwich in March, and constant rumours of other disagreements, including not being able to motivate his team of 'superstars', Malcolm Allison left City, struggling in the middle of another poor sequence of defeats, to manage Crystal Palace. A useful Blues star of the early Fifties and a back-room coaching stalwart at Maine Road for many years, Johnny Hart was appointed caretaker-manager and he led the Blues into the low key 88th derby match.

BEFORE THE GAME

	P	W	D	L	F	A	Pts
CITY	39	14	10	15	53	56	38
UNITED	39	12	12	15	43	57	36

Manchester United in 1972-73. The Reds season began under Frank O'Farrell and ended under Tommy Docherty, who made significant additions to this line-up. *Back:* Wyn Davies (inset), John Fitzpatrick, Tony Young, Tommy O'Neil, Sammy McIlroy, Carlo Sartori, Tony Dunne, Ted MacDougall (inset). *Middle:* Steve James, David Sadler, Alex Stepney, John Connaughton, Jimmy Rimmer, Brian Kidd, Martin Buchan. *Front:* Willie Morgan, Ian Moore, Denis Law, George Best, Bobby Charlton.

MATCH VERDICT

In a dour, petty encounter United extracted the grim satisfaction of arresting City's recent golden run at Old Trafford, but this seemed a very minor achievement when set against the deeds of some of the great United sides of all too recent memory.

At least United's defence seemed a tighter one under Tommy Docherty, and the towering, raw-boned crowd favourite Jim Holton gave another solid performance in this game. Martin Buchan, playing in an unusual position at left back, impressed with his pace and allowed Mike Summerbee little scope to cause any danger. But United's graceful midfield pair of the veteran Charlton - playing in his last derby - and Graham were totally overrun by their more youthful City counterparts, and with Doyle and Oakes outstanding in defence, the summary result was that United offered virtually no attacking threat all afternoon. The only suggestion of a goal to either side came late on. Holton showed a certain naivety and lack of concentration as, following his foul he remonstrated with the referee, while Summerbee rolled the free-kick to the unmarked Marsh whose shot clipped the outside of the post.

After some of the excellent derby games of recent years, The Manchester Evening News bemoaned the lack of entertainment from both sides:

"Sad for soccer that League football's biggest attendance of the season should have had to watch such a sterile, dismal derby. The fact that it went out on television on Sunday was another blow for the popularity of the game. Both Manchester United and Manchester City hit a low note and sustained it. This 0-0 draw wasn't vicious, simply petty and spoiling. At the same time I cannot see too many of the United fans in the huge 61,000 crowd being too down-hearted, particularly now that they have had time to reflect upon the significance of their team's performance. They have only to think back to the early season encounter at Maine Road to know what I mean. That day City won 3-0 with the help of three appalling defensive mistakes by a very ragged Reds team

On Saturday United presented a very different front. There was no question about the solidity of the defence for instance. Jim Holton at centre-half has made all the difference, dominating and decisive, and the reorganisation of the back four has clicked into a great understanding. Martin Buchan is immaculate in his new left-back role, even finding time for his constructive touches again. Tony Young has become a tough little nut at right-back and Steve James has been an enormous success in his new role of sweeper.

United lost James through injury at the interval but Mick Martin fitted in just as effectively. In fact United are looking a team again in the real meaning of the word, and that is the difference between now and the humiliation at Maine Road when United were intimidated and frightened. Up front and in midfield it was disappointing of course. Brian Kidd toiled well enough, but there was no flow from George Graham and Bobby Charlton. Willie Morgan was well held and Lou Macari also found the City defence in destructive mood.

But the improvement at the back is a start, and after the fright of relegation for a great deal of this season, most United fans will be content with that step forward. The rest will come in time".

Malcolm Allison - left City for Crystal Palace in March 1973.

Frank O'Farrell - dismissed by United in December 1972.

AT THE SEASON'S END

CITY: Finished 11th on 41 points

UNITED: Finished 18th on 37 points

Manchester City in 1972-73. *The Blues season began under Malcolm Allison and ended with Johnny Hart in charge.* **Back:** *Tommy Booth, Mike Doyle, Ron Healey, Joe Corrigan, Colin Barrett, Ian Mellor.* **Second Row:** *Harry Godwin (Chief Scout), Wyn Davies, Colin Bell, Derek Jeffries, Tony Book, Alan Oakes, Geoff Clarke, Frank Carrodus, Freddie Hill, Tony Towers, John Gannon, Glyn Pardoe, Malcolm Allison (Manager), Ken Barnes (Trainer).* **Third Row:** *Willie Donachie, Peter Bounds, Mike Brennan, Jed Coyne, Andy Black, George Dunlop, Steve Potter, Howard White, Duncan Kerr, Denis Leman, Eamon Kavanagh, Steve Coulson, Johnny Hart (Coach).* **Front:** *Francis Lee, Mike Summerbee, Rodney Marsh, Jimmy Madley, Paul Smith, George McBeth.*

89

MANCHESTER CITY 0
MANCHESTER UNITED 0

DATE	13th March 1974
DIVISION	One
VENUE	Maine Road
ATTENDANCE	51,331

Manchester City		Manchester United
Joe CORRIGAN	1	Alex STEPNEY
Glyn PARDOE	2	Alex FORSYTH
Willie DONACHIE	3	Stewart HOUSTON
Mike DOYLE	4	Mick MARTIN *
Tommy BOOTH	5	Jim HOLTON
Mick HORSWILL	6	Martin BUCHAN
Mike SUMMERBEE	7	Willie MORGAN
Colin BELL	8	Lou MACARI
Frank CARRODUS	9	Brian GREENHOFF
Alan OAKES	10	Gerry DALY
Dennis TUEART	11	Paul BIELBY
Denis LEMAN	12	George GRAHAM (4)

BACKGROUND

United were undergoing a period of immense change. It was almost a year since the last derby meeting, and Bobby Charlton had retired officially and George Best unofficially. More headlines were also made in the previous summer when Denis Law, the last of United's famous trio returned to City on a free transfer. Law commented later in his autobiography on his disquiet over the the way his illustrious United career finished, and it proved a shrewd short term move by Johnny Hart to bring the Scot to Maine Road. Younger players were still emerging. Brian Greenhoff won a place as a utility player and Docherty showed an ongoing natural flair for picking up good players from the lower divisions when he signed Stewart Houston from Brentford. However, with half the season gone last season's deep seated problems still remained and the Reds were rooted in the relegation zone. Unusually, the club was also gaining a reputation for rough and tough play as they battled to retain First Division status.

City had also already made many headlines this season. Early on, the popular Johnny Hart was forced to resign due to ill health. Hart's side, based around attractive forwards, were good to watch but inconsistent. His replacement was something of a surprise as City appointed the dour, disciplinarian Norwich City manager Ron Saunders. Within three months he was leading City out at Wembley as the Blues went all the way to the final of the League Cup, where they lost out 2-1 to Wolverhampton Wanderers.

However, the Blues did not carry this Cup form through into League games and the club languished in the wrong half of the table not far above their struggling neighbours. Ron Saunders decided to take action and, in the week preceding the derby, Tony Towers was transferred to Sunderland for £125,000 and, with a cash adjustment on the deal, Mick Horswill (£100,000) and the talented Dennis Tueart (£275,000) moved from Wearside in time to make their debuts in this important derby.

The week before the derby saw City manager **Ron Saunders** move into the transfer market and sign both **Dennis Tueart** (£275,000) and **Mick Horswill** (£100,000) from Sunderland. The pair made their debuts against United

BEFORE THE GAME

	P	W	D	L	F	A	Pts
CITY	30	11	8	11	30	28	30
UNITED	30	6	9	15	25	38	21

MATCH VERDICT

It was a match that made front page headlines for all the wrong reasons. 'Spare us more soccer shame' screamed the Manchester Evening News in the aftermath of one of the most notorious matches in the history of the fixture.

The bare facts of two players dismissed and four others booked do not begin to fully describe the disgraceful scenes that accompanied this game. Any football played was virtually irrelevant as both sides employed ale-house tactics, liberally sprinkled with deliberate intimidation and foul tackling. Following an unsavoury enough opening, the match exploded when, after another midfield brawl involving a number of players, referee Clive Thomas ordered chief offenders Macari and Doyle from the field. In full view of the large crowd both players stood their ground and in an appalling show of petulance refused to go. In the end Thomas led all the players from the field and there was a potentially ugly few minutes when the incensed crowd were left wondering what would happen next. Eventually, both teams returned, minus the miscreants, and the two players subsequently faced League disciplinary action. City, even with their expensive debutants, were unable to put any quality moves together, hardly surprising, as too many players were often embroiled in the spoiling tactics. Perhaps the saddest aspect of all was that United's desperation for League points had outweighed the proud sporting traditions of a great club. This, coupled with some subsequent crowd hooliganism, provided nothing but shameful memories of a derby match best forgotten.

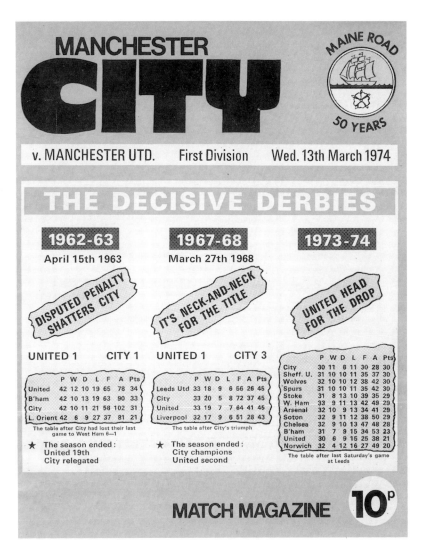

MANCHESTER **CITY**

MAINE ROAD
50 YEARS

v. MANCHESTER UTD.   First Division   Wed. 13th March 1974

THE DECISIVE DERBIES

1962-63
April 15th 1963
DISPUTED PENALTY SHATTERS CITY

UNITED 1   CITY 1

	P	W	D	L	F	A	Pts
United	42	12	10	19	65	78	34
B'ham	42	10	13	19	63	90	33
City	42	10	11	21	58	102	31
L. Orient	42	6	9	27	37	81	21

The table after City had lost their last game to West Ham 6—1

★ The season ended:
United 19th
City relegated

1967-68
March 27th 1968
IT'S NECK-AND-NECK FOR THE TITLE

UNITED 1   CITY 3

	P	W	D	L	F	A	Pts
Leeds Utd	33	18	9	6	56	26	45
City	33	20	5	8	72	37	45
United	33	19	7	7	64	41	45
Liverpool	32	17	9	6	51	28	43

The table after City's triumph

★ The season ended:
City champions
United second

1973-74
UNITED HEAD FOR THE DROP

	P	W	D	L	F	A	Pts
City	30	11	8	11	30	28	30
Sheff. U.	31	10	10	11	35	37	30
Wolves	32	10	10	12	38	42	30
Spurs	31	10	10	11	35	42	30
Stoke	31	8	13	10	39	35	29
W. Ham	33	9	11	13	42	49	29
Arsenal	32	10	9	13	34	41	29
Soton	32	9	11	12	38	50	29
Chelsea	32	9	10	13	47	48	28
B'ham	31	7	9	15	34	53	23
United	30	6	9	15	25	38	21
Norwich	32	4	12	16	27	49	20

The table after last Saturday's game at Leeds

MATCH MAGAZINE   **10ᵖ**

Spare us more soccer shame!

MANCHESTER today reflected on a night of savage soccer shame. In one of the worst derby games on record, City and United both had a player sent off and Glamorgan referee Clive Thomas was forced to call a five-minute halt for tempers to cool.

In addition, 51,000 spectators at Maine Road saw four other players booked as both sides provided an unsavoury spectacle that must never be repeated.

Unfortunately, both sides meet again in the final match of the season—at Old Trafford on April 27.

For the sake of football in general, the good name of the two clubs in particular, and the honour of Manchester itself, I hope we are not forced to see a repeat.

It was a wicked exhibition of petulance and bad temper by sides who, too often in recent years, have resorted to such ale-house football.

Derby matches generate sufficient passion and atmosphere . . . last night it was loaded even more, because United are struggling desperately for First Division survival.

That is why the hope is that their fate is decided before the sides meet again. If not, and they need the points to stay up, we could witness an even more bitter, shabby affair.

Lou Macari (above) and Mike Doyle (right) - both sent off

Referee Clive Thomas, who was forced to lead the teams off the field to 'cool off' following the scenes surrounding the dismissal of City's Mike Doyle and United's Lou Macari. Thomas said later: "When taking their names I told them 'off'. They both refused to come off the field and went further away. I called them back and said: 'off'. They refused and, therefore, I had no option but to pick up the ball, walk off the field of play and call off the two teams."

90

MANCHESTER UNITED 0
MANCHESTER CITY 1
(Law)

DATE	27th April 1974
DIVISION	One
VENUE	Old Trafford
ATTENDANCE	56,996

Manchester United		Manchester City
Alex STEPNEY	1	Joe CORRIGAN
Alex FORSYTH	2	Colin BARRETT
Stewart HOUSTON	3	Willie DONACHIE
Brian GREENHOFF	4	Mike DOYLE
Jim HOLTON	5	Tommy BOOTH
Martin BUCHAN	6	Alan OAKES
Willie MORGAN	7	Mike SUMMERBEE
Lou MACARI	8	Colin BELL
Sammy McILROY	9	Francis LEE
Jim McCALLIOG	10	Denis LAW *
Gerry DALY	11	Dennis TUEART
Mick MARTIN	12	Mick HENSON (10)

BACKGROUND

City's form dipped again following the last derby match in March, and there was a whiff of player-power as new Chairman Peter Swales ended Ron Saunders' brief management spell with the sack. Tony Book was the popular choice to succeed Saunders and he quietly led the Blues to safety with a number of unbeaten games, culminating in the 2-1 defeat of West Ham prior to the derby visit to Old Trafford. Denis Law was set to revisit his old stamping ground as skipper of the Blues and everything was poised for a nostalgic after-noon as one of Old Trafford's all time greats returned, were it not for the fact that United were battling to avoid the humiliation of a drop into the Second Division for the first time since 1938.

Tommy Docherty had tried his best to stop the rot, but did not look likely to save United for a sec-ond season and, if truth be told, relegation had looked a certainty since Christmas. United looked a doomed side of dubious quality, drastically short of both goals and confidence. Even so, with an injection of more young players United unexpect-edly hit a decent streak of form and an unbeaten run of six games featured a 3-0 win over Everton and 1-0 victory over Cup finalists Newcastle Unit-ed to give the long-suffering fans renewed hope. However, failure to score goals cost them dearly yet again as in the midweek match before the City game United went down 1-0 at Everton to leave further gloom enveloping Old Trafford. The stark reality was that United entered this critical derby contemplating the almost unthinkable prospect of relegation to the Second Division. They quite simply had to beat City and then hope fellow strugglers Southampton and Birmingham lost their matches. This scenario would enable the Reds to go into their final league game at Stoke City with a chance of staying up.

BEFORE THE GAME						
	P	W	D	L	F	A	Pts
CITY	41	13	12	16	38	46	38
UNITED	40	10	12	18	38	46	32

United fans started a fire in the Stretford End and then invaded the pitch again three minutes after the initial disturbance that followed Law's goal. Referee David Smith abandoned the match with five minutes left but the League ruled the result stood.

MATCH VERDICT

The stakes had never been so high since City faced a corresponding end of season fate back in 1963. Once again circumstances had conspired to turn the derby match into a crucial fixture upon which would depend the First Division survival of one of these famous clubs. United's desperate League position was certainly reflected in the nature of their play. Too often rushed and riddled with basic mistakes they exuded the aura of condemned men. As so often the case with teams on the slide, when the Reds did put their football together 'Lady Luck' was absent. Donachie and Barrett both cleared shots off the City line, but the Blues play also lacked any particular pattern amid all the tension. Following an uneventful first half, the game seemed to be meandering towards a tame goalless draw when Fate took a quite extraordinary hand. In one of the most controversial and famous derby incidents United's fate was settled at a stroke. Just as in 1963, when as a new United player he was brought down for a late penalty, Denis Law was at the centre of the action. United's former 'King of Old Trafford' had been warmly applauded by appreciative home fans on his return, as City skipper, to the scene of his many triumphs. Law had been virtually invisible in the preceding 81 minutes but the following moments changed all that. At the end of what was a sporadic City attack Bell found Lee, who passed the ball to Law standing back to goal near the penalty spot. They say instincts in old strikers die hard, and it was typical of Law that he should instantly, and quite brilliantly, back-heel the ball past a startled Stepney. A number of supporters invaded the pitch and, looking almost in a state of shock at the enormity of what he had done to his beloved old club, Law raced off the field and was replaced by

*The moment of relegation truth for United as former favourite **Denis Law** (No.10) back-heels the ball past a startled **Alex Stepney** for City's 82nd minute winner. What was to be Law's last touch in League football is watched by United's **Jim Holton**, **Gerry Daly** and City's **Colin Bell**.*

substitute Henson. Denis commented later in his autobiography; "it was no more than a reflex action which made me flick out my heel - and as it was I felt sick. I have seldom felt so depressed in my life as I did that weekend. After 19 years of giving everything I had to score goals, I had finally scored one which I almost wished I hadn't".

Law's goal looked sure to be the one which sent United down, but in effect they would have been relegated anyway because fellow strugglers Birmingham and Southampton both won the same afternoon. The final minutes of the match were marred by a second more ugly pitch invasion from disgruntled supporters and ended with the game abandoned. The League, quite rightly, later ruled the score should stand. Six years after winning the European Cup, United were in the Second Division for the first time since 1938.

AT THE SEASON'S END

CITY: Finished 14th on 40 points
(League Cup finalists, losing 1-2 to Wolves)

UNITED: Finished 21st on 32 points
(Relegated to Division Two)

Law has the last sad word

By ERIC TODD

Man U 0, Man C 1

Saturday's greatest irony at Old Trafford was without doubt or exception Denis Law's goal. It was " the most unkindest cut of all " in the words of Marcus Antonius — he was not in the press box of course — who in the same speech said " If you have tears, prepare to shed them now." Which seemed no less relevant.

Law, you may remember, used to play for Manchester United whose exclusive monarchy and lauded him in such excerpts as " We'd walk a million miles for one of your goals our De-he-nis." They gave him a generous encore when he returned from exile as captain for the day. They cheered him again when he trotted up for the spin of the coin.

Before that some of the younger supporters ran on to the pitch to greet the United players and to wish them luck in this most crucial game " Please keep off the pitch," uttered a disembodied voice which lacked the severity and anxiety of later repeats.

So the referee, Mr D W Smith, of Stonehouse — a replacement for Mr J Hunting of Leicester —, started his last game before he retires, in the event an uninspired game apart from good performances by Oakes, Barrett, Doyle, Macari, Daly and Houston. United did nearly all the attacking but their supporters' frustration was aggravated when Donachie and Barrett both cleared off their own goal line. Mercifully, however, there was no rough and tumble compared with that when United were on the United pitch. Doyle was booked for obstructing Macari, but this was solid stuff.

Eight minutes from time, Bell passed to Lee, and Lee to Law who backheeled the ball brilliantly past Stepney. Law did look a bit sheepish — " tsh now you weep and I perceive you feel the dint of pity " — but being Law he just had to score. The Stretford End had only a few yards let alone a million miles to walk after this goal and, reinforced by an auxiliary army from the old scoreboard end, they swarmed over the pitch in their hundreds. Mr Smith led the players to the touchline while the police, hopelessly outnumbered as they were, managed to repel boarders in a three-minute counter-attack.

The game was restarted, and the Stretford End started a fire of toilet paper and programmes hoping, perhaps that a smoke screen would help towards the abandonment for which obviously they were hoping. Sir Matt Busby, another of the Stretford End's unofficial kings, appealed for order when the second invasion got under way, but it was useless. According to the referee, four minutes remained when he abandoned the match By the that time, results from the other relevant matches had come through — they were not announced publicly which perhaps has as well — and United were down.

Two hundred spectators were ejected before and during the game ; 33 including 11 juveniles, will be required to answer accusations of disorderly conduct, assaulting the police, theft, and pocket-picking. If these be the loyal supporters of whom Tommy Docherty speaks so highly, few people will admire his choice.

Denis Law is surrounded by fans who invaded the pitch moments after he scored City's goal. "I didn't want to play in the match, but as a professional I had to" said Law who added he had never felt as depressed as he did that weekend.

91

MANCHESTER CITY 2
(Nicholl og, Royle)

MANCHESTER UNITED 2
(McCreery, Macari)

DATE		27th September 1975
DIVISION		One
VENUE		Maine Road
ATTENDANCE		46,931

Manchester City		Manchester United
Joe CORRIGAN	1	Alex STEPNEY
Kenny CLEMENTS	2	Jimmy NICHOLL
Willie DONACHIE	3	Stewart HOUSTON
Mike DOYLE	4	David McCREERY
Dave WATSON	5	Brian GREENHOFF
Alan OAKES	6	Martin BUCHAN
Asa HARTFORD	7	Steve COPPELL
Colin BELL	8	Sammy McILROY
Joe ROYLE *	9	Stuart PEARSON
Rodney MARSH	10	Lou MACARI
Dennis TUEART	11	Gerry DALY
Denis LEMAN (9)	12	Arthur ALBISTON

BACKGROUND

United spent only one season in the Second Division and returned revitalised as Champions. Tommy Docherty put his faith in the young players who had done so well to gain the club an instant return and his only major signing brought Stuart Pearson to the club from Hull City for £200,000. Ironically, United's drop down a division had actually increased their phenomenal support with an average gate of 48,000 (an increase of 5,000 on the relegation season). City, who might have hoped to take advantage of being the only Manchester First Division club that season averaged 33,000.

Three straight wins at the season's outset quickly showed the 'new' United would not be out of place back in the higher division and indeed, they were already up amongst the leaders.

Just as had happened with United, the great City side of the late 60's and early 70's was breaking up. Francis Lee had been sold to Derby County and promptly helped them to win the 1974-75 Championship while Mike Summerbee had joined Burnley. City had, partly by necessity, become big spenders as they replaced the old with known quality. Dave Watson, Sunderland's commanding centre-half cost £250,000; midfielder Asa Hartford the same price from West Bromwich Albion and centre-forward Joe Royle arrived from Everton for £175,000. Despite boasting eight internationals, the side had made only a modest start to the new season and were hoping for an improvement as the derby contests resumed.

BEFORE THE GAME							
	P	W	D	L	F	A	Pts
UNITED	9	6	1	2	16	7	13
CITY	9	4	1	4	13	6	9

*United's flying winger **Steve Coppell** avoids this lunge by another of City's new signings, midfielder **Asa Hartford** who cost £250,000 from West Bromwich Albion in August 1974.*

Dave Watson - the commanding centre-half was a £250,000 buy from Sunderland as City re-shaped their side

MATCH REPORT

In an excellent derby at Maine Road where City had become near invincibles against United, Tommy Docherty's adventurous young side were pleased to come away with a point. All the scoring in an exciting match was crammed into a spell-binding ten minute period during the first half. On 21 minutes United's youthful full-back Jimmy Nicholl was put under pressure to such an extent by the whole-hearted Joe Royle that, with Stepney off his line, the youngster spectacularly lobbed the ball over the stranded goalkeeper and into his own net. Despite this unnerving error, the Irish-man showed great character and generally enjoyed a sterling game. Indeed, the United side as a whole were not dispirited by the setback and took the game to their experienced hosts, who first became unsettled and then, dramatically, conceded two goals inside a minute to leave the home crowd stunned. City were slow to clear a United attack and little David McCreery nipped in like a flash to drill a shot past Corrigan. Then as City were busy adjusting, United raced away, forced a corner and with the home defence still at sixes and sevens, McIlroy's in-swinging flag-kick was expertly headed home by that veritable 'jack-in-the-box' Lou Macari. The United fans, now in good voice, were however, soon silenced as amaz-ingly in City's next real attack the Blues equalised. As Tueart's corner came across, Doyle hooked the ball into the box and big Joe Royle thumped it into the back of the United net. Not surprisingly, after such a goal glut, the remainder of the game seemed rather tame but there was still much good football to admire, suggesting this could well be a successful season for both Manchester clubs. In the final moments City might have snatched both the points as the veteran Oakes headed over an open goal. In truth though, on the day neither side deserved to lose.

City star **Rodney Marsh** makes it clear exactly where he wants the ball as United's **Alex Stepney** and **Jimmy Nicholl** organise the Reds defence.

Well done mate! City's **Dennis Tueart** rushes to congratulate new £175,000 signing **Joe Royle** after the big centre-forward had thumped his corner past Alex Stepney to level matters at 2-2.

92

MANCHESTER UNITED 2
(McIlroy, Hill)

MANCHESTER CITY 0

DATE	4th May 1976
DIVISION	One
VENUE	Old Trafford
ATTENDANCE	59,528

Manchester United		Manchester City
Alex STEPNEY	1	Joe CORRIGAN
Alex FORSYTH	2	Kenny CLEMENTS
Stewart HOUSTON	3	Michael DOCHERTY
Gerry DALY	4	Mike DOYLE *
Arthur ALBISTON	5	Tommy BOOTH
Martin BUCHAN	6	Ged KEEGAN
Steve COPPELL	7	Peter BARNES
Sammy McILROY	8	Paul POWER
Stuart PEARSON *	9	Joe ROYLE
Tommy JACKSON	10	Asa HARTFORD
Gordon HILL	11	Dennis TUEART
David McCREERY (9)	12	Alan OAKES (4)

BACKGROUND

United had enjoyed a tremendous first season back in the big time and their exciting brand of open attacking football had remarkably brought them within sight of achieving the coveted League and Cup 'double'. Unfortunately, by the time of the derby it was clear this was not to be. A shock 1-0 defeat by Second Division Southampton at Wembley three days earlier had stopped them winning the F.A. Cup and, shortly before this, League defeats by Stoke City and Leicester City ended the Reds' interest in the League title chase when they had looked favourites to win it. A consolation to such a promising campaign would be to beat City and record their first League victory over the Blues in five years.

City had disappointed in the League, mainly because only two away victories all season meant they were never in a position to seriously mount a challenge for the title. Colin Bell, injured in the November League Cup tie with United, had still not returned to the side and there were now long term fears for his future, while Rodney Marsh had moved on to play in the United States. Younger players such as Paul Power, Kenny Clements, Peter Barnes and Ged Keegan were now regulars in the side and had helped City to make up for League disappointments by winning the League Cup, beating Newcastle United 2-1 at Wembley in March. More headlines were made days before the derby when City signed Tommy Docherty's son Michael from Burnley to set up a unique father and son confrontation for this 92nd derby match.

BEFORE THE GAME							
	P	W	D	L	F	A	Pts
UNITED	41	22	10	9	66	42	54
CITY	41	16	11	14	64	44	43

Stuart Pearson - a new face in the top flight, the striker had cost United £200,000 from Hull and scored 17 goals as the Reds won promotion at the first attempt. A fine opportunist, he was soon to prove his worth in Division One.

Peter Barnes - now a regular as City's new side developed during this season, he won the PFA Young Player of the Year Award for 1975-76.

MATCH VERDICT

This game, which was played during the week following United's disappointing Cup Final defeat by Southampton was, perhaps understandably, a bit of an anti-climax. If anything it was the Blues who had more of an end-of-season look to them.

Had City shown more drive and appetite in the first half when United looked stale they could have been well in front. But it was United who put their disappointments behind them and, in a sparkling second half showing, claimed the top dog spot in Manchester.

Two goals scored in four second half minutes settled the matter. Hill, so disappointing at Wembley, showed what might have been when after 48 minutes he fired a spectacular shot from an acute angle into the City net. Four minutes later, Forsyth's through ball allowed McIlroy to run on and outpace Doyle, Booth and Docherty before beating Corrigan with a fine angled drive. From this point there was just one team in the game and only two brilliant Corrigan saves denied Coppell from doubling the Reds' winning margin.

AT THE SEASON'S END

UNITED: Finished 3rd on 56 points
(F.A. Cup Runners-up, losing 1-0 to Southampton)

CITY: Finished 8th on 43 points
(League Cup Winners, beating Newcastle United 2-1)

WELCOME TO OLD TRAFFORD

MANCHESTER UNITED v MANCHESTER CITY

SPECIAL DERBY REVIEW

United

4th May, 1976
Kick-off 7.30   No. 27

10p

*Split family loyalties over Red or Blue are not unusual in Manchester, but a unique family confrontation was thrown up in this derby as City's recent signing of full-back **Michael Docherty** from Burnley pitted the young defender against his father, United manager **Tommy Docherty**, who commented crisply :"I hope Michael is the best player on the losing side!"*

Gordon Hill - made up for a disappointing display in the F.A. Cup final with a thrilling goal to set United on their way to this end of season derby victory.

93

MANCHESTER CITY 1
(Tueart)

MANCHESTER UNITED 3
(Coppell, McCreery, Daly)

DATE		25th September 1976
DIVISION		One
VENUE		Maine Road
ATTENDANCE		48,861

Manchester City		Manchester United
Joe CORRIGAN	1	Alex STEPNEY
Mike DOCHERTY	2	Jimmy NICHOLL
Willie DONACHIE	3	Stewart HOUSTON
Mike DOYLE	4	Gerry DALY
Dave WATSON	5	Brian GREENHOFF
Paul POWER	6	Martin BUCHAN
Ged KEEGAN *	7	Steve COPPELL
Brian KIDD	8	Sammy McILROY
Joe ROYLE	9	Stuart PEARSON *
Asa HARTFORD	10	Lou MACARI
Dennis TUEART	11	Gordon HILL
Tommy BOOTH (7)	12	David McCREERY (9)

BACKGROUND

Both Manchester clubs made pleasing starts to the new season. Docherty had developed an entertaining and successful side that played fast one touch football with goals likely from a number of sources. Above all, in an era when too many teams served up sterile defensive tactics, the 'Doc' had made wingers fashionable again and, in Steve Coppell and Gordon Hill, had two of the very best currently playing the game, dangerous both as creators and finishers.

Only one defeat had been sustained, when Tottenham Hotspur mounted an amazing second-half comeback at Old Trafford to beat United 3-2 after being totally outclassed by a thrilling Reds' performance in the first 45 minutes.

Meanwhile, Tony Book had set the Manchester football world talking when in the summer he bought ex-United idol Brian Kidd from Arsenal for £100,000. Kidd, who had scored 70 goals in 264 games for United, had maintained an even better ratio at Arsenal. Although yet to open his City account, many wondered if he was saving it up for a meeting with his old team. City, with Tueart in explosive form, had raced to the top of the table and waited confidently to put this young United side in its place.

BEFORE THE GAME							
	P	W	D	L	F	A	Pts
CITY	6	3	3	0	8	3	9
UNITED	6	2	3	1	10	7	7

*Ouch! United's **Martin Buchan** winces as City's **Mike Doyle** puts in a strong tackle during the Reds' 3-1 win.*

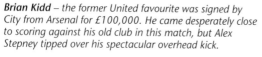

Brian Kidd – the former United favourite was signed by City from Arsenal for £100,000. He came desperately close to scoring against his old club in this match, but Alex Stepney tipped over his spectacular overhead kick.

Power DID score, claim Book's men

TOMMY DOCHERTY'S Red Army rule Manchester this morning after a derby classic which tortured the nerve ends of partisan and neutral alike **writes RICHARD BOTT.**

But until these two magnificently combative sides pit their wits and skills against each other again, City will argue that yesterday's game hinged on the goal that got away.

Was the ball over the line before United skipper Martin Buchan hooked it away in the 66th minute.

City's Paul Power who side-footed a shot past the diving Stepney when United were leading 2—1, told me: "I was sure it was a goal. I couldn't see if it was over the line because of Stepney, but Buchan seemed to hook it out of the back of the net."

Manager Tony Book said: "Can't say the ball was over. I chanced it entered: "In my opinion it wasn't. But the game is over now so it doesn't matter."

The game had to have controversy. It had everything else. Action, drama, skill, pace and a hero in United's 13th minute substitute David McCreery.

Nineteen last week, McCreery, an irrepressible bundle of energy and courage was pitch-forked into the fray when United's Stuart Pearson limped out of it with a pulled muscle.

His team had gone a goal down a few minutes earlier and the loss of Pearson left United with a mountain to climb. They scaled it magnificently and McCreery, with a foot in the first goal and scorer of the second, planted their flag at the summit.

"I didn't think we would be able to come back when we lost Stuart," said the diminutive Irishman.

But City lost their cutting edge in attack after the seventh-minute goal from Dennis Tueart which turned the Maine Road terraces into a blaze of blue and white. And United were never so negligent again as when they allowed Tueart to steal in at the far post and head home with Alex Stepney caught flat-footed.

Piercing

Perhaps United would not have recovered if they had been denied an equaliser so quickly.

It came in the 15th minute. Inspired by a typically audacious spurt by Gordon Hill. A tackle felled him, but the ball was already on its way to McCreery. He flicked it to many Nicholl and when another pass found Steve Coppell the wingman turned a sixpence to crack the ball

Minutes later Hill left defenders in his wake in with another piercing run and when he hit the ball inside hard and low McIlroy got a touch the ball seemed to come back off Doyle and McCreery stabbed it in.

City were knocked out of their stride but they came back before half-time so fiercely that United's goal had more lives than a cat.

Kidd, battling resolutely, saw a wonderful overhead kick tipped over by Stepney and then buried a header into the goalkeepers arms. And Royle

Man City 1, Man United 3

rose like a monolith only to see Stepney push the ball away.

There was no let up in the second half which began with another superb save by Stepney, against the bar from a second Royle header.

Then Doyle, always magnificent for City, finished in the back of his own net after clearing off the line from McIlroy.

Next came the over-the-line controversy. No goal, so it was United who swept away three minutes later for Gerry Daly to apply the coup de grace with a lethal finish to Hill's cross after the industrious Macari had begun the break with an intelligently-scooped, long pass.

City fought on bravely even after they had substituted Tomy Booth for young Ged Keegan in the 81st minute. But though they had contributed so much to an absorbing due, when it came to the punch they had not been able to provide it.

MANCHESTER CITY: Corrigan, Donachie, Doyle, Watson, Power, Keegan, Kidd, Royle, Hartford, Tueart. Sub.: Booth.

MANCHESTER UNITED: Stepney, Nicholl, Houston, Daly, Greenhoff, Buchan, Coppell, McIlroy, Pearson, Macari, Hill. Sub.: McCreery.

REFEREE: A Jones, Ormskirk.

MATCH VERDICT

This was a derby match which reflected the health of Manchester football circa 1976; two teams attractively committed to creative attacking football.

City started as one might expect of League leaders, and full of confidence they raced into a seventh minute lead. United's defensive cover was missing as Tueart stole up on the far post and his free header flew past a flat-footed Stepney. United's troubles doubled a few minutes later when centre-forward Pearson limped off to be replaced by substitute David McCreery. But United remained loyal to their attacking philosophy and, following a spell of neat football, drew level 15 minutes later. A typically audacious dash by winger Gordon Hill opened up the City right flank and as the ball transferred quickly from McIlroy to Nicholl it arrived at speed in the City penalty area. Coppell pirouetted on a sixpence and cracked it straight past Corrigan. Roared on by their jubilant following in the crowd, United carried the game to the Blues and deservedly went in front. Again Hill was the supplier as his jinking run and cross was met by McIlroy. The shot struck Doyle, but McCreery, following in, fired the rebound past Corrigan. In keeping with the nature of an excellent contest, City came back and they dominated the game either side of half-time with both Royle and Kidd going close. The final outcome of the game was shaped by contrasting fortunes on the hour. Following sustained City pressure Paul Power side-footed past Stepney but with the ball almost over the line, Buchan somehow scooped it clear as the City players desperately appealed for the goal. The referee waved away the protests, and three minutes later Macari's long through-pass released Hill whose run and cross found Daly and his crisp shot settled the issue.

Dennis Tueart – he had started the season in explosive form for City and headed the Blues into a 7th minute lead.

Was it a goal or wasn't it? City's Paul Power slots the ball past United 'keeper Alex Stepney, but Martin Buchan produces a balancing act right on the line to hook the ball clear and preserve the Reds' 2-1 lead.

The City 'goal' that got away . . .

94

MANCHESTER UNITED 3
(Pearson, Hill, Coppell)

MANCHESTER CITY 1
(Tueart)

DATE	5th March 1977
DIVISION	One
VENUE	Old Trafford
ATTENDANCE	58,595

Manchester United		Manchester City
Alex STEPNEY	1	Joe CORRIGAN
Jimmy NICHOLL	2	Kenny CLEMENTS
Stewart HOUSTON	3	Willie DONACHIE
Sammy McILROY	4	Mike DOYLE
Brian GREENHOFF	5	Dave WATSON
Martin BUCHAN	6	Paul POWER *
Steve COPPELL	7	Gary OWEN
Jimmy GREENHOFF	8	Brian KIDD
Stuart PEARSON	9	Joe ROYLE
Lou MACARI	10	Asa HARTFORD
Gordon HILL *	11	Dennis TUEART
David McCREERY (11)	12	Peter BARNES (6)

Jimmy Greenhoff – an inspired buy for £100,000 from Stoke City in November 1976 he was a quality player whose passing skills and goalscoring abilities could dictate the course of a match.

BACKGROUND

City were maintaining excellent progress in the League tucked into a group of teams all chasing for the title. Local boys Kenny Clements and Gary Owen had now established themselves in the first team and Book had merged a winning blend of international players and promising youth. Brian Kidd, after an embarrassingly long wait for his first goal, had hit form with 12 goals prior to the derby, four of them in a 5-0 defeat of Leicester City. The Blues' forward line was particularly potent at this time with Kidd, Tueart and Royle all spelling danger for United.

The Reds had struggled immediately after the September derby with five defeats in nine games.

Docherty then pulled off something of a masterstroke when he picked up Jimmy Greenhoff from Stoke City for the relatively cheap price of £100,000. The classy Greenhoff immediately settled into an impressive partnership with Pearson and there was a marked improvement in United's form. This was reflected in the convincing 4-0 defeat of championship hopefuls Everton on 27th December. The New Year saw this run continue and United once again had Wembley in their nostrils as, by the time of the derby, they had reached the last 16 of the F.A. Cup and were due to meet last season's Wembley conquerors Southampton in a replay three days after this derby.

BEFORE THE GAME							
	P	W	D	L	F	A	Pts
CITY	27	13	11	3	40	19	37
UNITED	26	12	7	7	47	35	31

Gary Owen – the City midfielder was now an established part of the Blues' successful short-passing game and linked up well with Peter Barnes down the left-flank.

MATCH VERDICT

This was a crushing blow to City's championship ambitions as United completed the seasonal 'double' over their big-spending neighbours simply by maintaining such an attacking pressure and momentum throughout the 90 minutes that City were unable to break clear and express their own attacking capabilities. The battle was won in the competitive midfield where the diminutive and talented Scots Hartford and Macari were pitted against each other. On this occasion it was the effervescent Macari who dominated proceedings and it was his persistent harrying that forced the two errors inside seven first half minutes which cost the Blues the game. Twice Macari panicked City defenders into over-hurried clearances that resulted in Pearson and then Hill both shooting past Corrigan to give United a cushion they retained for the rest of the match. United maintained the pressure in the second half and twice the brilliance of Corrigan stopped the Reds from further increasing their lead. However, the giant goalkeeper was powerless when the wily Jimmy Greenhoff sent Coppell through with a glorious defence splitting pass which the little winger smashed into the net. Little had been seen of the much vaunted City forward line who generally lacked cohesion and thrust. Tueart however, cheered the travelling fans with a late consolation goal but the Blues finished well beaten by 'the Doc's' young outfit. The result left a serious question mark over City's championship ambitions and shifted the focus so significantly that instead some now asked what price United for the 'double'.

AT THE SEASON'S END

CITY: Finished 2nd on 56 points
(1 point behind Champions Liverpool)

UNITED: Finished 6th on 47 points
(F.A. Cup Winners, beating Liverpool 2-1)

*Opposing skippers **Mike Doyle** and **Martin Buchan** shake hands before the start of the 94th League derby match.*

*United's **Steve Coppell** clears the danger watched by the Reds defender **Brian Greenhoff** (No.5).*

MACARI TAKES A SALUTE FROM DOC

MONDAY'S MAN

LOU MACARI . . . the genius behind Manchester United's revival, and a derby dazzler on Saturday

THERE was no holding little Lou Macari, as Manchester United's midfield maestro brought high-flying Manchester City crashing to a 3-1 defeat in the Old Trafford derby.

Early in the season, manager Tommy Docherty was almost at his wit's end trying to motivate Macari into action.

The manager and player were on a collision course with Macari's Old Trafford future in doubt, as the boss dropped his £200,000 Scot.

By DAVID MEEK

But Macari has been the inventive genius behind most of United's successes in their live-saving run of 14 games in League and Cup, with only one defeat.

He was certainly the key figure on Saturday, completely eclipsing his arch rival Asa Hartford and dominating the midfield with his hustling, twinkling style.

Television assessor Denis Law rated Macari his man-of-the-match, and Docherty declared: "His performance was as good as I have ever seen him play."

ERRORS

It was Macari's busy-bee work that led to two goals in seven minutes, that knocked the stuffing out of City.

Stuart Pearson grabbed the first and Gordon Hill smashed in the second, after errors forced by Macari.

Steve Coppell scored a gem of a goal in the second half, after a brilliant switch of play by Jimmy Greenhoff, but by this time City were a spent force.

They pulled a goal back in a scramble through Dennis Tueart, but for a team of championship contenders — tipped for the title by Docherty — they were disappointing.

The completion of a League double over City hoists the Reds into a challenging title position, themselves, but while victory in a derby match is satisfying, heady stuff for the winners, United would be well advised to play it cool.

Though they mastered these opponents, they should remember that they only scored the first two goals with the help of deflections, which played the ball right into the path of the scorers.

Until the first goal, the game was riddled with mistakes and spoiled by the wind.

All credit to United for making the most of their chances, the aspect of the game that is now worrying City chief Tony Book.

Once on top, United never let up. Steve Coppell played a valuable role in helping out in midfield when City were in possession, and attacking hard down the right flank to give the Reds a width in attack that was never matched by their opponents.

With Hill always dangerous on the other wing, and Pearson and Jimmy Greenhoff applying pressure down the middle, it was an uneasy afternoon for Mike Doyle and company.

In contrast, the United defence always looked in command. Martin Buchan was outstanding, and with Brian Greenhoff gave Brian Kidd and Joe Royle a thin time.

95

MANCHESTER CITY 3
(Kidd 2, Channon)

MANCHESTER UNITED 1
(Nicholl)

DATE	10th September 1977
DIVISION	One
VENUE	Maine Road
ATTENDANCE	50,856

Manchester City		Manchester United
Joe CORRIGAN	1	Alex STEPNEY
Kenny CLEMENTS	2	Alex FORSYTH
Willie DONACHIE	3	Arthur ALBISTON
Gary OWEN	4	Sammy McILROY
Dave WATSON	5	Jimmy NICHOLL
Tommy BOOTH	6	Martin BUCHAN
Peter BARNES	7	Steve COPPELL
Mike CHANNON	8	David McCREERY
Brian KIDD	9	Stuart PEARSON
Asa HARTFORD	10	Lou MACARI *
Paul POWER	11	Gordon HILL
Joe ROYLE	12	Chris McGRATH (10)

BACKGROUND

Sensationally Tommy Docherty was not in charge of United as the new season opened. He had been sacked in the summer, following revelations of an affair with the wife of the club physiotherapist. Unfortunately for 'the Doc's' fans they would never know if his stylish team could have won more trophies to add to the F.A. Cup which had been United's first major honour since the Busby days. United's choice as his managerial successor could not have been more different in character. A fine Coach, but a studious and much more reticent man, Dave Sexton inherited a useful side who had made a confident start, thrashing Birmingham 4-1 at St.Andrews, and still remained unbeaten by derby day.

City's reputation as Manchester's big spenders had continued as Book bought the charismatic England International Mike Channon from Southampton for £300,000. The Blues had similarly made a useful start to the new season. Following a disappointing home draw they entered the derby with three straight wins. Away victories at Aston Villa (4-1) and West Ham (1-0) were followed by a 4-0 thrashing of Norwich City. Dennis Tueart, a hat-trick hero at Villa, was in prime form and this early season derby looked set to be a real battle of the giants.

BEFORE THE GAME							
	P	W	D	L	F	A	Pts
CITY	4	3	1	0	9	1	7
UNITED	4	3	1	0	7	2	7

*Aerial action from Maine Road as **Kenny Clements**, **Steve Coppell** and **Dave Watson** challenge for the ball during City's convincing 3-1 win.*

Kidd's double act in a family at war!

by RICHARD BOTT

**Manchester City 3,
Manchester United 1**

Alex Stepney – United's long serving goalkeeper produced a series of fine saves

BRIAN KIDD, once as indelibly red as any Manchester United diehard could be, was the bushy-haired hero of the other half of Soccer's new capital city last night.

But after his two-goal salvo had shot down his old club in a stirring, raw-boned derby at Maine Road, Kidd joked : "This is going to split the family when we get together for breakfast tomorrow.

"Some are for City, some for United. I hope I get a word in."

Kidd spent seven seasons at Old Trafford before moving to Arsenal. Then he came home to Manchester in a £100,000 deal just over a year ago, only to change his allegiance.

"I would be a hypocrite to say it didn't mean anything special scoring goals against United," he said. "But there is no bitterness and I've nothing to prove. All that really matters is the result."

City manager Tony Book was as unemotional as ever. But, deep-down, there was immense pride and satisfaction in his team's performance — ending three consecutive derby victories by United, and keeping City at the top of the table.

"We looked full of goals," said Book. "A great team effort . . . the display I was looking for . . . the fans deserve the result."

United, well beaten on the day, went home with additional worries. Lou Macari, their Scottish fireball, hub of their midfield, has joined the queue for the treatment room. And, on Tuesday, United fly out to meet the pride of French football, St. Etienne.

Macari, who pulled a hamstring while playing for Scotland in East Berlin last week, was withdrawn after 70 minutes yesterday and said later : "I am going to struggle to make it for Wednesday."

That is grim news for United with the Greenhoff brothers still side-lined, and Stuart Pearson aggravating his neck and back injury.

Perhaps City had learned a sound lesson from the previous year when an early goal gave them starry eyes . . . and United roared back to beat them 3—1.

This time, after Kidd had rifled a free-kick wide of Alex Stepney in the 14th minute, City made sure they were ready for United's retaliatory surge. The Maine Road men marshalled their ranks superbly, tackling and covering brilliantly.

United's task was magnified within three minutes of the interval. Arthur Albiston miskicked. Kidd swooped again and the shot spun out of Stepney's grasp and over his shoulder into the net.

Only an infringement denied Kidd a spectacular hat-trick but, with 11 minutes left, Mike Channon made it 3—0 and it was party time for everyone in sky-blue on the Maine Road terraces.

United, beaten but not bowed, consoled themselves and their followers with a dramatic and totally unexpected 35-yard drive from Jimmy Nichol three minutes from the end. But for them the end had already come.

MATCH VERDICT

City gained revenge for United's derby 'double' the previous season with an emphatic victory that kept the Blues at the top of the table. It was United 'old boy' Brian Kidd who made the headlines and won over any lingering Kippax terrace doubts about his allegiance by scoring two goals.

Just as happened a year ago, City took an early lead as United's over-worked defence gave away a 14th minute free-kick in a dangerous location on the edge of their own penalty area. Kidd, taking a long run up, sent a thumping drive whistling past Stepney and directly into the net. Stung into response, United began to put their game together but it was City who continued to offer the greater threat and Stepney was obliged to make a series of fine saves to keep the Reds in contention. However, eleven minutes from the break he was defeated again as City netted a vital second goal. Following a spell of sustained City pressure Albiston's hasty mis-kick allowed Kidd a clear route to goal. His stinging drive was grasped at by Stepney but the ball spun out of the goalkeeper's hands and over his shoulder into the net.

City retained the initiative throughout the second half with a series of fluent moves which kept the Reds penned into their own half. It was no more than City deserved when, eleven minutes from time, Channon cleverly spotted a gap and finished coolly, before celebrating in typical style with his famous cartwheeling arm salute. United, who had frankly received something of a mauling, derived some late consolation when Nicholl's gallop up-field was concluded with a rasping shot into the City net.

*Manchester City in 1977-78. **Back:** Paul Power, Colin Bell, Joe Corrigan, Keith MacRae, Willie Donachie, Peter Barnes. **Middle:** Tony Book (Manager), Tony Henry, Kenny Clements, Tommy Booth, Dave Watson, Joe Royle, Bill Taylor (Coach). **Front:** Roy Bailey, Jimmy Conway, Ged Keegan, Brian Kidd, Mike Doyle, Gary Owen, Dennis Tueart, Asa Hartford, Freddie Griffiths (Physio).*

Mike Channon -– a cool finish and familiar cartwheeling arm salute.

DATE	15th March 1978
DIVISION	One
VENUE	Old Trafford
ATTENDANCE	58,398

Manchester United		Manchester City
Alex STEPNEY	**1**	Joe CORRIGAN
Jimmy NICHOLL	**2**	Kenny CLEMENTS
Stewart HOUSTON	**3**	Willie DONACHIE
Sammy McILROY	**4**	Tommy BOOTH
Gordon McQUEEN	**5**	Dave WATSON
Brian GREENHOFF	**6**	Gary OWEN
Steve COPPELL	**7**	Mike CHANNON
Jimmy GREENHOFF	**8**	Colin BELL
Joe JORDAN *	**9**	Brian KIDD
Lou MACARI	**10**	Asa HARTFORD
Gordon HILL	**11**	Peter BARNES
Arthur ALBISTON (9)	**12**	Paul POWER

Dave Sexton
Manager

I was hit by the full force of a Manchester derby soon after my arrival as manager of Manchester United.

For the fixture against Manchester City at Maine Road fell just five games after the start of the season, and I was caught up in excitement and tension.

I was involved in London as both a player and a manger in derby fixtures, and the rivalry was always fairly intense, but I must say that a Manchester derby seems to be out on its own as a special event.

RED AND BLUE

Perhaps it is because the two clubs belong to the same city and therefore football fans tend to divide up red or blue with no room for a neutral! London is slightly more cosmopolitan with several teams in the capital which probably eases the pressures.

Anyway, it is all happening again this evening as we welcome City to Old Trafford for our rearranged match. As a manager I have to remain slightly more detached and no doubt Tony Book is striving for an equally cool approach because no matter how important local prestige might be, the fact is that tonight's match carries just the two points like the rest of the League programme.

We need them after a disappointing run to give ourselves a boost as we blend our new players, Joe Jordan and Gordon McQueen, into the team and try to recapture our rhythm.

This is a critical phase of the season for us, even if some of our targets may now seem to be eluding us. We have got to get our game together for a confident campaign next season.

BACKGROUND

City's blistering start to the season had seen them top the table until mid-October before suffering a first defeat at Coventry City. This prompted a mediocre spell of form and a slight fall away from the upper reaches of the table, but a post-Christmas run of nine games without defeat positively re-activated the Blues' title challenge. The turning point coincided with a remarkable return to the team of their inspirational talisman Colin Bell. Just to prove the point, he made his comeback as a second-half substitute against Newcastle United in a game with City struggling at 0-0. Almost single-handedly Bell inspired the Blues to a rousing 4-0 scoreline. Somewhat surprisingly, Dennis Tueart, who scored a hat-trick that day was later in the season sold to New York Cosmos leaving United one less thorn to worry about.

United's league form meanwhile, was inconsistent and they seemed unable to build on the odd excellent performance such as an amazing 6-2 win at Everton. Dave Sexton decided the moment to strengthen his side's backbone had arrived and, after protracted negotiations, he purchased the expensive but powerful Leeds United pair Joe Jordan and Gordon McQueen. Leeds' players had never been great favourites with United fans and both men knew they would need to prove themselves to a demanding audience.

BEFORE THE GAME							
	P	W	D	L	F	A	Pts
CITY	30	17	5	8	56	33	39
UNITED	31	11	7	13	47	48	29

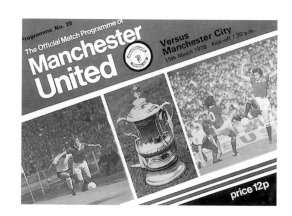

Gordon McQueen – the tall, attacking centre-half cost United £495,000 when he moved from Elland Road in February 1978.

Peter Barnes – first to react and put City back in the match at 2-1.

Thomas spoils derby sizzler

IF WORLD CUP referee Clive Thomas makes the same mistakes in Argentina this summer as he did at Old Trafford last night, he'll be lucky to see his native Wales again !

Right or wrong over the controversial Brian Kidd equaliser that gave Manchester City a 2-2 draw, it only compensated for the Treorchy official's abysmal decision to grant Manchester United a second penalty in an otherwise derby dazzler.

By PETER GARDNER

The over-fussy Thomas — nicknamed "Clive the Book" — will never get away with such indiscretions in South America come June.

However, the Reds can quit squealing about being robbed on the night. And neither can I wholeheartedly agree with City boss only Book's claim that his side should have won over 90 minutes.

The fact is that football was the winner on a night when Manchester soccer proved that the game can still be played in the right spirit of adventure and attacking ambition.

No one can grumble about a draw in the 90th meeting which ultimately became a memorable match and certainly one of the best of my clashes I have seen for years.

It was a game that had everything — penalty drama, superb goalkeeping at both ends, a sterling fightback from two down by the Blues and seven bookings although it was never the bitter, nasty struggle such a figure might suggest.

FADING

UNITED suddenly found the motivation they have been lacking for a long time simply because they were facing blue shirts once more.

CITY had the bit between their teeth because they could see their already fading title dream drifting even further into oblivion.

As it is the loss of another point — although in normal circumstances an Old Trafford draw is considered one gained — leaves City now firmly out on a limb so far as the championship is concerned.

The only way any sidecan top Nottingham Forest now is for Clough's runaways to hit a slump of disastrous proportions. "They'd have to lose four or five games on the trot to slip now," admitted Book today.

However, he can be proud of a side that fought so magnificently to grasp a point from a game that at one stage seemed beyond salvation.

And it was Asa Hartford who once more epitomised this spirit more than anyone. In his last match before a three-game suspension, the Scottish international worked heart and soul for success. How City will miss him.

LIMP

Gary Owen, too, magnificently shouldered the midfield burden in a red-blooded battle that revealed all that is best in the English game.

With Brian Kidd struggling from a right knee knock and Peter Barnes coming in for harsh punishment also the Blues front line had a limp alone look but the effort rarely flagged in a fighting finish which brought two goals in a minute from the injured pair.

At the back Joe Corrigan as did his opposite number Alex Stepney, made a string of world class saves while in front the City back four fought stubbornly to contain a revitalised United side that suddenly recaptured the glitter of the Docherty era.

G O A L S : Barnes (77 minutes). Kidd (78) for City; Hill (8 and 57 pens) for United.

Wakey, wakey .. Reds bungle it!

By DAVID MEEK

WORLD CUP referee Clive Thomas cost Manchester United victory against Manchester City at Old Trafford with a big-headed blunder.

The linesman flagged Brian Kidd offside, but having awarded a goal, Mr Thomas stubbornly refused to change his decision.

His reason after the match was that the linesman had flagged "too late." How late islate? In my view not a matter of second.

I believe Mr Thomas was right in every one of his seven bookings — three from City and four from United. It was good, strong refereeing but to my mind he let the power go to his head when he refused to take notice of the linesman who clearly flagged for offside.

But having said that the Welsh referee more or less handed City their equaliser for a 2-2 draw, the message must be equally blunt to Manchester United . . . wakey, wakey!

The Reds should never have allowed the game to have slip from a two-goal lead situation. With the help of Gordon Hill's two penalties they were in control until they suddenly went to pieces after the departure of Joe Jordan with a hamstring strain in the 5th minute.

Sub Arthur Albiston came on to play at left-back with Stewart Houston moving into the attack to replace Jordan.

Peter Barnes pulled a goal back after Alex Stepney had done well to parry a shot from Brian Kidd and this really seemed to throw the Reds into total confusion.

Houston was switched into midfield and I couldn't follow the rest of the tactical plan because chaos reigned and it was difficult to understand who in the United team was supposed to be doing what.

Manager Dave Sexton agreed later that things became disorganised.

What was so disappointing for United fans is that it was muddle that helped to lose them a point at Newcastle on Saturday after being in front for most of the game.

Either the understanding between bench and pitch needs working on or United need a player to get things sorted out in that kind of situation.

MATCH VERDICT:

In a match of no little incident it was controversial referee Clive Thomas who made the headlines. Two penalty decisions and a furore over an 'offside' goal contributed to the night's drama. It had all begun well enough for United as their crisp football had City back-peddling early on. The nerves evident in the City play surfaced after only eight minutes as Clements' albeit clumsy challenge on McIlroy was rather harshly ruled as illegal and Hill stepped up to confidently drive the penalty past Corrigan. Despite Hartford's tireless efforts United maintained a control from this point on, playing some attractive one touch football. It came as little surprise when shortly into the second half the Reds increased their lead. This time there was no doubt at all as Greenhoff's clever little shimmy in the box was greeted by a wild flail from Hartford and, once again, Mr Thomas pointed to the spot and Hill's powerful kick gave Corrigan no chance. However, when Jordan limped off, United seemed to lose some of the initiative and now it was City's turn to look the more likely side with some dangerous forays. The Blues' efforts were rewarded in quite dramatic fashion with two goals inside a minute. Firstly Kidd, with room to spare on the United right, sent in a blistering shot that Stepney brilliantly parried, but Barnes reacted first to the rebound and City were back in the match. Immediately after this Hartford cleverly exploited United's obvious disorientation and his through ball to Kidd, standing on his own up the field, allowed the former United favourite to race away and slot the ball past Stepney. Despite a linesman's flag, Mr Thomas saw no infringement and the goal stood despite United's protests. A game United appeared to be winning in a canter had been snatched away from them.

Joe Jordan ––the explosive Scottish international striker cost United £350,000 when he arrived from Leeds United in January 1978.

AT THE SEASON'S END

CITY: Finished 4th on 52 points

UNITED: Finished 10th on 42 points

97

MANCHESTER UNITED 1
(Jordan)

MANCHESTER CITY 0

DATE	30th September 1978	
DIVISION	One	
VENUE	Old Trafford	
ATTENDANCE	55,301	

Manchester United		Manchester City
Paddy ROCHE	1	Joe CORRIGAN
Arthur ALBISTON	2	Kenny CLEMENTS
Stewart HOUSTON	3	Willie DONACHIE
Brian GREENHOFF	4	Paul POWER
Gordon McQUEEN	5	Dave WATSON
Martin BUCHAN	6	Paul FUTCHER
Steve COPPELL	7	Mike CHANNON
Jimmy GREENHOFF	8	Gary OWEN
Joe JORDAN	9	Brian KIDD
Lou MACARI	10	Asa HARTFORD
Sammy McILROY	11	Peter BARNES
David McCREERY	12	Roger PALMER

BACKGROUND

Again a new season had meant changes at Maine Road. Following the move of Tueart, long-serving Mike Doyle now joined Stoke City, and in came the Futcher brothers from Luton Town. Defender Paul Futcher was Book's 'big buy' but the much admired player had a tough debut at Derby County and looked most uncomfortable in Liverpool's 4-1 win at Maine Road. That defeat apart, City again started the season well, as befitted a side which had now become a regular in the top half of the table during recent seasons.

There were also changes at United, who now had Paddy Roche in goal to replace Stepney who had left to play in America. Sexton decided on the pairing of Jordan and Jimmy Greenhoff up front, but even at this stage of the season, there were mumblings of concern about the side's ability to score enough goals. Three of the club's 13 goals had come in an impressive victory at Leeds United but other than this a series of frustrating draws reflected the supporters' concern.

	P	W	D	L	F	A	Pts
BEFORE THE GAME							
CITY	7	3	3	1	13	8	9
UNITED	7	2	4	1	8	9	8

Manchester United in 1978-79. *Back:* Jimmy Greenhoff, Joe Jordan, Stewart Houston, Jimmy Nicholl, Gordon McQueen. *Middle:* Tommy Cavanagh (Assistant Manager), Chris McGrath, Alex Forsyth, Brian Greenhoff, Alex Stepney, Paddy Roche, Stuart Pearson, Sammy McIlroy, Ashley Grimes, Dave Sexton (Manager), Laurie Brown (Physio). *Front:* Martyn Rogers, David McCreery, Lou Macari, Martin Buchan, Andy Ritchie, Steve Coppell, Arthur Albiston.

Aerial action at Old Trafford as City's defensive pair **Dave Watson** *and* **Paul Futcher** *get up above little* **Lou Macari** *to head clear.*

*A clash of the giants as United's powerful striker **Joe Jordan** wings in towards the ball challenged by City's muscular centre-half **Dave Watson**. The final word went to Jordan, who netted the Reds' last minute winner.*

MATCH VERDICT

It was a game of poor vintage, not in keeping with the recent entertaining derby matches, and United pinched the points with a goal in the last minute.

The Reds had the lion's share of possession but their play lacked both quality and direction. City on the other hand, were curiously subdued, missing the usual vitality they reserved for this fixture and, consequently, rarely looked like commanding the game.

Steve Coppell was clearly United's man of the match. His intelligent and speedy incursions down the right wing gave Donachie numerous problems and it was perhaps a surprise that no goal came from this productive quarter. Owen and Hartford still gave typically battling performances in the City midfield and Kidd once almost capitalised on a nervous fumble by Roche. Indeed, City felt they had won the game with Channon's clinical finish, and were not pleased to discover the strike rubbed out for an offside decision. The game was meandering comfortably towards a goalless draw when United, in one last assault, gained a corner. Coppell's accurate centre was met by the towering McQueen whose powerful header was brilliantly parried by Corrigan but then only half cleared as far as Jordan, who joyously drilled a fierce low shot into the City net through a crowd of players.

A postal first day cover issued to celebrate the derby meeting during Manchester United's Centenary Year in 1978.

***Paul Futcher** was City's big close-season buy at £350,000 from Luton Town. Here he signs for the Maine Road club watched by Chairman **Peter Swales** and Manager **Tony Book**.*

98

MANCHESTER CITY 0
MANCHESTER UNITED 3
(Coppell 2, Ritchie)

DATE	10th February 1979
DIVISION	One
VENUE	Maine Road
ATTENDANCE	46,151

Manchester City		Manchester United
Joe CORRIGAN	1	Gary BAILEY
Willie DONACHIE	2	Brian GREENHOFF
Paul POWER	3	Arthur ALBISTON
Gary OWEN	4	Sammy McILROY
Dave WATSON	5	Gordon McQUEEN
Paul FUTCHER	6	Martin BUCHAN
Mike CHANNON	7	Steve COPPELL
Colin BELL	8	Jimmy GREENHOFF
Brian KIDD	9	Andy RITCHIE
Asa HARTFORD	10	Lou MACARI
Peter BARNES	11	Mickey THOMAS
Ron FUTCHER	12	Jimmy NICHOLL

*City pair **Joe Corrigan** and **Dave Watson** combine to halt the threat of United youngster **Andy Ritchie** who netted the Reds' third goal.*

BACKGROUND

United's largely indifferent season was reflected in regular changes to the playing personnel. In goal, Paddy Roche had been jettisoned and blond 20-year-old Gary Bailey was now first team choice. In a move that perhaps reflected the marked change of style between the sort of line-ups preferred by Docherty and Sexton, the unpredictable but talented Hill left the club to rejoin Docherty at Derby County and the hard working Mickey Thomas was now installed on the left flank. With Joe Jordan injured, the promising Andy Ritchie (later to find more permanent fame with City's Roger Palmer at Oldham) was selected to play at centre-forward. The Reds actually entered the derby in the midst of a dreadful run of form having lost their previous four games.

City's season had been turned upside down. Despite the arrival of Polish international Kazimeira Deyna for £120,000 from Legia Warsaw in November, a miserable pre-Christmas run of two points from seven games had set the alarm bells ringing and Chairman Peter Swales, acting with his usual alacrity in these situations, decided on a change to the managerial set-up. Prodigal son Malcolm Allison was invited back to the club in January, in the capacity of 'coaching overlord', with the more introverted Book remaining as manager, but the arrangement somehow looked sure to have its drawbacks. Allison commented on his new position in typical fashion; "I'm not just a coach, I'm a scientist and like all good scientists I can make things work." Results did show a slight improvement from this point on, but a 3-0 defeat of Tottenham Hotspur at White Hart Lane seven days before the derby was City's only win in 14 games. Allison's heyday record against United had always been an impressive one and City fans naturally hoped that would continue in this important match.

BEFORE THE GAME

	P	W	D	L	F	A	Pts
UNITED	23	9	6	8	32	41	24
CITY	24	6	9	9	33	30	21

Willie Donachie (left) watches as City's **Dave Watson** and **Colin Bell** combine to hold off United's **Sammy McIlroy**. Allison's ploy of operating the experienced Bell as a sweeper in this derby was not however a success.

MATCH VERDICT

Malcolm Allison had of course talked a good derby in the press during the preceding week but when it came to the day in question his plans went awry. The idea of operating the experienced Bell as a sweeper in a mobile defence was typically imaginative, but it simply did not come off. Indeed, all it did in practice was to hand United the attacking initiative and give the Reds' play a direction and purpose it had seldom expressed all season. City's defensive scheme came unstuck after just 20 minutes with Bell's sweeping role rendered superfluous. Corrigan, in an unusual fluster, suddenly left his line in a forlorn attempt to dispossess McIlroy who simply fed Coppell with the ball and the winger side-footed into an empty net. City desperately sought to get back into the game but were effectively hamstrung by their system. United's response was to score a killer second goal.

This time Coppell was allowed far too much space and his fine angled shot from the right crept inside Corrigan's far post.

City looked a well beaten side in a lack lustre second half, and United won in a canter. With 20 minutes remaining Andy Ritchie showed what a useful prospect he might become when the wily Greenhoff set up a chance and Ritchie's instant volley soared into the City net.

AT THE SEASON'S END

UNITED: Finished 9th on 45 points.
(F.A. Cup finalists, losing 3-2 to Arsenal)

CITY: Finished 15th on 39 points

He's back! **Malcolm Allison** strolls back into Maine Road in January 1979 as City's new Chief Coach.

Steve Coppell – on target twice in United's 3-0 win.

A near miss for City as **Peter Barnes** curls a shot past United's **Gordon McQueen** and 'keeper **Gary Bailey**, but also wide of the post. Watching on the left are City striker **Brian Kidd** and United's **Sammy McIlroy**.

99

MANCHESTER CITY 2
(Henry, Robinson)

MANCHESTER UNITED 0

DATE	10th November 1979	
DIVISION	One	
VENUE	Maine Road	
ATTENDANCE	50,067	

Manchester City		Manchester United
Joe CORRIGAN	1	Gary BAILEY
Ray RANSON	2	Jimmy NICHOLL
Willie DONACHIE	3	Stewart HOUSTON
Dave BENNETT	4	Sammy McILROY
Tommy CATON	5	Kevin MORAN
Tommy BOOTH	6	Martin BUCHAN
Tony HENRY	7	Ashley GRIMES
Steve DALEY	8	Ray WILKINS
Michael ROBINSON	9	Steve COPPELL
Paul POWER	10	Lou MACARI
Kazimeira DEYNA	11	Mickey THOMAS
Dragoslav STEPANOVIC	12	Tom SLOAN

BACKGROUND

City made all the close-season headlines as Malcolm Allison undertook nothing short of a revolution at the club. In July Tony Book had moved up to general manager, while Allison took over as team manager. Flamboyant as ever, Allison bewildered the fans with a rapid series of deals that had a stream of players moving in and out of the Club. Out went crowd favourites Owen and Barnes to Ron Atkinson's West Bromwich Albion while Mike Channon returned to Southampton. The shock that accompanied this was almost minor compared to the extravagant prices paid for several virtual 'unknowns' who now arrived at Maine Road. Steve MacKenzie, with no League appearances under his belt, cost £250,000 from Crystal Palace; 20-year-old Michael Robinson came from Third Division Preston for a staggering £750,000 and then on 5th September Wolves' midfield player Steve Daley was signed for £1.4 million. So far however, the outcome of these extraordinary measures had not been overly impressive. City languished near the bottom of the table and, to rub it in, recently rejected players such as Owen and Barnes were outstanding as the Blues were thrashed 4-0 at West Bromwich Albion. Allison's re-structured team was still very much on trial as they entered this derby.

Things were rather quieter at Old Trafford, but England midfield player Ray Wilkins had joined the club from Chelsea for £850,000. Sexton's albeit rather methodical side had a well-balanced look to it and were proving hard to beat as they moved to the top of the League table. Former Gaelic footballer Kevin Moran was currently enjoying a run in the side, covering for the injured McQueen, but this did not stop United making the short trip across the city as clear favourites to increase Malcolm Allison's woes.

Manchester City in 1979-80. **Back:** *Steve Daley, Paul Futcher, Tommy Caton, Joe Corrigan, Keith MacRae, Tommy Booth, Michael Robinson.*
Middle: *Malcolm Allison (Chief Coach), Stuart Lee, Roger Palmer, Paul Power, Willie Donachie, Tony Henry, Dragoslav Stepanovic, Roy Bailey (Medical).*
Front: *Tony Book (Manager), Kaziu Deyna, Steve MacKenzie, Dave Bennett, Ray Ranson, Bobby Shinton, Barry Silkman, Colin Viljoen.*

BEFORE THE GAME							
	P	W	D	L	F	A	Pts
UNITED	14	8	4	2	19	8	20
CITY	14	5	3	6	13	21	13

ONE HORSE RACE, CITY!

*The headline from the **Manchester Evening News** which commented that "even the staunchest United fan had to admit it was almost a one-horse derby"*

__Kaziu Deyna__ – the Polish International had a hand in the build-up to both City goals in the derby.

*City's million pound man **Steve Daley** is put under pressure by United trio **Kevin Moran, Mickey Thomas** and **Stewart Houston**.*

MATCH VERDICT

It proved to be an unexpected afternoon of glory for Malcolm Allison's new-look City as League leaders United came unstuck in the Maine Road mud. City, much the more determined side, fully merited their victory. In the traditionally competitive spirit of these matches little was given away in a frenetic opening half. The nearest either side came to a goal was when Coppell's snap shot struck a post and bounced clear. Robinson, leading the City line with great gusto, also went close on a couple of occasions as Buchan and Moran struggled to contain him.

City gradually gained the upper hand and achieved the crucial first goal nine minutes into the second half. Power swung the ball in from the left, and when a dribble and shot by Polish International Deyna wrong-footed the United defence, the ball deflected into the middle where Tony Henry reacted quickly to clip a left foot shot past Bailey. City, visibly more confident, now put the Reds under severe pressure looking for the goal that would settle the issue. This duly arrived and was a fitting reward for Robinson who had had an excellent game. Deyna was again the source as he cleverly worked the ball towards the big striker who glanced up and sent a 20 yard drive beyond the stranded Bailey.

__Tony Henry__ drives the ball into the United net to give the Blues a 1-0 lead.

100

MANCHESTER UNITED 1
(Thomas)

MANCHESTER CITY 0

DATE	22nd March 1980
DIVISION	One
VENUE	Old Trafford
ATTENDANCE	56,387

Manchester United		Manchester City
Gary BAILEY	1	Joe CORRIGAN
Jimmy NICHOLL	2	Ray RANSON
Arthur ALBISTON	3	Nicky REID
Sammy McILROY	4	Tommy BOOTH
Gordon McQUEEN	5	Tommy CATON
Martin BUCHAN	6	Paul POWER
Steve COPPELL	7	Tony HENRY
Ray WILKINS	8	Steve DALEY
Joe JORDAN	9	Kevin REEVES
Lou MACARI	10	Dennis TUEART
Mickey THOMAS *	11	Dave BENNETT *
Ashley GRIMES (11)	12	Roger PALMER (11)

*United's **Joe Jordan** fires in a shot as City defender **Tommy Caton** tries to get across and cover.*

BACKGROUND

The early season derby victory had proved an utterly false dawn in a season of gloom for the Blues. Embarrassing defeats, caused largely by a combination of continually changing personnel and tactics, plummeted the club in the wrong direction. The real decline in form occurred from Christmas onwards and included a humiliating Third Round F.A. Cup exit at Fourth Division Halifax Town. This was followed by a 4-1 hammering at Southampton with former Blues Dave Watson and Mike Channon among the scorers. The misery continued when West Bromwich Albion beat City 3-1 the following week at Maine Road and Peter Barnes scored twice! Long serving Willie Donachie moved to American soccer during derby week, but former favourite Dennis Tueart had returned in January for a second spell at the club. With pressure mounting in March, Allison again resorted to the cheque book and forward Kevin Reeves was finally prised away from Norwich City for another huge fee of £1.2 million. The derby would be his second game as the Blues went to Old Trafford looking desperately for points that would relieve the growing crisis.

Sexton's hard-to-beat United were tucked into the title pursuit although, in honesty, their bid to catch a runaway Liverpool side lacked a certain validity. Convincing defeats at Liverpool (2-0) and at Ipswich where they were thrashed 6-0 (Bailey even saved two penalties!) left various question marks hanging over their title pedigree. The side was also not converting enough chances and entered the derby scoreless in the past three games. Off the field Chairman Louis Edwards had died and was officially due to be succeeded by his son Martin, who on this historic centenary derby day exchanged club pennants on the pitch before the match with City Chairman Peter Swales.

BEFORE THE GAME							
	P	W	D	L	F	A	Pts
UNITED	32	16	10	6	47	26	42
CITY	33	9	9	15	31	55	27

The real derby losers —the fans

United's **Martin Buchan** clears as City's new £1.2 million buy **Kevin Reeves** closes in to challenge.

Sheer determination from City's **Paul Power** as he holds off United star **Steve Coppell**.

City's **Paul Power** looks on as **Nicky Reid** attempts to block a hot-shot from United's **Lou Macari**.

MATCH VERDICT

As is so often the case with this type of historic footballing occasion, it did not live up to its billing.

Sadly, for two clubs with such great traditions, the centenary derby will never be recalled for the quality of its football. Instead it was characterised by a dour struggle between two sides needing the points for vastly different reasons. The first half was particularly poor with little creative play. City seemed particularly nervous and new boy Reeves had their only real shot at goal. United similarly lacked punch up front and seemed to rely solely on Jordan's aerial power to provide 'knock downs'. The game badly needed a goal and what proved to be the conclusive one arrived shortly after half-time. There seemed little danger as Mickey Thomas finished an aimless run with a shot that Corrigan had well-covered but, as the giant goalkeeper shaped to collect, Henry stuck out a boot and diverted the ball on a looping arc into the net. United players showed their obvious relief as they mobbed Thomas and the Reds' supporters in the Stretford end taunted their old adversary Allison with suggestions of the sack. The goal brought an increase in the frenetic activity of both sides but it was all too painfully apparent that neither team possessed a player whose guile and skill would trouble the scoreboard again.

In the Manchester Evening News, the writers who follow both clubs regularly bemoaned the standard of football served up for the centenary derby. United correspondent David Meek described the match as "a disaster for football as the defences dominated a dour struggle" while City man Peter Gardner was even more scathing:

"What a stinker to serve up for the 100th meeting between Manchester's big two. United and City fans have endured some dour derby clashes down the years - but this must surely rank as one of the worst. Neither side got to grips with a colourless tie in which the Reds looked far from title challengers, and the Blues struggled like the relegation battlers they are. And the losers were the fans who packed this famous Old Trafford stadium, scene of so many past glories, but who had so little to cheer about".

AT THE SEASON'S END

UNITED: Finished 2nd on 58 points.
(2 points behind Champions Liverpool)

CITY: Finished 17th on 37 points

101

MANCHESTER UNITED 2
(Coppell, Albiston)

MANCHESTER CITY 2
(Reeves, Palmer)

DATE	27th September 1980
DIVISION	One
VENUE	Old Trafford
ATTENDANCE	55,918

Manchester United		Manchester City
Gary BAILEY	1	Joe CORRIGAN
Jimmy NICHOLL	2	Ray RANSON
Arthur ALBISTON	3	Nicky REID
Sammy McILROY	4	Tommy BOOTH
Gordon McQUEEN	5	Tommy CATON
Martin BUCHAN	6	Tony HENRY
Ashley GRIMES	7	Paul POWER
Jimmy GREENHOFF	8	Steve DALEY
Steve COPPELL	9	Roger PALMER
Mike DUXBURY *	10	Dave BENNETT *
Mickey THOMAS	11	Kevin REEVES
Tom SLOAN (10)	12	Paul SUGRUE (10)

BACKGROUND

City had not made a happy start to the new season, and some pundits claimed Malcolm Allison's job was under threat. The team's instability was reflected in the fact that only five players had appeared in every game and, of those, only Steve Daley in the same position. The Blues were still looking for the season's first victory, and a home defeat by Stoke City in the game prior to the derby merely increased the crowd's discontent and also meant that Dennis Tueart, who had sustained a broken wrist, would miss this important fixture with the Reds.

Not that United had made the most convincing of starts either. The Reds had been involved in some sterile draws and there was gradual mounting criticism of what was considered by many to be the Reds' boring style of play. Not even the unusual spectacle of five goals in a September thrashing of Leicester City could compensate for the fear that United were not capable of scoring enough goals over a season to reap any real success. Even so, their fans were hopeful enough of collecting the points against crisis-ridden City.

BEFORE THE GAME

	P	W	D	L	F	A	Pts
UNITED	7	2	4	1	9	2	8
CITY	7	0	3	4	8	16	3

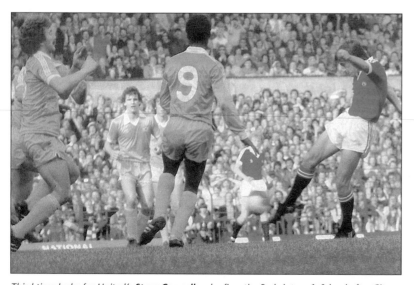

*Third time lucky for United's **Steve Coppell** as he fires the Reds into a 1-0 lead after City defenders had blocked his two other shots moments earlier.*

*City striker **Dennis Tueart** - missing from the line-up with a broken wrist.*

DING-DONG DERBY!

*United's **Mike Duxbury** shares his delight with the crowd after laying on the opening goal for **Steve Coppell**.*

*City's **Roger Palmer** prods the ball past advancing goalkeeper **Gary Bailey** for the Blues' dramatic last minute equaliser.*

MATCH VERDICT

City again illustrated their durability in this fixture by grabbing a last minute equaliser when all seemed lost. United set the tempo to the early part of the game and the only blemishes to their general control were bookings for Albiston's bad foul on Bennett and some dissent by McQueen to the referee. On the half hour United deservedly went in front. Duxbury's deep cross from the right was headed goalwards by McIlroy but Corrigan managed to block this with his legs and Coppell, playing centre-forward on this occasion, had one shot blocked by Ranson and another by Corrigan before his third attempt rocketed into the net. But United conceded a soft goal and lost their advantage in time added on to the half. Daley's in-swinging corner was expertly met by Reeves' header which bulged the net while the tall United defenders stood and gawped at each other.

United's attempts to reimpose their superiority in terms of goals were thwarted by some doughty defending from the Blues coupled with a fair helping of ineptitude and ill-luck from the United forwards. One illustration of this came as Grimes' goal-bound shot beat Corrigan but hit Duxbury and bounced clear to safety. The deadlock was finally broken on 72 minutes with what United fans believed would be the winner. Booth's clearance from McIlroy's corner went straight to the lurking Arthur Albiston whose 25 yard shot whistled past the advancing City defence and planted firmly in the net. After first disallowing the goal for offside, the referee, after consultation with the

*A delighted **Roger Palmer** hugs team-mate **Paul Power** as **Paul Sugrue** and **Tommy Booth** join in the celebrations.*

linesman, let it stand, and City players cast some accusing looks in the direction of Ranson who appeared to be the sluggish culprit. City however, were far from finished and gave the home crowd some anxious final moments. These efforts culminated in a corner which Caton headed downwards and, as Bailey raced off his line to claim the ball, Roger Palmer nipped in first and prodded home the equaliser.

102

MANCHESTER CITY 1
(MacKenzie)

MANCHESTER UNITED 0

DATE	21st February 1981
DIVISION	One
VENUE	Maine Road
ATTENDANCE	50,114

Manchester City		Manchester United
Joe CORRIGAN	1	Gary BAILEY
Tony HENRY	2	Jimmy NICHOLL
Bobby McDONALD	3	Arthur ALBISTON
Nicky REID	4	Mike DUXBURY *
Paul POWER	5	Kevin MORAN
Tommy BOOTH	6	Martin BUCHAN
Dave BENNETT	7	Steve COPPELL
Gerry GOW	8	Ray WILKINS
Steve MacKENZIE	9	Garry BIRTLES
Tommy HUTCHISON	10	Lou MACARI
Kevin REEVES	11	Sammy McILROY
Dennis TUEART	12	Scott McGARVEY (4)

*City Chairman **Peter Swales** introduces the Blues' new manager **John Bond** after the Autumn dismissal of **Tony Book** and **Malcolm Allison**.*

BACKGROUND

It was City who commanded all the major headlines between derbies. Malcolm Allison and Tony Book were both dismissed within a month of the September derby and their replacement - another man with a penchant for large cigars - John Bond, was handed the tough assignment of saving the Blues from relegation. In contrast to the previous years of big-spending, the former Norwich City manager made some shrewd initial signings, opting for the experience of Bobby McDonald and Tommy Hutchison from Coventry City, while Gerry Gow came from Bristol City and Phil Boyer from Southampton. This solid infusion seemed to do the trick and the Blues, playing good football into the bargain, had climbed away from the danger zone by derby day. Bond's attractive side had also made excellent Cup progress on two fronts. City were most unlucky to lose out to Liverpool in the semi-final of the League Cup while, incredibly in this season of stark contrasts, Wembley beckoned in the F.A. Cup. The rejuvenated Blues had reached the Sixth round with rousing victories over, with delicious irony, Allison's Crystal Palace (4-0) and Bond's old team Norwich City (6-0).

Meanwhile, United's season was turning into a massive anti-climax. With no less than 16 draws Dave Sexton's side had never much chance of being in real contention for the title and the all too often unexciting brand of football served up by the team was bringing pressure to bear on the United manager. The Cup had brought no relief either with a Fourth round F.A. Cup exit at Nottingham Forest. Sexton had attempted to improve the limited capabilities of United's strike force, something clearly apparent earlier in the season, by paying £1.2 million for Nottingham Forest's England forward Garry Birtles. It proved an altogether unhappy gamble for the United manager as by derby day Birtles was still looking for his first League goal after a run of 13 games. He did in fact remain scoreless in the League for the rest of the season and it was not until his 30th game that he notched up that first League goal, by which time the man who signed him had been moved on.

BEFORE THE GAME						
	P	W	D	L	F	A	Pts
UNITED	30	8	16	6	37	27	32
CITY	29	10	8	11	41	41	28

MAC THE KNIFE!

Steve's thrust ends deadlock

MATCH VERDICT

In a poor game City deservedly took the points. It was they who played the little good football on display while United produced a dreadfully uninspiring performance. The Reds, obviously trying to lift themselves out of their recent torpor, had started brightly but this soon faded as City began to win possession and put the United defence under pressure. Bennett, on the City right, provided most of the danger with some fast runs and accurate crosses. Martin Buchan, struggling manfully at the back of a rattled United defence, managed to keep the Reds level until half time. City maintained their grip on the game but seemed unable to apply the vital goal touch. Bailey's superlative tip around a post denied the persistent Bennett and perhaps prompted City fans' fears that this was not to be their day. But all these misgivings were forgotten when the Blues finally broke through on the hour and scored what would prove to be the game's only goal. Needless to say the tricky Bennett was instrumental in the goal. His link-up with Power enabled the City skipper to reach the by-line and swing over a low, swift cross which MacKenzie met with a sweet strike that sent the ball decisively past Bailey and into the net.

AT THE SEASON'S END

UNITED: Finished 8th on 48 points

CITY: Finished 12th on 39 points
(F.A. Cup Finalists, losing replay 3-2 to Spurs, after a 1-1 draw)

*The United defence is helpless as City's **Steve MacKenzie** (No.9) holds off a challenge from **Mike Duxbury** (No.4) and lets fly with a sweet shot for the only goal of the match.*

*A contrast in styles as United's expensive, but goalless, £1.2 million striker **Garry Birtles** holds off a challenge from **Gerry Gow**, City's tough-tackling £175,000 bargain buy from Bristol City during the Blues' 1-0 win at Maine Road.*

103

MANCHESTER CITY 0
MANCHESTER UNITED 0

DATE	10th October 1981
DIVISION	One
VENUE	Maine Road
ATTENDANCE	52,037

Manchester City		Manchester United
Joe CORRIGAN	1	Gary BAILEY
Ray RANSON	2	John GIDMAN
Kevin BOND	3	Arthur ALBISTON
Nicky REID	4	Ray WILKINS
Paul POWER	5	Kevin MORAN
Tommy CATON	6	Martin BUCHAN
Dennis TUEART	7	Bryan ROBSON
Martin O'NEILL	8	Garry BIRTLES *
Tommy HUTCHISON	9	Frank STAPLETON
Asa HARTFORD	10	Sammy McILROY
Kevin REEVES	11	Remi MOSES
Phil BOYER	12	Steve COPPELL (8)

*Asa Hartford, re-signed by City just a week earlier from Everton for £350,000 challenges United's England midfielder **Ray Wilkins**.*

BACKGROUND

It was all change at United over the summer and a very different team lined up for this 103rd derby. Dave Sexton, sacked in April, was replaced by the colourful Ron Atkinson. The new man soon showed a flair for the large headline as he decided on a big spending policy to rejuvenate the stagnant Reds. Frank Stapleton, at the time arguably the country's leading centre-forward was bought for nearly £1 million to replace the Italian-bound Joe Jordan. John Gidman arrived from Everton in exchange for Mickey Thomas and Remi Moses, now out of contract at Atkinson's old club West Bromwich Albion, also joined the squad for around £650,000. It took a while for the new team to gel, but the prospects looked good as the accent returned to attack and, in the game prior to the derby, a 5-0 thrashing of Wolverhampton Wanderers with a McIlroy hat-trick, suggested Atkinson was getting it right. The game with Wolves though had been partly overshadowed by the on pitch signing of Atkinson's biggest buy - his former Albion captain Bryan Robson - at a British record fee of £1.8 million. Was he to be the final part of the jigsaw?

John Bond too now showed a penchant for headlines and expensive buys. He bolstered his gallant Cup Final team with Martin O'Neill from his old club Norwich, but it was the signing of the richly-talented Trevor Francis for £1 million from Nottingham Forest that had the City fans streaming to watch his debut at Stoke City. Unfortunately, Manchester football supporters would be unable to compare City's million pound man with United's because by derby day Francis was sidelined with a bad knee injury. Bond had also recently re-signed the popular Asa Hartford from Everton for £350,000 and acquired his son Kevin from Seattle Sounders in America. Among those who left to make way for all this were Tony Henry, Dave Bennett and Steve MacKenzie. The new Blues had made a steady if unspectacular start to a season now offering three points for a win.

BEFORE THE GAME

	P	W	D	L	F	A	Pts
UNITED	9	4	3	2	12	5	15
CITY	8	3	2	3	12	12	11

GREAT SAVER JOE

Then City in big fightback

Joe Corrigan – a string of fine saves by the City goalkeeper kept the scoreline blank.

MATCH VERDICT

All the attention focussed on the country's costliest player as Bryan Robson ran out for his League debut at Maine Road. Steve Coppell had been manager Atkinson's surprising choice as to who would make way for 'Robbo', and the Reds' midfield trio of Robson, Moses and Wilkins had an imposing look to it. City seemed in awe of the threesome and United had all the early play as Robson demonstrated to his new fans the all-action style that would make him such a popular and successful player for the club. Firstly his late dash into the penalty area was ended by an untidy late lunge from Caton and the United fans howled in vain for a penalty. Then following Birtles' neat flick Robson galloped through with the goal at his mercy, but Joe Corrigan dived bravely at the United man's feet to save with his legs. With the United midfield in control, McIlroy rounded off a delightful move with a lob over Corrigan that clipped the crossbar, and the goalkeeper did well to push a powerful effort from Wilkins around a post for a corner.

United replaced the injured Birtles with Coppell on the half-hour, but City, so slow to start, gradually began to impose themselves on the game and it required a marvellous reaction save with his legs from Bailey to prevent Tueart giving the Blues an interval lead. With City's midfield getting a tighter grip the second period drifted towards an anti-climactic draw as the teams cancelled each other out. By full time it was the Blues who felt they might have won it as Caton and Hartford both went close with snap shots, but more of the talk on the way home surrounded the display of Robson who many believed could be the man to galvanise United towards further glory.

Remi Moses – the Manchester-born midfielder was another expensive cog in Ron Atkinson's re-built United

Two new faces in derby action as United's **Bryan Robson** makes his League debut at Maine Road and battles for the ball with **Martin O'Neill**, City's new signing from Norwich.

Big money signings **Bryan Robson** and **Frank Stapleton** both went close to giving United the lead at Maine Road.

104

MANCHESTER UNITED 1
(Moran)

MANCHESTER CITY 1
(Reeves)

DATE	27th February 1982	
DIVISION	One	
VENUE	Old Trafford	
ATTENDANCE	57,830	

Manchester United		Manchester City
Gary BAILEY	1	Joe CORRIGAN
John GIDMAN	2	Ray RANSON
Arthur ALBISTON	3	Bobby McDONALD
Ray WILKINS	4	Nicky REID
Kevin MORAN	5	Aage HAREIDE
Martin BUCHAN	6	Tommy CATON
Bryan ROBSON	7	John RYAN
Garry BIRTLES	8	Kevin REEVES
Frank STAPLETON	9	Gary JACKSON
Mike DUXBURY	10	Asa HARTFORD
Steve COPPELL	11	Paul POWER
Scott McGARVEY	12	Steve KINSEY

Tommy Caton – the young defender was at the heart of a sterling defensive display from City.

Nicky Reid – the competitive defender/midfielder was a great favourite with the City fans and enjoyed an outstanding match in this derby meeting.

BACKGROUND

Atkinson was leading United in a determined bid to win the title in his first season. By derby day the Reds were in a useful second place and four points behind leaders Southampton, with two games in hand. Robson was proving an inspirational player in a strong midfield while Stapleton and Birtles had netted 20 goals between them. A disappointing Cup exit at Watford meant however, that the old adage of concentrating on the League would now be the major United aim.

City were also in contention for the League. Indeed, an excellent 3-1 victory at Liverpool on Boxing Day left the Blues only two points behind early season leaders Swansea City. Trevor Francis, particularly during home appearances, was in outstanding form, and he and Reeves were proving a daunting strike force that might well be a worry to United on derby day. However, a bad injury to the talented Tueart, who would be unavailable for the rest of the season, was a big blow to City. On the day, Manager Bond also sprang a surprise for the pundits by selecting unknown local boy Gary Jackson to play in the Old Trafford cauldron.

BEFORE THE GAME							
	P	W	D	L	F	A	Pts
UNITED	25	13	7	5	38	19	46
CITY	26	12	6	8	40	30	42

MORAN'S STRIKE PEGS BACK CITY

MATCH VERDICT

Football's biggest provincial crowd for four seasons certainly got value for money in a rip-roaring derby at Old Trafford. United opened splendidly, serving up a tidal wave of fast fluent football that had City virtually encamped in their own half throughout the first 20 minutes. It needed a desperate save by Corrigan to keep out an effort from Stapleton, while Moran struck a post with a header. Traditionally however, City are never more dangerous than when they are written off and sterling defensive work by Caton, Reid and the ever dependable Corrigan allowed the Blues to weather this opening and then begin to play some good football themselves. The Blues had detailed the Norwegian Hareide to do a close marking job on the dangerous Robson and the plan seemed to work as it stifled United's momentum. Indeed, it was the Norwegian who broke off from his close shadowing to spark the goal which silenced the previously enthusiastic home fans. His pass released Ranson on an enterprising run which took the full back past Albiston and, despite Robson's lunge, he pulled back a dangerous pin-point centre for Reeves to beat Bailey's right hand with a glorious glancing header into the net. This million pound man might have had his critics but his goal record against the Reds was proving impressive.

United were not downcast by this setback and the goal merely served to increase the intensity of the assault on the City goalmouth. An equaliser looked inevitable and, sure enough, it arrived on the stroke of half-time. City thought they had cleared the danger following a United corner but Gidman returned the ball to the middle from the right and Moran powered through to squeeze a header just inside a post from 12 yards.

United maintained an attacking momentum throughout the second half but the brave resistance of the City rearguard repeatedly frustrated their attempts to secure all the points. In the end it was a hard earned draw for the Blues, but neither Caton, Reid nor Corrigan deserved to be on a losing side.

AT THE SEASON'S END

UNITED: Finished 3rd on 78 points

CITY: Finished 10th on 58 points

The front cover of *Manchester United's* programme for the 104th derby.

Kevin Reeves – a striker with a fine scoring record against United, he put City ahead with a superb glancing header.

Kevin Moran – on target with United's equaliser when he squeezed a header just inside a post shortly before half-time.

105

MANCHESTER UNITED 2
(Stapleton 2)

MANCHESTER CITY 2
(Tueart, Cross)

DATE	23rd October 1982
DIVISION	One
VENUE	Old Trafford
ATTENDANCE	57,334

Manchester United		Manchester City
Gary BAILEY	1	Joe CORRIGAN
Mike DUXBURY	2	Ray RANSON
Arthur ALBISTON	3	Bobby McDONALD
Ray WILKINS	4	Kevin BOND
Kevin MORAN	5	Paul POWER
Gordon McQUEEN	6	Tommy CATON
Bryan ROBSON	7	Dennis TUEART
Arnold MUHREN *	8	Kevin REEVES
Frank STAPLETON	9	David CROSS
Norman WHITESIDE	10	Asa HARTFORD
Steve COPPELL	11	Graham BAKER
Lou MACARI (8)	12	Peter BODAK

BACKGROUND

Trevor Francis left the Blues in the summer for Italy and Bond moved in the less exotic talents of Graham Baker who cost £225,000 from Southampton and much-travelled striker David Cross from West Ham. City made an encouraging start with three straight wins but this was followed by more uncertain form and some disappointing defeats that moved the club down the table. The experienced Cross was proving something of a bargain with five goals thus far and the City fans were cheered by the return of favourite Dennis Tueart.

Ron Atkinson maintained his import of quality players to United with the acquisition of the skilful midfield player Arnold Muhren on a free transfer from Ipswich Town. United's midfield, based on the England pair of Wilkins and Robson, now had a truly awesome look to it, and United underlined why they were the bookmakers' favourites for this season's title with an impressive start to the new campaign which saw them top of the table by derby day. A certain Norman Whiteside, capped at the almost unbelievably young age of 16 in the previous summer's World Cup in Spain, was now Frank Stapleton's striking partner.

BEFORE THE GAME							
	P	W	D	L	F	A	Pts
UNITED	10	6	3	1	15	6	21
CITY	10	5	1	4	13	14	16

*City's **Kevin Bond** keeps a close eye on United striker **Frank Stapleton**, but it wasn't close enough as the Irishman scored twice to drag the Reds back from 0-2 down.*

***David Cross** – City's new signing made his derby mark early by slotting the Blues into a 2-0 lead.*

*United's **Frank Stapleton** slides in his second goal of the afternoon to earn the Reds a 2-2 draw despite the efforts of City's **Asa Hartford** (No.10) and grounded goalkeeper **Joe Corrigan**. United's **Bryan Robson** and substitute **Lou Macari** prepare to celebrate the home recovery.*

MATCH VERDICT

In a rousing match, which was very much in keeping with the improved football played by the Manchester sides in the previous season United, having dominated the game, had to come from two goals down to snatch the point. The Reds' confident opening was shattered on 12 minutes as City scored in their first attack. Ranson won the corner and, when Power's in-swinging kick curled over, Reeves' neat flick was met at the far post by Tueart's dramatic diving header into the net. For the remainder of the half United's fluent play threatened to demolish the Blues but some wayward finishing by the United strikers only increased the home crowd's frustration. There was a sense of incredulity as, on the stroke of half-time, City's second major attack put them into a crucial two goal lead. Reeves released Baker with a short pass and the midfield player's low centre into the six yard box was met expertly by the veteran Cross who flicked the ball over the line.

With United's early fluency transforming into second half desperation, Frank Stapleton chose the moment to score his first goal in ten games. Trapping Muhren's pass, he pivoted and lost Caton in one movement and then drifted a memorable 20 yard shot past the diving Corrigan and high into the net. The scenario of the first half now continued as United resumed their encampment in the City half and the Blues pulled everyone back to protect their lead. Stapleton was not finished though and, following a United corner with ten minutes left, Coppell and Moran combined with the Irishman and a dangerous ball was dragged back into the six yard box for Stapleton to joyously stab home the equaliser.

***Arnold Muhren** – United's classy Dutchman arrived from Ipswich Town in the close season to give the Reds midfield an even more awesome look to it.*

***Graham Baker** – City's modest £225,000 buy from Southampton in the wake of Trevor Francis' departure to Italian football.*

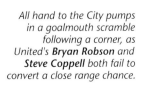

*All hand to the City pumps in a goalmouth scramble following a corner, as United's **Bryan Robson** and **Steve Coppell** both fail to convert a close range chance.*

106

MANCHESTER CITY 1
(Reeves)

MANCHESTER UNITED 2
(Stapleton 2)

DATE	5th March 1983	
DIVISION	One	
VENUE	Maine Road	
ATTENDANCE	45,400	

Manchester City		Manchester United
Joe CORRIGAN	1	Gary BAILEY
Ray RANSON	2	Mike DUXBURY
Bobby McDONALD	3	Arthur ALBISTON
Nicky REID	4	Remi MOSES
Kevin BOND	5	Paul McGRATH
Tommy CATON	6	Gordon McQUEEN
Dennis TUEART	7	Ray WILKINS
Kevin REEVES	8	Arnold MUHREN
David CROSS	9	Frank STAPLETON
Asa HARTFORD	10	Norman WHITESIDE
Graham BAKER *	11	Steve COPPELL
Peter BODAK (11)	12	Lou MACARI

BACKGROUND

United were enjoying mixed fortunes. Already through to a League Cup Final appearance with Liverpool they had also reached the Sixth round of the F.A. Cup. The only disappointment had been maddeningly inconsistent League form which had seen them drop vital points and hence lose ground on runaway leaders Liverpool. Disappointing defeats at relegation-threatened Brighton & Hove Albion and mid-table Coventry and Stoke City put something of a question mark over the side's ability to play well on the more mundane occasions. The absence through injury of the mercurial Robson was another key factor in the equation.

By this stage the season had turned rather sour on City. Inconsistent League form saw a gradual falling away in the table, from a lofty second place in November to 14th by derby day. By now manager John Bond was also no longer with the club. Following a hugely disappointing F.A. Cup defeat in January at Brighton when the Blues had been beaten 4-0 he had, albeit somewhat surprisingly, decided to quit. Peter Swales accepted the resignation and appointed a former Blue, Bond's assistant John Benson, as the new manager. The fans however, were not at all happy and, following a demoralising 1-0 home defeat by Notts County, there were crowd demonstrations. The unthinkable prospect of relegation was surely not possible but without a victory in the League for seven games it was a worried City that faced the Reds.

BEFORE THE GAME							
	P	W	D	L	F	A	Pts
UNITED	28	13	9	6	37	22	48
CITY	30	10	8	12	38	48	38

Joe Corrigan – City's loyal and long-serving last line of defence, is watched by striker David Cross as he turns this effort from United's Frank Stapleton over the crossbar. It was to be the final derby for both players, who within weeks of this match had left the relegation struggles at Maine Road for new careers in American soccer.

BIG DROP IS CITY'S FEAR

*United's **Frank Stapleton** tussles for the ball with City's **Kevin Bond**. The talented Reds' striker emulated his feat in the October derby by again scoring twice.*

*City left-back **Bobby McDonald** clears from United's **Steve Coppell**, but the Reds winger got away from his marker to set up the visitors opening goal for Frank Stapleton.*

MATCH VERDICT

In a typically close-fought contest United's more fluent football merited the victory, but it was a desperately disappointing defeat for the Blues and left many fans wondering if the ten point cushion between the club and the dreaded relegation spot might be eroded if these sort of results continued.

It had all started so promisingly for the Blues. They competently resisted United's assured start and through the outstanding Hartford began to win the important midfield supremacy. A series of near misses finally culminated in a City goal on the half hour. Hartford's corner was flicked on at the near post by Reeves and reached McDonald at the far post. Finding the angle too tight the City full-back hooked the ball back into the middle where Reeves stooped to force a header under McQueen's diving body and into the net. But the Blues' joy was not to last. The influential Hartford was now hampered by an injury and, minutes into the second half, United gained the equaliser with a delightfully old fashioned goal. Coppell showed McDonald a clean pair of heels as he raced down the right wing and hit an arcing cross on the run towards Stapleton who rose majestically and hung in the air above Caton long enough to send a thunderous header into the back of the City net. With the Blues visibly wilting United grasped the midfield initiative through Moses and Wilkins and within 15 minutes were in front. Muhren's in-swinging corner picked out Stapleton and the Irishman, who had developed quite a taste for scoring against the Blues this season, sent his curving header past Corrigan. City's desperate attempts to retrieve something from the game were doomed to failure. Certainly the home fans cursed their luck as, in one desperate last rally, Caton's powerful shot clattered against a post.

Peter Gardner writing in the 'Manchester Evening News' had little doubt about the worrying direction of City's season:

"Manchester City must today wake up to the growing realisation that an inglorious and desperate scramble to avoid relegation is staring them starkly in the face.

More than parochial pride was lost against Manchester United at Maine Road on Saturday when a 2-1 defeat sent the Blues tumbling to the brink of a place among the last half dozen strugglers.

Their cushion is a 10 point margin, although City's current slide in which they have lost four of the last five games and won only once in the League in 1983 is that of a side going in only one direction....down!

Whether the Blues actually hit rock bottom remains to be seen. However, there is grave cause for concern with an ominous fixture list facing the club in the weeks that remain of what has become a disastrous and critical campaign. Two demanding away matches at Swansea and Southampton provide the immediate threat for a team who are in a losing rut.

And kicking the habit is the major problem for manager John Benson who has now got to persuade his players to provide the same sort of commitment they revealed against the Reds in less mundane, but equally important forthcoming games".

Asa Hartford – the City man fought a desperate battle for midfield control and set up City's goal from a corner but, when he was slowed by an injury early in the second half, the match slipped away from the Blues.

AT THE SEASON'S END

UNITED: Finished 3rd on 70 points
(F.A. Cup Winners, beating Brighton 4-0 in a replay after a 2-2 draw. League Cup finalists, losing 2-1 to Liverpool)

CITY: Finished 20th on 47 points
Relegated to Division Two

*Looking to the future – United's **Frank Stapleton** and City's **Mick McCarthy** in October 1986.*

MODERN TIMES

More Memorable Matches 1985-1991

107

MANCHESTER CITY 0
MANCHESTER UNITED 3
(Robson pen, Albiston, Duxbury)

DATE	14th September 1985
DIVISION	One
VENUE	Maine Road
ATTENDANCE	48,773

Manchester City		Manchester United
Alex WILLIAMS	1	Gary BAILEY
Andy MAY	2	Mike DUXBURY
Clive WILSON	3	Arthur ALBISTON
Kenny CLEMENTS	4	Norman WHITESIDE
Mick McCARTHY	5	Paul McGRATH
David PHILLIPS	6	Graeme HOGG
Mark LILLIS	7	Bryan ROBSON
Paul POWER	8	Gordon STRACHAN
Steve KINSEY *	9	Mark HUGHES
Sammy McILROY	10	Frank STAPLETON *
Paul SIMPSON	11	Peter BARNES
Jim MELROSE (9)	12	Alan BRAZIL (10)

*United's powerful young striker **Mark Hughes** swerves away from City full-back **Clive Wilson**.*

BACKGROUND

United fans believed their long wait for the League title was coming to an end as Ron Atkinson's revamped United opened the season in devastating form and entered the derby with seven straight wins. Furthermore, victory over the Blues would set a club record for a best ever start to a season. In the two seasons since the last derby Atkinson had fashioned several more changes to his talented squad. Youngsters Mark Hughes and Graeme Hogg were now established first team players. Hughes looked a tremendous prospect up front and, already endowed with a Cup-winners medal, had started the season in brilliant form. Following the departure of Ray Wilkins to Italy at the end of 1983-84, Atkinson had purchased the creative and competitive Gordon Strachan for £600,000 and also Danish international Jesper Olsen as exciting wide players and they had enjoyed excellent first seasons. In another imaginative move Atkinson had acquired the former Blues winger Peter Barnes and he was due a warm reception on his return to Maine Road in red colours!

City had found their return to the big time under Billy McNeill and Jimmy Frizzell a mixed one. Following a promising opening five games with only one match lost, some ominous cracks appeared during two defeats before the derby. In common with Peter Barnes' arrival at Old Trafford, City now had ex-United idol Sammy McIlroy playing for them. He was one of many modest buys that characterised the now careful spending Blues. Kenny Clements returned after six years with Oldham, whilst Mick McCarthy (Barnsley), David Phillips (Plymouth) and City supporter Mark Lillis (Huddersfield) were the other new derby faces who aimed to put a stop to United's runaway start to the season.

BEFORE THE GAME							
	P	W	D	L	F	A	Pts
UNITED	7	7	0	0	18	2	21
CITY	7	2	2	3	8	12	8

City's **Andy May** clashes with United's early penalty scorer **Bryan Robson** while former Reds favourite **Sammy McIlroy** - now in Blues colours - leads the chase for the loose ball.

MATCH VERDICT

In what many critics thought might be United's hardest game yet in their record-breaking start to the season, City proved no match for the Reds and were simply outclassed. If there was any criticism of this impressive United side it was with regard to some sketchy finishing for, in truth, they could have doubled the scoreline, such was their superiority.

In an ominous start for the Blues, United's midfield men seemed to be first to every ball and, through quick release to Strachan and Barnes, it was clear City would have their hands full. Peter Barnes who had received a mixed reception from his old fans quickly showed up as he moved the ball towards Whiteside on the right. McCarthy intercepted but then put Williams in trouble with a poor back pass. The goalkeeper compounded the error by panicking and pulling down the menacing Hughes. Up stepped Robson and drove the penalty firmly into the net. The Blues tried to rally but it was one-way traffic as United poured forward and killed off the game with a spectacular second goal. City thought they had cleared the danger as the ball looped out of their penalty area but Albiston, arriving at speed, struck a powerful 25 yard drive with his right foot that fizzed past the helpless Williams. There was no come-back route now for a City side which looked bereft of any guile or confidence. United were able to relax a little, and seemed happy to store up further energies to maintain their incredible opening run. Late in the second half the score gained a more realistic look as, following another difficult moment for the City defence, Stapleton struck the bar from close in when to many it appeared easier to hit the target, but Duxbury followed in and spared his blushes by drilling the rebound past the disconsolate Williams. By this point the home fans were on their way out. It had been United's day, and this eighth consecutive victory was the club's best ever start to a season.

Billy McNeill – now manager of City.

Mike Duxbury slots in the loose ball for United's third goal with City 'keeper **Alex Williams** prostrate after **Frank Stapleton** (also grounded) had hit the crossbar.

Mick McCarthy, City's uncompromising central defender plunges in to clear from United's **Norman Whiteside**.

108

MANCHESTER UNITED 2
(Gibson, Strachan pen)

MANCHESTER CITY 2
(Wilson, Albiston og)

DATE	22nd March 1986
DIVISION	One
VENUE	Old Trafford
ATTENDANCE	51,274

Manchester United		Manchester City
Chris TURNER	1	Eric NIXON
Mike DUXBURY	2	Nicky REID
Arthur ALBISTON	3	Paul POWER
Norman WHITESIDE	4	Kenny CLEMENTS *
Paul McGRATH	5	Steve REDMOND
Mark HIGGINS	6	David PHILLIPS
Colin GIBSON	7	Mark LILLIS
Gordon STRACHAN	8	Andy MAY
Mark HUGHES	9	Steve KINSEY
Peter DAVENPORT	10	Neil McNAB
Peter BARNES *	11	Clive WILSON
Frank STAPLETON (11)	12	Paul SIMPSON (4)

Irresponsible United left with red faces

*Neil McNab who was outstanding in midfield for the Blues takes on United's **Peter Barnes** (left) and **Arthur Albiston**.*

BACKGROUND

United's record-breaking start to the season saw them win the first ten games outright and then go 16 matches before Sheffield Wednesday became the first team to beat them in November. Unbelievably some three months later the Reds entered the derby struggling to stay in contention for the title, having slipped down in third place, four points behind leaders Everton. A dreadful run of inconsistent form had cost the club dearly. Two factors seemed to contribute to the sad demise. 'Captain Marvel', Bryan Robson, had hardly played since October, sidelined by another injury jinx. Then the club were forced, following continued Press speculation, to announce just days before the derby meeting that the popular and talented Mark Hughes would leave the club in the summer. In what smacked slightly of desperation, Atkinson rather tarnished his impressive buying record with a series of hasty purchases in an attempt to bolster both morale and the diminishing title challenge. In came utility man Colin Gibson from Aston Villa, little striker Terry Gibson from Coventry City, and defender John Sivebaek. Then, two weeks before the City game, Peter Davenport, Hughes' intended successor, arrived from Nottingham Forest for a major fee.

Meanwhile City were enjoying some modest success by establishing themselves in mid-table and indeed, were due to play Chelsea at Wembley the next day in the Final of the low-key Full Members' Cup competition. McNeill had developed a side based very much on local talent with the backbone of the team being Nixon, Reid, Power, Clements, May, Simpson and Clive Wilson. The promising youth skipper Steve Redmond had also won a defensive place in the line-up by derby day. There were still some question marks about the side's lack of scoring power as McNeill juggled Gordon Davies and Steve Kinsey in an attempt to gain more goals, and consequently The Blues still entered the derby against the now rather unpredictable Reds as underdogs.

BEFORE THE GAME

	P	W	D	L	F	A	Pts
UNITED	32	19	5	8	54	25	62
CITY	33	11	8	14	36	43	41

MATCH VERDICT

This was a significant match in the annals of United's 1985-86 season as the Reds further frustrated their supporters by losing a two goal lead and dropping further vital points in pursuit of that elusive title. City featured in a great come-back which said much about their pride and determination for these parochial affairs. It had all started so well for the Reds. With just 90 seconds gone City conceded a careless free kick some 25 yards out, and new boy Colin Gibson sent a swerving shot around the wall and beyond Nixon into the net. United generally had the better of a tense first half, although careless finishing by Hughes and Davenport would prove costly. The combative Neil McNab kept the Blues in the game with some timely tackles and useful prompting of his forwards that kept the United defence on alert. However, the anxiety of United's fans seemed to be eased when Strachan's penalty appeared to put the game beyond the Blues' powers of recovery. City though, did not view it that way and, with 19 minutes left the United defenders were conspicuously absent as Clive Wilson stooped to head the Blues back into the game. All the anxiety and nervousness so evident in United's recent performances returned almost at once as City proceeded to place them under constant pressure.

This general lack of composure was graphically illustrated in the final minutes of the game when Albiston, chased back for a loose ball and under pressure from Simpson, sent an injudicious back-pass curling wide of Turner and into the back of his own net.

AT THE SEASON'S END

UNITED: Finished 4th on 76 points

CITY: Finished 15th on 45 points

Gordon Strachan puts the Reds 2-0 up with a firmly struck 58th minute penalty.

City's *Clive Wilson* (just out of picture) sends a bobbling header past the United defence and goalkeeper *Chris Turner* to put City back in contention after 71 minutes.

City's *Kenny Clements* challenges for the ball with the Reds' skipper *Norman Whiteside* during the 2-2 draw.

More despair for *Chris Turner* as *Arthur Albiston's* misguided back-pass whizzes past his hands and into the net for the own goal that handed City a 78th minute equaliser.

109

MANCHESTER CITY 1
(McCarthy)

MANCHESTER UNITED 1
(Stapleton)

DATE	26th October 1986	
DIVISION	One	
VENUE	Maine Road	
ATTENDANCE	32,440	

Manchester City		Manchester United
Perry SUCKLING	1	Chris TURNER
John GIDMAN	2	John SIVEBAEK
Clive WILSON	3	Arthur ALBISTON
Kenny CLEMENTS	4	Norman WHITESIDE
Mick McCARTHY	5	Paul McGRATH
Steve REDMOND	6	Graeme HOGG
David WHITE	7	Bryan ROBSON
Neil McNAB	8	Remi MOSES
Imre VARADI	9	Frank STAPLETON
Tony GREALISH *	10	Peter DAVENPORT
Paul SIMPSON	11	Peter BARNES
Ian BRIGHTWELL (10)	12	Terry GIBSON

BACKGROUND

Both Manchester clubs found themselves down among the final four in the table on derby day; City were rock bottom with United just three places above. For the Blues this was a major disappointment after establishing themselves in solid enough fashion the previous season. After the promising start of a victory over top-flight newcomers Wimbledon and a draw against Liverpool at Anfield, the familiar scenario of poor performances, lost confidence and managerial change had the Blues downcast by derby day. By the end of September Billy McNeill's constant failure to find successful goalscorers was clearly illustrated by just two goals in six matches, but at this point the manager resigned and walked out on Maine Road to take up an appointment at Aston Villa.

Jimmy Frizzell was appointed as the new manager and immediately made a series of transfer moves. Much travelled Imre Varadi joined the club from West Bromwich Albion and scored within six minutes of his debut at Chelsea. Tony Grealish, who also arrived from The Hawthorns for a bargain £20,000 was due for a derby debut along with John Gidman who also joined the ranks of those who have played for both Manchester clubs when he moved across to Maine Road. Manager Frizzell was naturally hopeful these players would improve the dire situation which the club now faced.

After several years of Cup success and healthy challenges in the League, Ron Atkinson was facing mounting criticism as United made a poor start to the new season. Without an injured Robson, and with Mark Hughes now transferred to Barcelona, United lost the first three games and, although Southampton were beaten 5-1 on Robson's return, the side seemed strangely dull and lacking in both flair and confidence. Atkinson must have hoped the corner had been turned in October as the Reds beat Sheffield Wednesday and Luton Town and were looking for a further win against City to give the season a belated lift-off.

BEFORE THE GAME

	P	W	D	L	F	A	Pts
UNITED	11	3	2	6	14	14	11
CITY	11	1	4	6	8	13	7

Jimmy Frizzell - a first derby as manager for City's new boss.

John Gidman - *crossed Manchester from Old Trafford to join the Blues.*

*City's **Mick McCarthy** and **David White** combine to clear from the threat of United's **Paul McGrath** and **Frank Stapleton** (above).*

*Imre Varadi (No.9) and **Steve Redmond** congratulate City defender **Mick McCarthy** after he had headed a splendid goal to level the score at 1-1.*

MATCH VERDICT

The first 'live' derby proved to be anything but a television spectacular and the arm-chair viewer was subjected to a gritty and uninspiring game between two struggling teams. The City fans must have drawn some comfort from a battling display by their 'new' players and had a case in claiming the performance merited three points. For United this was just another mediocre showing in a disappointing season. McNab and Grealish showed a hungry appetite for the fray and generally got the better of Robson and Moses in midfield. This enabled City to set up a series of attacks that fully extended the United defence and only brilliant saves by Turner kept Varadi and White from scoring. After half-time United finally managed to put their game together and on 50 minutes Frank Stapleton, a man with a great derby scoring record, did it yet again. As Barnes eventually broke clear of his marker and put over a teasing cross, Stapleton timed his run perfectly and sent a dipping header into the City net. Much to their credit, City did not allow this reverse to stifle their attacking instincts and quickly hit back. Simpson's short corner reached McNab and his centre was met by McCarthy who outjumped Hogg and powered in a header with such force the ball rebounded out into the field of play. It was at least a goal to savour in what was a largely forgettable match.

*United's **Bryan Robson** tangles for possession with City's new signing **Tony Grealish**.*

110

MANCHESTER UNITED 2
(Reid og, Robson)

MANCHESTER CITY 0

DATE	7th March 1987
DIVISION	One
VENUE	Old Trafford
ATTENDANCE	48,619

Manchester United		Manchester City
Gary BAILEY	1	Perry SUCKLING
John SIVEBAEK	2	Nicky REID
Colin GIBSON	3	Clive WILSON
Mike DUXBURY	4	Kenny CLEMENTS
Paul McGRATH	5	Mick McCARTHY
Kevin MORAN	6	Ian BRIGHTWELL
Bryan ROBSON	7	Graham BAKER
Gordon STRACHAN *	8	Neil McNAB
Norman WHITESIDE	9	Imre VARADI
Terry GIBSON	10	Paul MOULDEN *
Liam O'BRIEN	11	Paul SIMPSON
Peter DAVENPORT (8)	12	Steve REDMOND (10)

BACKGROUND

Just ten days after the October derby United sprang a shock and sacked manager Ron Atkinson, who seemed to have paid the penalty as much for the previous season's dramatic fade-out in the League as for any disappointments of the current campaign. Immediately the respected Aberdeen manager Alex Ferguson was installed as the new boss. Without setting the world alight the Scot saw his team climb the table despite a mixture of results. Good ones, such as the now almost annual victory at Liverpool, were mixed with indifferent performances, including a home defeat by Norwich City, which followed the Anfield success. By the date of the derby the new manager was still assessing his staff and had made no real moves to change playing personnel.

Jimmy Frizzell meanwhile had clearly worked hard at City in a gallant effort to try and turn around a seemingly impossible situation and the club, although still precariously placed, were now in 17th place. By the time of the derby, many of City's highly promising Youth Cup-winning side of 1986 had graduated to the first team including Ian Brightwell, Paul Moulden and Steve Redmond. The Blues' fans were also delighted with the form shown by ex-Red John Gidman, although sadly injury ruled out his selection for this match. Peter Barnes had also moved back from United to City, following in the steps of the celebrated Billy Meredith and Denis Law as players who had started out with City, played for United, and then returned to the Blues.

BEFORE THE GAME

	P	W	D	L	F	A	Pts
UNITED	29	9	11	9	37	30	38
CITY	29	6	11	12	26	38	29

MANCHESTER UNITED F.C. P.L.C.
OLD TRAFFORD, MANCHESTER

TODAY LEAGUE — DIVISION 1

MANCHESTER UNITED
v.
MANCHESTER CITY

SATURDAY, 7th March, 1987
Kick-off 3-00 p.m.

Secretary.

Issued subject to the Rules, Regulations and Bye-Laws of the Football Association. No ticket exchanged nor money refunded.
This portion to be retained Enter via Turnstile 94-98

PADDOCK SCOREBOARD ADULT

Nᵒ 0848

ADMISSION
£2.80

As a capacity attendance is expected, it is strongly recommended that patrons ENTER THE GROUND not less than 30 minutes before kick-off

Alex Ferguson - in charge at Old Trafford for the past four months following the November dismissal of Ron Atkinson.

City's **Kenny Clements** and **Ian Brightwell** are helpless as United skipper **Bryan Robson** slots in a pass from **Peter Davenport** to seal the Reds 2-0 victory.

Paul Moulden - one of a number of highly promising City youngsters thrown into the first team fray by manager Jimmy Frizzell. His Youth team scoring exploits earned the nickname 'Goalden Moulden' and earlier, with Bolton Lads, he entered the 'Guinness Book of Records' after netting 289 goals in 40 games!

MATCH VERDICT

The pre-match headlines were made by Peter Barnes who was prevented from emulating the unusual derby record of Meredith and Law when he was dropped from the expected line-up. Jimmy Frizzell subsequently fined the winger for his indiscreet comments on the matter. In a one-sided game of dubious quality United dominated without ever impressing, while City ambitions seemed to be based purely on survival. The main feature of a sterile first half was the battle between United's centre forward Whiteside and the City centre half McCarthy. Whiteside, showing a typical mixture of aggression, skill and craft, generally had the better of the tussle and McCarthy's frustration boiled over with a wild tackle that resulted in a booking. As United upped the tempo, Suckling distinguished himself with a series of fine saves - two from Duxbury and Robson were particularly noteworthy - but on the hour City's resistance was finally broken. Strachan's floated corner was met by McGrath's downward header which threaded its way through the crowded area but flew into the roof of the City net courtesy of a sliced deflection from an attempted clearance by the unfortunate Reid. City responded with a rather indeterminate search for an equaliser but their efforts were all far too hurried and seemed unlikely to gain much reward. With the subsequent room now afforded to their forwards, United settled the game. Terry Gibson released Davenport with a quick pass and the substitute's neat pull-back from the by-line was met just outside the six yard box by Robson whose firm low shot put the game beyond the reach of the saddened Blues.

AT THE SEASON'S END

UNITED: Finished 11th on 56 points

CITY: Finished 21st on 39 points
Relegated to Division Two

Delight for United and despair for City as **Paul McGrath's** header from a corner is deflected off **Nicky Reid** into the Blues' net to make it 1-0 after 62 minutes.

111

MANCHESTER CITY 5
(Oldfield 2, Morley, Bishop, Hinchcliffe)

MANCHESTER UNITED 1
(Hughes)

	DATE	23rd September 1989
	DIVISION	One
	VENUE	Maine Road
	ATTENDANCE	43,246

Manchester City		Manchester United
Paul COOPER	1	Jim LEIGHTON
Gary FLEMING	2	Viv ANDERSON
Andy HINCHCLIFFE	3	Mal DONAGHY
Ian BISHOP	4	Mike DUXBURY
Brian GAYLE	5	Mike PHELAN
Steve REDMOND	6	Gary PALLISTER
David WHITE	7	Russell BEARDSMORE *
Trevor MORLEY	8	Paul INCE
David OLDFIELD	9	Brian McCLAIR
Ian BRIGHTWELL	10	Mark HUGHES
Paul LAKE *	11	Danny WALLACE
Jason BECKFORD (11)	**Sub**	Lee SHARPE (7)
Gary MEGSON	**Sub**	Clayton BLACKMORE

BACKGROUND

On the eve of City's return to the big time it was United who made all the off-field headlines. Manager Alex Ferguson who, in City's Second Division years, had already lavished out a lot of money purchasing new players in pursuit of a team to bring lasting success, now spent the summer and early season in a massive shake-up of the club. Out went crowd favourites Norman Whiteside and Paul McGrath to Everton and Aston Villa respectively and, by the time of the derby match Neil Webb (£1.5 million from Nottingham Forest) and Mike Phelan (£750,000 from Norwich City) had been joined by Gary Pallister (£2.3 million from Middlesbrough), Paul Ince (£1.7 million from West Ham) and Danny Wallace (£1.2 million from Southampton).

Even this incredible spending spree was actually overshadowed by a proposed Boardroom takeover as Martin Edwards surprisingly announced, on the very eve of the season, that mystery business tycoon Michael Knighton was to buy him out and would ultimately become the new Chairman. As if this was not sensation enough, the new 'Chairman' then trotted out onto the Old Trafford pitch before United's opening game against Arsenal, blowing kisses and scoring a goal in the Stretford end.

United maintained the optimism with an impressive 4-1 defeat of the reigning champions. It was not to last. Familiar problems appeared as United gained just one point from the next four matches. There was a much needed return to form in the last game before the derby as United, inspired by a Hughes hat-trick, thrashed surprise League leaders Millwall 5-1. Had United turned the corner and was this expensive side going to use the Maine Road game to re-launch their season?

Mel Machin was the man who had guided City back into the First Division after a two year spell in Division Two. His pre-season spending saw the experienced striker Clive Allen join the club from Bordeaux for £1 million followed by Bournemouth's talented midfield player Ian Bishop who came for £750,000, although fans' favourite Paul Moulden had joined the Cherries as part of the deal. City also felt they had at last settled their goalkeeping worries as Welsh international Andy Dibble had served them well during the Second Division campaign. Even so, it looked as if it was going to be a difficult first season for the Blues who gained just one point from the opening four games, and had to wait until their fifth match to collect a welcome 1-0 win over Queen's Park Rangers. City therefore were poised to renew the series of derby contests locked in joint bottom spot with Tottenham Hotspur and Sheffield Wednesday.

MATCH VERDICT

In one of the most remarkable results in the long history of derby football City, the clear underdogs, inflicted a humiliating defeat of record-breaking proportions on their long time rivals. It was the most complete of victories by City who simply played United off the park, equalling their record home victory in this fixture and, in so doing, exposed Alex Ferguson's misfit millionaire side who would ultimately be unable to make any realistic impression on the title challenge this season.

Few City fans could have been optimistic as United opened brightly, before some ugly crowd disturbances forced the players to leave the field for a few minutes. When the teams returned, City embarked on a spell of football that produced two goals inside 60 seconds, left the Reds devastated, and enabled the rampant home side to gain a stranglehold on the game which they never relinquished.

Firstly White highlighted Duxbury's discomfort at left-back by turning him inside out and sending a low dangerous centre into the box which the lanky Pallister missed and Oldfield, following in, cracked the ball into the United net. With the Reds barely able to draw breath, City found there was more joy to be had probing United's other suspect flank. Anderson was caught out of position as Lake and Morley tore a great hole in the visiting defence and the exposed Leighton's initial save only resulted in Morley firing the rebound home.

United attempted to rally but without Robson the midfield was rudderless and City, with Bishop, Lake and White outstanding, played all the penetrative football. United attempted to attack, but it was all rather ineffective, and City countered brilliantly to take a three goal half-time lead. Redmond, collecting the ball on the edge of his own area, sent a glorious long ball out to Oldfield who gathered up the ball in his stride, and sent an instant cross into the penalty area where Bishop, timing his run to perfection, headed superbly past a bewildered Leighton.

The second half started explosively as United, with a piece of individual magic, pulled a goal back and scented a possible recovery. Beards-

more's tricky run on the right turned Hinchcliffe and his high cross was met by an airborne Mark Hughes whose magnificent bicycle-kick flew over Cooper into the net. City though were not to be denied and went further ahead on the hour. Again the Blues made inroads on the United right flank where Anderson fatally hesitated for the referee's whistle as Lake raced through and teed up the ball for Oldfield to score easily from close range.

With the Blues' fans chants of 'easy easy' ringing in their ears, City rubbed it in with a magnificent fifth goal. In a sweeping move from the half-way line Bishop found White and, with Duxbury out of position, the City winger pulled over a pin-point centre which was met by the onrushing Hinchcliffe whose bullet header shot past the hapless Leighton and the Reds' humiliation was complete.

3-0

4-1

5-1

1-0. David Oldfield thumps City's first goal from 10 yards.

2-0. United defenders **Mal Donaghy** and **Gary Pallister** are helpless as City's **Trevor Morley** makes it 2-0.

3-0. **Ian Bishop** meets *David Oldfield's* cross with a flying header to make it 3-0 to City.

4-1. United's grounded **Gary Pallister** can only watch as **David Oldfield** slots in his second of the match to make it 4-1 to City.

5-1. Pallister and Donaghy are mere spectators as City's **Andy Hinchcliffe** powers in a decisive header to make it 5-1.

112

MANCHESTER UNITED 1
(Blackmore)

MANCHESTER CITY 1
(Brightwell)

DATE	3rd February 1990
DIVISION	One
VENUE	Old Trafford
ATTENDANCE	40,274

Manchester United		Manchester City
Jim LEIGHTON	1	Andy DIBBLE
Viv ANDERSON	2	Alan HARPER
Lee MARTIN	3	Andy HINCHCLIFFE
Mal DONAGHY *	4	Ian BRIGHTWELL
Mike PHELAN	5	Colin HENDRY
Gary PALLISTER	6	Steve REDMOND
Clayton BLACKMORE	7	David WHITE
Mike DUXBURY	8	Mark WARD
Brian McCLAIR	9	Wayne CLARKE *
Mark HUGHES	10	Gary MEGSON
Danny WALLACE *	11	Paul LAKE
Russell BEARDSMORE (4)	Sub	Jason BECKFORD (9)
Mark ROBINS (11)	Sub	Gary FLEMING

*Oh yes! City's **Ian Brightwell** can't contain his delight at netting the Blues' equaliser with a spectacular 25 yard drive. **Alan Harper**, **Steve Redmond** and **Paul Lake** join the celebrations.*

BACKGROUND

Amazingly, just two months after the so-called 'Maine Road Massacre', the manager who had planned one of City's greatest derby triumphs was dismissed. Indeed, by the time of this February derby many of the Blues team who had played such a vital role in the defeat of United had either left the club or were out of favour. In fact, City started the match with only four of the players that had humiliated the Reds so severely in September. Despite the derby victory City's form had not picked up, and instead the team suffered some demoralising defeats such as a 6-0 reverse at Derby County. A disappointing home exit to Coventry in the League Cup and a 1-1 draw at lowly Charlton Athletic proved the final straw for Mr Swales and Mel Machin was sacked at the end of November. After former City striker Joe Royle had turned down the job, the vastly experienced Howard Kendall was appointed with the task of saving the Blues from yet another relegation. Mr Kendall decided on some immediate changes. Tactically he employed a sweeper which had the desired effect as City's over generous defence tightened up, and in addition to this came a wholesale change in personnel with a heavy influx of players he knew and understood - several of them his former Everton players. Out went derby heroes Bishop, Morley and Oldfield quickly followed by McNab and Gayle. In came Peter Reid, Alan Harper, Mark Ward and Wayne Clarke. Kendall's changes seemed to work and the club, although not safe by derby day, had moved up the table to 14th place. One major blow for City was the suspension of the influential Peter Reid who, ironically, was serving a ban for an incident when playing with his old club Q.P.R. against City!

United's League season was fading miserably. The Michael Knighton 'take over' had fallen through although continual rumblings of boardroom unrest persisted and Martin Edwards made clear his controlling shares in the club were still for sale. The indiscreet nature of these boardroom shenanigans had held the club up to public ridicule and none of it could have helped the playing side of things. Alex Ferguson needed all the help he could get as his expensively assembled squad's much acclaimed title ambitions came to nothing, and now the stark reality of relegation had loomed as a genuine possibility. The Reds were in the midst of a record spell of games without a win, something the club had not endured since the 1930's. Entering the derby match they had not won in the League since a 3-1 defeat of Luton Town in November - a run of ten matches. With only four points collected during this run, Ferguson's misfits plummeted down the table to 17th place, just one position and two points above the dreaded 18th place relegation spot. Confidence, and goals, were at rock bottom as United entered yet another vital derby match without long-term injured midfielders Webb and Robson. In the memories of older fans there were shades of 1963 as the current Reds had also embarked on a critical F.A. Cup run which, the media assured, would determine Alex Ferguson's future. Character had been shown in the Third round victory at fancied Nottingham Forest and, in further away ties, Hereford United had been beaten in round Five and Newcastle United were waiting in the Sixth round. The stage was set for an historic 100th derby in the First Division. Could City continue their climb to safety or would an increasingly desperate United gain that elusive League victory?

*United's **Mike Phelan** holds off City's new striker **Wayne Clarke**.*

BEFORE THE GAME

	P	W	D	L	F	A	Pts
CITY	23	7	5	11	25	37	26
UNITED	23	6	6	11	27	33	24

MATCH VERDICT

It was a game which reflected the perilous state of the two Manchester teams and it was dominated by nervous play, unforced errors and a general lack of creativity. On the chances alone, City should have won it comfortably, but in the end were indebted to a marvellous equaliser from Brightwell. The inconclusive result meant both teams' grim struggle to avoid the drop continued.

United made a determined start with close early efforts by McClair and Hughes, but further openings were few and far between, and it was City's confident play which gained a series of opportunities that the Blues then proceeded to squander. Firstly, Pallister's badly struck back pass put Leighton under pressure and City seemed sure to score through Clarke but under Donaghy's lunging challenge the ball skidded wide. Clarke again went close with a header from Megson's corner which whistled past the right hand post, and Brightwell was guilty of a shocking miss when, put clean through and with Leighton off his line, he feebly lobbed the ball wide. The chances kept coming City's way in the second half and White, operating as City's centre-forward in Kendall's plan, squandered another chance when sent clear by Redmond as, with only Leighton to beat, he shot tamely wide of the post. City were made to pay for such waste as United, so lacking in confidence and direction, suddenly took the lead with a fine goal. Wallace who had been virtually anonymous all afternoon suddenly found himself with the ball on the right wing. A little shimmy, followed by a swerving cross hit cleverly behind the City defenders, was met by a diving header from Clayton Blackmore and Old Trafford exploded in relief. It was not to last though and, within five minutes, City were level. Ward found Brightwell on the right and from fully 25 yards the City man sent a quite stunning shot searing past Leighton and into the net.

*United winger **Danny Wallace** takes on City's **Paul Lake**.*

AT THE SEASON'S END

UNITED: Finished 13th on 48 points
(Better goal difference than City.
F.A. Cup Winners, beating Crystal Palace 1-0
in replay after 3-3 draw)

CITY: Finished 14th on 48 points

Howard Kendall - his first derby in charge of City.

***Clayton Blackmore** flings himself in front of City defender **Alan Harper** to put United 1-0 ahead with a superb diving header.*

113

MANCHESTER CITY 3
(White 2, Hendry)

MANCHESTER UNITED 3
(Hughes, McClair 2)

DATE	27th October 1990
DIVISION	One
VENUE	Maine Road
ATTENDANCE	36,427

Manchester City		Manchester United
Tony COTON	1	Les SEALEY
Alan HARPER	2	Dennis IRWIN
Neil POINTON	3	Lee MARTIN
Peter REID *	4	Steve BRUCE
Colin HENDRY	5	Clayton BLACKMORE
Steve REDMOND	6	Gary PALLISTER
David WHITE	7	Neil WEBB
Adrian HEATH	8	Paul INCE
Niall QUINN	9	Brian McCLAIR
Gary MEGSON	10	Mark HUGHES
Mark WARD	11	Lee SHARPE *
Ian BRIGHTWELL (4)	Sub	Danny WALLACE (11)
Clive ALLEN	Sub	Mal DONAGHY

BACKGROUND

Just prior to the opening of the new season, the whole football world, and City fans in particular, were saddened to hear of the death of the legendary Joe Mercer. There were poignant verses of 'Joe Mercer's aces' sung as City opened their campaign at Tottenham. Unfortunately for the Blues, they ran into World Cup heroes Gary Lineker and Paul Gascoigne and Spurs were 3-1 victors.

Manager Howard Kendall had however, revitalised the Maine Road club with an impressive run of results at the end of the previous season, and injected a fresh sense of belief. Indeed, the defeat at White Hart Lane was their only reverse prior to the derby, while home form was particularly strong with five straight wins over Everton, Aston Villa, Norwich, Coventry and Torquay (in the League Cup).

Kendall had strengthened his squad with the close season signings of goalkeeper Tony Coton (£1 million from Watford), Neil Pointon from Everton and Mark Brennan from Middlesbrough. Some fans remained critical of the high number of former Goodison Park imports, particularly as popular left-back Andy Hinchcliffe went to Everton as part of the Pointon deal. There were also mutterings about the rejection of the equally popular Andy Dibble in favour of Coton in goal, but the experienced Kendall was not concerned by any of these criticisms as he could point to a side that had made rapid progress since his arrival and indeed, would enter the derby as favourites.

United were hoping that their record equalling F.A. Cup win of the previous season would prove to be the platform for a serious assault on the still much yearned for Championship title. However, by this the tenth League game their hopes already looked rather forlorn as, saddled by unconvincing form, they trailed along a dozen points behind leaders Liverpool. Useful victories had been achieved against modest mid-table sides, but more telling was a reverse against Liverpool and the pair of home defeats inflicted by other likely contenders Forest and Arsenal.

Sealey, Irwin and Webb were set to make derby debuts, but once again long term injury had deprived United of midfield powerhouse Bryan Robson. With the bitter memory of their humiliation at Maine Road a year previously, the Reds needed little incentive to show a marked improvement.

*Veteran midfielder **Peter Reid**, soon to be appointed City manager in the wake of Howard Kendall's shock departure, holds off a challenge from United's rising young star **Lee Sharpe**.*

BEFORE THE GAME							
	P	W	D	L	F	A	Pts
CITY	9	4	4	1	12	9	16
UNITED	9	4	1	4	10	11	13

Adrian Heath whose deft header set up City's second goal, battles for the ball with United's **Clayton Blackmore**.

MATCH VERDICT

The 113th derby proved to be one of the most exciting and fluctuating contests in the long history of the fixture. City, with the previous season's derby triumph fresh in their minds, seemed assured of another memorable victory as they led the Reds 3-1 with only ten minutes remaining of what had been a pulsating match. United however, managed to avert a further dose of Maine Road misery by staging a remarkable grandstand finish that all but won them the game.

City started as the more purposeful and direct team and there were shades of the rout a year earlier as the Blues raced into a two goal lead inside 27 minutes. City's closely-knit team-work pegged United back in their own half, and but for Sealey's agility, Reid's shot would have given the home side an early lead. As it was, City did not have to wait long as, shortly after this, some ragged defending saw several United men spurn opportunities to clear Ward's low cross before Quinn, the previous season's signing from Arsenal, diverted the ball to White who curled a shot round the exposed Sealey and into the net. There was no mistake about the quality of City's second goal though, as an excellently conceived move split the United back-line wide open. Redmond's lob forward found the diminutive Heath, whose deftly flicked header cleared the statuesque United defence and the quick-thinking White raced on to drive beyond the advancing goalkeeper.

Clearly shaken, United struggled to show any real cohesion or pattern in their play, but after 37 minutes gained a lifeline which turned the game from a one-sided contest into a true full-blooded derby. Initially, there seemed little threat to City from a free-kick conceded 30 yards out, but Irwin's precise chip found Hughes who out-jumped Redmond to direct a powerful header into the top right corner of Coton's net.

The second half saw United with an increased share of possession, but it was City who created the better chances. Twice Sealey had to be alert to save from Megson and Heath, and only the intervention of the crossbar stopped White from becoming the first player for 20 years to notch a derby hat-trick. However, on 79 minutes a top

drawer move convinced City's fans that victory was theirs. Hendry broke through Webb's limp tackle some 35 yards from the Reds' goal and, as he advanced on the back-peddling Bruce and Pallister, the centre-back exchanged passes with Quinn before stroking the ball wide of Sealey. Manager Howard Kendall decided this was a safe enough moment to substitute Reid, his influential midfield maestro, but within two minutes substitute Brightwell dithered with the ball ten yards outside his own box, and in an instant McClair's predatory instincts had dispossessed the City man and defenders were left trailing in his wake before Coton was beaten with a clinical finish. With the stunned home crowd barely able to draw breath, United forced a corner and from Webb's flag-kick Bruce touched the ball on for McClair to head United level at 3-3. United scented the chance of a sensational victory and would have achieved it, had Coton not produced a splendid save to smother Pallister's last minute volley and conclude an outstanding derby with honours even.

As if such a remarkable match were not enough, just nine days later Howard Kendall shocked City by walking out on the club to rejoin Everton where he had spent so many years as both a successful player and manager. His deputy Peter Reid who had studied Kendall's methods so carefully was appointed as City's new manager soon after.

David White - netted twice for City and was denied by the crossbar from becoming the first man for 20 years to notch a derby hat-trick.

*New faces for the derby future. City's Eire international striker **Niall Quinn** is crowded out by United's talented young winger **Lee Sharpe** and defender **Lee Martin**.*

114

MANCHESTER UNITED 1
(Giggs)

MANCHESTER CITY 0

DATE	4th May 1991
DIVISION	One
VENUE	Old Trafford
ATTENDANCE	45,286

Manchester United		Manchester City
Gary WALSH	1	Martyn MARGETSON
Denis IRWIN	2	Andy HILL
Clayton BLACKMORE	3	Neil POINTON
Steve BRUCE	4	Adrian HEATH
Mike PHELAN	5	Colin HENDRY
Gary PALLISTER	6	Steve REDMOND
Bryan ROBSON	7	David WHITE
Neil WEBB	8	Mark BRENNAN *
Brian McCLAIR	9	Niall QUINN
Mark HUGHES	10	Alan HARPER
Ryan GIGGS *	11	Mark WARD *
Mal DONAGHY (11)	12	Peter REID (8)
Mark ROBINS	13	Wayne CLARKE (11)

United 'keeper **Gary Walsh**, making his derby debut, punches clear from City's **Niall Quinn** who is closely shadowed by Reds centre-back **Gary Pallister**.

BACKGROUND

Manchester football entered this the 114th derby match on a footballing high; not since the 1976/77 season had both clubs finished in the top six. In different ways both clubs could look back on a highly pleasing season. City, stunned by Howard Kendall's November desertion to Everton had, under his successor Peter Reid, enjoyed one of their finest campaigns for many years and indeed, entered this derby on the crest of a sparkling run of seven games unbeaten. During this spell City drew with Arsenal and had impressive victories over Cup Finalists Nottingham Forest and high-flying Leeds United and Crystal Palace. All this culminated in a resounding 5-1 thrashing of Aston Villa, when David White, a constant thorn in United's flesh in recent years, became the first City player since the war to score four goals in an away game.

However, it was the beanpole figure of centre forward Niall Quinn who had become the 'Maine' attraction. The unassuming Irishman had proved a revelation as he plundered 20 goals prior to the derby and made many more for grateful colleagues. City's Player of the Year it seemed could do no wrong and his remarkable deeds in April against Derby County simply underlined this. First his well-taken goal put City ahead and then, following the sending-off of goalkeeper Coton, Quinn donned the green jersey and proceeded to save the Dean Saunders' penalty! However, the dismissal did have repercussions for the Blues as Coton, who had won over the fans with a series of excellent displays, was suspended and out of the derby match. Surprisingly, Reid selected 19 year old Martyn Margetson to replace Coton and make his League debut in the Old Trafford cauldron, while the manager's only move in the transfer market had been the modest acquisition of former United reserve Andy Hill from Bury.

In many respects the October derby was a watershed for United's season. The stirring Maine Road come-back had proved a launch-pad for improved performances in all competitions - a complete reversal of the previous winter's dismal losing run

BEFORE THE GAME

	P	W	D	L	F	A	Pts
CITY	36	16	11	9	61	50	59
UNITED	34	15	11	8	55	38	55

(United had one point deducted by The Football League)

- as Alex Ferguson's rapidly developing side put together an impressive 16 match unbeaten sequence from late November to mid-February. Once again the team reserved their best performances for Cup competitions. The cream of the First Division were dispatched in a League Cup run which saw United reach Wembley for the second year in succession. Liverpool were well beaten, Arsenal were thrashed 6-2 at Highbury - their heaviest home defeat for 69 years, and a replay saw the end of Southampton. Further delight was derived from the semi-final ejection of old rivals Leeds. Although all were impressive team displays, two players particularly stood out. Lee Sharpe's audacious displays on the left wing were a refreshing throw back to the days of great attacking wingers and the mercurial Mark Hughes led the line with vast strength and skill. Accolades followed both players as they picked up P.F.A. Player of the Year awards. Unfortunately for United the League Cup retained its elusiveness as Sheffield Wednesday caused an upset by winning the final.

There was more than a silver lining left to United's season. Following in the great English tradition, Alex Ferguson's team had reached the final of the European Cup-Winners' Cup. Victories over Pecsi Munkas, Wrexham, Montpellier and Legia Warsaw had set up a glorious final with Spain's Barcelona on 15th May in Rotterdam.

Unfortunately for the Manchester public there would be no opportunity to compare City's White and United's winger Sharpe who had suffered an injury, and in a surprise move Alex Ferguson nominated 17 year old Ryan Giggs to make his debut. Like City, United were without their regular goalkeeper. Les Sealey had been injured at Wembley, and his place went to Gary Walsh - his first derby appearance.

MATCH VERDICT

In a moment reminiscent of Sammy McIlroy's 1971 derby debut, United's precocious young talent Ryan Giggs was officially credited with the goal that sealed City's fate in this typically competitive match. He was appropriately placed to flick on McClair's right wing cross after 22 minutes following a superb volleyed pass by Hughes. It was questionable if Giggs actually got a meaningful touch to the ball as it flashed past Margetson and was diverted into the net by the unfortunate Hendry but a delighted manager was later quick to claim the goal for his young starlet. "He made a smashing debut" enthused Ferguson.

The goal was one of the few highlights of a scrappy first half, where enthusiastic tackling showed little quarter given by either side. City, largely disappointing in the opening period, had a wonderful opportunity to get back into the game immediately on the resumption. The combative little Ward outstripped Blackmore down the City right wing and his piercing cross to the near post seemed a formality to the normally deadly Quinn but his diving header flashed well wide. As if jolted by this turn of events, United

responded with their best football of the match. City's debutant Margetson showed his talents with a splendid finger-tip save to deny Webb's goal-bound shot. Following this, Webb found space to advance and square the ball to the onrushing Hughes whose instant shot defeated Margetson but smashed against the post. McClair, following in, sent the rebound high into the crowd. United's pressure seemed to have told in the 70th minute as Webb escaped the City offside trap and, collecting Blackmore's punt in his stride, stroked the ball under the advancing 'keeper and into the net. However, referee Tyldesley had already blown for a free kick to United on the halfway line.

Giggs' substitution to a standing ovation marked the final quarter of the match when United fell back on defence and, with the appearance of City's manager Peter Reid, it was the Blues who finished the game in storming fashion. A series of aerial assaults saw the Reds penned back into their penalty box but, with Pallister enjoying a marked superiority in his contest with the subdued Quinn, United appeared to have the points secured. However, in typical derby fashion there remained a sting in the tail. With the City pressure mounting and the seconds ticking away, one last City centre found the head of substitute Clarke whose glancing header flashed past Walsh but thudded against the foot of a post and rebounded to safety.

Martyn Margetson - City's young goalkeeper made his debut in the derby but was beaten by United's newcomer *Ryan Giggs*.

AT THE SEASON'S END

CITY: Finished 5th on 62 points

UNITED: Finished 6th on 59 points
League Cup Finalists, losing 0-1 to Sheffield Wednesday. European Cup Winners' Cup winners, beating Barcelona 2-1

United's powerful striker **Mark Hughes** clashes with City defender **Colin Hendry** who many fans felt got the decisive touch for the Reds' winning goal.

INTRODUCTION

The Cup matches between the two clubs have been occasions when the derby contest has meant 'sudden death' with no opportunity, as in the League meetings, to redress the balance or avenge a defeat at a later stage in the season.

The first derby Cup match occurred in a competition which still exists today, the F.A. Cup or 'English Cup' as it was better known when Newton Heath (United) beat Ardwick (City) 5-1 in a First Round Qualifying tie back in October of 1891.

Since then, perhaps surprisingly, considering the growing stature and Cup traditions of both clubs, there have only been another nine Cup meetings, four in the F.A. Cup, and four (including two matches in a two-legged semi-final) in the League Cup. The Charity Shield match of 1956 is also included as it represents a form of knockout game between the Football League Champions and F.A. Cup Holders.

As one might expect, the majority of these Cup contests were typically tight and tense affairs, usually backed by a big crowd. United have just got the edge in the F.A. Cup with three victories to City's two. However, City have quite clearly done better in the League Cup, and in fact are unbeaten by United in this competition which was inaugurated in the early 1960's.

There are often various quirks associated with Cup runs, and as far as City are concerned, a derby Cup meeting has always proved a lucky omen. On no less than four occasions, City have gone on to reach Wembley following a defeat of United along the way. United on the other hand, despite a grand F.A. Cup record, have not found derby Cup meetings part of a path to trophy successes. Unlike Merseyside rivals Liverpool and Everton, United and City have never met at Wembley in a major Cup Final. The nearest either have got to this have been semi-final meetings in the 1926 F.A. Cup and the 1969 League Cup, both of which were won by City. No doubt it will be something to savour one day in the future!

CUPS TO CHEER

JUST OUR CUPPA!

United v City in Cup Competitions 1891-1987

NEWTON HEATH 5
(Sneddon, Doughty, Farman 2, Edge)

ARDWICK 1
(Pearson)

DATE	3rd October 1891
COMPETITION	F.A. Cup 1st Rd (Qual)
VENUE	North Road
ATTENDANCE	10,000

Newton Heath		Ardwick
J.F. SLATER	1	William DOUGLAS
R. McFARLANE	2	Archie FERGUSON
John CLEMENTS	3	David ROBSON
Roger DOUGHTY	4	Jack PEARSON
William STEWART	5	Daniel WHITTLE
Jack OWEN	6	Harry DAVIDSON
A.H. FARMAN	7	Joe DAVIES
Alfred EDGE	8	William McWHINNIE
J. SNEDDON	9	Hugh MORRIS
William SHARPE	10	John MILNE
A. HENRYS	11	Bob MILARVIE

BACKGROUND

This was to be the first true meeting between the two clubs in a prestigious Cup competition which still exists today. Both teams were playing in the Football Alliance, a competition set up to rival the Football League. It was Ardwick's first season in the Alliance and the club were hoping for great things. Success had already been achieved in the Manchester Cup Final, where Newton Heath had been defeated 1-0 with a goal from Dave Weir. A number of professional players had been recruited from Scotland, including their talented goalkeeper Douglas. So it was Ardwick who entered this First Qualifying round contest confident of progressing in the 'English Cup' as it was referred to at the time.

As far as the Heathens were concerned this derby Cup tie was an ideal opportunity to gain revenge for their shock defeat in the previous season's Manchester Cup. It should perhaps be said at this stage that their commitment to the English Cup competition was a trifle indifferent. Four years earlier, following a 2-2 draw with Fleetwood Rangers, the Heathens refused to play extra time and so forfeited the tie! Similarly in 1890, in a tie against Bootle, the Heathens fielded their entire reserve side and lost the match. Even so, nobody doubted that for this first derby Cup tie the Heathens would be fully prepared.

*Newton Heath in 1891-92. **Back:** Mr. Preddy (Trainer), H. Jones, Mr. Bird, R. McFarlane, J. F. Slater, J. E. Clements, Unknown, Unknown. **Middle:** R. Doughty, W. Stewart, J. Owen. **Front:** A. H. Farman, W. Hood, R. Donaldson, J. Sneddon, A. Edge.*

SATURDAY'S PASTIMES.

FOOTBALL.

ASSOCIATION.

ENGLISH CUP—QUALIFYING COMPETITION.

DIVISION 1.

Bishop Auckland, 4 goals; Southwick, 3.
Gateshead North-Eastern, 3 goals; Ashington, 2.
Newcastle East End, 5 goals; Tow Law, 1.
Whitburn, 3 goals; Sunderland Olympic, 2.
Birtley scratched to Shankhouse.

DIVISION 2.

South Bank, 3 goals; St Augustine's, 3.
Darlington, 3 goals; Port Clarence, nil.
Spennymoor, 4 goals; Whitby, 3.

DIVISION 3.

Newton Heath v. Ardwick. — At Newton Heath, before 12,000. Among the spectators were Sir James Fergusson, M.P., and Mr. C. P. Scott, the two candidates for North-East Manchester division. The former gentleman kicked off. The home team were the first to take up the attack, and Douglas had to fist out. He acquitted himself creditably, however, and from his return the Ardwick forwards made a rush towards their opponents' goal, but the lengthy Stewart got his head to the ball and transferred operations to the opposite end. The play did not remain there long, for Furgerson put in a huge kick, which carried play into mid-field. An unfortunate accident occurred here to Milarvie, one of the visiting forwards. It was not of a serious nature, however, for he returned to the fray, after a few minutes stoppage. Newton were now having the best of matters, but they could not penetrate. The sound defence of the men proved equal to the pressure and they cleared the stronghold splendidly. A regular bombardment was now made on the Ardwick goal, and Douglas, who was apparently in one of his best moods, saved repeatedly in marvellous fashion on numerous occasions with the bulk of his opponents around him. Doughty now had to leave the field, he having had an old injury to his hand hurt. He only remained absent for about ten minutes, but when he returned he was apparently suffering very greatly. Ardwick were now awarded the new penalty kick, and what was regarded as a certain goal was fisted out. From this the home forwards went away with great determination, and eventually Sneddon scored with a simple shot. Half-time arrived, the score being credited :— Newton, 1 goal; Ardwick, nil. Sneddon restarted, and the opening was all in favour of Newton Heath. From a nice pass by Sharp, Sneddon scored the second point. The homesters at once returned to the attack, and Sharp, putting in a high shot, Doughty succeeded in scoring a third. By the aid of a free kick Pearson scored the first and only point for Ardwick. After this Farman and Edge each scored. Final :

NEWTON HEATH .... 5 goals.
ARDWICK .... 1 „

How 'The Umpire' newspaper of the day reported on Newton Heath's emphatic victory in the English Cup. Note: This report credits Sneddon with a second goal, but all other sources contradict this and credit Farman.

MATCH VERDICT

It was quite a civic occasion at North Road as M.P. Sir James Ferguson kicked off the game. In a typical Cup-tie atmosphere there were chances for both sides in a frantic opening. Newton Heath had slightly the better of it but weak shooting, coupled with some inspired goalkeeping by Douglas, kept the game scoreless.

This was the first year that the penalty kick was introduced to the game (at the suggestion of a Mr J. Read, Honorary Secretary of the Irish F.A.), and a turning point in the tie seemed to have arrived with the application of the new rule and the award of a penalty to Ardwick. As local scribes pointed out this should have meant a 'certain' goal, but Heathens' goalkeeper Slater did not see it this way and dramatically fisted the kick to safety. To make matters worse for Ardwick the Heathens almost immediately went to the other end and scored. Sneddon's low bobbling shot deceived Douglas and entered the net. The Heathens dominated the second half, bombarding the Ardwick goal with a series of corners. The second goal was merely a question of time and it duly arrived as Farman took Sharpe's pass in his stride and beat Douglas with a low shot. Doughty seemed to have decided the contest with a third goal immediately after this but Ardwick, in true Cup fighting tradition, immediately pulled a goal back. Awarded a free kick some yards from the Heathens' penalty area, Pearson scored with a direct shot. But there was no denying the Heathens on the day and, in a final flourish, Farman and Edge scored goals that gave the scoreline a more emphatic appearance.

Jack Owen – another of Newton's winning side against rivals Ardwick.

Roger Doughty – a tough half-back whose brother Jack also played for the club, he was on target in the 5-1 defeat of Ardwick.

THE WINNER'S PROGRESS

Date	Round		Att.	Opponents	F	A	Goalscorer
24/10/91*	Two	H	Unknown	Heywood	3	2	Unknown
14/11/91	Three	A	2,000	South Shore	2	0	Farman, J. Doughty
5/12/91	Four	H	4,000	Blackpool	3	4	Edge (2), Farman

*Match staged as friendly

MANCHESTER CITY 3
(Browell 2, Roberts)

MANCHESTER UNITED 0

DATE	27th March 1926	
COMPETITION	F.A. CUP Semi-final	
VENUE	Bramall Lane	
ATTENDANCE	46,450	

Manchester City		Manchester United
Jim GOODCHILD	1	Alf STEWARD
Sam COOKSON	2	Charlie MOORE
Philip McCLOY	3	Jack SILCOCK
Charlie PRINGLE	4	James McCRAE
Sam COWAN	5	Frank BARSON
Jimmy McMULLAN	6	Frank MANN
Billy AUSTIN	7	Joe SPENCE
Tommy BROWELL	8	Thomas SMITH
Frank ROBERTS	9	Frank McPHERSON
Tom JOHNSON	10	Clat RENNOX
George HICKS	11	Henry THOMAS

*Controversy in the 14th minute as City's **Tommy Browell** (centre with ball) sees his header hooked clear – but the referee was already signalling for a goal as the ball had crossed the line.*

*Tommy Browell follows up to force the ball in after his header was cleared from behind the line. United goalkeeper **Alf Steward** protests, but to no avail as City were 1-0 ahead. Note United's white strip with a red V that was worn between 1923-27.*

*United goalkeeper **Alf Steward** safely gathers this first half header from City's airborne **George Hicks**. Other players featured are City's other goalscorer, **Frank Roberts** (left), United 'hard man' **Frank Barson** (centre) and United full-back **Charlie Moore** (right).*

CITY'S PROGRESS

Date	Round		Att.	Opponents	F	A	Goalscorers
9/1/26	Three	A	29,700	Corinthians	3	3	Cookson, Roberts, Hicks
13/1/26*	Three	H	42,303	Corinthians	4	0	Austin (2), Johnson, Hicks
30/1/26	Four	H	74,789	Huddersfield Town	4	0	Hicks (2), Browell, Roberts
20/2/26	Five	H	51,630	Crystal Palace	11	4	Roberts (5), Browell (3), Austin, Johnson, Hicks
6/3/26	Six	A	24,600	Clapton Orient	6	1	Johnson (3), Hicks, Roberts, Browell

UNITED'S PROGRESS

Date	Round		Att.	Opponents	F	A	Goalscorers
9/1/26	Three	A	14,841	Port Vale	3	2	Spence (2), McPherson
30/1/26	Four	A	40,000	Tottenham Hotspur	2	2	Spence, Thomas
3/2/26*	Four	H	45,000	Tottenham Hotspur	2	0	Rennox, Spence
20/2/26	Five	A	50,500	Sunderland	3	3	McPherson, Smith (2)
24/2/26*	Five	H	58,661	Sunderland	2	1	McPherson, Smith
6/3/26	Six	A	28,699	Fulham	2	1	Smith, McPherson

*Replay

Sam Cowan – an outstanding display in the City midfield.

MATCH VERDICT

City justifiably won the first ever semi-final between the great Manchester rivals. The more fancied United simply did not perform on the day and City, with half-backs Cowan, McMullan and Pringle outstanding, dominated throughout.

Nerves, which so often accompany this penultimate round before Wembley seemed to particularly affect United. On too many occasions their play was riddled with the anxiety of misplaced passes, hasty shots and badly timed tackles.

After a scrappy opening the game turned in City's favour with a goal that the United players bitterly contested. City won a corner kick and, as Hicks curled the ball into the box, Browell jumped above the United defenders and headed firmly past Steward. Although the ball was bundled out it had clearly crossed the line first. The United defenders were not at all happy with this and vehemently claimed to the referee that Browell had pushed to gain an advantage, but their appeals were in vain and the goal stood. From this point on the soured attitude of United's players' seemed to have an adverse effect on their efforts to get back into the game.

Barson their inspirational defender, and a player with the reputation of a 'hard man', soon showed his angry feelings about the goal when he cynically flattened Cowan, and then annoyed the City fans by feigning injury himself.

As United lost both their shape and tempers, City, playing good open football, began to have things all their own way and only the slack finishing by the Blues enabled United to go in at half time only one goal down. After the break, City continued to squander chances as Johnson put Browell clean through, but the usually deadly inside right failed to control the ball and Silcock cleared. The woodwork also came to United's aid as Austin's firm shot slammed against a post and rebounded to safety.

With just 15 minutes remaining City settled the tie. Barson's unfortunate afternoon was compounded as he missed Hicks' through ball to Browell and this time the City forward struck the ball cleanly first time past Steward into the net.

Just two minutes later United's wilting Wembley dreams were destroyed. Roberts broke free down the middle, but his mis-hit shot from 15 yards did not appear dangerous until Steward, in a misguided attempt to turn the ball around a post, merely succeeded in diverting it into the net.

City may have had little short of a disastrous time in the League this season but they were clearly enjoying the mastery of Manchester. Having humiliated their neighbours 6-1 at Old Trafford in January, they now had eliminated United from the Cup and had made it through to the new Wembley stadium for a re-run of City's 1904 Final - this time however, the score would be reversed.

THE WINNER'S PROGRESS

Date	Round		Att.	Opponents	F	A	Goalscorers
24/4/26	Final	At Wembley	91,547	Bolton Wanderers	0	1	None

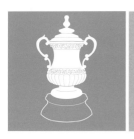

MANCHESTER CITY 2
(Hayes, Revie)

MANCHESTER UNITED 0

DATE	29th January 1955
COMPETITION	F.A. CUP 4th Round
VENUE	Maine Road
ATTENDANCE	74,723

Manchester City		Manchester United
Bert TRAUTMANN	1	Ray WOOD
Jimmy MEADOWS	2	Bill FOULKES
Roy LITTLE	3	Roger BYRNE
Ken BARNES	4	Don GIBSON
Dave EWING	5	Allenby CHILTON
Roy PAUL	6	Duncan EDWARDS
Paddy FAGAN	7	Johnny BERRY
Joe HAYES	8	Jackie BLANCHFLOWER
Don REVIE	9	Tommy TAYLOR
Johnny HART	10	Dennis VIOLLET
Roy CLARKE	11	Jack ROWLEY

City's Joe Hayes is fatally unmarked as he drills the ball past Ray Wood in the United goal to put the Blues 1-0 ahead from Johnny Hart's centre.

United's Dennis Viollet fires in a shot despite the efforts of City's Dave Ewing (right) to intervene, but Bert Trautmann in the Blues' goal came to the rescue with a fine save.

CITY'S PROGRESS

Date	Round		Att.	Opponents	F	A	Goalscorers
8/1/55	Three	A	23,409	Derby County	3	1	Barnes, Hayes, Revie

UNITED'S PROGRESS

Date	Round		Att.	Opponents	F	A	Goalscorers
8/1/55	Three	A	26,000	Reading	1	1	Webster
12/1/55*	Three	H	24,578	Reading	4	1	Webster (2), Viollet, Rowley

*Replay

MATCH VERDICT

In a splendid Cup tie that would be remembered for years to come by all who witnessed it, City deservedly knocked United out of the ring in what was another triumph for the 'Revie plan'.

United started brightly in front of a huge all-ticket crowd with thousands still not able to get into the ground until the beginning of the second half. Berry caught the eye with some dangerous runs during the opening 15 minutes when City looked strangely nervous. However once settled it was the intricately combined moves of the Blues that dominated the game and City went close on a number of occasions. Only a dramatic overhead clearance by Edwards, after Clarke's shot had hit the bar and a timely header off the line by Byrne, enabled United to go into the interval on level terms.

The second half brought a continuation of City's domination as Revie's promptings, and intelligent runs by Clarke and Hart, kept the Reds' defence at full stretch. On the hour, with the home crowd starting to wonder whether all City's superiority would ever bring a goal, the Blues broke the deadlock with a controversial opener. Hart beat Foulkes and carried the ball down the by-line but, as the United defenders fatally stood still believing the ball had run out of play, the City man continued and centred into the penalty area where the unattended Hayes shot past Wood. United's woes continued when eight minutes later Chilton was sent off following a midfield tangle with Hart. Even the City players begged with referee Oxley to reverse his decision but the big centre half was forced to leave the field accompanied by a stunned silence from the crowd.

United now attempted a gallant last ditch attempt to save the tie and Berry went close to snatching a dramatic equaliser but City were altogether too wily for them and, with two minutes remaining, settled the tie. Hart's corner found Revie whose shot passed through team-mate Clarke's legs and into the net.

City had won the vital derby Cup tie, but was this an omen for a great Cup run?

Berry missed a gilt-edged chance ♔ United bothered and breathless ♔ Triumph for the deep Revie plan

HAIL CITY'S TRIUMPH!

When Manchester United goalkeeper, Wood, failed to gather a corner-kick taken by Fagan, Hayes put in a header which had "goal" written all over it until Byrne popped up to head away from underneath the bar.

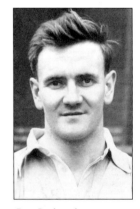

Don Revie – *the master behind City's tactics and scorer of the Blues second decisive goal.*

	THE WINNER'S PROGRESS						
Date	**Round**		**Att.**	**Opponents**	**F**	**A**	**Goalscorers**
19/2/55	Five	A	23,104	Luton Town	2	0	Clarke (2)
12/3/55	Six	A	58,000	Birmingham City	1	0	Hart
26/3/55	S/F at Villa Park		58,498	Sunderland	1	0	Clarke
7/5/55	Final at Wembley		100,000	Newcastle Utd	1	3	Johnstone

MANCHESTER UNITED 3
(Morgan pen, Kidd 2)

MANCHESTER CITY 0

DATE	24th January 1970
COMPETITION	F.A. Cup 4th Round
VENUE	Old Trafford
ATTENDANCE	63,417

Manchester United		Manchester City
Alex STEPNEY	1	Ken MULHEARN
Paul EDWARDS	2	Tony BOOK
Francis BURNS	3	Glyn PARDOE
Pat CRERAND	4	Mike DOYLE
Ian URE	5	Tommy BOOTH
David SADLER	6	Alan OAKES
Willie MORGAN	7	Mike SUMMERBEE *
Carlo SARTORI	8	Colin BELL
Bobby CHARLTON	9	Francis LEE
Brian KIDD	10	Neil YOUNG
John ASTON	11	Ian BOWYER
Shay BRENNAN	12	Tony TOWERS (7)

Brian Kidd gives United a blistering start to the second half by outpacing City's Tommy Booth to fire a powerful shot beyond Ken Mulhearn.

KIDD BORN TO BE KING!

United win back pride

Willie Morgan strokes his penalty to the left of City goalkeeper Ken Mulhearn to give United a 1-0 lead on the stroke of half-time after Glyn Pardoe had tripped Bobby Charlton at the end of a surging run.

Delight for Bobby Charlton and despair for Tommy Booth as Brian Kidd's shot enters the net to make it 2-0.

Brian Kidd beats Ken Mulhearn with a superb lob to make it 3-0 to United and seal a place in round five.

UNITED'S PROGRESS						
Date	Round	Att.	Opponents	F	A	Goalscorers
3/1/70	Three A	29,552	Ipswich Town	1	0	McNeil (og)

CITY'S PROGRESS						
Date	Round	Att.	Opponents	F	A	Goalscorers
3/1/70	Three A	30,271	Hull City	1	0	Young

"You'd better wait out here—my dad's a City supporter !"

The passions of the Manchester public always run high where derby Cup ties are concerned. A local cartoonist here captured the mood of United's comprehensive victory.

MATCH VERDICT

In this season of derby clashes United gained sweet revenge for their defeat in the League Cup semi-final by dumping the reigning Cup holders out of this year's competition and at the same time restoring their pride in the contest between the Manchester clubs.

The match, eagerly anticipated since the Cup draw, was played to a capacity Old Trafford audience. United, without Best, Law and Stiles started nervously, perhaps somewhat intimidated by the League humiliation inflicted by the Blues earlier in the season. However, the dangerous City forwards seemed strangely muted on the day and it was the Reds, with the old firm of Charlton and Crerand influential, who dominated the game. Indeed, it was United who gained the psychological boost of a goal on the stroke of half time. Charlton's surging run was ended by a trip from Pardoe and Willie Morgan stroked the penalty to the left of Mulhearn and United were ahead.

United sensed victory and, with a blistering opening twenty minute spell in the second half, it was the newly crowned king, Brian Kidd, who provided it with two quality goals that sank the Blues. Two minutes into the second period Kidd beat Booth in a race for a loose ball and his powerful shot beat Mulhearn to put the Reds two up. Then on 64 minutes City, desperately looking for a goal to put them back in the tie, were awarded a free kick some thirty yards from the United goal. The resulting shot fired straight into the defensive wall, and was subsequently hooked up the field to reach Kidd standing on the half way line.

Instinctively Kidd turned and raced away towards the City goal with Oakes and Book in vain pursuit and, as Mulhearn raced off his line to meet the threat, the United man kept his cool and brilliantly lobbed the ball over the 'keeper and into the net. That was effectively the end of the contest with City finishing up as a well-beaten side. United were warmly applauded off the pitch at the final whistle, and there were high hopes the victory might lead to glory in this year's competition.

*Bobby Charlton, whose vast experience helped United to dominate the tie here flies in to challenge City's **Mike Doyle** (No.4) and **Alan Oakes** during the Reds' 3-0 victory.*

THE WINNER'S PROGRESS							
Date	Round		Att.	Opponents	F	A	Goalscorers
7/2/70	Five	A	21,771	Northampton Town	8	2	Best (6), Kidd (2)
21/2/70	Six	A	40,000	Middlesbrough	1	1	Sartori
25/2 70*	Six	H	63,418	Middlesbrough	2	1	Charlton, Morgan
14/3/70	S/F at Hillsborough		55,000	Leeds United	0	0	None
23/3/70*	S/F at Villa Park		62,500	Leeds United	0	0	None
26/3/70**	S/F at Burnden Park		56,000	Leeds United	0	1	None
10/4/70	†at Highbury		15,105	Watford	2	0	Kidd (2)
*Replay	**Second Replay		†Experimental Third Place Play-off				

MANCHESTER UNITED 1
(Whiteside)

MANCHESTER CITY 0

DATE	10th January 1987
COMPETITION	F.A. Cup 3rd Round
VENUE	Old Trafford
ATTENDANCE	54,294

Manchester United		Manchester City
Chris TURNER	1	Perry SUCKLING
John SIVEBAEK	2	John GIDMAN
Colin GIBSON	3	Clive WILSON
Norman WHITESIDE	4	Kenny CLEMENTS
Billy GARTON	5	Mick McCARTHY
Kevin MORAN	6	Steve REDMOND
Mike DUXBURY	7	David WHITE *
Gordon STRACHAN	8	Neil McNAB
Frank STAPLETON	9	Imre VARADI
Peter DAVENPORT *	10	Tony GREALISH *
Jesper OLSEN	11	Paul SIMPSON
Terry GIBSON (10)	12	Ian BRIGHTWELL (7)
Liam O'BRIEN	13	Graham BAKER (10)

BACKGROUND

This was United manager Alex Ferguson's first Cup tie with United after replacing Ron Atkinson in November 1986. Meanwhile, City were becoming involved in a desperate struggle to avoid relegation back to Division Two despite the brave efforts of Jimmy Frizzell to turn things around with an influx of experienced players. The Blues were hoping for a Cup run to boost flagging morale.

*United goalkeeper **Chris Turner** goes down to save and deny City striker **Imre Varadi** who is shadowed by the Reds' **Billy Garton**.*

Whiteside incision leaves City prostrate

Manchester United, like President Reagan, found themselves attacked both from the front and the behind but managed to come up smiling. It was never a breeze, but on chances created Ferguson's team just about deserved to sneak through.

Saturday night brought an hour of that increasingly elusive beast, the televised football highlight. A cut here, a replay there, and this looked a passably exciting match. In fact it was 54,000 good Manchester folk in search of an occasion. The seething masses oohed and aahed, willing the boys in red and blue to great deeds, but the game refused to respond.

With two substitutes on each side the touchline often became a more exciting place than the pitch as the quartet limbered up. Terry Gibson was on the point of coming on when Whiteside scored. On a warmer day he would have made it onto the pitch earlier but it must have taken him at least three minutes to

peel off assorted tracksuits and jumpers. On such finer points of undress are cups won.

City, deciding offence was the best form of defence, had much the better of a disappointing first half, yet United had the better chances. Suckling saving from Whiteside and Davenport. Colin Gibson had tied up White, but Simpson looked capable of the unexpected. Alas, like Peter Barnes, who may soon be returning to Maine Road, his deceptions are short-lived.

United's goal owed everything to Whiteside's refusal to take anything for granted. Redmond's temporary loss of concentration had allowed the Northern Ireland international to launch an attack, and when Davenport stumbled under a challenge certain red shirts froze, awaiting a penalty. Not Whiteside.

Television might have illuminated the finer points of Varadi's disallowed header, but all Brian Moore could come

up with in the studio was the unanswered question : Was there a push ? Prolonged examination could have provided an answer, but it was on with the show.

And there was quite a show after the whistle. Microphones here, cameras there, journalists everywhere. Frizzell sucked deep on a cigarette and chuntered about the referee. "One decision has cost us a lot of money. We deserved a replay." Ferguson was elated, much of the tension of the last few weeks falling from his shoulders. Everybody wanted to talk to him. As he was hauled off for yet another interview he was heard to ask somewhat plaintively : "Just how many radio stations are there in Manchester ? ".

SCORERS— Manchester United : Whiteside (54)
Manchester United : Turner, Sivebaek, C Gibson, Whiteside, Garton, Moran, Duxbury, Strachan, Stapleton, Davenport (T Gibson 66) Olsen
Manchester City : Suckling, Gidman, Wilson, Clements, McCarthy, Redmond, White (Brightwell 85) McNab, Varadi, Grealish (Baker 78), Simpson.
Referee : B Hill (Kettering)

The moment that *most* of Old Trafford hoped for finally arrives as Norman Whiteside scores the only goal of the match.

MATCH VERDICT

In a game that lacked real quality, United grabbed the all important goal that allowed them to progress in this year's competition. As is always the case when Manchester pride is at stake, a capacity all-ticket crowd was gathered at Old Trafford. They paid record receipts for a derby match. However the match as a spectacle disappointed. Stephen Bierley, reporting in The Guardian, summed it up thus: "54,000 good Manchester folk in search of an occasion. The seething masses 'oohed' and 'aahed' willing the boys in Red and Blue to great deeds, but the game refused to respond".

A lack lustre first half saw City play the more coherent football but United create the clearer chances as Suckling made excellent saves from Whiteside and Davenport. The major action of the game came in the final half hour. Whiteside, playing at centre forward, and, not for the first time in recent derby history, embroiled in a rather 'macho' battle with McCarthy for most of the afternoon, increasingly gave the Blues' defence problems and it was his quick thinking on the hour which settled the tie. The Northern Ireland international launched the move himself with a quick pass to Davenport on the edge of the City box. As Davenport stumbled under a challenge, several Red shirts froze and claimed the penalty, but Whiteside pounced on to the loose ball and swept it past Suckling.

That proved to be enough, although the City fans joined manager Frizzell's claims that they were 'robbed' when the referee disallowed a Varadi goal that would have earned a replay at Maine Road. Certainly, there was an air of mystery about Mr Hill's decision to rule out Varadi's header for a 'pushing' offence. Alex Ferguson did not worry about that however, as indicated by his comments shortly afterwards in the tabloid press claiming United were on their way to Wembley.

Imre Varadi – a goal disallowed for a mysterious pushing offence.

THE WINNER'S PROGRESS

Date	Round		Att.	Opponents	F	A	Goalscorers
31/1/87	Four	H	49,082	Coventry City	0	1	None

MANCHESTER CITY 2
(Bell, Lee pen)

MANCHESTER UNITED 1
(Charlton)

DATE	3rd December 1969
COMPETITION	League Cup S/F leg 1
VENUE	Maine Road
ATTENDANCE	55,799

Manchester City		Manchester United
Joe CORRIGAN	1	Alex STEPNEY
Tony BOOK	2	Paul EDWARDS
Glyn PARDOE	3	Tony DUNNE
Mike DOYLE	4	Francis BURNS
Tommy BOOTH	5	Ian URE
Alan OAKES	6	David SADLER
Mike SUMMERBEE	7	George BEST
Colin BELL	8	Brian KIDD
Francis LEE	9	Bobby CHARLTON
Neil YOUNG	10	Nobby STILES
Ian BOWYER	11	John ASTON
Dave CONNOR	12	Jim RYAN

A diabolical verdict says Ian Ure

CONTROVERSY raged long after the penalty that put Manchester City into a one-goal lead three minutes from the end of last night's League Cup-tie against Manchester United at Old Trafford.

By DAVID BARNES

City's Francis Lee fell heavily as he bore down on the United goal after a clash with centre-half Ian Ure.

Ure maintained: 'It was a diabolic decision. A terrible thing for the match to hinge on.

'You have got to go for the ball in these situations and that is what I did.'

United chief coach Wilf McGuinness said: 'Lee pushed the ball into a ruck of players and I think he got exactly what he was aiming for. Someone was kidded.

'I thought we were unlucky to lose. We created more chances and were much the better side in the second half.'

But Lee staunchly defended his right to the penalty which he took himself to put City ahead.

'I took the ball and turned on it and would have got my shot in when Ian took my legs away. It was a clear penalty

and I can't understand what all the arguments are about.

'To be frank I thought we should have had another penalty before that when Nobby Stiles caught me in the six-yard box.'

But if United were bitter about City's winner the Maine Road side were equally convinced that Bobby Charlton's equaliser in the 65th minute should not have been allowed.

Skipper Tony Book said: 'As the ball came across George Best pushed me. I was off balance and could not make my clearance properly when it ran to Bobby to shoot in.'

United's Ian Ure walks sadly off the pitch last night —only minutes after giving away the penalty that won the first leg.

				CITY'S PROGRESS			
Date	Round		Att.	Opponents	F	A	Goalscorers
3/9/69	Two	A	11,215	Southport	3	0	Oakes, Bell, Lee
24/9/69	Three	H	28,019	Liverpool	3	2	Doyle, Young, Bowyer
15/10/69	Four	H	45,643	Everton	2	0	Bell, Lee (pen)
29/10/69	Five	H	42,058	Queen's Park Rangers	3	0	Bell (2), Summerbee

				UNITED'S PROGRESS			
Date	Round		Att.	Opponents	F	A	Goalscorers
3/9/69	Two	H	38,939	Middlesbrough	1	0	Sadler
23/9/69	Three	H	48,347	Wrexham	2	0	Kidd, Best
14/10/69	Four	A	27,959	Burnley	0	0	None
20/10/69*	Four	H	50,275	Burnley	1	0	Best
12/5/69	Five	A	38,895	Derby County	0	0	None
19/5/69*	Five	H	57,393	Derby County	1	0	Kidd

*Replay

*United's **Bobby Charlton** hammers the ball past City goalkeeper **Joe Corrigan** to level it up at 1-1.*

***Francis Lee** drills in the controversial late penalty that gave City a slender 2-1 lead to take to Old Trafford.*

MATCH VERDICT

City gained a slender one goal lead to take with them to the vital second leg game at Old Trafford a fortnight later. City, who early on had looked capable of inflicting another heavy defeat on their neighbours following a 4-0 League mauling at Maine Road in November, were in the end grateful for a controversial last-minute penalty.

United started in very nervous fashion and it was the Blues who dominated the opening half-hour playing fast, flowing football. After just 13 minutes the hard-pressed United defence cracked and City went in front. Lee made a typically bustling run down the left and, after evading a number of United tackles, sent in a fierce shot which deflected and spun high into the air. Bell, following in, met the loose ball on the half volley and crashed it past Stepney. Having gained the initiative the Blues poured forward and Bell, Lee and Oakes all had shots which Stepney did well to save.

But United's defence withstood the intense pressure and as the teams entered the second half it was the Reds, with Charlton outstanding, who began to look the more likely side in what was fast developing into a pulsating contest. United held the territorial advantage with much of the danger to the Blues' back line coming from Best's skilful sorties over the mud. Indeed, it was the Irishman who finally broke the home resistance and set up United's deserved equaliser on 66 minutes. As Book struggled to recover, Best dribbled past him and sent an inviting pass out to Kidd on the right, who instantly pulled the ball into the penalty area where Charlton had timed his run

*__George Best__ (left) is ushered away by United Trainer **Jack Crompton** and manager **Wilf McGuinness** after an ugly exchange with referee **Jack Taylor** (right).*
In one of the very first cases of a player later being charged with bringing the game into disrepute, Best, whose disciplinary record was at this time excellent, was dealt with most severely, suffering a £100 fine and a month's suspension.

to perfection and drove the ball beyond Corrigan.

The game seemed certain to end in a draw when, with just two minutes left, City gained a vital second goal. Lee set off on another of his typically probing runs which ended inside the penalty area with what United believed was a theatrical fall as Ure put in a tame but rather desperate lunge. Lee seemed to have already lost control of the ball which ran out of play but referee Jack Taylor pointed to the spot. Despite all the fierce United protests Lee kept his cool and dispatched the penalty with his usual efficiency low to Stepney's right.

All this provided a somewhat sour ending as far as United were concerned. The arguments continued shortly after the final whistle. Best, frustrated in the final seconds when his header was cleared off the line, got involved in animated discussion with referee Taylor as they left the pitch. In a rather ugly ending to the exchange, Best appeared to knock the ball out of Taylor's hands and McGuinness and trainer Jack Crompton rapidly ushered the United player down the tunnel. Best was subsequently fined and banned for the incident. Poor Ian Ure complained the penalty decision was "diabolical" while United manager Wilf McGuinness, rather caustically claimed Lee had "got what he was aiming for". It was a somewhat unfortunate footnote to what had been a splendid match that in reality left both sides still able to entertain dreams of making it through to Wembley.

MANCHESTER UNITED 2
(Edwards, Law)

MANCHESTER CITY 2
(Bowyer, Summerbee)

DATE	17th December 1969
COMPETITION	League Cup S/F leg 2
VENUE	Old Trafford
ATTENDANCE	63,418

Manchester United		Manchester City
Alex STEPNEY	1	Joe CORRIGAN
Paul EDWARDS	2	Tony BOOK
Tony DUNNE	3	Glyn PARDOE
Nobby STILES	4	Mike DOYLE
Ian URE	5	Tommy BOOTH
David SADLER	6	Alan OAKES
Willie MORGAN	7	Mike SUMMERBEE
Pat CRERAND	8	Dave CONNOR
Bobby CHARLTON	9	Francis LEE
Denis LAW	10	Neil YOUNG
George BEST	11	Ian BOWYER
Brian KIDD	12	Bobby OWEN

SUMMERBEE SEES CITY HOME IN CLASSIC 'DERBY'

Alex Stepney fumbles and Mike Summerbee slots the ball into the net to make it 2-2 with nine minutes left and take City through to the League Cup Final at Wembley.

City youngster Ian Bowyer beats diving United goalkeeper Alex Stepney to the loose ball to put the Blues 1-0 ahead on the night.

Delight for City and misery for United after **Ian Bowyer's** early goal made it 3-1 on aggregate.

*United's young goalscorer **Paul Edwards** heads clear watched by **Pat Crerand** and City's **Ian Bowyer**.*

MATCH VERDICT

It hardly seemed possible but in an even more dramatic match than the first leg game City won through to Wembley, although yet again the ending of the tie was shrouded in controversy.

In a bright opening there was much good football from both sides to entertain an excited and expectant capacity crowd. City looked particularly dangerous on the break and seemed to have settled the tie after just 17 minutes when they took a two goal aggregate lead. Summerbee's skilful run on the right carved an opening in the penalty area for Young. His shot beat Stepney but was blocked on the line by Ure. The goalkeeper made a desperate dive to rescue the loose ball but Ian Bowyer, following up, got there first and slotted it into the net. Despite the scale of the uphill task now faced United returned undeterred to the attack and, within six minutes, had the home fans singing with delight after a goal from a rather unlikely source. Paul Edwards, a 21 year old full back with just five games behind him, moved upfield to collect Crerand's piercing pass and, after a brief glance up, struck a fine shot from 20 yards high into the roof of the net. Although United were now back in the game, it was City who twice went close before the interval. Lee's powerful drive was saved by Stepney and, when put clean through the United defence, a fatal moment's hesitation by City's cube-sized forward allowed Edwards to nick the ball off his toe.

The second half though saw an irresistible increase in United's momentum as they penned the Blues back into their own half in an attempt to score the elusive goal that would keep their Wembley dream alive. Following a series of near misses, the home crowd went into raptures as United finally obtained the reward such sustained pressure had merited. Best's brilliant incursion down the right left the City defence floundering and when his fierce shot proved too hot for Corrigan Law appeared, with characteristic speed and instinct, to stab the loose ball into the net. For the first time over the two epic matches United now sensed they might be destined for victory. With a discernible spring in their step the Reds placed City's defence under ever-increasing pressure. However, the third goal simply would not come and with only eight minutes left it suddenly all went wrong for United and for goalkeeper Alex Stepney in particular. Morgan's foul on Bowyer 20 yards out from United's goal gave City an indirect free kick. Lee slammed the kick past United's defensive wall, and if Stepney had simply let the ball pass unmolested straight into the net, it would not have counted. However, in the heat of the moment the goalkeeper attempted to catch the ball. Unfortunately he fumbled and Summerbee, who could barely believe his luck, followed in to gleefully bury it in the net with the crest-fallen Stepney helpless on his knees. There was no come-back for United this time and for the second time in the history of the derby contest City had frustrated United's Wembley ambitions at the penultimate hurdle.

*Relief for United's **Ian Ure** (left), **Paul Edwards** and goalkeeper **Alex Stepney** as City's **Ian Bowyer** just fails to reach a low centre from **Neil Young**.*

THE WINNER'S PROGRESS

Date	Round	Att.	Opponents	F	A	Goalscorers
7/3/70	Final at Wembley	97,963	West Bromwich Albion	2	1*	Doyle, Pardoe

*After extra time

MANCHESTER UNITED 1
(Daly pen)

MANCHESTER CITY 0

DATE	9th October 1974
COMPETITION	League Cup Round 4
VENUE	Old Trafford
ATTENDANCE	55,159

Manchester United		Manchester City
Alex STEPNEY	1	Keith MacRAE
Alex FORSYTH	2	Geoff HAMMOND
Arthur ALBISTON	3	Glyn PARDOE *
Brian GREENHOFF	4	Mike DOYLE
Jim HOLTON	5	Jeff CLARKE
Martin BUCHAN	6	Alan OAKES
Willie MORGAN	7	Mike SUMMERBEE
Sammy McILROY	8	Colin BELL
Stuart PEARSON *	9	Rodney MARSH
Jim McCALLIOG	10	Asa HARTFORD
Gerry DALY	11	Dennis TUEART
Lou MACARI (9)	12	Peter BARNES (3)

BACKGROUND

This is the only Cup tie to have taken place whilst the two teams have been in different divisions. United had been relegated to Division Two the previous spring, but Tommy Docherty's young side had made a highly promising start in their attempt to return to the top flight at the first attempt. With 11 games completed the Reds topped the division by three points and had sustained just one defeat. The only major change to their personnel was in the shape of striker Stuart Pearson, purchased from Hull City in the summer for £180,000. Although the priority was clearly the League, United fans were delighted to have been given such an early opportunity to put one over the old enemy and show City they were now equipped to return to the First Division.

Tony Book as manager at Maine Road had developed a useful Blues side that were up with the leaders in the First Division at the time of this tie. The City management were well aware of the opportunities afforded by their more famous neighbour's demotion and with entertainers of the calibre of Marsh, Summerbee and Bell, here surely was a chance to steal a march on United and narrow the attendance gap between the clubs. The very last thing City would have wanted was to be knocked out of this year's competition at Old Trafford.

FIRST-RATE, UNITED

UNITED'S PROGRESS

Date	Round		Att.	Opponents	F	A	Goalscorers
11/9/74	Two	H	21,616	Charlton Athletic	5	1	Macari (2), McIlroy, Houston, Warman (o.g.)

CITY'S PROGRESS

Date	Round		Att.	Opponents	F	A	Goalscorers
10/9/74	Two	H	14,790	Scunthorpe United	6	0	Bell (3), Barrett, Marsh, Doyle

MATCH VERDICT

United gained some revenge for the League indignity imposed by their First Division neighbours the previous April by knocking them out of the Cup.

Docherty's side showed scant signs of any inferiority complex as they opened with some brisk, intelligent football. However, as the half progressed it was the silky touches of Rodney Marsh that caught the eye as he dictated much of the play and created a series of openings that kept Stepney at his most alert. Docherty's decision to give a debut to 17 year old Arthur Albiston could have backfired when the youngster's underhit backpass gave City their best opening, but Stepney smothered Summerbee's shot. United had to resume the second half without the injured Pearson, but began to look increasingly dangerous, particularly through the jinking runs of McIlroy. With just 15 minutes remaining and a draw on the cards, United grabbed the winner with young Albiston playing a major part in it. His run down the left flank caught City out and as the ball entered the box it struck the hand of City defender Jeff Clarke and the referee immediately blew for a penalty. Gerry Daly reflected the growing quality of 'Doc's' young team as he kept his nerve and drove the important kick unerringly past MacRae.

David Meek writing in the Manchester Evening News had no doubts about the positive aspects of United's victory:

*Wrong way! City goalkeeper **Keith MacRae** guesses wrong as United's **Gerry Daly** slots in the all-important 75th minute penalty.*

*Delight for **Gerry Daly** who raises his fist in salute and is congratulated by team mate **Sammy McIlroy**. City's goalkeeper **Keith MacRae** turns away glumly after being beaten by the spot-kick that decided the Blues' fate.*

Winners, losers and fans can walk tall after last night's 'derby' classic in the League Cup at Old Trafford. Manchester United should feel especially proud because they showed that their newly fashioned team can live with First Division opposition. The penalty that put Manchester City out of this tremendous third round tussle was a hard decision but the Reds matched their rivals in every department and provided more action near goal. The 75th minute penalty came when referee Gordon Kew penalised Jeff Clarke for handling. There was no doubt about the ball striking the young centre-half's hand, but it did not look deliberate to me and therefore should not have been a penalty. But at least it did not come from a fluke breakaway against the run of play.

Spot-king Gerry Daly faced his toughest test yet in front of a 55,000 crowd with record League Cup receipts outside Wembley of £83,000. But the youngster beat Keith MacRae to make it six out of six with his penalty kicks this season - and for the sixth time he sent the goalkeeper diving the wrong way.

City also came through the penalty test with credit, not a murmur of protest and a sporting handshake from skipper Rodney Marsh for the referee at the end. This spirit spread to the terraces to make it a splendid night of stirring partisan sport without violence.

No doubt the arguments will rage over the penalty, but at least victory went to the team spelling more danger near goal in a match that was also won by the game of football.

Lou Macari – a player of refreshing zest on the United substitute's bench.

THE WINNER'S PROGRESS

Date	Round		Att.	Opponents	F	A	Goalscorers
13/11/74	Four	H	46,275	Burnley	3	2	Macari (2), Morgan
4/12/74	Five	A	36,005	Middlesbrough	0	0	None
18/12/74*	Five	H	49,501	Middlesbrough	3	0	Pearson, Macari, McIlroy
15/1/75	S/F leg 1	H	58,010	Norwich City	2	2	Macari (2)
22/1/75	S/F leg 2	A	31,621	Norwich City	0	1	None

*Replay

Gerry Daly – spot on success for United

MANCHESTER CITY 4
(Tueart 2, Hartford, Royle)

MANCHESTER UNITED 0

DATE	12th November 1975
COMPETITION	League Cup 4th Round
VENUE	Maine Road
ATTENDANCE	50,182

Manchester City		Manchester United
Joe CORRIGAN	1	Paddy ROCHE
Kenny CLEMENTS	2	Jimmy NICHOLL
Willie DONACHIE	3	Stewart HOUSTON
Mike DOYLE	4	Tommy JACKSON *
Dave WATSON	5	Brian GREENHOFF
Alan OAKES	6	Martin BUCHAN
Peter BARNES	7	Steve COPPELL
Colin BELL *	8	Sammy McILROY
Joe ROYLE	9	Stuart PEARSON
Asa HARTFORD	10	Lou MACARI
Dennis TUEART	11	Gerry DALY
Tommy BOOTH (8)	12	David McCREERY (4)

*Anxious looks on the faces of the City backroom staff as **Colin Bell** is carried off after just five minutes by **Roy Bailey** and **Freddie Griffiths** while manager **Tony Book** hurriedly re-organises the team. The injury was to prove so serious that Bell played only four games during the following two years, and would never regain full fitness.*

BACKGROUND

Both Manchester clubs had gained notable scalp on the way to this encounter. City eventually saw off the previous year's losing finalists Norwich City, while United went one better and beat the reigning League Cup holders Aston Villa on their own ground.

City were also seeking a little revenge following their exit from this competition at Old Trafford a year earlier in a Third round tie.

MATCH VERDICT

United were soundly thrashed as City handed out a soccer lesson to cruise through into the quarter finals. The Blues effectively ended the game as a contest inside the opening 30 minutes when they ran the Reds' defence ragged with some highly skilful football, with Hartford and Tueart really outstanding.

United fans must have known it would not be their night as the Reds conceded a dreadful goal inside the first 35 seconds - one of the quickest derby goals on record. It was not the kind of start that much criticised goalkeeper Paddy Roche would have wanted, as he was among United's defensive spectators who stood and dithered as Tueart pulled down a pass and comfortably drove the ball into the net. Five minutes later tragedy struck the Blues when Colin Bell did not get up following a tackle with Buchan and he was stretchered off with badly torn thigh muscles and took no further part in the match. Indeed, it was to prove a most serious long term injury. However with substitute Booth drafted into an orthodox midfield role City did not lose momentum and kept the Reds under constant pressure. After 28 minutes a City attack was barely cleared, the ball was lobbed back into the United box and Royle outjumped Greenhoff and headed down for the outstanding Hartford to sweetly half-volley past Roche into the corner of the net. With the United fans standing in glum silence, worse was to come as on 36 minutes a slip by the usually impeccable Buchan allowed the ball to reach Tueart who instantly drilled it beyond Roche to put City in an unassailable position.

There was something approaching greater parity between the teams in a quieter second half but Joe Royle merely underlined City's superiority with a fourth goal nonchalantly clipped in from Barnes' cross that sent the City fans home

CITY'S PROGRESS

Date	Round		Att.	Opponents	F	A	Goalscorers
10/9/75	Two	A	18,332	Norwich City	1	1	Watson
17/9/75*	Two	H	29,667	Norwich City	2	2	Royle, Tueart
24/9/75†	Two	–	6,238	Norwich City	6	1	Tueart (3), Doyle, Royle, opp. o.g.
8/10/75	Three	H	26,536	Nottingham Forest	2	1	Bell, Royle

Replay, †Second Replay – at Stamford Bridge

UNITED'S PROGRESS

Date	Round		Att.	Opponents	F	A	Goalscorers
10/9/75	Two	H	25,286	Brentford	2	1	Macari, McIlroy
8/10/75	Three	A	41,447	Aston Villa	2	1	Macari, Coppell

delighted.

Peter Garner in the Manchester Evening News was quick to praise the outstanding contribution of Hartford to City's success:

"Asa Hartford gave a World-class midfield performance as Manchester City breathtakingly turned on the League Cup power. It was a dazzling flashback to the vintage years when the champagne Blues were at their rampaging best as they tore Manchester United to shreds.

City not only beat United, they massacred them to reach the quarter finals for the second time in three seasons. Yet it was victory achieved at considerable odds for the Blues who lost Colin Bell after just five minutes. A goal after 35 seconds by Dennis Tueart gave the Blues the flying start they wanted, and it owes much to the character and spirit moulded in the side that they were able to overcome the blow to Bell.

Yet it was from that moment when Bell was carried off on a stretcher that Hartford took the game by the scruff of the neck to provide a display never seen at Maine Road in years. I single out Hartford because his contribution stood out head and shoulders as he hit 40-yard passes that found the target with radar precision. His short-ball game too was exemplary, providing the vital link between defence and attack that saw City turn in their most blistering all round display in years."

United's **Paddy Roche** and **Jimmy Nicholl** are helpless as City's **Dennis Tueart** makes it 1-0 after just 35 seconds.

Man of the Match **Asa Hartford** dashes in to beat **Paddy Roche** with a left foot shot to make it 2-0.

Joe Royle is surrounded by United defenders as he casually clips a **Peter Barnes** cross into the net to wrap it up at 4-0.

THE WINNER'S PROGRESS

Date	Round		Att.	Opponents	F	A	Goalscorers
3/12/75	Five	H	30,022	Mansfield Town	4	2	Hartford, Royle, Tueart, Oakes
13/1/76	S/F leg 1	A	35,000	Middlesbrough	0	1	None
21/1/76	S/F leg 2	H	44,426	Middlesbrough	4	0	Oakes, Keegan, Barnes, Royle
28/2/76	Final at Wembley		100,000	Newcastle United	2	1	Barnes, Tueart

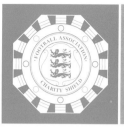

MANCHESTER CITY 0
MANCHESTER UNITED 1
(Viollet)

		DATE	24th October 1956
		COMPETITION	F.A. Charity Shield
		VENUE	Maine Road
		ATTENDANCE	30,495

Manchester City		Manchester United
John SAVAGE	1	Ray WOOD
Bill LEIVERS	2	Bill FOULKES
Roy LITTLE	3	Roger BYRNE
Don REVIE	4	Eddie COLMAN
Dave EWING	5	Mark JONES
Roy PAUL	6	Duncan EDWARDS
Paddy FAGAN	7	Johnny BERRY
Joe HAYES	8	Billy WHELAN
Bobby JOHNSTONE	9	Tommy TAYLOR
Jack DYSON	10	Dennis VIOLLET
Roy CLARKE	11	David PEGG

BACKGROUND

This meeting of the previous season's F.A. Cup and League Championship winners has proved to be the only Charity Shield match between the clubs in the history of the derby. Prior to this encounter City had appeared in two Charity Shield games, winning the Shield when they beat Sunderland in 1937. By contrast, United had won the Shield in three of their four appearances; against Queen's Park Rangers (1908), Swindon Town (1911), and Newcastle United (1952).

It was not until 1974 that the Charity Shield moved to the prestigious Wembley site and acted as the curtain raiser to the new season. The 1956-57 season was already well under way when this midweek game was played and there was much speculation as to how popular it might prove in soccer mad Manchester.

Certainly it had all the ingredients of a fascinating match. The 'Busby Babes' were the talk of the football world, League Champions and a vastly talented team that had yet to reach its peak and appeared to have the football world at its feet. City, convincing F.A. Cup winners with the revolutionary 'Revie plan' were one of the few teams who had enjoyed any success against the Babes in recent seasons. One man who missed the contest was the charismatic City goalkeeper Bert Trautmann, still recuperating from the broken neck sustained in City's Cup Final triumph over Birmingham City the previous May.

LEAGUE CHAMPIONS JUST HOME

Over-Elaboration Nearly Proves Costly

FROM OUR SPECIAL CORRESPONDENT

Manchester C. 0, Manchester U. 1

Extravagance, even when it brings with it a certain reckless excitement, is a sad fault on the football field, and Manchester United, who might have scored half a dozen goals in their F.A. Charity Shield match with Manchester City at Moss Side last night, committed the sin to excess. In fact, they scored only once, but that single goal seemed a small reward for all the striving with which the League champions sought to vanquish the F.A. Cup winners. In the end we were disappointed, because so much of what we were promised came to nought.

The match began like one which seemed likely to yield goals galore. Early on and for most of the rest of the match it was United who did the greater part of the attacking. There were long passes down the middle and fierce chases by Whelan and Viollet, which unavoidably threatened ill to Savage in the City goal. And there were neat shots from Pegg and Taylor—but from too far off to cause any real fear.

The City forwards countered this swift menace by individual strivings, but nearly ten minutes went by before Wood was seriously tested. It was end-to-end stuff, but the United made three attacks to every one of City's.

In this way the game progressed for a quarter of an hour, the excitement coming from the pace and keenness of the struggle rather than from contrived surprises and subtleties. There was little

apart from the extreme unhappiness of one or two of the missed chances by the United inside forwards, to remember until Revie, who is now a right half, struck three bold and splendid blows. They were all rather similar. He would collect a loose ball on his side of the half-way line and move forward with the United defence falling back before him. Each time he was allowed to come near the penalty area. Twice he made Wood leap desperately to punch the ball and the third time he lost his chance with a poor pass. After that he returned to defence.

These bold strokes heartened City and in the time that remained before half-time they attacked in full force. Dyson, one of those footballers who moves with the ball rather than merely to the ball, made a splendid semi-circular run which finished up with a fine shot just over the bar and Johnstone worried Wood with a couple of neat headers. After a goalmouth scramble the United goalkeeper left the field with an injured hip and Gaskell, a fifteen-year-old schoolboy international, took his place.

After half-time the match became a matter of seeing whether the City defence could hold out against the continued pressure of United's attacks. For a time the pattern was unchanged, but in the seventy-fifth minute Whelan put the ball out to Berry on the right wing; Berry returned it, and the City defenders suddenly stood still and watched some neat inter-passing which ended in Viollet's shooting neatly past Savage. After that the play was fierce and hard, but it brought no profit to anyone.

MANCHESTER CITY.—Savage; Leivers, Little; Revie, Ewing, Paul; Fagan, Hayes, Johnstone, Dyson, Clarke.
MANCHESTER UNITED.—Wood; Foulkes, Byrne; Colman, Jones, Edwards; Berry, Whelan, Taylor, Viollet, Pegg.

Dennis Viollet – his 75th minute goal was enough to win the Charity Shield for United's 'Busby Babes'.

MATCH VERDICT

The modest crowd of Mancunians that gathered to see this midweek game were captivated by a treat of end to end football. League champions United dominated proceedings, mounting on average three attacks to every one mustered by the Blues. The Reds though, appropriately in the circumstances, showed far too much charity to their neighbours with some decidedly lack-lustre finishing which let down a wealth of impressive approach play.

Whelan, Pegg, Viollet and Taylor all went close in an opening half hour during which the Cup holders had a problem getting out of their own half. As the break neared, some cultured sorties by Revie, playing at right-half, attempted to restore the balance and indeed, Wood was twice forced to make impressive saves. Shortly after this Wood had to retire hurt following a goalmouth scramble and United were allowed to send on 15 year old Youth International David Gaskell for the remainder of the game. In an unofficial sense, he became the first substitute to appear in a derby contest.

The pattern of the game remained much the same in the second half, but just when United must have been rueing all their missed chances a splendid move that characterised the youthful Champions settled the match. Whelan initiated a razor sharp passing movement on the right wing, Berry was prominent as the ball flashed through a static City defence and arrived at the feet of Viollet whose first time shot gave goalkeeper Savage no chance.

*City's midfield maestro **Don Revie** who twice brought fine saves from United goalkeeper **Ray Wood**.*

*A cartoon by George Butterworth previewed the **Charity Shield** game in the United programme. It is worth noting that the game should have taken place at Old Trafford, but as Maine Road had the floodlights at this time, the game was switched to City.*

errata

In a project of this size the occasional slip-up is unfortunately inevitable - well not even George Best and Colin Bell were right all the time! Those we have spotted too late for correction include the following:

p.102 Player's name missing on the front row (extreme right) of City team picture is **E. Eastwood**.

p.163 Caption to picture of Roger Byrne says he succeeded Johnny Carey as captain of United. **Allenby Chilton** in fact succeeded Carey.

p.175 Caption to top colour picture should read **Tony Towers** and not Willie Donachie.

p.217 Caption to colour picture at foot of page should read **Sammy McIlroy** and not Ray Wilkins.

p.220 The player celebrating with Ian Bishop is **Paul Lake** and not David White.

DERBY
STATISTICS

Aggregate Derby Results

	Played	United Won	City Won	Drawn	United Goals	City Goals
League	114	41	32	41	161	159
FA Cup	5	3	2	0	9	6
League Cup	4	1	2	1	4	8
Charity Shield	1	1	0	0	1	0
Total	124	46	36	42	175	173

Highest Individual Team Scores
City: 6 goals, (6-1 at Old Trafford 23/1/26)

Widest Victory Margin
5 goals: 23/1/26 - United 1 City 6
           12/2/55 - United 0 City 5

Highest Aggregate Derby Score
7 goals: 3/11/1894 - City 2 Newton Heath 5
           23/1/1926 - United 1 City 6
           5/5/1971 - City 3 United 4

Largest Home Win
United: 5-1 on 31/12/60
City: 5-1 on 23/9/89

Largest Away Win
United: 5-2 on 3/11/1894
City: 6-1 on 23/1/1926

Longest Derby Sequence Without a Win
City: 9 games 6/4/07 - 7/9/12
United: 8 games 19/1/52 - 31/12/55

Longest Derby Sequence Without a Team Scoring
United: 4 games, 18/11/72 - 27/9/75
City: 2 games, 25/12/97 - 26/12/98, 2/9/11 - 7/9/12,
           28/12/12- 11/4/14, 11/9/48 - 3/9/49, 21/4/73 -
           27/4/74, 30/9/78 - 10/11/79.

Bobby Charlton – the most derby appearances for United (27) and the top United scorer in derby games with 9 goals.

Most Derby Appearances
Overall: William Meredith - 14 for City, 15 for United.
           Total: 29
United: Bobby Charlton - 27
           First: 28/12/57 (scored in 2-2 draw at Maine Road)
           Last: 21/4/73 (0-0 at Old Trafford)
City: Joe Corrigan - 26
           First: 15/11/69 (kept a clean sheet in 4-0 win at
           Maine Road)
           Last: 5/3/83 (2-1 defeat at Maine Road)

Most Derby Goals
United: Bobby Charlton - 9 goals (27 games)
City: Joe Hayes - 10 goals (17 games)
           (Plus 1 goal in abandoned game of 1960)
           Francis Lee - 10 goals (15 games)

Joe Hayes - *joint top scorer for City in derby matches alongside Francis Lee with a total of 10 goals.*

The First League Derby Goal
Richard Smith for Newton Heath (United) in the 5-2 victory at
Hyde Road in the first ever derby.

The First Player Sent Off in a Derby
Sandy Turnbull (United) on 21/12/07 during a 3-1 United
victory at Clayton.

The First Substitute used in a Derby
Mike Doyle (City) for Bobby Kennedy - 17/9/66

Derby Appearances For United – The Top Fifty

Player	Seasons	League	Cup	Total
CHARLTON, R.	1956-73	24	3	27
STEPNEY, A.C.	1966-78	20	4	24
FOULKES, W.A.	1952-70	21	2	23
BUCHAN, M.M.	1972-83	18	2	20
COPPELL, S.J.	1974-83	16	1	17
McILROY, S.B.	1971-82	15	2	17
ALBISTON, A.R.	1974-88	15	1	16
DUNNE, A.P.	1960-73	14	2	16
MACARI, L.	1972-84	14	2	16
BEST, G.	1963-74	13	2	15
BYRNE, R.W.	1951-58	13	2	15
MEREDITH, W.H.	1906-21	15	0	15
SADLER, D.	1963-73	12	3	15
STILES, N.P.	1960-71	13	2	15
VIOLLET, D.S.	1952-62	13	2	15
BERRY, J.J.	1951-58	12	2	14
CHILTON, A.C.	1939-55	13	1	14
SPENCE, J.W.	1919-33	13	1	14
WALL, G.	1905-15	14	0	14
KIDD, B.	1967-74	11	2	13
SILCOCK, J.	1919-34	12	1	13
STACEY, G.	1907-15	13	0	13
DUCKWORTH, R.	1903-14	12	0	12
ROBERTS, C.	1903-13	12	0	12
WOOD, R.E.	1949-58	10	2	12
BAILEY, G.R.	1978-86	11	0	11
BRENNAN, S.A.	1957-70	11	0	11
DUXBURY, M.	1980-90	10	1	11
EDWARDS, D.	1952-58	9	2	11
LAW, D.	1962-73	10	1	11
ROWLEY, J.F.	1937-55	10	1	11
TURNBULL, A.	1906-15	11	0	11
ASTON, J. (Snr)	1946-54	10	0	10
CAREY, J.J.	1937-52	10	0	10
CRERAND, P.T.	1962-71	8	2	10
ERENTZ, F.C.	1892-1901	10	0	10
HOUSTON, S.M.	1973-80	9	1	10
NICHOLL, J.M.	1974-82	9	1	10
PEARSON, S.C.	1937-54	10	0	10
CARTWRIGHT, W.G.	1895-1904	9	0	9
GREENHOFF, B.	1973-78	7	2	9
HILDITCH, C.G.	1919-32	9	0	9
MOORE, C.	1919-30	8	1	9
MORGAN, W.	1968-75	6	3	9
STEWARD, A.	1920-32	8	1	9
TAYLOR, T.	1952-58	7	2	9
WEST, E.J.	1910-15	9	0	9
BENNION, S.R.	1921-32	8	0	8
GREGG, H.	1957-66	8	0	8
PEGG, D.	1952-58	7	1	8
QUIXALL, A.	1958-64	8	0	8

Note: All appearances also include any outings as a substitute.

Johnny Carey - played in 10 League derby matches for United during his career at Old Trafford.

UNITED SCORERS

United's Derby Goalscorers

Player	Seasons	League	Cup	Total	Derbies
CHARLTON, R.	1956-73	8	1	9	27
SPENCE, J.W.	1919-33	8	0	8	14
VIOLLET, D.	1952-62	6	1	7	15
SMITH, R.	1894-1900	6	0	6	6
COPPELL, S.	1974-83	5	0	5	17
KIDD, B.	1967-74	3	2	5	13
LAW, D.	1962-73	4	1	5	11
STAPLETON, F.	1981-86	5	0	5	7
CASSIDY, J.	1892-1900	4	0	4	8
CLARKIN, J.	1893-96	4	0	4	4
DAWSON, A.	1958-62	4	0	4	2
HILL, G.	1975-78	4	0	4	5
PEARSON, S.C.	1937-54	4	0	4	10
TAYLOR, T.	1952-58	4	0	4	9
TURNBULL, A.	1906-15	4	0	4	11
WEST, E.J.	1910-15	4	0	4	9
BERRY, J.J.	1951-58	3	0	3	14
BEST, G.	1963-74	3	0	3	15
ALBISTON, A.	1974-88	2	0	2	16
ANDERSON, G.	1911-15	2	0	2	4
BRADLEY, W.	1958-62	2	0	2	3
DALY, G.	1973-77	1	1	2	7
DONALDSON, R.	1892-98	2	0	2	5
EDWARDS, D.	1952-58	2	0	2	11
FARMAN, A.H.	1889-95	0	2	2	1
HUGHES, M.	1985-91	2	0	2	6
LIVINGSTONE, G.	1908-14	2	0	2	1
McCLAIR, B.	1987-91	2	0	2	4
McCREERY, D.	1974-79	2	0	2	4
McILROY, S.	1971-82	2	0	2	17
RENNOX, C.	1924-27	2	0	2	3
ROBSON, B.	1981-91	2	0	2	7
WALL, G.	1905-15	2	0	2	14
WHELAN, L.	1954-58	2	0	2	4

The following players have each scored one goal in the League derby matches:
Bamford T., Blackmore C., Blanchflower J., Boyd H., Bryant W., Buchan M., Carey J., Chisnall P., Delaney J., Downie J., Duxbury M., Foulkes W., Gibson C., Giggs R., Gillespie M., Goodwin F., Gowling A., Halse H., Herd D., Hodge J., Hopkin F., Johnston W., Jordan J., Macari L., Manley T., McShane H., Miller T., Moran K., Nicholl J., Pearson M., Pearson S., Pegg E., Quixall A., Rawlings W., Reid T., Ritchie A., Roberts C., Rowley J., Scanlon A., Schofield A.J., Stiles N., Strachan G., Thomas H., Thomas M., Turnbull J., Wilson J.

The following players have each scored one goal in Cup derbies:
Doughty R., Edge A., Edwards P., Morgan W., Sneddon J., Whiteside N.

*Top scorer for United in derby matches, **Bobby Charlton** is congratulated by Pat Crerand and Denis Law (hidden), after one of his two League goals against City at Maine Road in September 1967. United won the match 2-1.*

CITY APPEARANCES

Derby Appearances For City – The Top Fifty

Player	Seasons	League	Cup	Total
CORRIGAN, J.T.	1966-83	23	3	26
OAKES, A.	1958-76	20	5	25
DOYLE, M.	1962-78	19	5	24
TRAUTMANN, B.C.	1949-64	22	1	23
BELL, C.	1966-79	17	4	21
BOOTH, T.A.	1965-81	17	4	21
CLARKE, R.J.	1947-58	16	2	18
SUMMERBEE, M.G.	1965-75	14	4	18
HAYES, J.	1953-65	15	2	17
BOOK, A.K.	1966-74	13	3	16
DONACHIE, W.	1968-80	15	1	16
YOUNG, N.J.	1959-72	13	3	16
EWING, D.	1949-62	13	2	15
LEE, F.H.	1967-74	12	3	15
POWER, P.	1973-86	15	0	15
BARNES, K.H.	1950-61	13	1	14
HARTFORD, R.A.	1974-79 &1981-84	12	2	14
MEREDITH, W.H.	1894-1906 &1921-24	14	0	14
PARDOE, G.	1961-76	10	4	14
FLETCHER, E.	1911-26	13	0	13
LEIVERS, W.E.	1953-64	12	1	13
PAUL, R.	1950-57	11	2	13
SMITH, W.E.	1906-20	13	0	13
CLEMENTS, K.H.	1971-79 &1985-88	10	2	12
JONES, W.L.	1903-19	12	0	12
TUEART, D.	1974-78 &1980-83	10	2	12
EADIE, W.P.	1906-14	11	0	11
REVIE, D.	1951-56	9	2	11
BROWELL, T.	1913-26	9	1	10
LITTLE, R.	1949-58	8	2	10
COWAN, S.	1924-35	8	1	9
DORSETT, J.H.	1910-20	9	0	9
FAGAN, F.	1953-60	7	2	9
HART. J.P.	1944-63	8	1	9
HENRY, W.A.	1911-20	9	0	9
WILLIAMS, C.A.	1894-1902	9	0	9
BRANAGAN, K.F.	1948-60	8	0	8
BROOK, E.F.G.	1928-40	8	0	8
MEADOWS, J.	1951-57	7	1	8
REDMOND, S.	1986-91	7	1	8
REID, N.S.	1977-87	8	0	8
SEAR, C.	1955-68	8	0	8
WATSON, D.	1975-79	7	1	8
WESTWOOD, E.	1937-53	8	0	8
BARLOW, C.J.	1956-63	7	0	7
CATON, T.	1979-83	7	0	7
DORSETT, G.	1904-12	7	0	7
HOLFORD, T.	1908-14	7	0	7
MARSHALL, R.S.	1928-39	7	0	7
RANSON, R.	1976-84	7	0	7
REEVES, K.P.	1980-83	7	0	7
THORNLEY, I.	1904-12	7	0	7

Steve Redmond - holds the record for the most derby appearances by a current City player with a total of 8 outings against United.

Ian Brightwell - one of a number of City players who have netted once in a derby match, he struck a spectacular equaliser in the 1-1 draw at Old Trafford in February 1990.

City's Derby Goalscorers

Player	Seasons	League	Cups	Total	Derbies
HAYES, J.	1953-65	9	1	10	17
LEE, F.H.	1967-74	9	1	10	15
BELL, C.	1966-79	7	1	8	21
BARNES, H.	1914-24	5	0	5	6
BROWELL, T.	1913-26	3	2	5	10
MEREDITH, W.H.	1894-06 &1921-24	5	0	5	14
HART, J.P.	1944-63	4	0	4	9
JOHNSON, T.C.F.	1919-30	4	0	4	7
ROBERTS, F.	1922-29	3	1	4	5
TUEART, D.	1974-78 &1980-83	2	2	4	12
AUSTIN, S.W.	1924-31	3	0	3	5
FAGAN, F.	1953-60	3	0	3	9
JONES, W.L.	1903-19	3	0	3	12
KIDD, B.	1976-79	3	0	3	6
MARSHALL, R.S.	1928-39	3	0	3	7
REEVES, K.P.	1980-83	3	0	3	7
ROYLE, J.	1974-77	2	1	3	5
SUMMERBEE, M.G.	1965-75	2	1	3	18
BROADIS, I.A.	1951-53	2	0	2	3
BROOK, E.F.G.	1928-40	2	0	2	8
CLARKE, R.J.	1947-58	2	0	2	18
DOYLE, M.	1962-78	2	0	2	24
HARLEY, A.	1962-63	2	0	2	2
HILL, R.	1895-97	2	0	2	3
McADAMS, W.J.	1953-60	2	0	2	6
MURPHY, W.	1918-26	2	0	2	6
OLDFIELD, D.	1988-90	2	0	2	1
REVIE, D.G.	1951-56	1	1	2	11
STEWART, G.	1906-11	2	0	2	2
TAIT, T.	1928-30	2	0	2	2
WHITE, D.	1986-91	2	0	2	6

The following players have each scored one goal in the League:
Barnes K.H., Barnes P.S., Barlow C.J., Bishop I., Black A., Bray J., Brightwell I., Channon M.R., Conlin J., Cowan S., Cross D., Cumming J.F., Dobing P., Dorsett G., Dougal D., Dyson J., Eadie W.P., Gillespie W.J., Halliday D., Hannah G., Heale J.A., Hendry C., Henry A., Herd A., Heslop G., Hicks G.W., Hill F., Hinchcliffe A., Howard F.J., Johnstone R., Kennedy R., Law D., Linacre W., McCarthy M., McCourt F.J., Mackenzie S., Marsh R.W., Mellor I., Morley T., Munro J.F., Palmer R.N., Ray R., Robinson M.J., Rowan A., Sharples J., Taylor H.G., Thornley I., Toseland E., Wagstaffe D., Warner J., Williams F., Wilson C., Wynn G.A., Young N.J.

The following players have each scored one goal in the League Cup:
Bowyer, I., Hartford, R.A.

The following player has scored one goal in the F.A. Cup:
Pearson, J.

Note: Cups column for both City and United refers to the FA Cup, League Cup and Charity Shield competitions.

CITY AND UNITED DEBUTS

The following players all made their **full** first team debuts for **City** in the Manchester derby:-

City's Debutants Player	Date	Derby Number
Bert Read	7/12/1895	4
John McMahon	25/12/1902	11
Robert Davies	2/9/1911	21
Sid Hoad	2/9/1911	21
Frank Knowles	11/10/1919	29
Sid Scott	18/10/1919	30
Jackie Bray	8/2/1930	40
Bill Sowden	30/8/1952	53
Dave Ewing	3/1/1953	54
Ken Mulhearn	30/9/1967	77
Mick Horswill	13/3/1974	89
Dennis Tueart	13/3/1974	89
Michael Docherty	4/5/1976	92
Gary Jackson	27/2/1982	104
John Gidman	26/10/1986	109
Tony Grealish	26/10/1986	109
Martyn Margetson	4/5/1991	114

The following players made their **full** first team debuts for **United** in the Manchester derby:

United's Debutants Player	Date	Derby Number
Thomas Morrison	25/12/1902	11
Harold Hardman	19/9/1908	17
George Livingstone	23/1/1909	18
Jack Grimwood	11/10/1919	29
Frank Hodges	18/10/1919	30
William Roughton	12/9/1936	43
Alex Stepney	17/9/1966	75
Tommy O'Neil	5/5/1971	84
Sammy McIlroy	6/11/1971	85
Paul Bielby	13/3/1974	89
Arthur Albiston	9/10/1974	League Cup
Mike Duxbury	27/9/1980	101
Bryan Robson *	10/10/1981	103
Ryan Giggs	4/5/1991	114

* Robson made his 'full' debut for United three days earlier in a League Cup match against Tottenham Hotspur.

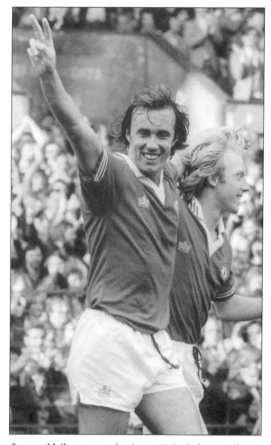

Sammy McIlroy – one of only two United players to have marked their derby debut with a goal. Called up on the morning of the match, he netted the Reds first in a thrilling 3-3 draw at Maine Road in November 1971.

Tony Grealish - a 1986 derby debut for City.

OWN GOALS AND SENDINGS-OFF

Nobby Stiles – the only player in derby history to score two own goals.

Own Goals

Listed below are all the own goals scored in derby matches with the names of all those who have suffered the ultimate calamity of having the opposing supporters singing their praises! United's competitive midfielder Nobby Stiles holds the unenviable derby record of having scored twice for City.

Player	Date	Derby No.
William Holmes	10/4/1903	12
Bill Foulkes	28/12/1957	64
Dave Ewing	23/9/1961	71
Nobby Stiles	23/9/1961	71
Nobby Stiles	21/1/1967	76
David Sadler	15/11/1969	81
Martin Buchan	18/11/1972	87
Jimmy Nicholl	27/9/1975	91
Arthur Albiston	22/3/1986	108
Nicky Reid	7/3/1987	110

Sendings-Off

The passion of the derby match has brought many cautions down the years, but only six players have ever been dismissed from the field during a game between the Manchester rivals.

Player	Team	Date	Derby No.
Sandy Turnbull	United	21/12/1907	15
Billy Linacre	City	3/9/1949	49
Henry Cockburn	United	3/9/1949	49
Allenby Chilton	United	29/1/1955	FA Cup Rd 4
Mike Doyle	City	13/3/1974	89

HAT-TRICKS AND 100-UP

Derby Hat-Tricks

Player	Team	Derby Number	Date	Goals	Result
Richard Smith	N. Heath	1	3/11/1894	4	Ardwick 2 N. Heath 5
Horace Barnes	City	33	22/10/1921	3	City 4 United 1
Joe Spence	United	34	29/10/1921	3	United 3 City 1
Alex Dawson	United	69	31/12/1960	3	United 5 City 1
Francis Lee	City	83	12/12/1970	3	United 1 City 4

One Hundred Up

The 100th goal in derby League contests was scored by Tommy Johnson (City). It was the winner in City's 2-1 success at Old Trafford in derby no. 38 (5/1/1929).

The 100th United goal in League derby contests was scored by Denis Law. It was United's first goal in derby no. 71 (23/9/1961) which saw United win 3-2 at Old Trafford.

The 100th City goal in League derby contests was scored by Alex Harley. It was City's early goal in the tense 1-1 draw at Maine Road in derby no. 74 (15/5/1963)

The 100th derby goal in all League and Cup contests:
for United - was scored by Alex Dawson. It was United's third goal in their 5-1 victory at Old Trafford in derby no. 69 (31/12/1960)

for City - was scored by David Wagstaffe. It was City's only goal in a 3-1 defeat at Maine Road in derby no. 70 (4/3/1961)

Abandoned Derbies

The only abandoned derby match was the First Division League match between the sides in the 1960/61 season. This game was played on 27th August 1960 and was abandoned due to a waterlogged pitch during a torrential downpour with the score standing at 2-2. City's scorers were Denis Law and Joe Hayes, while on target for United were Dennis Viollet and Alex Dawson. Attendance 51,927.

The match was replayed on 4th March 1961, the result being City 1 United 3.

Strictly speaking the notorious relegation derby match of 27th April 1974 could be considered an abandoned match. Following a crowd invasion the referee finally took the players off (with some minutes still left to play) and due to the disturbances they did not return. However, the result, United 0 City 1, was allowed to stand.

NEWTON HEATH v. ARDWICK DISTRICT

This match was played at Belle Vue Gardens last night before a tremendous crowd, the "gate" being for the benefit of the Hyde Explosion Fund. There were twenty of the Wells's lights round the ground, but still there seemed to be some difficulty in seeing the ball at times, especially when it was off the ground. It was stated that there had been quite 6,000 tickets sold, and the gates were crowded for over two hours before the time for starting, so that there would be quite 10,000 people present, and it ought to result in a considerable addition to the fund. Mr. Charles Jennison kicked off, and R. G. Barlow was referee. The game was not a success as an exhibition of football, but still at times there was some good bits of play, which were applauded by the spectators, who seemed to be quite enthusiastic. The chief feature of the match was the cheering when the ball was kicked either over the bar or outside, as most of the spectators were sure it went through. The scoring done was four goals by Newton Heath and one by the District, but, unfortunately for the former, one of theirs was put through his own goal by Powell. Score:—Newton Heath, three goals; Ardwick and District, two goals.

A match report from the first floodlight derby in 1889 - not that it seems the 10,000 crowd could see a great deal of the game!

First Floodlight Derby

The first floodlight derby between the two clubs was a friendly played at Belle Vue on 26th February 1889, and was an exhibition match to raise money for a local charity fund set up after the death of 23 miners in the Hyde coalmine explosion.

The first 'modern day' floodlight derby was the Charity Shield match played at Maine Road on 24th October 1956.

First 'Live' Television Derby

The first derby between City and United screened 'live' on television was played on Sunday 26th October 1986 at Maine Road. Shown on Independent Television, the match kicked-off at 2.35pm and ended in a 1-1 draw.

The only derby to be abandoned in August 1960 provoked this humorous cartoon in the local paper about the legendary Manchester rain!

*United's muscular striker **Mark Hughes** has won the P.F.A. accolade twice, first in 1988-89 and then again in 1990-91.*

Manchester Players Honoured

The two major awards which are available to Manchester United and Manchester City players within the domestic game are the Football Writers 'Footballer of the Year' (instigated in the 1947-48 season) and the Professional Footballers' Association 'Footballer of the Year' (instigated in 1974).

The following United and City players have won these awards:

United
Johnny Carey	1948-1949	(Football Writers award)
Bobby Charlton	1965-1966	(Football Writers award)
George Best	1967-1968	(Football Writers award)
Mark Hughes	1988-1989	(P.F.A. award)
Mark Hughes	1990-1991	(P.F.A. award)

City
Don Revie	1954-1955	(Football Writers award)
Bert Trautmann	1955-1956	(Football Writers award)
Tony Book*	1968-1969	(Football Writers award)

won jointly with Dave Mackay

The following City and United players have won the P.F.A. Young Player of the Year award:

United
Mark Hughes	1984-1985
Lee Sharpe	1990-1991

City
Peter Barnes	1975-1976

*City's **Bert Trautmann**, winner of the Football Writers Award in 1955-56.*

PLAYED FOR BOTH CLUBS

Players Who Have Played For Both City And United

Listed below are all direct transfers between the two clubs, with the exact date of signing specified where known. It is perhaps interesting to note that the majority of moves were before the Second World War, which is possibly an indication not only of the increased competitiveness between the two clubs in the modern age but also the worry that a player may cross Manchester and do embarrassingly well for the rival club! There has also never been a major fee involved. The most expensive move was made by Wyn Davies back in September 1972 when United paid City £60,000 for his services in the first cash transfer transaction between the clubs for 41 years.

Wyn Davies – his £60,000 move from Maine Road to Old Trafford in 1972 is the record fee to pass between the two Manchester clubs. He is also the only player United have bought directly from City in the past 57 years!

Signed for City from United

Player	Date Signed
Milarvie, Robert	c/s 1891
Carson, A.	15/3/1893
Cassidy, Joe	20/4/1900
Morgan, Hugh	31/7/1901
Christie, John	5/5/1904
Buckley, F.	2/9/1907
Broomfield, Herbert	11/7/1908
Knowles, Frank	6/10/1919
Woodcock, Wilf	5/5/1920
Albinson, George	19/5/1921
Meredith, Billy	25/7/1921
Dale, Billy	23/12/1931
Rowley, Harry	23/12/1931
Westwood, Eric	13/11/1937
Walsh, Billy	5/5/1936
Gemmell, Eric	23/5/1946
Fidler, Dennis	28/11/1956
Whelan, Tony	15/3/1973
Law, Denis	2/7/1973
Bodak, Peter	18/1/1983
Gidman, John	21/10/1986
Barnes, Peter	13/1/1987

Signed for United from City

Player	Date Signed
Douglas, William	26/1/1894
Caines, J.	c/s 1894
Stones, Harry	c/s 1894
Hurst, Daniel	30/5/1902
Williams, Fred	4/6/1902
Read, Bert	28/8/1902
Meredith, Billy	5/12/1906
Turnbull, Sandy	5/12/1906
Bannister, Jimmy	5/12/1906
Burgess, Herbert	5/12/1906
Quinn, John	11/6/1908
Ridding, Bill	23/12/1931
Langford, Len	1/6/1934
Davies, Wyn	14/9/1972

*Former Reds favourite **Sammy McIlroy** with ex-Blues star **Peter Barnes** - two players who have turned out for both Manchester clubs.*

Record transfer fee between the two clubs:

Wyn Davies on 14/9/1972 from City to United for £60,000.

Others who have played for both clubs without a direct transfer:

Frank Barrett	United 1896-1900, City 1901-02
Mick Hamill	United 1911-1913, City 1920-24
Di Jones	United pre-1888, City 1898-1902
Brian Kidd	United 1967-1973, City 1976-1979
George Livingstone	City 1903-1907, United 1908-1913
Sammy McIlroy	United 1971-1981, City 1985-1987

The following were Juniors at United and went on to play for City:

Daniels, Bernard	joined City 1973
Ward, Ashley	joined City 1989
Hill, Andy	joined City 1990

Frank Haydock was a United player in the early 1960's when his brother William Haydock played for City. Their appearances were limited however, and they did not meet on derby duty.

Family Connections

There have been a number of players - or their families - who have played for one Manchester club yet have supported the other. Among more modern players was City striker Paul Stewart who was a United supporter as a youngster, and United forward Mark Robins who was a member of City's Junior Blues club! There have also been a number of players whose relatives have played for the opposition. The most recent of these involves the Docherty family. Tommy, then the United manager, witnessed his son Michael make his debut for the Blues against the Reds in May 1976. At the time, 'The Doc' told reporters he wanted Mike to "be the best player on the losing side."

Another father and son combination was the Herd family. Alec Herd was part of the highly successful City side of the 1930's when he helped the club to two F.A. Cup Finals and a League Championship. His son, David emulated his father's success when, throughout United's successful 1960's, he played a major part in the Reds team. At one stage in their respective careers father and son actually played on the same side. They were both, at the time, with Stockport County and on the last day of the 1950-51 season were selected to play as inside-forwards against Hartlepool.

Another unusual combination was that of the Haydock brothers. William, the elder of the two brothers, was a City player between March 1959 and March 1961, whilst his brother Frank was with United from December 1958 to August 1963. However, they did not get to play against each other in a derby as their appearances for the Manchester clubs were limited. Two other brothers were Matt and Billy Gillespie who even played against each other at the turn of the century when Billy played for City and Matt for Newton Heath.

Harry Rowley - started out with United and, after a spell with City, returned to Old Trafford after a brief stint at Oldham. He is pictured here wearing the cherry and white hooped shirts worn by United during their Second Division days in the 1930's.

Maine Road To Old Trafford And Back Again

There are three players in the long history of the local rivalry who started their derby career playing for City, then at some stage played for United before returning to the Blues.

They are Billy Meredith, Denis Law and Peter Barnes.

These players featured in derby matches at each stage of their Manchester career.

Billy Meredith was in fact an even greater journeyman between the two clubs. He started his long career with City in 1894 as an amateur, and moved to United in December 1906. During the First World War he returned to the Blues, but once League football resumed in 1919 he was back with United until July 1921 when he returned to Maine Road to finish his career with City.

A player who has done the reverse and started out with the Reds and returned to Old Trafford via a spell with the Blues is Harry Rowley who first joined United in 1928. He moved to the Blues in 1931 and then, after a brief spell with Oldham Athletic, returned to United in 1934.

DERBY MANAGERS

Note: *To enable a fair comparison of a manager's derby record in the following lists, 2 points are given for a win and 1 point for a drawn game. Those who were not at the helm for a derby match are not included.*

United Managers

Manager	Seasons	Played	Won	Drawn	Lost	Points
Alf Albut	1889-1900	11	6	3	2	15
James West	1900-1903	2	1	1	0	3
Ernest Mangnall	1903-1912	10	4	5	1	13
J.J. Bentley	1912-1914	4	2	0	2	4
John Robson	1914-1921	6	1	4	1	6
John Chapman	1921-1926	5	1	1	3	3
Herbert Bamlett	1927-1931	6	1	1	4	3
Scott Duncan	1932-1937	1	1	0	0	2
Walter Crickmer	1931-1932 &1937-1945	1	0	0	1	0
Sir Matt Busby	1945-1969 & 1970-1971	39	16	13	10	45
Wilf McGuinness	1969-1970	6	1	1	4	3
Frank O'Farrell	1971-1972	3	0	1	2	1
Tommy Docherty	1972-1977	9	4	3	2	11
Dave Sexton	1977-1981	8	3	2	3	8
Ron Atkinson	1981-1986	7	2	5	0	9
Alex Ferguson	1986-1991	6	3	2	1	8

Note: *Clarence Hilditch (1926-27) was manager but never took charge of a derby side.*

*A giant figure in United's derby history, **Sir Matt Busby** was in charge of the club for 39 derby matches and lost only 10 of them.*

City Managers

Manager	Seasons	Played	Won	Drawn	Lost	Points
Lawrence Furniss	1889-1893	1	0	0	1	0
Joshua Parlby	1893-1895	2	0	0	2	0
Sam Ormerod	1895-1902	8	2	3	3	7
Tom Maley	1902-1906	2	0	1	1	1
Harry Newbould	1906-1912	10	1	5	4	7
Ernest Mangnall	1912-1924	12	4	4	4	12
David Ashworth	1924-1925	1	0	1	0	1
Peter Hodge	1926-1932	6	4	1	1	9
Wilf Wild	1932-1946	2	1	0	1	2
Jock Thomson	1947-1950	6	0	4	2	4
Leslie McDowall	1950-1963	26	8	7	11	23
Joe Mercer	1965-1972	15	7	4	4	18
Malcolm Allison	1972-1973 & 1979-1980	4	2	1	1	5
Johnny Hart	1973	1	0	1	0	1
Ron Saunders	1973-1974	1	0	1	0	1
Tony Book	1974-1979	11	3	2	6	8
John Bond	1980-1983	4	1	3	0	5
John Benson	1983	1	0	0	1	0
Billy McNeill	1983-1986	2	0	1	1	1
Jimmy Frizzell	1986-1987	3	0	1	2	1
Mel Machin	1987-1989	1	1	0	0	2
Howard Kendall	1989-1990	2	0	2	0	2
Peter Reid	1990-1991	1	0	0	1	0

Note (1): *Sam Cowan (1946-47) and George Poyser (1963-65) were managers but never took charge of a derby side..*

Note (2): *The League game of 23/1/26 (United 1 City 6) and the F.A. Cup semi-final game of 27/3/26 (City 3 United 0) were played out under the rather unlikely management team of the Board of Directors. It could therefore be said that City Chairman Albert Alexander Snr., who took the leading role, was responsible for two of City's greatest victories.*

Les McDowall - *renowned for his coolness when he joined City as a player before World War Two, he led the club to promotion in his first season in charge in 1950 and two F.A. Cup finals followed as he then developed the revolutionary deep-lying centre-forward tactics around Don Revie. He managed City in 26 derby games - more than any other City boss - between 1950 and 1963.*

DERBY DOUBLES

The following are the seasons in which one of the Manchester clubs won both derbies played:

United	City
1894-95*	1930-31
1908-09	1954-55
1949-50	1969-70
1956-57	
1960-61	
1961-62	
1976-77	
1978-79	

* as Newton Heath

Colin Bell in action against United at Maine Road in November 1972 when the Blues won 3-0 and the midfielder scored twice. The 1972-73 season was one of the 22 occasions that City have finished above United in the League table.

Despite the near misses or disasters of a particular season, the burning issue for most City or United fans is that they finished the campaign in a higher position than their rivals.

To solve any arguments, here is the complete record of which club finished top dog for all the seasons when both clubs shared the same division. These details, when compared alongside page 324 (Different Divisions) gives an overall record for both clubs.

City placed above United (22 times)

1895-96*/ 1897-98*/ 1898-99*/1902-03*/1913-14/ 1914-15/ 1919-20/ 1920-21/ 1921-22/ 1928-29/ 1929-30/ 1930-31/ 1936-37/ 1957-58/ 1961-62/ 1967-68/ 1971-72/ 1972-73/1973-74/ 1976-77/ 1977-78/ 1990-91

United placed above City (35 times)

1894-95*/ 1896-97*/ (both as N. Heath) 1906-07/ 1907-08/ 1908-09/ 1910-11/ 1911-12/ 1912-13/ 1925-26/ 1947-48/ 1948-49/ 1949-50/ 1951-52/ 1952-53/ 1953-54/ 1954-55/ 1955-56/ 1956-57/ 1958-59/ 1959-60/ 1960-61/ 1962-63/ 1966-67/ 1968-69/ 1969-70/ 1970-71/ 1975-76/ 1978-79/ 1979-80/ 1980-81/ 1981-82/ 1982-83/ 1985-86/ 1986-87/ 1989-90

* Refers to when clubs were in Division Two

The following attendance facts and figures all relate solely to the Manchester derby. We have taken the most accurate information located from many sources on both the City and United sides to provide a comprehensive list of all relevant statistics. As can be seen from the lowest all-time derby figure, we have had, in some cases, to rely on the reports of the period to show an attendance estimate. For that reason, we have provided the additional figures for games played at Maine Road and Old Trafford. Again, all average attendance detail is based on information available and, again, we have shown averages for both teams at home as well as averages at Maine Road and Old Trafford.

The Cup averages are based on all F.A. Cup, League Cup and Charity Shield matches between the two clubs, with all City's home games played at Maine Road, whilst four United home games were played at Old Trafford and one at North Road.

As is clear from all this information, the Manchester Derby has always been well attended - the 10,000 in 1891 and 1895 were large attendances for the period. The two 'low' attendances at Old Trafford and Maine Road listed below are a result of two factors: firstly, the Maine Road game was the only derby match to be 'live' on television, and secondly, segregation problems at Old Trafford following the Hillsborough disaster restricted City's allocation of tickets. Perhaps the most interesting statistic of all is the last which reveals that a total of more than 6 million people have seen the Manchester rivals meet in the first class competition.

Derby Attendance Records

Record	Gate	Venue	Date	Derby Number
League highest	78,000	Maine Road	20/9/1947	45
League highest	68,796	Old Trafford	12/9/1936	43
Highest other than League	74,723	Maine Road	29/1/1955	F.A.Cup Rd 4
Lowest League	32,440	Maine Road	26/10/1986	109
Lowest League	40,274	Old Trafford	3/2/1990	112
Lowest all-time derby *(based on newspaper reports of the period)*	10,000	North Road	3/10/1891	F.A.Cup Rd 1 Q
	10,000	Bank Street	5/10/1895	3

Average League Derby Attendance

Overall	48,719	(5,553,917)	
With City at home	47,696	(2,718,660)	57 games
With United at home	49,741	(2,835,251)	57 games (inc. 2 matches at Maine Road)
At Maine Road	55,758	(2,341,835)	42 games (inc. 2 matches with United 'at home')
At Old Trafford	53,480	(2,460,076)	46 games

Average Cup Derby Attendance

Overall	50,394	(503,937)	10 games
With City at home	52,800	(211,199)	4 games
With United at home	49,258	(246,288)	5 games

Average Overall Attendance
(Inc. League, FA Cup, League Cup & Charity Shield)

48,854	(6,057,854)	124 games (inc. 1 match at Bramall Lane)

What a difficult but enthralling task it was to choose the best United and City elevens from the near century of derby matches. In the end we could have chosen six teams to represent the Reds and Blues, there were so many good players to choose from. Obviously our final choice was going to be somewhat subjective and we are sure we will have left out lots of people's favourites, but as the man said football is a game all about opinion.

The sides on the following pages are NOT meant to be the greatest ever United and City teams. The sole criteria for selection is performance in the derby match. Selection is based on; number of appearances, position played and goals scored. The players with the maximum scores within this context were those selected. One or two corners have been cut and in some positions a number of players had similar claims, but as authors we had the final power of managerial decision.

MANCHESTER UNITED TEAM

1) ALEX STEPNEY
2) JOHNNY CAREY (Captain)
3) ROGER BYRNE
4) DUNCAN EDWARDS
5) BILL FOULKES
6) MARTIN BUCHAN
7) STEVE COPPELL
8) JOE SPENCE
9) BOBBY CHARLTON
10) DENIS LAW
11) GEORGE BEST

Substitutes:
Dennis Viollet and Arthur Albiston
Manager:
Sir Matt Busby CBE

Traditionally, United have never been recognised as a club famed for its goalkeepers and selection for this position was uncluttered. The defence has a stable and experienced look to it and in the tradition of the Club the accent of this side is on attack. The Club has had such marvellous forwards over the years that selection for these positions was particularly difficult. However, with an inspirational midfield of Edwards and Charlton playing behind such a potent forward line goals would be assured. With Sir Matt Busby at the helm and playing a daring 4-2-4 this team would take some beating.

Steve Cawley

ALEX STEPNEY (Goalkeeper)

Alex started his impressive Old Trafford career against the Blues in 1966 and went on to make the second highest number of derby appearances of all United players. A cool and agile 'keeper he became one of the few United players to win virtually all the major honours of the game; League Championship medal, European Cup winners medal and an F.A. Cup winners medal. In terms of derby confrontation Alex would not like reminding of the gaffe which allowed City to progress to the 1970 League Cup Final. Happily for United fans this was not in line with the usual dependability he afforded the United defence throughout his career, as his six derby clean sheets testify.

JOHNNY CAREY (Right back)

A mark of this player's stature in the annals of great United players is that he is chosen captain despite the presence of other great United skippers in this line up. Gentleman John was epitomised as Busby's brain on the field as he captained the

As far as United were concerned I can hear the cries now: what no Robson, Hughes, Stapleton, Kidd, Macari, Stiles, Taylor, Delaney, Rowley just to name a few. Well, I did say selection was difficult. Certain factors determined selection and in the process this meant certain 'greats' didn't make it. For instance there are times when one of the sides is in the Second Division and so players could be enjoying superb careers but in derby terms they are unable to gain credit points. Bryan Robson is a good example of this as in his first eight seasons with United, City were in Division Two for four of them. The tragedy of the Munich air crash meant many great players could not be considered, although there are two wonderful exceptions to this.

maestro's first great side to the F.A. Cup in 1948 and the League Championship in 1952. The 1948-49 season saw him named Footballer of the Year. Carey had the rare distinction of playing for both the Republic of Ireland and Northern Ireland. All his derby appearances came after the war and he was on the losing side on only one occasion. A mark of the all round ability that he would offer

this side was the fact that he turned out in nine different positions for the club over his career. However in this team of all the talents, he takes the right back spot where his cool resourcefulness, intelligent reading of the game and immaculate distribution would enhance any side.

ROGER BYRNE (Left back)

Local boy Roger Byrne, the 'father of the Babes', takes the left back spot. A fast, stylish, intelligent player, good in the air and a strong tackler with whom few wingers relished a battle. As a full back he was ahead of his time, overlapping and initiating forward movements, particularly in combination with Duncan Edwards with whom he had an almost tele-

pathic understanding. In this team he would probably be entrusted with the penalty kicks, where he had the reputation as a lethal marksman who rarely missed. From the time of his debut in 1951 he was involved in many derby contests and he had captained the 'Babes' to two Championships and one Wembley appearance to add to his thirty three England Caps, before his untimely death in the Munich air crash in 1958. However his indomitable spirit would live on in this side.

BILL FOULKES (Central defender)

The long serving Bill Foulkes would play centre half despite playing a lot of his earlier career at full back. Another one of the home produced 'Babes', he was a survivor of the Munich crash and, as captain of the side in the immediate aftermath, his qualities of leadership allowed United to get through one of the most testing times in their history.

Although maybe not as polished as a Hilditch or a Roberts his qualities of utter reliability and no-nonsense defensive talents enabled the skilful forwards Busby assembled to win the trophies in the 50's and 60's. Bill did not score many goals in his record 682 appearances for the Club, but one of his nine goals came in the 1967 derby and it helped United win their last Championship.

MARTIN BUCHAN (Central defender)

Martin Buchan seems the ideal player to operate just behind the redoubtable Foulkes. It may have surprised some fans how many derby appearances this polished defender made in his

11 year United career. Joining United in 1972 from Aberdeen he saw the Reds through the troubled early 70's, was captain and, some would say, the inspiration behind the exciting young Docherty side of the mid 1970's. He captained United in three F.A. Cup Finals in '76, '77 and '79. Thirty four Scottish caps seems a modest reward for a defender of true international class. Intelligent reading of the game allied to the

perfectly timed tackle or interception meant that Buchan was rarely embarrassed by any forward. He completes an authoritative defence of players who had all captained United at some point in their post war history.

DUNCAN EDWARDS (Midfield)

Perhaps the greatest United player of all time, this giant of a player makes an awesome combination with Charlton in the midfield of this team. Considered by many to have been the most complete player to have graced not just United, but the whole Football League, Duncan made his debut in 1953 at the tender age of sixteen. Within two years he

was an England international and by the age of twenty one had two Championship medals and a Wembley appearance behind him. An immaculate passer of the ball, particularly over long distance, a shuddering tackler, possessor of a thunderous shot and an excellent header of the ball he was the nucleus of the immortal Busby Babes. Duncan had a penchant for spectacular long range goals and two strikes in derbies in 1957 helped United to memorably crushing wins. Like Roger Byrne, Duncan was tragically killed in the Munich crash. There is no saying what he might have achieved in the game, had he lived on. As it is, what he did achieve stands as a wonderful testimony to a unique player.

STEVE COPPELL (Right winger)

It might surprise some to see Steve Coppell take this position, where he just edges out the legendary Billy Meredith (who suffered from making rather too many appearances for the other lot!). Certainly the unassuming Coppell would not be the first name on many lists for a forward position, given the wealth of talent the Reds have enjoyed. How-

ever, the facts speak for themselves and against the Blues Steve Coppell was a mightily effective player. Not just in terms of his many appearances, which stand testimony to his consistency at the club, but also with his goals tally, a very healthy ratio for a winger. If one bears in mind his premature retirement at the age of 28, his feats are all the more impressive. So Coppell, probably playing as a straight winger, as he began his United career in '75, would be expected to provide the darting run, accurate cross and of course the odd goal.

JOE SPENCE (Forward)

In this line-up Joe Spence, hero of United in the 20's and 30's would effectively be playing at centre forward. In one of the leanest periods in United's history Spence shone out as a player of real class and charisma. In derby terms his record is simply second to none. He was a first choice player throughout his fourteen years at the club. Operating mainly at centre forward his chief attribute was a nose for goals. An excellent header of the ball, his intelligent, positional play around the penalty area meant he was always a man to be watched. As City threatened to dominate Manchester football in the inter-war years Spence was often United's only reprisal. His derby hat-trick of 1921, coming just seven days after the famed Horace Barnes and the Blues had humiliated United, probably stands as one of the highlights of Joe's career.

BOBBY CHARLTON (Midfield)

Having the most appearances and goals against the Blues the legendary Bobby Charlton has no trouble getting into this side. He would play in the midfield with Edwards. Bobby Charlton **is** Manchester United and a side without him would be incomplete. In a career with United from 1955 to 1973 he won virtually every honour the game had to offer. In this line-up he would be given the slightly more forward role to Edwards and would be expected to put that left foot to good effect. Although renowned for his feats with United and his century-plus caps with England, Bobby always proved a thorn in the side of City - firstly as a flying winger, then as a sharp-shooting inside left and, from '66 onwards, as a masterly midfield schemer. Throughout the period he retained that characteristic balance of grace and power that was unique to one of the maestros of the game.

DENIS LAW (Forward)

Denis the 'King' would play as an out and out forward, next to Spence in this team. A brilliant striker, Law was probably at his playing peak in his United years between 1963 and 1967. Indeed during these years he would probably have walked into any World XI. Brilliant in all areas where one would expect a striker to excel, he had a good shot in either foot, was a magnificent leaper and header of the ball and had the all-round skill to create as well as to score. However, many would claim his most special talent was his unerring anticipation of the half chance. Wherever this occurred the quicksilver Scot was onto it first, goal scored, arm speared into the air. A mark of his stature is that, of course, he did have two seasons with the Blues and scored a rather notorious goal in 1974 - yet he has always been held in the highest regard by United fans.

GEORGE BEST (Left winger)

For a short time in the late 60's George Best was, in many people's opinion, one of - if not the greatest - players in the world. Genius can be an over used term (especially when selecting all-time great teams) but George possessed this gift. A rare talent who could win games by, seemingly, feats of sheer magic. By only remembering this marvellous goal, or that amazing dribble, many forget what a complete player Best was. He was an excellent header of the ball, often out-jumping bigger men to score. A vastly under-rated tackler, he was capable of defence-splitting passes from any part of the field and could be lethal in any dead ball situation. That said, George's *tour de force* was the mazy dribble, cutting in off either foot or wing, leaving countless defenders in his wake and as often as not the ball in the net. Georgie simply strolls into this side.

MANCHESTER CITY TEAM

1) BERT TRAUTMANN
2) TONY BOOK (Captain)
3) WILLIE DONACHIE
4) MIKE DOYLE
5) TOMMY BOOTH
6) ALAN OAKES
7) MIKE SUMMERBEE
8) COLIN BELL
9) FRANCIS LEE
10) JOE HAYES
11) ROY CLARKE

Substitutes:
Roy Paul and Tommy Browell
Manager:
Joe Mercer OBE

As far as City were concerned, selection for every position was extremely difficult commencing with probably the most difficult of all - the goalkeeper. With such greats as Joe Corrigan, Frank Swift, Bert Trautmann and, before them, Walter Smith and Charlie Williams all playing in derbies, it was certainly not easy. I eventually had a straight choice between the derby record-appearance holder, Joe Corrigan, and the legendary Bert Trautmann. Sadly, Frank Swift, like so many players from City's Sam Cowan inspired successful 1930's, had featured in too few derbies, as United were in the Second Division for much of this period. I chose Trautmann, as his reputation was often enhanced by his brilliance in derby matches.

Moving on to the rest of the team, I have chosen a particularly strong back four, with Tony Book adopting the captaincy. The midfield, in my opinion, is extremely exciting with Mike Summerbee just beating Billy Meredith to the right-wing place by a whisker, whilst loyal servant Roy Clarke attacks down the left-flank. The two centre-forwards in this 4-2-4 formation are Francis Lee and Joe Hayes, who between them have scored twenty goals in just thirty-two derby matches.

As well as the standard eleven players we decided to choose two substitutes. My first thoughts were to include City's legendary Billy Meredith, who was the main reason for Manchester's first successes. However, I doubt if Meredith would have 'approved' of substitutes and so reluctantly left him for United's possible selection as he actually featured in more League derbies for The Reds. I chose a defender and a forward, with Fifties hero Roy Paul at the back and Twenties star Tommy Browell providing the necessary fire up-front. In my opinion, the side, with manager Joe Mercer controlling things, is unbeatable. It would take an extremely strong defence to hold back City's skilful forwards and attacking midfielders and, if in the unlikely event, United were to beat the Blues' strong defence, they would still have to face one of the world's all-time greatest goalkeepers! City will play a simple 4-2-4 formation.

Gary James

he featured in was the 1968 'Championship Match' which the Blues won 3-1 against the odds at Old Trafford. He also featured in the League Cup Semi-Final derbies of 1969/70. After his playing career finished he first became Assistant Manager and then Manager of the Blues. His first derby match as Manager was the unforgettable 1-0 victory at the tail end of the 1973/4 season. After Book's highly successful spell as City Manager had ended, more derby success was achieved when, whilst he was Youth Team Coach, the Blues beat United in the FA Youth Cup Final of 1986. This was the first ever national final between City and United and it was fitting that Tony Book, along with Glyn Pardoe, was responsible once again for bringing honour to his beloved City.

With Tony Book influencing this 'all-time best' derby line-up the Blues simply cannot fail to win.

WILLIE DONACHIE (Left back)

Donachie's introduction to the derby came in May 1971 when he was just nineteen years old. Over the course of the next nine years he played in 15 League derbies and in the League Cup derby of the 1975/76 season. He was acclaimed as one of the best full-backs of the period and became a regular in the Scottish national squad, winning thirty-five full caps and three at Under-23 level. Donachie joined City as a junior in 1968, with the high points of his City career coming in the League Cup Finals of 1973/74 (when he was also ever-present in the League) and 1975/76. He, along with Joe Corrigan, was also ever-present in the 1976/77 season when the Blues finished runners-up to Liverpool, in spite of losing both derby matches to United 3-1. With his fast play and skilful ball control Donachie delighted the supporters whilst maintaining a strong defensive record. His performance in the derby remained consistent throughout his City career and it was somewhat fitting that his last match against United ended in a 2-0 victory for the Maine Men. Donachie was greatly missed when he left City in March 1980, although City supporters were pleased when, in 1990, he helped former team-mate Joe Royle take Oldham Athletic to Wembley and then in 1991 to the Second Division championship title.

BERT TRAUTMANN (Goalkeeper)

Bert Trautmann, one of the world's truly great 'keepers, joined the Blues from St. Helens Town in November 1949. His first taste of a Manchester derby came on New Year's Eve 1949 when he was still attempting to overcome the hostility of the crowd. Many supporters were against him at first because of his German nationality, but over the course of the next fifteen years his performances for City, and his friendly nature, made him one of the most popular players of all time. He kept six clean sheets in the derby, including the 1955 Cup match and, from the time of his signing right up to his retirement, he featured in all but three derby matches. He only missed two of these games (one being in the Charity Shield) because he was still recovering from a broken neck sustained in the 1956 FA Cup Final.

As well as appearing in 23 derbies, Trautmann won representative honours when he played two matches, with City team mate Denis Law, for The Football League in 1960. It is generally accepted that he would have regularly featured in West Germany's national side if it had not been for the fact that he was playing in England so soon after the war. In 1956 he was deservedly voted Footballer of the Year, and in 1964 his testimonial was watched by a crowd of almost 48,000 with many more locked out. Such was the popularity of the derby's greatest goalkeeper.

TONY BOOK (Right back)

Tony Book's influence on the derby is remarkable. Of the 16 derbies he played in eight ended in a City victory, whilst four others were drawn. As captain during this period, he led the club through one of its most successful times, not just in the derby but also nationally. Probably the most important derby

MIKE DOYLE (Central defender)

Doyle featured in an amazing total of 24 derby matches for City between 1962 and 1978, only two short of record holder Joe Corrigan. He also scored two derby goals - the first coming in the 2-1 victory in March 1970, and the second in the following derby, City's 4-1 win in December of the same year.

Locally-born Doyle joined the club from Stockport Boys and progressed through the team until he made his debut against Cardiff in 1965. In September 1966 he made history with his first derby appearance as he came on as substitute for Bobby Kennedy. This was the first substitution ever in a Manchester derby. For the next derby Doyle was included in the starting line-up, and from then on established himself as a regular in the City side. In 1975 he became captain, and a year later he made the first of his five international appearances for England. In addition to these honours Doyle played in eight Under-23 Internationals and two Football League matches. His final derby match was on 5th March 1977 and the following year he was signed by Stoke for £50,000 after injury had reduced his appearances with the Blues. Mike Doyle's single-minded determination clearly helped the rest of the City side although he was perhaps a little too zealous in 1974 when, along with United's Lou Macari, he was sent off in controversial circumstances. None could fault, however, his overall performance in the derby matches when his partisan influence was much needed and, more often than not, greatly in evidence.

TOMMY BOOTH (Central defender)

Booth would probably be the surprise choice of this derby line-up; yet what few people fail to realise is that he featured in seventeen League and four Cup derbies, making him the fifth most selected City player. His first derby appearance came when just nineteen, in the 1-0 City victory at Old Trafford on March 8th 1969. In between that appearance and his last, over a decade later, Booth established himself, first as a centre-half and then, after Colin Bell's horrific injury, as a midfielder. Whilst playing as a centre-half he was often compared by his manager Joe Mercer to the old fashioned exponents of the art such as Stan Cullis, and was certainly admired by many as he made four international appearances for the England Under-23 side. Booth's career at City was highly successful as he won an FA Cup Winners medal as well as winners' medals in the European Cup Winners' Cup, and two in the League Cup. Despite the success, there were also periods of major upheaval and change at City. Booth played under no less than six different Managers at Maine Road, and yet adapted well and remained with the club right up to September 1981 when he moved to Preston North End for £30,000.

Booth, the typical 'Local Hero', made his final derby appearance on 21st February 1981 when the Blues beat the Reds 1-0, just as they had when his derby career commenced all those years before.

ALAN OAKES (Midfield)

Quite surprisingly Alan Oakes has not appeared in the most derbies for City, although he is second placed with 25 outings. The main reasons for this are twofold. Firstly, City and United were in different divisions for four of his seasons with the club and secondly, he only appeared in four derbies in his first four full seasons. When he joined City in 1958 he joined a team in decline as the side that had won the FA Cup only two years earlier were struggling in Division One. Oakes' first derby appearance was in the no-score draw on February 6th 1960 and because of the overall performance of City at that time, he had to wait until 27th March 1968 before he played in a derby-winning side. From that point on glory followed. Oakes appeared for the Football League in 1969 as he was rewarded for quietly going about his business, helping to turn City into a dominant side. His powerful style of play and skilful passing ensured his place in the team throughout his City career. In fact in his last season (1975/76) Oakes was one of the driving forces in the side that won the League Cup.

After a City career that proved highly successful his last match was, of course, the Manchester derby on 4th May 1976 when he came on as substitute (for only the third time in his City career) for Mike Doyle. What a way to go out!

MIKE SUMMERBEE (Right wing)

Summerbee's pride and passion when playing for City against United was always noticeable. Without doubt he loved the Blues and always gave his full commitment to the task of seeing City win - nothing else would do. Joe Mercer bought him from Swindon Town during City's Second Division days. He was in fact Mercer's first signing, and Summerbee soon became a hero for the masses of Blues fans. He played at centre-forward in his first derby on 17th September 1966, but was in his regular number 7 shirt for the next match against United. Over the course of the next nine years he played in fourteen League and four Cup derbies scoring three goals. His first derby League goal was in the 1-0 victory on 8th March 1969, but his most important derby goal had come in the second leg of the 1969 League Cup semi-final which ended with a 2-2 draw and the Blues going through to the final 4-3 on aggregate.

His last League derby was the controversial 1-0 City victory on 27th April, 1974, with his last ever derby being the 1-0 League Cup defeat on 9th October 1975. His career at City ended on 13th June 1975 when he joined Burnley for £25,000.

Summerbee's determination and love of everything Blue is still missed at Maine Road today. No doubt he is proud of the fact that the Blues were only defeated in four of the eighteen derbies he appeared in.

COLIN BELL (Midfield)

Colin Bell is not only the third highest derby goalscorer and joint fifth in the table of appearances, he is also, arguably, the greatest player ever to play in a sky-blue shirt in the derby. His courage, stamina, speed, skill, enthusiasm and strength all combined to make him probably the most important player in the club's long history. His derby career commenced in September 1966 and, from that point on, his influence and exceptional skill helped the Blues to great success over the Reds. Bell, naturally, featured in all the major derbies, yet it was usually at a cost. In 1968, he scored one of City's goals in the 3-1 victory at Old Trafford that set them up for the League Championship, but was later stretchered off, missing the next four League games. In truth, the rigours of the Manchester derby cost Colin Bell much too dearly. No City supporter can ever forget the sad League Cup derby match of November 1975. The Blues won the game 4-0, yet the result was overshadowed by Bell's devastating knee injury which caused him to miss the whole of the following season. He fought hard in an endeavour to return to full-fitness and, on Boxing Day 1977, the supporters flocked to Maine Road to see his return. He came on as substitute against Newcastle to one of the greatest and most richly deserved ovations ever heard at Maine Road and, once again, his influence helped the Blues to a convincing 4-0 victory. Although Bell was never quite the same mobile force again he did play in two more derby matches, and his commitment and enthusiasm for the game was still unflagging. During 1990 he returned to City as Coach to the 'B' Team - a move greatly approved of by the supporters. Colin Bell, with his 48 England caps and his regularly outstanding performances, remains, in the eyes of thousands who saw him play, simply, "The Greatest".

ton mill in August 1953. He scored four early goals in a trial match and was quickly signed up by Manager Les McDowall whose own knowledge of the game was outstanding. Joe Hayes' career with City spanned twelve years and he played in two contrasting periods. The first was City's highly successful mid-fifties when he featured in two FA Cup finals, scoring in the second when the Blues won the Cup. The second period was City's struggling early Sixties spell when the Blues were relegated in 1963. Hayes was consistent, twice finishing the season's leading scorer, a record that marked him out as one of the greatest goal-poachers of his period. His last derby was the 1-1 draw on 15th May 1963 and at the age of 27 he should have gone on and played in many more derbies. However, a serious knee injury in a game against Bury the following season limited his chances with the Blues and in June 1965 he moved on to Barnsley. Who knows how many goals and what rewards he may have earned had his Maine Road career lasted until City's return to the First Division in 1966.

FRANCIS LEE (Forward)

Lee's derby record is incredible; of the 15 League and Cup derbies he played in, only two ended in defeat (the 1970 FA Cup match and the League game on 5th May 1971) and he scored a total of 10 goals, making him the joint highest scorer with Joe Hayes. Lee joined City on 9th October 1967 for £60,000 from Bolton, and made his first derby appearance in the 'Championship derby' of 27th March 1968. In that game he scored the first of his 10 derby goals, ironically from the penalty spot, where he became "something of an expert". His bustling, mischievous style of play was loved by the supporters and helped City attain success after success during his seven season career at Maine Road. On 12th December 1970, Lee made history in the derby by becoming only the fifth player to score a derby hat-trick as City won the game 4-1. With his determined attitude Lee became a regular for England whilst with the Blues, making 27 appearances for his country as well as representative appearances for The Football League and a United Kingdom XI.

His last ever League appearance for City was in the derby match on the last day of the 1973/74 season before he was transferred to Derby County where he helped The Rams to the League Championship. Francis Lee's determination helped him to succeed where others would have failed, and his penalty expertise and goalscoring prowess are vital in this line-up.

ROY CLARKE (Left winger)

Roy Clarke joined City on 23rd May 1947 and between then and his transfer to Stockport in September 1958 he made 18 derby appearances for the Blues. His first taste of derby rivalry came on 20th September 1947 when he played in the no-score draw before 78,000 supporters - a record for the derby. The powerful left-winger featured in all the major derbies of the period, including the Cup match of 1955, and even scored two goals in League derbies - one on 30th August 1952 and one other on 2nd February 1957. Before joining City, Clarke worked in the South Wales coal mines and became noted for his footballing skills whilst playing for Cardiff City. He was an outstanding attacker with a terrific shot and was, undoubtedly, one of City's greatest players as they were re-born, after a brief spell in the Second Division. Clarke became a regular Welsh International winning 22 caps and he also won international recognition for a different sport when, in 1939, he was a Welsh Schools' Baseball International.

Roy Clarke's last derby for the Blues was on 31st August 1957 when City were defeated 4-1. After his distinguished career was over he returned to Maine Road to run the City Social Club. After years of success in that job Clarke retired, although even now nothing can keep him away from the excitement of Maine Road on match days. Roy Clarke was, without doubt, one of the greatest wingers ever to play in a Manchester derby.

JOE HAYES (Forward)

Although records show that Joe Hayes scored 10 goals in 17 derby games for City, he did actually score an eleventh goal. Sadly, the extra goal will never count, as it was scored in the abandoned League game played on 27th August 1960. Nevertheless Hayes' record in the derby is tremendous and he even scored in his very first derby, the FA Cup match on 29th January 1955. His career with City began while he was working at a cot-

When They Were Apart

Listed below are the details of what happened to the two clubs when they were in different divisions.

Year	CITY Division	Position	Trophies	UNITED Division	Position	Trophies
1892/93	+2	5	-	*1	16	-
1893/94	+2	13	-	*1	16	-
1899/1900	1	7	-	*2	4	
1900/01	1	11	-	*2	10	-
1901/02	1	18	-	*2	15	-
1903/04	1	2	FA Cup Winners	2	3	-
1904/05	1	3	-	2	3	-
1905/06	1	5	-	2	2	-
1909/10	2	1	2nd Div.Champs	1	5	-
1922/23	1	8	-	2	4	-
1923/24	1	11	-	2	14	-
1924/25	1	10	-	2	2	-
1926/27	2	3	-	1	15	-
1927/28	2	1	2nd Div.Champs	1	18	-
1931/32	1	14	-	2	12	-
1932/33	1	16	FA Cup Finalists	2	6	-
1933/34	1	5	FA Cup Winners	2	20	-
1934/35	1	4	-	2	5	-
1935/36	1	9	-	2	1	2nd Div.Champs
1937/38	1	21	Charity Shield	2	2	-
1938/39	2	5	-	1	14	-
1946/47	2	1	2nd Div.Champs	1	2	-
1950/51	2	2	-	1	2	-
1963/64	2	6	-	1	2	-
1964/65	2	11	-	1	1	League Champions
1965/66	2	1	2nd Div.Champs	1	4	Joint Charity Shield
1974/75	1	8	-	2	1	2nd Div.Champs
1983/84	2	4	-	1	4	Charity Shield
1984/85	2	3	-	1	4	FA Cup Winners
1987/88	2	9	-	1	2	-
1988/89	2	2	-	1	11	-

The above record shows that City have spent 16 seasons in a higher division than United, whilst the Reds themselves have been a division above the Blues on 15 occasions.

Whilst in a different division to United, City have won:-

2 F.A. Cups, 1 Charity Shield, 4 Second Division Championship's and have been F.A. Cup Finalists.

Over the same period United have won:-

The League Championship, 1 F.A. Cup, the Charity Shield (twice - once as joint holders) and 2 Second Division Championship's.

*Note: + = as Ardwick, * = as Newton Heath*

Manchester's Glory

Detailed below are the occasions when Manchester first won each of the major trophies. In addition we have provided Manchester's most recent success in each trophy.

Trophy	First success	Most recent success
Division Two Champions	City 1898/99	United 1974/75
F.A. Cup	City 1903/04	United 1989/90
League Championship	United 1907/08	City 1967/68
Charity Shield	United 1908/09	United 1990/91*
F.A. Youth Cup	United 1952/53	City 1985/86
European Cup	United 1967/68	-
European Cup-Winners' Cup	City 1969/70	United 1990/91
League Cup	City 1969/70	City 1975/76

Shared with Liverpool

Manchester City in 1903-04. A season of achievement for the Blues, but no derby meetings with United who were at that time in Division Two. They were also the first of the two great Manchester clubs to lift the F.A. Cup in this season.
Back: *T.E. Maley (Manager), S. Frost, W. Gillespie, J. McMahon, T. Hynds, J. Hillman, S. Ashworth, J. Broad (Trainer).* **Front:** *H. Burgess, G. Livingstone, W. Meredith, A. Turnbull, F. Booth.*

A joint fixture list for **Manchester United** *and* **Manchester City** *in 1935-36, but the Blues were in Division One and United in Division Two.*

Date	Attendance	Result		City	United
25/09/15	20,000	United 1	City 1	Barnes	Halligan
25/12/15	20,000	City 2	United 1	Taylor, Barnes	Halligan
25/03/16	15,000	United 0	City 2	Taylor, Cartwright	-
29/04/16	18,000	City 2	United 1	Barnes, opp.o.g.	Crossley
18/11/16	8,000	United 2	City 1	Hoad	Woodcock, Anderson
03/03/17	15,000	City 1	United 0	Barnes	-
07/04/17	14,000	United 5	City 1	Newton	Anderson 3, Woodcock 2
21/04/17	15,000	City 0	United 1	-	Anderson
29/09/17	20,000	City 3	United 1	Lomas 2, Jones	Anderson
06/10/17	10,000	United 1	City 1	Lomas	Woodcock
29/03/18	10,000	City 3	United 0	Fletcher, Royle, Mann	-
01/04/18	10,000	United 2	City 0	-	Woodcock, Buckley
05/10/18	12,000	United 0	City 2	Kenyon, Cartwright	-
12/10/18	15,000	City 0	United 0	-	-
18/04/19	35,000	City 3	United 0	Barnes 2, Wynn	-
21/04/19	35,000	United 2	City 4	Barnes 2, Browell, Lomas	Potts, Spence
21/10/39	7,000	United 0	City 4	Herd, Heale, Doherty, Brook	-
10/02/40	5,000	City 1	United 0	Herd	-
20/04/40	21,874	**United 0	City 1	Worsley	-
22/04/40	21,596	**City 0	United 2	-	Wrigglesworth, Pearson
28/09/40	10,000	City 4	United 1	Doherty, 2, Brown, Currier	Smith
05/10/40	10,000	United 0	City 2	Currier, McShane	-
14/04/41	7,000	City 1	United 7	Currier,	Rowley 4, Pearson 2, Smith
20/12/41	7,000	City 2	United 1	Boothway 2	Morris
25/12/41	20,000	United 2	City 2	Boothway 2	Smith, Rowley
23/05/42	6,000	City 1	United 3	Stuart	Worrall 2, Whalley
07/11/42	9,301	United 2	City 1	Clark	Pearson, opp.o.g.
14/11/42	5,674	City 0	United 5	-	Bryant 2, Smith 3
06/02/43	17,577	*City 0	United 0	-	-
13/02/43	16,326	*United 1	City 1	Herd	Smith
06/03/43	28,962	**United 0	City 1	Currier	-
13/03/43	36,453	**City 2	United 0	Currier, Doherty	-
06/11/43	15,157	City 2	United 2	Burke, Boothway	Smith, Pearson
13/11/43	8,958	United 3	City 0	-	Morris, Bryant, Smith
22/01/44	12,372	*United 1	City 3	Boothway 2, Heale	Smith
29/01/44	18,569	*City 2	United 3	Williamson, Heale	Rowley 2, Smith
10/04/44	18,990	City 4	United 1	McDowall 3, Bardsley	Bryant
18/11/44	20,764	United 3	City 2	Smith 2	Morris 2, Mycock
25/11/44	18,657	City 4	United 0	Williamson 2, Smith, Doherty	-
03/02/45	30,000	*United 1	City 3	Herd 2, Dunkley	Mitten
10/02/45	22,923	City 2	United 0	Williamson, Smith	-
06/04/46	62,144	United 1	City 4	Smith 4	Aston
13/04/46	50,440	City 1	United 3	Smith	Pearson, Hanlon, Rowley

* Match counted towards League War Cup qualifying rounds
** LeagueWar Cup knock-out competition.

Notes:

During both World Wars the Football League was suspended and the Manchester clubs played each other in the League regional competitions.

Obviously, during war time attendances were much reduced due to Government crowd limits, although by the 1945-46 season, with hostilities in Europe over and most of the troops back home, the attendances returned to normal.

City came to the rescue of their neighbours in 1941. United's Old Trafford ground had been badly blitzed by bombs and City allowed United to play their home games at Maine Road.

United's 7-1 victory at Maine Road on 14th April 1941 was City's heaviest defeat at Maine Road since its opening in 1924.

Guest players were a feature of wartime soccer, particularly during the Second World War. The following lists both the Reds and the Blues who played for the 'other side'.

City players who guested for United during World War Two: P. Doherty, A. Herd, A. Emptage, S. Barkas, E. Eastwood, J.J. Robinson, G. Scales, W. Williams, W. Bootle, P. Robinson.

United players who guested for City during World War Two: J.J. Carey, J. Breedon, G. Vose, W. Porter.

W. Meredith and W. Woodcock were United players who guested for City during the First World War.

JUBILEE DERBIES

These were two matches played pre-season in 1938 and 1939 in celebration of the Football League jubilee. Nearly all the games played in August of 1938 and 1939 were some form of derby match. The aim was to raise money for a League Trust Fund that had been set up to bolster the finances of the game, although one of the main aims was that proceeds would go to assist players when their careers were over. A forerunner of the players Provident Fund, it was the idea of the then President of the Football League Charles E. Sutcliffe. The Manchester matches proved quite attractive as they allowed the Reds and Blues to meet in a season when, with City in the Second Division in 1939, this would not have occurred.

The details of these games were:

City 2 (Bray, Howe) **United 1** (Baird)
Date: 20th August 1938
Venue: Maine Road
Attendance 27,788
City: Swift, Clarke, Eastwood, McDowall, Neilson, Bray, Dunkley, Herd, Howe, Doherty, Brook.
United: Breen, Redwood, Porter, Warner, Vose, McKay, Bryant, Baird, Smith, Craven, Rowley.

United 1 (Smith)**City 1** (Milsom)
Date: 19th August 1939
Venue: Old Trafford
Attendance 20,000 (est.)
United: Breedon, Redwood, Roughton, Gladwin, Chilton, McKay, Bryant, Carey, Smith, Asquith, Wrigglesworth.
City: Swift, Sproston, Westwood, McDowall, Cardwell, Bray, Dunkley, Herd, Milsom, Doherty, Brook

MANCHESTER INTERNATIONAL TOUNAMENT

Manchester International Football Tournament
at Maine Road, Manchester
Tuesday 4th and Wednesday 5th August 1987.

TOURNAMENT BROCHURE 60p

OFFICIAL CLUB SPONSORS.
brother
The future at your fingertips.

The tournament brochure for the first and to date, only Manchester International Football Tournament.

The International Tournament was basically arranged to ensure that the Reds and the Blues met each other at some competitive level during 1987-88. City had been relegated at the end of the previous season and were keen, under new manager Mel Machin, to face United. For both teams the tournament was to be used to see how English clubs could compare to the world's top teams. At the time of the tournament it was hoped that it would become a regular feature in the Manchester football calendar. The 'Maine Road Academy' and the Old Trafford 'Theatre of Dreams' would take it in turns to stage the event. Sadly, this never materialised as, the following year, the Old Trafford pitch was relaid, preventing United from staging the competition.

The tournament, the first of its kind in England, provided Manchester's two clubs with the chance of playing against top European and South American sides with PSV Eindhoven and Athletico Mineiro providing the opposition. On the first night, the two overseas teams played each other, with Mineiro beating the Dutch to reach the final, while United beat City 3-1 in the other semi-final before a crowd of 27,000.

On the second night, before a slightly lower crowd, the Blues cheered their loyal supporters by beating the Dutch champions 3-1 to gain third place, while United easily overpowered their South American rivals 3-1 in the final.

Manchester's first, and so far only international tournament was ended by Sir Matt Busby presenting his beloved United with the trophy. This style of tournament, popular on the continent, has since been copied by the English authorities who now arrange a similar competition each year at Wembley.

FRIENDLIES AND TESTIMONIALS

This is a complete list of the 'friendly' matches played between the two Manchester clubs from pre-League days right up to the more familiar present day 'Testimonial' matches held for long-serving players from both clubs, who not surprisingly, tend to pick their Manchester rivals when choosing benefit match opposition.

Season	Team	Team
1881/82		
Nov 12	Newton Heath 3	West Gorton 0
	Att: 3,000	
Mar 4	West Gorton 2	Newton Heath 1
	Att: 5,000	
1884/85		
Jan 17	Gorton AFC 1	Newton Heath 3
	Att: 7,000	
1888/89		
Feb 26	Newton Heath 3	Ardwick 2
	Att: 12,000	
May 20	Ardwick 2	Newton Heath 1
	Att: 3,000	
1889/90		
Feb 1	Ardwick 0	Newton Heath 3
	Att: 18,000	
1890/91		
Nov 15	Newton Heath 4	Ardwick 1
	Att: 7,000	
Jan 2	Ardwick 1	Newton Heath 1
	Att: 9,000	*(Abandoned - fog)*
Feb 28	Ardwick 1	Newton Heath 3
	Att: 11,000	
1892/93		
Jan 2	Ardwick 3	Newton Heath 5
	Att: 10,000	
Mar 27	Newton Heath 3	Ardwick 2
	Att: 2,000	
Apr 10	Newton Heath 2	Ardwick 1
	Att: 3,000	
Apr 29	Ardwick 3	Newton Heath 0
	Att: 2,000	
1893/94		
Dec 25	Newton Heath 2	Ardwick 1
	Att: 6,000	
Apr 9	Ardwick 1	Newton Heath 2
	Att: 600	
1895/96		
Dec 25	City 3	Newton Heath 1
	Att: 10,000	
1896/97		
Apr 30	City 2	Newton Heath 5
	Att: 6,000	*(Manchester and Salford Cup Final)*
1897/98		
Apr 27	Newton Heath 2	City 4
	Att: 3,000	*(Healey Cup Final)*
1898/99		
Oct 29	City 2	Newton Heath 1
	Att: 6,000	
Jan 7	Newton Heath 2	City 0
	Att: 4,000	
Apr 24	Newton Heath 1	City 2
		(Healey Cup Final)

Bert Trautmann's Testimonial match at Maine Road on 15th April 1964 does not quite qualify for the list above but is of interest as players from both City and United combined to take on an All International XI. Here the great City goalkeeper greets United's **Denis Law** and **Bobby Charlton** who both donned blue shirts for the night!

*A newspaper report of an early friendly between **Ardwick** and **Newton Heath** on 29th April 1893. Ardwick won the last of four friendlies played that season 3-0.*

> **Ardwick v. Newton Heath.**—At Ardwick, before 3000 persons. The Newton Heath team were :— Rattigan, goal; Brown and Clements, backs; Hood, Perrins, and Holt, half-backs; Mathieson, Coupar, Stewart, Fitzsimmons, and Erentz, forwards. The Ardwick team was a representative one, except that Bowman deposed Milarvie. The game opened rather tamely, neither side exerting themselves particularly, although Rattigan got away a good shot from Bowman. With 15 minutes gone by, however, Morris put the finishing touch to some clever work by the Ardwick forwards, among whom Mooney and Carson were seen to advantage. Good work by Coupar and Stewart next gave the visitors a look in, but Steele saved at the expense of a corner, and the ball was taken to the other end, where Bowman was cruelly fouled when a goal seemed inevitable Displaying by far the better football, however, Ardwick soon gained their second point, Brown, in attempting to get rid of a good effort by Whittle, kicking through his own goal. The home team, who were playing with a gusty wind, were continually dangerous, but after an attack on the Heathen's citadel, Stewart and Coupar made a desperate effort to score. They were accounted for by M'Vickers, however, just as they appeared to possess a chance, and a little later Erentz put the ball out, and at half-time Ardwick led by 2 goals to nil. Playing with the wind, the Newton Heath men had the better of some tame business for the first five minutes, but at the expiration of that time the Ardwick men began to play much better, and some fool tactics were resorted to, particularly by the visitors, and from one of the free kicks which were awarded, Hopkins almost scored. After a little further pressure by the Ardwick men, which was brought about principally as the result of hard play by Whittle, Hopkins, Morris, Yates, and Carson, Mathieson by a fine run took operations to the other end, where free kicks for fouls in dangerous positions against Ardwick almost resulted in Newton Heath scoring The visitors at this point made strenuous efforts to score, and some keen struggles took place immediately in front of the home goal, but the defence came out of the ordeal manfully, and some capital combined play by Middleton, Morris, and Yates caused Newton Heath to fall back, when Yates and Carson experienced ill-luck with good shots. After some attacking by the visitors, during which Steele made a plucky save, Hopkins, amid much applause, scored Ardwick's third point. Some exciting and fairly even play went on to the finish. Final :—
>
> ARDWICK .... 3 goals
> NEWTON HEATH .... Nil

1899/90		
Nov 29	Newton Heath 0	City 1
	Att: 2,800	
Jan 1	City 2	Newton Heath 1
	Att: 7,000	
Feb 27	Newton Heath 1	City 0
	Att: 2,000	
1900/01		
Sept 26	Newton Heath 0	City 0
	Att: 600	
1915/16		
May 6	City 2	United 2
	Att: 15,000	
1916/17		
Dec 26	United 1	City 0
Jan 1	City 0	United 0
1917/18		
Dec 25	City 0	United 2
Jan 1	United 2	City 0
1918/19		
Dec 25	City 2	United 1
Jan 1	United 2	City 0

1922/23		
Mar 10	City 5	United 0
	Att: 18,000	
1938/39		
Aug 20	City 2	United 1
	Att: 27,788	*(Jubilee Fund)*
1939/40		
Aug 19	United 1	City 1
	Att: 20,000	*(Jubilee Fund)*
Sept 30	United 2	City 3
	Att: 5,000	
Dec 25	City 1	United 1
	Att: 12,000	
Dec 26	United 3	City 1
	Att: 8,000	
1942/43		
Aug 22	City 1	United 5
	Att: 5,000	
1943/44	City 2	United 2
	Att: 12,000	
1944/45		
Aug 19	City 2	United 2
	Att: 12,000	
1951/52		
Feb 23	United 4	City 2
	Att: 25,002	
1953/54		
Apr 28	City 3	United 2
	Att: 10,261	
1959/60		
Mar 12	City 1	United 3
	Att: 29,476	
1970/71		
Nov 10	United 0	City 3
	Att: 26,161	*(Bill Foulkes Testimonial)*
1971/72		
May 3	City 1	United 3
	Att: 30,429	*(Alan Oakes Testimonial)*
1973/74		
Oct 24	United 1	City 2
	Att: 17,859	*(Tony Dunne Testimonial)*
1975/76		
Sept 2	City 3	United 4
	Att: 20,309	*(Mike Summerbee Testimonial)*
1976/77		
Mar 25	City 4	United 2
	Att:7,654	*(Glyn Pardoe Testimonial)*
1987/88		
Aug 4	City 1	United 3
	Att: 20,000	*(Manchester International Tournament)*
May 8	United 0	City 2
	Att: 14,898	*(Arthur Albiston Testimonial)*
1988/89		
Aug 21	United 5	City 2
	Att: 25,436	*(Kevin Moran Testimonial)*
1989/90		
Aug 13	United 0	City 2
	Att: 19,958	*(Mike Duxbury Testimonial)*

*When both City and United got knocked out of the F.A. Cup in 1960, the clubs arranged a friendly to fill the spare Saturday on 12th March at Maine Road. United won 3-1, and here the City defence is under pressure as **Albert Quixall's** shot beats **Bert Trautmann**, but **Bill Leivers** clears off the line. **Dennis Viollet** is the United player in the background.*

*Most of the friendlies between the clubs during modern times have taken the form of Testimonial matches for long-serving players. This is the cover of the brochure for **Alan Oakes'** match for which more than 30,000 people turned out to see City beaten 1-3 by United.*

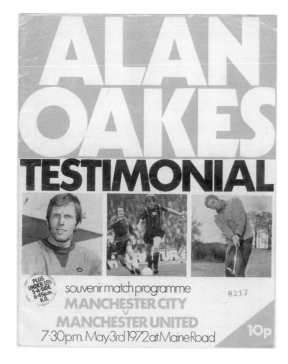

Lancashire Combination

1892/93

Jan 14	Ardwick 1	N. Heath 1
	Att: 1,500	
Mar 11	N. Heath 3	Ardwick 1

1893/94

Sept 16	N. Heath 6	Ardwick 0
	Att: 2,000	
Dec 2	Ardwick 2	N. Heath 1

1894/95

Oct 13	City 3	N. Heath 4
	Att: 2,000	
Dec 15	N. Heath 4	City 1

1895/96

Nov 9	N. Heath 3	City 1
	Att: 3,000	
Dec 28	City 4	N. Heath 2
	Att: 600	

1896/97

Sept 19	N. Heath 1	City 3
	Att: 3,000	
Jan 9	City 2	N. Heath 0
	Att: 4,000	

1897/98

Sept 4	City 1	N. Heath 3
	Att: 2,000	
Dec 11	N. Heath 1	City 1
	Att: 6,000	

1898/99

Sept 3	N. Heath 2	City 1
	Att: 2,000	
Nov 26	City 1	N. Heath 1
	Att: 4,000	

1899/1900

Nov 25	N. Heath 3	City 3
	Att: 1,000	
Apr 17	City 5	N. Heath 0

1900/01

Mar 9	N. Heath 1	City 2
	Att: 2,000	
Mar 16	City 2	N. Heath 0
	Att: 4,000	

1901/02

Sept 14	N. Heath 4	City 2
	Att: 2,000	
Dec 21	City 6	N. Heath 2
	Att: 6,000	

1902/03

Nov 8	United 3	City 3
	Att: 10,000	
Jan 3	City 2	United 0
	Att: 12,000	

1903/04

Dec 25	City 0	United 1
	Att: 12,000	
Apr 1	United 3	City 1
	Att: 20,000	

1904/05

Jan 2	City 5	United 0
	Att: 5,000	
Apr 21	United 2	City 0
	Att: 12,000	

1905/06

Dec 25	City 2	United 1
	Att: 6,000	
Apr 13	United 0	City 3
	Att: 12,000	

1906/07

Jan 1	City 1	United 2
	Att: 4,000	
Mar 29	United 2	City 3
	Att: 19,000	

1907/08

Dec 25	City 0	United 0
	Att: 7,000	
Jan 1	United 1	City 0
	Att: 5,000	

1908/09

The teams did not play during this season. City were in Div. 2 and United in Div. 1

1909/10

Dec 27	United 1	City 7
	Att: 6,000	
Feb 9	City 1	United 0
	Att: 5,000	

1910/11

Dec 26	City 4	United 5
	Att: 8,000	
Apr 14	United 2	City 0
	Att: 12,000	

Central League

1911/12

Dec 25	City 1	United 1
	Att: 5,000	
Apr 5	United 1	City 4
	Att: 3,000	

1912/13

Dec 25	United 2	City 1
	Att: 4,500	
Mar 21	City 2	United 3
	Att: 15,000	

1913/14

Mar 4	City 0	United 1
	Att: 10,000	
Apr 10	United 0	City 3
	Att: 6,000	

1914/15

Dec 26	United 4	City 0
	Att: 2,000	
Apr 2	City 2	United 1
	Att: 15,000	

1919/20

Apr 2	City 1	United 4
	Att: 7,000	
Apr 6	United 4	City 0
	Att: 8,000	

1920/21

Nov 20	City 1	United 2
	Att: 10,000	
Nov 27	United 3	City 1
	Att: 9,000	

1921/22

Oct 22	United 0	City 0
	Att: 4,000	
Oct 29	City 1	United 0
	Att: 5,000	

1922/23

Dec 30	United 2	City 0
	Att: 5,000	
Jan 6	City 1	United 2
	Att: 10,000	

1923/24

Nov 17	United 1	City 1
	Att: 4,000	
Apr 9	City 3	United 0
	Att: 6,000	

1924/25

Oct 8	City 1	United 0
	Att: 4,000	
May 2	United 1	City 0
	Att: 8,000	

1925/26

Oct 21	United 2	City 1
	Att: 5,000	
Apr 19	City 3	United 1
	Att: 4,000	

1926/27

Aug 30	United 1	City 1
	Att: 7,000	
Sept 8	City 2	United 4
	Att: 5,000	

1927/28

Oct 1	United 0	City 2
	Att: 6,000	
Feb 11	City 1	United 3
	Att: 6,000	

1928/29

Aug 29	United 4	City 3
	Att: 4,000	
Sept 26	City 2	United 2
	Att: 5,000	

1929/30

Sept 30	City 2	United 4
	Att: 1,000	
Feb 8	United 3	City 0
	Att:4,000	

1930/31

Oct 4	United 2	City 3
	Att: 2,000	
Feb 7	City 4	United 3
	Att: 6,000	

1931/32

Sept 3	City 3	United 0
	Att: 6,000	
Jan 16	United 3	City 1
	Att: 4,000	

1932/33

Sept 3	United 1	City 0
	Att: 2,000	
Jan 7	City 2	United 1
	Att: 7,000	

1933/34

Sept 2	City 2	United 1
	Att: 6,000	
Jan 6	United 1	City 0
	Att: 5,000	

1934/35

Sept 22	City 0	United 1
	Att: 4,000	
Feb 2	United 2	City 2
	Att: 4,000	

1935/36

Sept 28	United 5	City 1
	Att: 6,000	
Feb 1	City 2	United 4
	Att: 4,000	

1936/37

Sept 12	City 2	United 5
	Att: 5,000	
Jan 9	United 2	City 0
	Att: 6,000	

1937/38

Sept 25	City 0	United 0
	Att: 7,000	

Date	Home	Away
Feb 5	United 1	City 1
	Att: 5,000	

1938/39

Date	Home	Away
Sept 10	United 2	City 2
	Att: 6,000	
Jan 14	City 1	United 2
	Att: 6,000	

1945/46

Date	Home	Away
Apr 6	City 4	United 0
Apr 13	United 3	City 4

1946/47

Date	Home	Away
Sept 28	City 4	United 1
Feb 1	United 2	City 2

1947/48

Date	Home	Away
Sept 20	United 6	City 2
Feb 7	City 1	United 2

1948/49

Date	Home	Away
Sept 11	United 3	City 1
Jan 22	City 1	United 8

1949/50

Date	Home	Away
Sept 3	City 1	United 1
	Att: 4,709	
Dec 31	United 0	City 3

1950/51

Date	Home	Away
Sept 23	United 1	City 2
Feb 3	City 2	United 2
	Att: 3,572	

1951/52

Date	Home	Away
Sept 15	United 2	City 2
Jan 19	City 3	United 1
	Att: 1,997	

1952/53

Date	Home	Away
Aug 30	United 0	City 0
Jan 3	City 1	United 1
	Att: 1,594	

1953/54

Date	Home	Away
Sept 5	United 0	City 1
Jan 16	City 1	United 0
	Att: 1,264	

1954/55

Date	Home	Away
Sept 25	United 2	City 2
Feb 12	City 5	United 2
	Att: 1,284	

1955/56

Date	Home	Away
Sept 3	United 6	City 2
Dec 31	City 0	United 3
	Att: 4,036	

1956/57

Date	Home	Away
Sept 22	City 1	United 1
	Att: 5,300	
Feb 2	United 3	City 1

1957/58

Date	Home	Away
Aug 31	City 3	United 4
	Att: 4,377	
Dec 28	United 4	City 0

1958/59

Date	Home	Away
Sept 27	United 3	City 3
Feb 14	City 2	United 2
	Att: 3,844	

1959/60

Date	Home	Away
Sept 19	United 3	City 2
	Att: 10,102	
Feb 6	City 2	United 2
	Att: 3,261	

1960/61

Date	Home	Away
Aug 27	United 1	City 0 (aban-
doned 45 mins)	*Att: 4,709*	
Feb 15	United 1	City 0
	Att: 9,588	
Mar 13	City 5	United 2
	Att: 4,855	

1961/62

Date	Home	Away
Sept 23	City 2	United 2
	Att: 2,317	
Feb 10	United 2	City 3
	Att; 2,863	

1962/63

Date	Home	Away
Sept 15	City 0	United 5
	Att: 2,276	
Mar 25	United 0	City 0
	Att: 7,181	

1963/64

Date	Home	Away
Oct 2	United 2	City 2
	Att: 11,334	
Apr 25	City 3	United 1
	Att: 2,873	

1964/65

Date	Home	Away
Aug 29	United 5	City 2
	Att: 10,106	
Mar 8	City 0	United 2
	Att: 5,765	

1965/66

Date	Home	Away
Dec 4	City 1	United 0
	Att: 1,787	
Apr 30	United 2	City 0
	Att: 1,743	

1966/67

Date	Home	Away
Sat 16	City 1	United 4
	Att: 5,658	
Jan 20	United 2	City 1

1967/68

Date	Home	Away
Feb 17	United 3	City 2
Apr 15	City 6	United 5
	Att: 2,503	

1968/69

Date	Home	Away
Aug 16	United 2	City 1
	Att: 10,174	
Mar 7	City 2	United 0
	Att: 5,720	

1969/70

Date	Home	Away
Nov 14	United 3	City 0
	Att: 5,260	
Mar 24	City 0	United 3
	Àtt: 1,774	

1970/71

Date	Home	Away
May 3	United 4	City 0
	Att: 1,275	
May 10	City 2	United 0
	Att: 1,117	

1971/72

Date	Home	Away
Nov 5	United 0	City 1
	Att: 4,701	
Feb 26	City 0	United 0
	Att: 2,696	

1972/73

Date	Home	Away
Nov 17	United 1	City 0
	Att: 2,589	
Apr 11	City 0	United 2
	Att: 445	

1973/74

Date	Home	Away
Dec 11	United 1	City 0
	Att: 385	
Apr 26	City 3	United 1
	Att: 2,191	

1974/75

Date	Home	Away
Oct 14	United 2	City 2
	Att: 2,076	
Mar 5	City 1	United 1
	Att: 3,398	

1975/76

Date	Home	Away
Sept 26	United 1	City 3
	Att: 1,848	
Apr 2	City 0	United 1
	Att: 864	

1976/77

Date	Home	Away
Sept 11	United 3	City 1
	Att: 1,604	
Feb 19	City 0	United 2
	Att: 1,959	

1977/78

Date	Home	Away
Sept 10	United 1	City 1
	Att: 1,208	
Mar 14	City 3	United 5
	Att: 2,194	

1978/79

Date	Home	Away
Sept 30	City 0	United 2
	Att: 1,721	
Feb 10	United 2	City 0
	Att: 462	

1979/80

Date	Home	Away
Nov 10	United 2	City 0
	Att: 763	
Mar 22	City 1	United 2
	Att: 818	

1980/81

Date	Home	Away
Sept 27	City 2	United 2
	Att: 1,067	
Feb 21	United 2	City 3
	Att: 541	

1981/82

Date	Home	Away
Nov 21	United 0	City 1
	Att: 571	
Apr 17	City 0	United 3
	Att: 579	

1982/83

Teams did not meet. The Central League was split into two divisions with City in Division Two.

1983/84

As above

1984/85 (Div. One)

Date	Home	Away
Nov 29	City 0	United 3
	Att: 1,240	
Apr 10	United 1	City 2
	Att: 1,111	

1985/86

Date	Home	Away
Sept 24	City 1	United 1
	Att: 1,785	
Dec 28	United 2	City 0
	Att: 963	

1986/87

Date	Home	Away
Oct 4	United 2	City 0
	Att: 741	
Mar 28	City 3	United 1
	Att: 694	

1987/88

Date	Home	Away
Mar 5	United 0	City 1
	Att: 861	
Apr 16	City 6	United 1
	Att: 3,022	

1988/89

Date	Home	Away
Sept 6	City 1	United 0
	Att: 1,879	
Jan 4	United 3	City 4
	Att: 2,770	

1989/90

Date	Home	Away
Dec 9	City 0	United 1
	Att: 862	
Apr 14	United 2	City 3
	Att: 1,081	

1990/91

Date	Home	Away
Nov 17	City 2	United 2
	Att: 1,200	
Feb 16	United 0	City 1
	Att: 3,579	

For the first time in history a national final was played between the two Manchester giants in 1986. Although the competition was not the F.A. or League Cup it aroused the same passion from both sets of supporters. The competition was the F.A. Youth Cup and Manchester's two brilliant young sides fought their way through in style to the final.

The first leg, played at Old Trafford on 24th April before a crowd of 7,602, was a passionate affair with both the Boy Blues and the Young Reds eager to prove themselves. The game was still goalless at half-time, although it must be said that Gary Walsh, in the United goal, was outstanding and had saved the Reds on a number of occasions.

The second half started in terrific style with United's Aidan Murphy scoring in the 49th minute. Sadly, for Murphy, this was his finest moment as, later in the game, an incident with City's Andy Thackeray resulted in both players being sent off. The game continued in fine style with City searching for the equaliser and in the 82nd minute fate was on their side as the buoyant Blues were awarded a penalty. Denton-born Paul Lake took the penalty but Man of the Match Gary Walsh, once again, showed great skill as he dived to his right to block the shot. The ball rebounded and Lake followed up, burying the ball into the net. City's defence then held the United attack at bay, keeping the score at 1-1 until the final whistle.

The second leg at Maine Road on 29th April captured the imagination of the Manchester public with 18,158 spectators paying a total of almost £28,000 to see the game. The attendance was actually greater than expected and it was almost 30 minutes before the crowd were all inside. The stewards had a tricky time finding everyone places, as City had only planned to open the Main Stand and Platt Lane, but the decision was soon taken to also make use of the North Stand. The game commenced with the Blues eager to take the lead and, in only the second minute, they gained the advantage as Paul Moulden's cross was headed into the United net by David Boyd. The City youth then dominated with shots by Boyd, Brightwell, Hinchcliffe, Moulden, Scott and White all brilliantly saved by United's tremendous Gary Walsh. United, themselves, did have a few more chances but it was not to be their day as, in the 86th minute, Paul Moulden followed up from a David White shot to put the Blues two up, and at full time young captain Steve Redmond climbed the Maine Road stairs to collect the trophy. The young Blues were then sent on a lap of honour and both teams were, deservedly, cheered from the field.

It is worth mentioning that many of the players who participated in this final went on to play significant roles at senior level for their respective clubs over following seasons.

The most obvious being:-

Steve Redmond who has featured in every League and Cup derby since.

David White who scored twice in the derby in October 1990.

Gary Walsh who became United's regular first team 'keeper in 1987 before a series of injuries restricted his chances;

Lee Martin who, in 1990, scored the winning goal for the Reds in the F.A. Cup Final replay.

The Teams
1st Leg:

United: Walsh, Gill, Martin, Scott, Gardner, Bottomley, Murphy, Todd, Cronin, Wilson (sub. Hopley), Harvey.

City: Crompton, Mills, Hinchcliffe, Brightwell, Redmond, Thackeray, White, Moulden, Lake, Scott, Boyd.

2nd Leg:

City: Crompton, Mills, Hinchcliffe, Brightwell, Redmond, Thackeray, White, Moulden, Lake, Scott, Boyd.

United: Walsh, Gill, Martin, Scott, Gardner, Harvey, Murphy, Todd, Cronin, Bottomley (sub. Hopley), Goddard.

Season	Round	Team	Team
1954/55			
Nov 17	2	City 1	United 2
1958/59			
Dec 15	3	City 0	United 4
1961/62			
Nov 30	2	United 3	City 0
1963/64			
Apr 8	S/F leg 1	United 4	City 1
Apr 20	S/F leg 2	City 3	United 4
1965/66			
Dec 13	2	City 0	United 5
1966/67			
Feb 8	4	City 0	United 3
		Att: 19,111	
1979/80			
Mar 31	S/F leg 1	United 0	City 0
		Att: 5,119	
Apr 14	S/F leg 2	City 3	United 1
		Att: 8,503	
1985/86			
Apr 24	F leg 1	United 1	City 1
		Att: 7,602	
Apr 29	F leg 2	City 2	United 0
		Att: 18,164	

*Young City skipper **Steve Redmond** shows off the **F.A. Youth Cup** after the Blues second leg win at Maine Road in April 1986.*

LANCASHIRE SENIOR CUP

Derby Meetings in the Lancashire Senior Cup

Season	Round	Team	Team
1897/98			
Jan 22	2	N. Heath 1	City 0
Att: 18,000			
1900/01			
Oct 22	2	City 2	N. Heath 0
Att: 4,000			
1907/08			
Sept 23	1	United 3	City 0
Att: 4,000			
1913/14			
Nov 10	S/F	City 1	United 1
Att: 8,000			
Nov 24	S/F replay	United 2	City 0
Att: 11,000 (at City's Hyde Rd ground)			
1925/26			
Dec 2	3	City 3	United 2
Att: 15,000			
1929/30			
Dec 11	S/F	City 3	United 1
Att: 7,000			

Season	Round	Team	Team
1931/32			
Oct 7	1	United 2	City 3
Att: 3,500			
1945/46			
May 1	S/F	United 3	City 0
Att: 32,231			
1949/50			
Oct 12	1	United 2	City 1
Att: 5,556			
1950/51			
Apr 18	S/F	City 0	United 0
Att: 8,357			
May 7	S/F replay	United 2	City 1
Att: 6,000			
1962/63			
Oct 24	2	City 0	United 0
Att: 5,356			
Nov 12	2 replay	United 2	City 0
Att: 6,381			

Note: *City and United did not enter after 1973/74 season*

LANCASHIRE YOUTH CUP

Derby Meetings in the Lancashire Youth Cup

Season	Round	Team	Team
1972/73			
Apr 25	F leg 1	City 2	United 0
Apr 30	F leg 2	United 0	City 3
1974/75			
Nov 12	2	City 1	United 2
1975-76			
Mar 29	S/F leg 1	United 1	City 0
Att: 8,385			
Apr 5	S/F leg 2	City 4	United 4
1977/78			
Nov 22	2	United 3	City 2
Att: 10,924			
1978/79			
Apr 9	S/F	United 3	City 0
Att: 950			
1979/80			
Nov 12	2	City 3	United 2
Att: 728			
1980/81			
Apr 13	F	City 0	United 2
Att: 2,235			

Season	Round	Team	Team
1982/83			
May 13	F	United 1	City 2
Att: 2,203			
1983/84			
Mar 3	S/F	United 0	City 4
1984/85			
Apr 18	S/F	United 1	City 3
Att: 535			
1989/90			
Mar 26	S/F	United 1	City 3

City v United in 'Friendly' Youth Matches

Season	Round	Team	Team
1967/68			
Sept 27	-	United 1	City 1
1976/77			
Nov 2	-	City 3	United 0
(Manchester Evening News Cup)			
1979/80			
Sept 11	-	City 1	United 1
(Manchester Evening News Cup)			

Manchester football was still in its infancy when The Manchester Cup was introduced in 1884/85. Rugby was the city's main sport at that time and it must have seemed unlikely that, within twenty years, the FA Cup would be paraded through the city by a local side. The Manchester Cup itself was, over the next decade, to become one of the area's top competitions, as most of the other fixtures were simply friendly matches, arranged often in an haphazard way. It was not until 1887 that the two sides, who would become such important rivals, were to meet in the competition. Newton Heath (United) had already won the trophy in 1886, whilst Gorton AFC (City) had struggled to make an impression in local football. Newton Heath were clear favourites and they duly demolished the inexperienced Gorton 11-1.

Despite this defeat, the Gortonians were not demoralised and set about the task of consolidating their future. In the close-season the club moved to Hyde Road, their first true football enclosure, and re-formed under the name of Ardwick AFC. By 1891 Ardwick were a force to be reckoned with, and the whole of Manchester was delighted when Ardwick trotted out to face the much-fancied Newton Heath for the 1891 Manchester Cup Final.

The Heathens had already featured in every Manchester Cup Final and had won the trophy on four occasions, but the 1891 result was a surprise 1-0 victory to Ardwick before a crowd of 10,000 (receipts of £216)

Both Newton Heath, in their 'Green and Gold' and Ardwick in their 'Cambridge Blue', were now major forces in local football.

It was the Manchester Cup that had really developed Newton Heath as a club, and now the same competition started to help Ardwick build up a local reputation.

Perhaps inevitably, as the two clubs grew in stature, the competition itself diminished in importance. Many of the teams from the early years began to disappear, and by the 1930's the competition was reduced to little more than the equivalent of friendlies between local football League teams.

1963/64 was the last season that Manchester's two main teams competed for the Cup with United defeating City 5-3 in the final at Maine Road before a crowd of 36,434. Ironically, this was the biggest crowd the two clubs had ever attracted in the competition, one reason probably being that it was the only Manchester derby available that season.

Manchester Senior Cup Honours
City: Winners - 1891*, 1892*, 1901, 1903, 1907, 1911, 1928, 1929, 1932, 1933, 1949.
Finalists - 1896, 1898, 1902, 1904, 1924, 1925, 1926, 1930, 1934, 1950, 1958, 1959, 1962, 1964.
  * competed as Ardwick

United: Winners - 1886*, 1888*, 1889*, 1890*, 1893*, 1902*, 1908, 1910, 1912, 1913, 1920, 1924, 1926, 1931, 1934, 1936, 1937, 1939, 1948, 1955, 1957, 1959, 1964.
Finalists - 1885*, 1887*, 1891*, 1901*, 1905, 1911, 1921, 1925, 1927, 1928, 1933, 1935, 1938.
  * competed as Newton Heath

Derby Meetings in the Manchester Senior Cup			
Season	**Round**	**Team**	**Team**
1886/87			
Feb 19	2	N. Heath 11	Gorton AFC 1
Att: 3,000			
1888/89			
Mar 16	3	N. Heath 4	Ardwick 1
Att: 2,000			
1890/91			
Apr 18	F	Ardwick 1	N. Heath 0
Att: 10,000		(at Whalley Range)	
1896/97			
Jan 16	1	City 0	N. Heath 1
Att: 18,000			
1897/98			
Mar 5	S/F	N. Heath 1	City 1
Att: 18,000		(at Newton's Clayton ground)	
Mar 12	S/F replay	N. Heath 1	City 2
Att: 14,000			
1900/01			
Apr 29	F	City 4	N. Heath 0
Att: 5,000			
1901/02			
Apr 26	F	City 1	N. Heath 2
Att: 15,000			
1903/04			
Apr 4	S/F	City 1	United 1
Att: 8,000			
Apr 7	S/F replay	United 1	City 2
Att: 1,000			
1906/07			
Apr 17	S/F	City 2	United 1
Att: 14,000			
1907/08			
Mar 18	1	United 1	City 0
Att: 6,000			
1909/10			
Feb 2	1	City 2	United 6
Att: 3,000			
1910/11			
Dec 14	F	City 3	United 1
Att: 6,500			

1914/15			
Mar 17	2	United 3	City 1
Att: 1,500			
1923/24			
May 10	F	United 3	City 0
Att: 12,000			
1924/25			
Mar 18	3	United 2	City 2
Att: 12,000			
Mar 25	3 replay	City 7	United 4
Att: 15,000			
1925/26			
May 6	F	United 2	City 0
Att: 7,000			
1927/28			
May 9	F	City 4	United 2
Att: 5,000			
1932/33			
May 15	F	City 2	United 1
Att: 20,000			
1933/34			
May 7	F	United 1	City 0
Att: 6,000			
1934/35			
Apr 24	S/F	United 3	City 1
Att: 5,000			
1938/39			
Apr 19	S/F	City 0	United 1
Att: 15,000			
1953/54			
Dec 16	S/F	City 0	United 2
Att: 8,054			
1956/57			
Nov 28	S/F	City 1	United 9
Att: 3,654			
1958/59			
Apr 13	F	United 4	City 0
Att: 23,509			
1963/64			
May 7	F	City 3	United 5
Att: 36,434			

Note: The Manchester Senior Cup was called the Manchester & District Cup until 1891/92. City and United did not enter after 1964.

DERBY MEMORIES

Many players down the years have experienced the thrill and excitement of playing in a Manchester derby match. We have collected together a sample of thoughts, comments and memories from some of the key figures involved since the Second World War to try and capture the flavour of just what it is like to turn out in front of a huge crowd on derby day. Enjoyment, triumph, heartbreak, injury and disappointment are just some of the results of the eternally passionate encounters between Red and Blue.

BRIAN KIDD (*United & City*)

"I used to sport City's colours from the age of about six when I went with my father. Then after Munich, perhaps out of sympathy, my boyhood enthusiasm switched to United. I never dreamed in those days I might play in derbies. When my own first derby came around I'm sorry to say I was booked as I got caught up in all the derby day tension. The game I remember best for personal reasons is the FA Cup game at Old Trafford in 1970 which United won 3-0. Sir Alf Ramsey was at the game and I scored a couple of goals. The Press said that was the game which sent me to Mexico. I don't know whether that is true, but it must have helped. I'm a local lad so I always got built up a long time beforehand - sometimes as much as a week before a derby game."

SAMMY McILROY (*United & City*)

"My first game and my first derby was when United drew 3-3 at Maine Road and I scored. I wouldn't say I can quite remember every move, but it has always stuck in my mind. The boss told

Brian Kidd - "I always got built up a long time beforehand - sometimes as much as a week before a derby game."

me to get out and enjoy myself, and the other players were great and did their best to take any of the nervous strain away. And the goal? Under pressure I think I might remember it! Brian Kidd went on a run down the left and played the ball inside to George Best who was being pulled from behind by a City defender. George wasn't getting anywhere so I rushed in and took the ball off him. Left foot, not much time to think about it, but I don't think I'll ever forget that. It was a dream start to a League career."

DENIS LAW (*City & United*)

"Scoring goals always gave me immense pleasure but my last for City against United in 1974 did nothing for the adrenalin because it was the end of season, deprived them of victory and was the reason they ended in the Second Division. Perhaps on reflection now it did them a favour because they were able to reorganise and go from strength to strength after coming back at the first time of asking. Again it balanced the books because ironically in 1963 I won a late penalty for United in a 1-1 derby draw at Maine Road. It was another end of season affair and we were both struggling against relegation. We won our next game to finish fourth from bottom but City lost theirs and went down. One thing is for sure - derby games are much too serious to recall any funny moments."

PETER BARNES (*City & United*)

"I remember my first outing for City at Old Trafford in a League Cup tie in October 1974 when I was put on for about the last 15 minutes, but a lot of things had happened! Our Jeff Clarke had han-

Denis Law - "derby games are much too serious to recall any funny moments."

dled the ball in the penalty area and Gerry Daly scored from the penalty, while big Jim Holton was stretchered off with a bad knee injury. For me it all flew by; I'd scarcely been on the field long enough to draw breath when it seemed the match was over!"

ALEX STEPNEY *(United)*
"I remember the first derby I played in best as it came in the same week that I signed for United, Tuesday September 13th 1966. Then on the 17th we played City at Old Trafford and won 1-0. It was the first derby City had played since they got back in the First Division, and some say it wasn't much of a game, but it was a good enough start for me!"

FRANCIS LEE *(City)*
"I always looked forward to them. There was something that lifted them above the run-of-the-mill League games and really put you on your toes. City didn't have much experience of losing derbies in my time at Maine Road, but I recall a few taunts coming my way when we did lose one. I can't recall a miserable derby because we had such good results and I look back with a lot of satisfaction on the matches I played in. One that perhaps stands out was the Old Trafford derby the year we won the championship. Colin Bell was superb that night and hit the heights of his well-known brilliance. I would have hated to have been on the United side when he was in that sort of form."

STEVE JAMES *(United)*
"Apart from the 3-3 draw at Maine Road in 1971, one of the games I remember best was a Youth Cup tie at Maine Road when we won 3-0. Brian Kidd and Francis Burns were in the side at the same time. Just because it's a Youth Cup tie doesn't mean to say there isn't the tension or the needle. There's just as much personal pride at stake, but that was one I really enjoyed."

KEN BARNES *(City)*
"It was the fear of losing, the fear of letting your fans down in front of their biggest rivals that turned those days into such an ordeal. As I grew more experienced I began to take it more in my stride, but the big job then was to ease the worries of the younger players. Just thinking about the result could keep you awake at night. You never knew if you would have a good Cup run, but you always knew you had to face those two really big games every season. My worst moment came in a 1-1 draw we played before our own fans in 1958. I will never forget missing the penalty which would have won us the match. There were only ten minutes left and it was a terrible experience for me to see Harry Gregg leap to the ball and clutch it at the second attempt. It was a tremendous save, but I felt sick with despair."

DAVID SADLER *(United)*
"They are not games I enjoyed a lot. Perhaps the

Ken Barnes - "It was the fear of losing, the fear of letting your fans down in front of their biggest rivals."

end of season 4-3 win at Maine Road in 1971 stands out as there was less tension than usual. But best of all were the two legs of the Youth Cup semi-final the year we won it in 1964. They were magnificent games which we won 4-3 and 4-1 which is always a consideration in these things. the crowds were up to the 30,000 mark and those were derby games I really did enjoy."

DAVE EWING *(City)*
"There can be few greater thrills than being pitched in at the deep end in front of 70,000 people, but that's how I felt when Les McDowall selected me at centre-half for the visit to Old Trafford on New Years Day in 1953. There were far more eventful derbies in the years that followed, but I'll never lose sight of that Manchester memory. Twenty four hours before the trip to Old Trafford I was told I'd be taking over at centre-half from Jack Rigby, and although I slept reasonably well that night the nerves were on edge and stayed on edge until it was all over. City got a draw and my finest moment came when I headed off the line. Although I was nervous at the prospect of such an important debut, I found that I worried a lot more about occasions like these as I got older, although I still savour the time we went to Old Trafford with our Revie plan and stuck five goals past United. The players and fans were jubilant for weeks afterwards."

TONY DUNNE *(United)*
"The 3-3 draw at Maine Road was the most exciting derby I'd been involved in and the best football too. It was like a cup game, with tremendous atmosphere, both sides wanting to win, and none of the fear that makes some derby games dull. The fact that I was injured and didn't play in the second half doesn't change my opinion of the game."

Ken Mulhearn - "I must have been the most nervous person ever to appear at a football ground."

MIKE DOYLE *(City)*

"We've never had any Red supporters in the family. We are all Blue, parents, aunts, uncles, even all the in-laws. My first local derby was the season we came back into the First Division and we drew 1-1 at Maine Road and Billy Foulkes scored their goal and we equalised when Nobby Stiles put in his own goal. Then he cleared a shot from me off the line. I was playing centre-forward which I can't say I particularly enjoyed much. I remember the next match at Maine Road as well because they beat us 2-1 and it was my mistake which gave them the winning goal. I was dead sick. That was the championship winning season of course, so our win at Old Trafford was very sweet revenge."

BOBBY CHARLTON *(United)*

"When we drew 1-1 at Maine Road in 1963. Alex Harley scored for City and we equalised late on from a penalty. There hadn't been such an important derby game for years. We were in the Cup Final, but we were both in danger of going down. I never worried about a game more than this one. I don't think we really deserved a draw, but what a relief to get a point - although it didn't do City much good!"

JOHN ASTON Jnr *(United)*

"The game at Maine Road in 1968 when I broke my leg. It was just after the European Cup Final, an early Saturday in the season and I was so looking forward to the coming months when it happened. It put me back quite a bit, so my memories of derby games are not too cheerful!"

ALAN OAKES *(City)*

"A derby provided my worst football moment. A draw with United at Maine Road in 1963 made it virtually certain we would be relegated. We were leading 1-0 and then Harry Dowd was penalised for a tackle on Denis Law. I don't know whether it was a penalty or not, I was too far away, but a draw was no good to us and in the end we were easily relegated."

GEORGE BEST *(United)*

"I don't really remember too many of them, but the one that made the most impression on me was one I didn't play in - I think I was suspended or something! It was the 1970 FA Cup game when Brian Kidd got a couple and we won at Old Trafford. I never got worked up before a game, not even before my first game for United, but that day I understood some of the tensions involved. Before the match I went into the dressing-room and I could feel - and see - that something extra was involved here. For me it was always a much easier atmosphere out on the pitch, but apart from that, a derby game was just like any other for me".

KEN MULHEARN *(City)*

"Within about a week of my signing from Stockport in September 1967 Harry Dowd dislocated a finger in training and I was told I was in for my debut against United on the Saturday at Maine Road. United were top and we were second, but one of the things I remember most vividly about the day was my arrival at the ground. Everything had happened so quickly; I had hardly got over the thrill of signing when I was in the team! I turned up ridiculously early - it must have been an hour and a half before any of the other players. Malcolm Allison took one look at me and locked me in the medical room! He obviously saw how white-faced I was. I must have been the most nervous person ever to appear at a football ground, so he just locked me up out of the way until the rest of the team reported and were getting changed. The game flew by and I can't remember any real incidents apart from the shots from Bobby Charlton which went past me. United won 2-1 but it was quite an experience. There were something like 63,000 at the game, and not many days earlier I'd been playing for Stockport in front of a few thousand. The noise and the atmosphere were unbelievable, the first time I'd sampled anything like it."

JOHNNY CAREY *(United)*

"It was all a matter of pride and honour. You just didn't want to lose to the other team in the city. The players felt that way, but the supporters seemed to feel it even more. The games were generally hard, irrespective of where the two sides might have been in the League. I don't think there can ever have been an easy derby game. The tension is terrific. The players may try and keep calm and try and avoid the tension, but it's impossible. The dressing room was usually a quiet place but it was always different on derby day; the crowd is noisier and there's more atmosphere and this gets through to the players. The pain of losing was tremendous, which is why the ideal derby result was always a draw!"

MIKE SUMMERBEE *(City)*

"Too many of the matches were something of an anti-climax. It is like everything in life. You expect too much from something and it usually lets you down. The main trouble was that the players were so eager to live up to the build up that it was hard to play a natural game. One match where that certainly wasn't true was City's 3-1 win at Old Trafford in the championship year, and it's that sort of game and the 3-3 draw at Maine Road that I prefer to remember."

NOBBY STILES *(United)*

"I was all for the United cause right from the start. In those boyhood days Johnny Carey and Stan Pearson were among my idols. When I used to go along with my father and brother, derby day was really special. I remember feeling crushed when City thrashed United by 5-0 at Old Trafford in the mid-Fifties. I always wanted that drubbing to be avenged, and as a young player, I got a great sense of satisfaction out of it when later we beat City by 5-1. Later I grew to hate derbies because there wasn't enough scope for genuine football because of all the tension. The accent was more on not losing than winning, which made the perfect result a draw."

ROY LITTLE *(City)*

"The one for me was a Fourth Round FA Cup tie at Maine Road in 1955. Although we won the game 2-0 (that in itself was worth remembering), the outstanding incident was the sending off of United's captain Allenby Chilton. It was the only occasion in my time at Maine Road that anyone had been given marching orders in a derby game. He did not deserve to go. It was an altogether curious decision because the ref sent him off for mouthing a word. He had not actually heard it. A few of us pleaded with the ref because we didn't want their fans to have the slightest excuse for explaining away a defeat such as 'you only beat ten men' but the ref waved us to one side and Chilton went off. To prove the point about our superiority that season we hammered them 5-0 at Old Trafford!"

PAT CRERAND *(United)*

"My first Manchester derby game will never be forgotten. It was a knockout. At least it was for City winger Dave Wagstaffe after I clouted him one on the chin as the teams trooped into the tunnel during the 1962-63 meeting at Maine Road. I'm not proud of my actions that evening. It wasn't a vicious first half, but I'd become riled with Wagstaffe who I thought had punched me and my Celtic temper boiled up. It was not a distinguished way to enter the Manchester rivalry, but the worst was still to come. Sir Matt came into the dressing-room and he was raging. "Did you hit David Wagstaffe?". Fool that I was, I didn't realise that Sir Matt knew I had landed the blow… in fact there were few people who didn't know! "No, I didn't" I lied. Matt was stumped. He knew I had

Pat Crerand - *"my first Manchester derby game will never be forgotten. It was a knockout."*

done the deed but was flabbergasted to hear me denying it. The reason was that I was so frightened I thought Matt was going to strike me. He looked in the mood to do so, and on the spur of the moment it seemed a good idea to deny it. I have always regretted doing so."

TONY BOOK *(City)*

"One match dominates my thoughts whenever people talk of the derby. City were competing neck and neck for the championship when we went to Old Trafford in 1968. An unforgivable error on my part let in George Best early on with a mistimed back-pass. I knew I should have stopped him and what's more I knew that had I been alert I could have stopped him. It didn't need the groans of our fans to make me aware of what a zero-rating I was getting because this was one meeting where neither side could afford slip-ups. As captain my team mates looked to me for example, but on this occasion it was their attitude, their example which promptly put behind me any thoughts of getting depressed about the incident. By the finish City had played some great stuff and turned disaster into delight. That derby was a thrill to play in, despite my early reverse, and I rate it as one of the best games of football I have ever played in."

STAN PEARSON *(United)*

"My best pal was City's centre-forward George Smith. We were brought up together in Salford and our careers ran parallel. I remember us beating City 2-0 at Old Trafford and I had the pleasure of scoring both goals, but the first was the most controversial I ever netted. Frank Swift was in goal for City and he swore I had punched the ball into the net. He chased the referee Arthur Ellis all the way to the half-way line protesting bitterly, but the goal counted. Although I never said as much at the time, he was one hundred per cent correct!"

"HIGHLIGHT OF THE YEAR"

(An extract from a letter sent to one of the Manchester clubs in 1957 by an anonymous 79 year old supporter from Sale. For all true football supporters and avid derby followers of both clubs the sentiments expressed surely still ring true today.)

"I hope to be at Maine Road for the derby game, as I have always regarded it as a highlight of the year to watch two fine teams from the same city in action. I like to hear the comments of the rival supporters, and I like it best of all when they applaud good work by the opposing side. I like it less when they criticise one of their own men who is having an off day, and when they expect a player or the team to do well every game.

Sometimes City are on top of the world, sometimes United. Which is just as it should be. Nobody with the interests of the game at heart could honestly wish for one side to win everything all the time.

I'd just like to say 'all the best' to both teams for the future, and I hope the name Manchester will long remain at the top of the football world."

BIBLIOGRAPHY

A-Z of Manchester Football, Derek Brandon, Boondaggle, 1978
Soccer at the Top, Matt Busby, Weidenfield & Nicholson, 1973
There's Only One United, Geoffrey Green, Hodder & Stoughton, 1978
Back Page Football, Stephen Kelly, Macdonald Queen Anne Press, 1988
An Autobiography, Denis Law, Queen Anne Press, 1979
Manchester City, A Complete Record, Ray Goble, Breedon Books, 1987
Heathens & Red Devils, Keith Mellor, Temple Press, 1987
Rothmans Football Yearbooks (1970-90), Queen Anne Press
Football from the Goalmouth, Frank Swift, Sporting Handbooks, 1948
Winners and Champions, Alec Shorrocks, Arthur Barker, 1985
The Manchester City Story, Andrew Ward, Breedon Books, 1984
The Football Man, Arthur Hopcraft, Collins, 1968
Manchester City - My Team, Mike Doyle, Souvenir Press, 1977
Football Wizard, John Harding, Breedon Books, 1985
Manchester United, Percy Young, Heinemann, 1960
Manchester United - A pictorial record, Charles Zahra, Joseph Muscat, Iain McCartney, Keith Mellor, Temple Press, 1987
Manchester United, A Complete Record, Ian Morrison & Alan Shury, Breedon Books, 1986 & 1990
From Maine Men to Banana Citizens, Gary James & Keith Mellor, Temple Press, 1989
Steppes to Wembley, Bert Trautmann, Robert Hale, 1956
Trautmann the Biography, Alan Rowlands, Breedon Books, 1990
A Red Dragon of Wales, Roy Paul, Robert Hale, 1956
Manchester City, Eric Thornton, Robert Hale, 1969
The Day a Team Died, Frank Taylor, Heinemann, 1960
The Manchester City Football Books, Peter Gardner, Stanley Paul
The Manchester United Football Books, David Meek, Stanley Paul
The Football League 1888-1988, Bryon Butler, Macdonald Queen Anne Press, 1988

PICTURE ACKNOWLEDGEMENTS

Allsport, Colorsport, Bob Thomas Sports Photography, David Munden, Cliff Butler, John Peters, Syndication International, The Hulton Picture Library, Manchester Evening News, The Daily Mail, The Daily Express, The Daily Mirror, Manchester United F.C., Manchester City F.C., British Library Newspaper library at Colindale, Stuart Renshaw.
There are a number of other photographs included in this book, the source of which we have been unable to trace. The owners are cordially invited to contact the publishers in writing providing proof of copyright.

SUBSCRIBERS

1   The Football League
2   Sir MATT BUSBY C.B.E.
3   NORAH MERCER
4   MARTIN EDWARDS
5   PETER SWALES
6   CLIFF BUTLER
7   PHIL CRITCHLEY
8   GEOFF DURBIN
9   GARY JAMES
10   STEVE CAWLEY
11   RAY GOBLE
12   MIKE DAVAGE
13   PETER GARDNER
14   DAVID MEEK
15   BRIAN CLARKE
16   STUART RENSHAW
17   IAIN McCARTNEY
18   BERNARD GEORGE HOLLOWAY
19   GEORGE CLIFFORD HALL REVILL
20   GERALD TOON, Scraptoft, Leicester
21   TONY & JENNY ROSSA, Anstey, Leicester
22   NORMAN GREENOP, Gamblesby, Cumbria
23   ELAINE WEINTRAUB, Fallowfield, Manchester
24   JAMES MICHAEL WOOLLEY
25   NEIL & CAROL FOWLER, Brassington, Derbyshire
26   CHICK FOWLER, Hockley, Essex
27   ALASTAIR & HELEN GREIG, Hale, Cheshire
28   ALISTAIR & JANET DOUGLAS, Framlingham, Suffolk
29   DAVE SMITH, Oadby, Leicester
30   JOHN ATKINSON, Old Colwyn, Clwyd
31   ROBERT SHAW, Plumstead, London
32   ROBERT COLIN HUYTON, Reddish, Stockport
33   JOHN SMITH, Bury, Lancashire
34   CHARLES H.ASHWORTH, Thornton Cleveleys, Lancs
35   JEFFREY & HOWARD SHULKIND, Liverpool
36   PAUL JACKSON, West Ewell, Surrey
37   HECTOR C.FRASER, Flixton, Manchester
38   IAN ROBERTS, Warrington, Cheshire
39   EDWIN SPARROW, Sale, Cheshire
40   TINA ROBERTSON
41   STAN RATCLIFFE, Poynton, Cheshire
42   DAVID GREEN, Thurnby Lodge, Leicester
43   JULIA BYRNE,Clarendon Park, Leicester
44   RICHARD BRADY
45   SEAN & JANE RILEY, Oldham, Lancashire
46   JOHN ROWLINSON
47   RALPH MORTIMER, London NW4
48   MARK LYON, Sandiway, Northwich, Cheshire
49   GARY ALAN NEILE, Carlisle, Cumbria
50   ANDREW DOLAN, Carlisle, Cumbria
51   RORY SKINNER, Leicester
52   STEPHEN IRISH, Stockton-on-Tees, Cleveland
53   ALAN LLOYD, Blackthorn, Northampton
54   DAVID FLATLEY, Denton, Manchester
55   SCOTT JAMES HUDSON, Blackpool, Lancashire
56   FIONA O'CONNOR, Cosby, Leics
57   NEIL SOFFE, Portslade, East Sussex
58   TONY BRUNT, Northenden, Manchester
59   IAN MALCOLM JONES, Bury, Lancashire
60   E.KENEHAN, Newport Pagnell, Bucks
61   NEIL MUSGRAVE, Headingley, Leeds
62   'THE BLUE'
63   HEIDI WARD, Hyde, Cheshire
64   ANDREW MALCOLM MACDONALD, Stockport, Cheshire
65   KEITH HARGREAVES, Ashton-under-Lyne, Lancashire
66   HELEN & ALICE LEES, Cheadle, Cheshire
67   LEE GRAHAM MANSFIELD, Droyslden Tameside, Manchester
68   MARK STANFORD, Croydon, Surrey
69   JOHN BENFIELD, Brooklands, Manchester
70   GEOFF GREENSTREET, West Didsbury, Manchester
71   JOHN McCADDEN, Worsley, Manchester
72   DEREK LEONARD, Macclesfield, Cheshire
73   IAN SHEARN, Midsomer Norton, Bath
74   JONATHAN ROBIN LEWIN, Failsworth, Manchester
75   CHRISTOPHER ROBIN BERWICK, Blaby, Leicester
76   PETER SANDERSON, Kendal, Cumbria
77   WAYNE NOONE, Fareham, Hampshire
78   MICHAEL FLANDERS, Margate, Kent
79   R.WELCH, Chapelfields, Coventry
80   G.HOLMES, Lincoln
81   BRIAN BARNETT, Brockworth, Gloucester
82   KARL HOLLYHEAD (Harry), Farncombe, Godalming, Surrey

83   GARETH PRITCHARD, Rhyl, Clwyd
84   JOHN KELLY, Timperley, Altrincham, Cheshire
85   DAVID J.FOWLER, Cranbrook, Kent
86   CHRISTOPHER R.HALLIWELL, Cheadle, Cheshire
87   STEPHEN BIGGS, London EC1
88   MICHAEL WILLIAM SMITH, Leek, Staffordshire
89   ANDREW LYNCH, Castleford, West Yorkshire
90   ROBERT BOLTON, Brentford, Middlesex
91   MICHAEL ATKIN, Blackpool, Lancashire
92   NEIL CRAIG STURLAND, Stone, Staffordshire
93   JOHN MARTIN FOLLON, Widnes, Cheshire
94   GORDON HINDLE, Chorlton, Manchester
95   IAN D.WHITTAKER, Newbury, Berkshire
96   JOHN CHAMBERLAIN, Navenby, Lincoln
97   PAUL & MARJORIE JAMES, Denton, Manchester
98   STEPHEN CHARLES HANDLEY, West Point, Manchester
99   DAVID JOHN FEELEY, Biggleswade, Beds
100   SEAN C.DOYLE, Stotfold, Hertfordshire
101   DAVID WILLIAM PEARSON, Hexham, Northumberland
102   ALISTAIR HENDERSON, Aylesbury, Bucks
103   MICHAEL AITCHISON, Heaton, Bradford, W.Yorks
104   PETER S.WILSON, Leominster, Herefordshire
105   BILLY McFARLAND, Ahoghill, Co.Antrim
106   DAVID N.ROBERTSON, Northolt, Middlesex
107   COLIN BACON, Keelby, South Humberside
108   STUART MARTIN, Stanwell, Staines, Middlesex
109   BRENDAN ANSELL, Wyken, Coventry, Warwickshire
110   JAMES KIRWIN, Bury, Lancashire
111   ALAN LEE, Offerton, Stockport
112   ANDY TANNER, Lower Earley, Reading
113   IAN PICKUP, Timperley, Altrincham
114   CHRISTOPHER HOGG, Davyhulme, Manchester
115   STEVEN J.MILLS, North Reddish, Stockport
116   CRAIG DAVIES, Skipton, North Yorkshire
117   BRIAN WAINWRIGHT, Unsworth, Bury, Lancs
118   DEREK PARRY, Old Colwyn, Clwyd
119   MICHAEL NICHOLAS, Rassau, Ebbw Vale
120   J.S.MOORE, Northallerton, North Yorkshire
121   W.GEORGE RENSHAW, Burnage, Manchester
122   ALAN DRYSDALE, Heywood, Lancashire
123   JASON ALLCROFT, Droylsden, Manchester
124   DAVE MARCINIAK, Minchinhampton, Glos.
125   ANDREW DOBNEY, Gosberton, Spalding, Lincs
126   RAYMOND M.CAWLEY, Fallowfield, Manchester
127   CHRISTOPHER GORDON MARSHALL, Shepherds Bush, London
128   IAN WOODLEY, London
129   JOE GLANVILLE, London
130   JANET & ANDREW BROWN, Harwood, Bolton, Lancs
131   PETER PICKUP, Pudsey, West Yorkshire
132   FRANCES GUNDRY, Dorchester, Dorset
133   DANIEL MILLER, New Mills, Stockport, Cheshire
134   KIM PAPADOPOULOS, Chorlton, Manchester
135   HANS M.KRISTOFFERSEN, Stabekk, Norway
136   IAN BULLOCK, Wigston Fields, Leicester
137   DAVID THOMAS, Banbury, Oxon
138   RICHARD J.FORD, Simonstone, Burnley, Lancs
139   JOHN E.BRADER, Stamford, Lincs
140   JAMES BRIGGS, Aston, Sheffield, South Yorks
141   BILLY O'NEILL, Thornley, County Durham
142   IAIN K.RICHARDSON, Douglas, Isle of Man
143   FRANK CROSSLEY, Upton, Chester
144   TONY CROSSLEY, Upton, Chester
145   PETER REEVES SCARRATT, Crewe, Cheshire
146   ANTHONY J.EVANS, Oundle, Peterborough
147   JOHN A.BEIRNE, Winton Eccles, Manchester
148   WAYNE GREEN, Tamerton Foliot, Devon
149   FLOYD WESTON, Byfleet, Surrey
150   DARREN KARL YOUENS, Swindon, Wiltshire
151   DARREN PHILIP HAMER, Leyland, Lancashire
152   STAN GRANT, Leicester
153   MICHAEL RANCE, Melton Mowbray, Leics
154   PETER HOCKENHULL, Great Glen, Leics
155   MARCUS SWAN, St.Budeaux, Plymouth, Devon
156   LINDA & PETER BRADLEY, Harrogate, N.Yorkshire
157   GARY STILL, Chadwell Heath, Essex
158   DEREK McNALLY, Chorlton, Manchester
159   DEREK ROBERTS & DAVID & SANDRA MARLOR, Manchester
160   LAWRENCE BINNS, Connecticutt, U.S.A.
161   WAYNE MARK JACKETT, Timperley, Manchester
162   WILLIAM B.KILMURRAY, Rathmines, Dublin
163   WILLIAM B.KILMURRAY, Rathmines, Dublin
164   WILLIAM B.KILMURRAY, Rathmines, Dublin
165   WILLIAM B.KILMURRAY, Rathmines, Dublin
166   LESLIE ALAN SMITH, St. Helens, Lancashire
167   PAUL TONNA, Tarxien, Malta
168   MICHAEL JOHN WILD, Bury, Lancashire
169   FRANK O'FARRELL, Gloucester
170   PAUL NAGEL, Stockton-on-Tees, Cleveland

171 MICHAEL EDROFF, Petts Wood, Kent
172 COLIN EDROFF, Stevenage, Herts
173 MIKE BILLINGTON, Stretford, Manchester
174 EINAR GUTTORMSSON, Iceland
175 MARTIN RICHARD BUSH, Reading, Berkshire
176 ROBERT J.BRIMICOMBE, Plymouth, Devon
177 T.A.GREEN, Hornchurch, Essex
178 DEREK HEYES, Horwich, Bolton, Lancashire
179 BARRIE SCOTT, Eaton Vale, Norwich
180 JOSEPH BURKE, Moston, Manchester
181 COLIN HALL, Harrogate, North Yorks
182 frank sidebottom, (timperley bigshorts)
183 RICHARD STOCKEN, Holmes Chapel, Cheshire
184 RICHARD CHORLTON, Worsley, Manchester
185 CHARLES ZAHRA, Rabat, Malta
186 WILLIAM PETER HARVEY
187 CAMILLA BASKCOMB & DAVE GILLAN, Battersea, London
188 MICHAEL BURNS, London
189 STEVEN HAMPSON, Sunnybank, Bury, Lancs
190 J.F.TUCKETT, Shirehampton, Bristol
191 ERIK LEES, Roundhay, Leeds
192 SHAY ALLEN, Wellingborough, Northamptonshire
193 LES TAYLOR, Tideswell, Buxton, Derbyshire
194 RUPERT J.BASKCOMB, Kingsdown, Bristol
195 RICHARD M.DENTON
196 MICHAEL HOPKINS, Southport, Lancashire
197 KENNETH G.C.HARTLEY, Lutterworth, Leics
198 ANDY FLACK, Horsham, West Sussex
199 STEVEN BOYD, Didsbury, Manchester
200 CANDIDA BASKCOMB, Sydney, Australia
201 R.N.BRAID, Heaton Park, Prestwich, Manchester
202 KEITH TOWNSEND, Bare, Morecambe, Lancashire
203 MARTIN SPENCER, Wythenshawe, Manchester
204 MARTIN DAVID HURST, Fallowfield, Manchester
205 JOHN HOARE, Worsley, Manchester
206 M.E.CUMMINGS, Heaton Mersey, Stockport, Cheshire
207 HARRY HOLLAND
208 VINCE MILLER, Heaton Chapel, Stockport, Cheshire
209 ANTHONY JOHN BONTER, Failsworth, Manchester
210 MICHAEL D.NANCE, Altrincham, Cheshire
211 KEVIN M.BOULD, Marple, Stockport, Cheshire
212 PHIL WATSON, Newton, Hyde, Cheshire
213 KEVIN FOWLES, Brooklands, Wythenshawe, Manchester
214 MARTIN CUSWORTH, Halifax, West Yorkshire
215 DARREN MICKLEWRIGHT, Bradmore, Wolverhampton
216 BILL & PHILIP ROYLE, Salford, Manchester
217 JOSEPH HULME
218 JULIE MANNS, Ashton-under-Lyne, Lancashire
219 DAVID MINETT, Herne Hill, London
220 T.FLETCHER, Batley, West Yorkshire
221 BRENDAN GAHAN, Cleveleys, Lancashire
222 PETER GRESTY, Birkdale, Southport
223 CARL GILMORE. Davyhulme, Manchester
224 PHILIP BROWN, Fleetwood, Lancashire
225 S.J.BELCHER, Bishops Cleeve, Cheltenham, Glos
226 NICK NAYLOR, Alderley Edge, Cheshire
227 DAVID ARTHUR DICKMAN, Disley, Stockport, Cheshire
228 ROBERT CRABB, Aberdeen
229 KEVIN A.LEATHER, Offerton, Stockport, Cheshire
230 DAVID KEATS, Thornton Heath, Surrey
231 BRIAN STIMPSON, Fallowfield, Manchester
232 STEVEN BRIAN SAVAGE, Heaton Mersey, Stockport
233 ANDREW ROBERT MILARVIE, Bramhall, Stockport
234 MIKE KIBBLE, Chatham, Kent
235 J.A.SHARPLES, Luton, Bedfordshire
236 A.R.GROOME, Harlow, Essex
237 JOHN A.HARRIS, Enfield, Middlesex
238 PETER T.CHAPMAN, Reydon, Southwold, Suffolk
239 ROBERT CHARLTON NEILL, Blackburn, Lancashire
240 KENNETH MILWARD, Heaton Chapel, Stockport, Cheshire
241 MICHAEL SLADE, Horsham, West Sussex
242 GARY CARTER, Little Lever, Bolton, Lancashire
243 C.DUNHILL, Bingley, West Yorkshire
244 JOHN SUTCLIFFE, Harrogate, North Yorkshire
245 OLE MORTEN EGEDAL, Notodden, Norway
246 PAUL MARTIN ELLIS, Mottingham, London
247 WILLIAM E.LIPPIATT, Bradford-on-Avon, Wiltshire
248 CHRIS WILDMAN, Penwortham, Preston, Lancs
249 RICHARD E.G.NEWTON, Exeter, Devon
250 SPORTSPAGES, London WC2
251 GARY SLACK, Bakewell, Derbyshire
252 NICK CHILD, Bromsgrove, Worcestershire
253 JAMES HEARD, Morecambe, Lancashire
254 SHAUN O'LEARY
255 ROBERT L.GRETTON, Chorlton, Manchester
256 JOHN FITZHUGH, Blaby, Leicestershire
257 MARK HARRISON, Lancashire
258 KEVIN MULVANEY, Kippax, Leeds

259 JOHN BADHAM, Ledbury, Herefordshire
260 IAN GRIFFITHS, Esless Park, Wrexham, Clwyd
261 CARL DAVID THORLEY, Sale, Trafford, Manchester
262 CHRIS THOMPSON, Merstham, Redhill, Surrey
263 JEFFREY COLIN SLATER, Mancot, Deeside, Clwyd
264 MARTIN E.JAMES, Ross-on-Wye, Herefordshire
265 DENNIS CHAPMAN, Chelston, Torquay, Devon
266 JAN ADAM WOLINSKI, Urmston, Manchester
267 JOHN S.DINSDALE, Stretford, Manchester
268 PAUL BISHOP, Stalybridge, Cheshire
269 GEOFFREY MARK CORCORAN, Heywood, Lancashire
270 STEPHEN HAUGHTON, Stretford, Manchester
271 MARK SMITH, South Reddish, Stockport, Cheshire
272 NORMA WORTON, Kenilworth, Warwickshire
273 LARS-OLOF WENDLER, Hoganas, Sweden
274 MATTEO TONNA, Soragna, Parma, Italy
275 NICHOLAS ALAN CUTLER, East Moseley, Surrey
276 ALAN WINTER, Coventry, Warwickshire
277 CLIFFORD JOHN PRICE, Kidlington, Oxford
278 DONALD ASHWOOD, Armadale, West Lothian, Scotland
279 ROBERT BOSWELL, Newton, Hyde, Cheshire
280 KEN CALLAGHAN, Halifax, West Yorkshire
281 AUSTIN N.FLETCHER, Urmston, Lancashire
282 STEPHEN ROBERTS, Bicester, Oxon
283 OLIVER SLATTERY, Fermoy, County Cork, Eire
284 DAVID TOMES, St. John, Jersey, Channel Islands
285 JOHN POND, Leigh-on-Sea, Essex
286 PAUL ROUGHLEY, Kirkby Overblow, Harrogate, N.Yorks
287 M.SWART, En Wieringerwerf, The Netherlands
288 C.J.KENNINGTON, Bolton, Lancashire
289 MARK ASH, Fakenham, Norfolk
290 SHAUN MICHAEL CROWLEY, Swinton, Manchester
291 DANIEL DAVID BRAY, Stalybridge, Cheshire
292 P.A.DAVIES, Tunstall, Stoke on Trent, Staffs
293 T.H.HOPE, Kinson, Bournemouth, Hampshire
294 ANDREW BRINDLE, Stockport, Cheshire
295 ROBERT BRINDLE, Stockport, Cheshire
296 GORAN SCHONHULT, Trelleborg, Sweden
297 D.R.BROWN, Cheadle Hulme, Stockport, Cheshire
298 HOWARD COOMBER, Chatham, Kent
299 JOHN, LYN, ADRIAN & EMMA BROCKLEHURST, Eccles
300 PAUL PHEBY, Burnage, Manchester
301 D.J.NELSON, Wythenshawe, Manchester
302 SEAN BRAY, Anstey, Leicester
303 GEOFF GREATOREX, Braunstone Frith, Leicester
304 ANDREW VIDEGRAIN, St.Brelade, Jersey
305 MICHAEL VIDEGRAIN, St.Brelade, Jersey
306 DERMOT BOYLAN, St.John, Jersey
307 PAUL BERNADINI, St.Helier, Jersey
308 ANDY ELLIOTT, St Helier, Jersey
309 ALISON & IAN McCLEVERTY, Ashton-under-Lyne, Lancs
310 GEORGE BIRD, Mellor, Cheshire
311 GEORGE BIRD, Mellor, Cheshire
312 MIKE DOBBIN, Palmers Green , London
313 BOB & PAT STONE, Leeds, West Yorkshire
314 NEIL A.SHAW, Whaley Bridge, Cheshire
315 GERALD HILL, Blurton, Stoke-on-Trent, Staffs
316 NORMAN JONES, Holywell, Clwyd
317 DAVID ROSE, Southampton, Hampshire
318 KEVIN MALLINSON, Blyth, Nottinghamshire
319 STANLEY MALLINSON, Dallas, U.S.A.
320 DEAN C. COMBS, Ramsgate, Kent
321 IAN DREW, Portsmouth, Hampshire
322 MICHAEL J.WELLS, Earls Barton, Northamptonshire
323 IAN Le DANTEC, St. Helier,Jersey
324 CLIFF MILLS, London SE17
325 R.J.McPAKE, Stapleton, Bristol, Avon
326 CHARLES JAMES McCORMICK, Northern Moor, M/chester
327 DAVID MORGAN, Kelvedon Hatch, Brentwood, Essex
328 BOBBY BASKCOMB, Worth Matravers, Swanage, Dorset
329 LEONARD ANTHONY LAVELLE, Heaton Moor, Stockport
330 L.M.McDONALD, Unsworth, Bury, Lancashire
331 MICHAEL BRETT, Thurles, Co.Tipperary
332 J.TWEDDELL, Barnes, London
333 NORMAN JOHN COOPER, North Watford, Herts
334 ROBERT BEARD, Peaslake, Guildford, Surrey
335 R.J.GODDARD, Wrecclesham, Farnham, Surrey
336 ANDREW WILSON, Offerton, Stockport, Cheshire
337 DAVID JOHN SMITH, Peel Green, Eccles, Manchester
338 JAMES NEIL GREGG, South Reddish, Stockport, Cheshire
339 KEITH TURK, Guiseley, Leeds, West Yorkshire
340 MICHAEL RICKETTS, Withington, Manchester
341 STUART HAMILTON, Keyham, Plymouth, Devon
342 LOUISE BURGESS, West Park, Lytham, Lancashire
343 PETER A.NEWTON, Sale, Cheshire
344 NIREUS FORD, Dukinfield, Cheshire
345 R.G.WOOLMAN, Windsor, Berkshire
346 JONATHAN & JUDITH POOLE, Alderley Edge, Cheshire

347   MARTIN COONEY, Tyldesley, Manchester
348   TONY BLUFF, Thurnscoe, Rotherham, South Yorkshire
349   STEVEN WORTHINGTON
350   ROBERT BEEL, Scunthorpe, South Humberside
351   MARTIN SIMONS, Bekkevoort, Belgium
352   JOHN REKIA, Beswick, Manchester
353   BRIAN MALPAS, Denton, Manchester
354   TONY OSTELL, Chadderton, Oldham, Lancashire
355   KARL LINGHAM, St.Athan, Barry, South Glamorgan
356   ADRIAN WILLEY, Ashton-under-Lyne, Tameside
357   ADRIAN LOVE, Rusthall, Tunbridge Wells, Kent
358   KELVIN SOMERS, Brompton Barracks, Chatham, Kent
359   RICHARD WORSLEY, Cheadle Hulme, Cheshire
360   KEITH HURSTHOUSE, Bussage, Stroud, Gloucs
361   JOHN SULLIVAN, New Barnet, Herts
362   KING of the KIPPAX, Leigh, Greater Manchester
363   I.G.ROBERTS, Sale, Cheshire
364   MARK M.FOSTER, Sale, Cheshire
365   BENNY RAYNER, St. Clements, Channel Islands
366   JOHN DAWSON, Moston, Manchester
367   Mr. & Mrs.J.DELANEY, Sale, Cheshire
368   CRAIG HANSON, Poynton, Cheshire
369   DAVID K.SMITH, Stepney Green, London
370   VIC MORLEY, Harwood, Bolton, Lancashire
371   CHRISTOPHER DEWEY, Thurmaston, Leicester
372   MAXWELL CARRUTHERS, Oadby, Leicester
373   SEAN WALSH, Failsworth, Manchester
374   GREG M.SMITH, Witham, Essex
375   BRIAN HUGH JONES, Sutton, Surrey
376   MICHAEL W.SHONN, Crumpsall, Manchester
377   STEVEN WIGLEY, Driffield, North Humberside
378   PAUL SHAW, Pwllheli, Gwynedd
379   RICHARD A.IKIN, Moulton, Cheshire
380   DAVID JOHN HENRY OWEN HOWL
381   CHRISTOPHER DAVID HOWL, London EC1
382   JOSEPH I.ATKINSON, Hooton, Cheshire
383   LEE LAWTON
384   DARREN LAWTON, Failsworth, Manchester
385   MARTYN C.PEACOCK, St.James, Northampton
386   MARK ANTONY ROUTH, Bury, Lancashire
387   J.THOMAS, Electrical & Mechanical Services, Denton, Manchester
388   TERRY THIRLWALL, Burnage, Manchester
389   PHILIP JAMES DRINKWATER, Levenshulme, Manchester
390   ALAN FORD, Marple, Cheshire
391   NICHOLAS T. & GARETH D.McHENRY, Woodley, Stockport
392   ANDREW SHEPARD, Cheadle Hulme, Cheshire
393   PAUL TAYLOR, Newton Heath, Manchester
394   TONY WALFORD, Blackley, Manchester
395   SIMON ASHLEY MIFFLIN, Putson, Hereford
396   STEVEN ALAN MIFFLIN, Putson, Hereford
397   Dr.JOHN McLOUGHLIN, Sale, Greater Manchester
398   ANDREAS LARSSON, Malmo, Sweden
399   ALAN BOUCH, Langwarrin, Victoria, Australia
400   Dr.BARRY SHMEIZER, Senderwood, Johannesburg, R.S.A.
401   HAYDEN, ELENNI, SAUL & NATHAN FOY, Failsworth
402   FRANCIS JAMES COOKSON, Crewe, Cheshire
403   NEIL REILLY, Wythenshawe, Manchester
404   KEVIN ROBINSON, Mitcham, Surrey
405   GEOFFREY T.ALLMAN, Wolverhampton
406   MICHAEL CRICK, Swerford, Oxford
407   STEVE MACKINNON, Timperley, Cesire
408   BRIAN EDWARD WHITE, Irchester, Northamptonshire
409   G.R.CAIN, London E9
410   VINCENT BARRY MOLLOY, East Didsbury, Manchester
411   J.H.MOGG, Uxbridge, Middlesex
412   FRANK COX, Ballyboden, Dublin, Eire
413   PETER D.TURNER, Knowle, Bristol
414   Mrs SYLIVIA O'BRIEN, Whaley Bridge, Stockport
415   CRAIG DAVIES, Swinton, Manchester
416   BETH ATKIN, London SW1
417   IAN SHEPHERD, Ranskill, Nottinghamshire
418   BRIAN JOHNSON
419   STEVE CRITCHLEY, Smithfield Plains, South Australia
420   STEIN SORENSEN, Mandal, Norway
421   PAUL KELVIN THOMPSON, Waltham, Grimsby
422   DAVID POVERELLO, Sydenham, Johannesburg, R.S.A.
423   BJORN HURST, Mitchell Park, Adelaide, Australia
424   PHIL WILLIAMS
425   NIGEL G.APPLETON, Mold, Clwyd
426   HARRY GEORGIADIS, Richmond, Melbourne, Australia
427   GARETH DAVID HAMER, Tottington, Bury, Lancs
428   KEITH HOOK, Houghton Regis, Bedfordshire
429   MARTIN JOHN STEPHENS, Heaton Moor, Stockport
430   TONY GEORGIOU, Hastings, Sussex
431   ROBERT POVERELLO, Sydenham, Johannesburg, R.S.A.
432   R.J.TOWNSEND, Scale Hall, Lancaster
433   NEALE A.BURNS, Balham, London SW12
434   NIKLAS DOHSE, Gothenbourg, Sweden

435   JENS ROEN WINKEL, Thyboroen, Denmark
436   JAMES RYAN COOPER, Shrewsbury, Shropshire
437   CENTRAL LIBRARY, St.Peter's Square, Manchester
438   BLACKWELL'S ACADEMIC BOOKSHOP, Oxford Road, Manchester
439   GINO DE RELAND, Rose Hill, Mauritius
440   GRAHAM SPACKMAN, Pinner, Middlesex
441   PER HARALD LARSEN, Bergen, Norway
442   HANS LOKOY, Hafrsfjord, Norway
443   OLE P.PEDERSEN, Oslo, Norway
444   LASSE OLSEN, Trondheim, Norway
445   KETIL KARLSEN, Fredrikstad, Norway
446   ATLE JOHANSEN, Andebu, Norway
447   BENT S.PEDERSEN, Skien, Norway
448   NIGEL BRIDGE, Hyde, Cheshire
449   S.J.GREATBANKS, Heaton Chapel, Stockport
450   SIMON L.HARROP, Cheadle Hulme, Cheshire
451   DEREK CLARKE, Shrewsbury, Shropshire
452   PETER BURKE, Channel Islands
453   ANTHONY JOHN MORRIS, Higher Blackley, Manchester
454   STEVEN NEIL MARTIN, Royton, Oldham, Lancs
455   SIMON HOWARD, Uppermill, Oldham, Lancs
456   CHRIS BUNKER, Birstall, Leicester
457   MURRAY ROBBINS, Cheltenham, Glos
458   PAUL COWMAN, Ashton-under-Lyne, Lancs
459   ALAN GILBERT, Bury, Lancs
460   G.W.COOPER, Fallowfield, Manchester
461   G.W.COOPER, Fallowfield, Manchester
462   N.J.S.SMITH, Buxton, Derbyshire
463   ANDREW WHELAN, Derbyshire
464   COLIN BALDWIN, Buxton, Derbyshire
465   SIMON COLLINGS, Middleton, Manchester
466   JOHN READ, Fixby, Huddersfield, W.Yorkshire
467   RICHARD PLUNKETT, Almondbury, W.Yorkshire
468   WAYNE DAVID JOHN SCHOFIELD, Clarksfield, Oldham
469   ALAN BRADLEY, Ashton-under-Lyne, Lancashire
470   NICK WEST, Springhead, Oldham, Lancashire
471   DANNY DRONSFIELD, Lees, Oldham, Lancs
472   STUART H.RENSHAW, Davenport, Stockport
473   LILLIAN JAMES, Haughton Green, Denton, Manchester
474   FRED & MARY BURDEN, Denton, Manchester
475   IAN S.FLETCHER, Buxton, Derbyshire
476   H.W., Manchester
477   B.HOURSTON, St. Ola, Orkney
478   J.H.WOOD, Rickmansworth, Herts
479   MARTIN DUNDON
480   TIM CHADWICK, Kentish Town, London
481   GARY THOMPSON, Belfast, Northern Ireland
482   LIONEL JAMES MAJOR, Chorlton, Manchester
483   FRANK O'NEILL
484   ATHOL JAMIESON, Brizlincote, Burton upon Trent
485   DAVID HICKMAN, Hebden Bridge, Yorkshire
486   DANIEL LINGARD, Banbury, Oxon
487   MATTHEW LINGARD, Bradford, West Yorkshire
488   ARNOLD VICTOR, Athlone, Cape Town, R.S.A.
489   Mrs E.A.THOMPSON, Bradford, West Yorkshire
490   B.BRANNEN, Cheadle Hulme, Cheshire
491   MICHAEL GREENHALGH, Hattersley Hyde, Cheshire
492   ROBERT O'CONNOR, Glossop, Derbyshire
493   MAURA CROSLAND, Pudsey, West Yorkshire
494   TONY CUTHBERTSON, Leeds, West Yorkshire
495   F.PYE, MSS (NORTH WEST) LTD, Salford, Manchester
496   THOMAS MOORE, Hitchin, Herts
497   GARY PICK, Melton Mowbray, Leics
498   MARTIN LARTY, Leigh, Lancashire
499   PAUL A.LOVELY, Grimsby, South Humberside
500   ROY MURPHY, Bolton, Lancashire
501   DAVID S.ALLEN, Bolton, Lancashire
502   CARL V.THOMAS, Bolton, Lancashire
503   ANDREW J.MITCHELL, Rochdale, Lancashire
504   HAPPY 34th BIRTHDAY BARN!
505   ROBERT MacFARLANE, South Knighton, Leicester
506   MERTON FISHER, Glenfield, Leicester
507   DONALD MacKAY, Greetland, Halifax, W.Yorkshire
508   CROSLAND & BARBARA WARD, Broadbottom, Hyde, Cheshire
509   JOHN CLANCY, Charlton Kings, Cheltenham, Glos.
510   RICHARD DONLAN, Hazel Grove, Southport
511   THEODORE MANTZOURANIS, Filothei, Athens, Greece
512   ANDREW C. SLIM, Alkrington, Middleton, Manchester
513   DAVID BORTHWICK, Manchester
514   NEIL ISHERWOOD
515   A. KEVIN LOVETT, Manchester
516   TOM & JANE BURGESS, Selsted, Essex
517   Mrs NORMA HEYWOOD, Gorton, Manchester
518   ANTHONY HEYWOOD, Denton, Tameside
519   IAN WILKINSON, Hopwood Heywood, Lancashire
520   KENNETH JOHN DOODSON, Smithy Bridge, Littleborough, Lancs
521   JANICE & EAMON HEIGHWAY, Thurmaston, Leicester
522   JULIAN BASKCOMB, Clarendon Park, Leicester